GEORGE HERBERT AND THE SEVENTEENTH-CENTURY RELIGIOUS POETS

AUTHORITATIVE TEXTS
CRITICISM

➤➤ A NORTON CRITICAL EDITION ◀◀

GEORGE HERBERT AND THE SEVENTEENTH-CENTURY RELIGIOUS POETS

AUTHORITATIVE TEXTS
CRITICISM

➤➤ ◀◀

Selected and Edited by

MARIO A. DI CESARE

HARPUR COLLEGE, STATE UNIVERSITY OF
NEW YORK AT BINGHAMTON

W · W · NORTON & COMPANY

New York · London

W. W. Norton & Company, Inc., 500 Fifth Avenue, New York, N.Y. 10110

Library of Congress Cataloging in Publication Data
Main entry under title:
George Herbert and the seventeenth-century religious poets.
  (A Norton critical edition)
  Bibliography: p.
  1. English poetry—Early modern, 1500–1700. 2. Christian poetry,
English. 3. English poetry—Early modern, 1500–1700—History and
criticism—Addresses, essays, lectures. 4. Religion in literature—Addresses,
essays, lectures. I. Herbert, George, 1593–1633. II. Di Cesare, Mario A.
PR1209.G4 1978   821'.7'0931   77–28074
ISBN 0-393-04398-3
ISBN 0-393-09254-2 pbk.

PRINTED IN THE UNITED STATES OF AMERICA
9 0

W. H. Auden: from *George Herbert: Selected by W. H. Auden* (London: Penguin Books, 1973). Reprinted by permission of Penguin Books Ltd. and Curtis Brown Ltd. on behalf of the Estate of W. H. Auden.

M. C. Bradbrook and M. G. Lloyd Thomas: From *Andrew Marvell* (1940). Reprinted by permission of the Cambridge University Press.

Douglas Bush: From *English Literature in the Earlier Seventeenth Century* (Second Edition), © Oxford University Press, 1962. Reprinted by permission of the Oxford University Press.

A. L. Clements: From *The Mystical Poetry of Thomas Traherne* (Cambridge, Mass.: Harvard University Press), © 1969 by the President and Fellows of Harvard College. Reprinted by permission of the author and the publishers.

Dennis Davison: From "Introduction" to *Andrew Marvell: Selected Poetry and Prose* (1952). Reprinted by permission of George G. Harrap & Company Ltd.

T. S. Eliot: From *George Herbert: Writers and Their Work* (London, 1962). Reproduced by permission of the British Council.

Robert Ellrodt: From "George Herbert and the Religious Lyric," in *English Poetry and Prose 1540-1674*, edited by Christopher Ricks (London, 1970). Reprinted with the permission of Sphere Books Limited.

William Empson: "Marvell's 'Garden,'" from *Scrutiny*, I (1932). Reprinted by permission of the Cambridge University Press.

E. B. Greenwood: From "George Herbert's Sonnet 'Prayer': A Stylistic Study," *Essays in Criticism*, XV (1965). Reprinted by permission of the author and the publisher.

Aldous Huxley: From *Texts and Pretexts* (New York: Harper & Row, 1932). Reprinted by permission of Harper & Row.

Frank Kermode: From "The Argument of Marvell's 'Garden,'" from *Essays in Criticism*, II (1952). Reprinted by permission of the author and the publisher.

L. C. Knights: From *Explorations* (London: Chatto & Windus, 1946). Reprinted by permission of the publisher.

Edward S. Le Comte: "Marvell's 'The Nymph Complaining for the Death of her Fawn,'" from *Modern Philology*, L (1952), 97–101. Reprinted by permission of the University of Chicago Press and the author. Copyright 1952 by The University of Chicago. All rights reserved.

H. M. Margoliouth: From Introduction to *Thomas Traherne: Centuries, Poems, and Thanksgivings*, © Oxford University Press, 1958. Reprinted by permission of the Oxford University Press.

E. C. Pettet: From *Of Paradise and Light* (New York: Cambridge University Press, 1960). Reprinted by permission of the Cambridge University Press.

S. Sandbank: "Henry Vaughan's Apology for Darkness," from *Studies in English Literature 1500-1900*, VII (1967). Reprinted by permission of the author and the publisher.

Stanley Stewart: From *The Expanded Voice: The Art of Thomas Traherne* (San Marino, 1970). Reprinted with permission of the author and the Henry E. Huntington Library and Art Gallery.

Richard Strier: From "Crashaw's Other Voice," *Studies in English Literature 1500-1900*, IX (1969). Reprinted by permission of the author and the publisher.

Joseph H. Summers: "Marvell's 'Nature'" from *ELH*, XX (1953), 121–35. © The Johns Hopkins University Press. Reprinted by permission of the author and the publisher.

Joseph H. Summers: "The Poem as Hieroglyph," from *George Herbert: His Religion and Art* (Cambridge, Mass.: Harvard University Press, 1954). Reprinted by permission of the author, Harvard University Press, and Chatto & Windus Ltd.

Austin Warren: From *Richard Crashaw: A Study in Baroque Sensibility* (1939). Reprinted by permission of Faber and Faber Ltd. and The University of Michigan Press.

Helen C. White: From *The Metaphysical Poets: A Study in Religious Experience*. Copyright 1936 by Macmillan Publishing Co., Inc.; renewed by Helen C. White, 1964. Reprinted by permission of the publisher.

Karina Williamson: "Marvell's 'The Nymph Complaining for the Death of her Fawn': A Reply," from *Modern Philology*, LI (1954), 268–71. Reprinted by permission of the University of Chicago Press. Copyright 1954 by The University of Chicago. All rights reserved.

For Douglas Bush
who has taught us all

Contents

Preface   xiii

The Texts of the Poems   1

George Herbert   3

From *The Temple* (1633)   4
  The Altar   4
  The Sacrifice   4
  The Thanksgiving   11
  The Reprisal   13
  The Agony   13
  Good Friday   14
  Redemption   14
  Sepulchre   15
  Easter Wings   17
  Easter   18
  H. Baptism (I)   18
  H. Baptism (II)   19
  Sin (I)   19
  Affliction (I)   20
  Prayer (I)   21
  [Prayer (II)]   22
  The H. Communion   22
  [Church Lock-and-Key]   23
  Love I   23
  Love II   24
  The Temper (I)   24
  The Temper (II)   25
  Jordan (I)   25
  Employment (I)   26
  The H. Scriptures I   27
  The H. Scriptures II   27
  Whitsunday   27
  Grace   28
  Church Monuments   29
  Church Music   30
  The Windows   30
  The Quiddity   30
  The Star   31

Sunday	32
Anagram	33
Employment (II)	33
Denial	34
Christmas	35
The World	36
Vanity (I)	36
Virtue	37
The Pearl. Matth. 13. 45	38
Affliction (IV)	39
Man	40
Life	41
Mortification	41
Jordan (II)	42
Obedience	43
The British Church	44
The Quip	45
Iesu	46
Dialogue	46
Dullness	47
Sin's Round	48
Peace	48
The Bunch of Grapes	49
The Storm	50
Paradise	51
The Size	51
Artillery	52
The Pilgrimage	53
The Bag	54
The Collar	55
Joseph's Coat	56
The Pulley	57
The Search	57
The Flower	59
The Son	60
A True Hymn	60
Bitter-sweet	61
Aaron	61
The Forerunners	62
Discipline	63
The Banquet	64
The Elixir	65
A Wreath	66
Death	66
Doomsday	67

Judgement 68
Heaven 68
Love (III) 69
Sonnets from Walton's *Lives* (1670) 69
[My God, where is that ancient heat . . .] 69
[Sure Lord, there is enough . . .] 70

Richard Crashaw 71

From *Steps to the Temple* (1646) 71
To the Infant Martyrs 71
Upon the Infant Martyrs 72
On the Water of Our Lord's Baptism 72
To Our Lord, Upon the Water Made Wine 72
Upon the Ass That Bore Our Saviour 72
I Am the Door 72
Upon Lazarus His Tears 73
Matthew 27: And He Answered Them Nothing 73
Upon Our Saviour's Tomb Wherein Never
  Man Was Laid 73
On Mr. G. Herbert's Book 73
From *Delights of the Muses* (1646) 74
Music's Duel 74
From *Carmen Deo Nostro* (1652) 78
In the Holy Nativity of Our Lord God:
  A Hymn Sung as by the Shepherds 78
Saint Mary Magdalene or The Weeper 80
A Hymn to the Name and Honor of the
  Admirable Saint Teresa 84
From *The Flaming Heart* 88
To the Noblest and Best of Ladies,
  The Countess of Denbigh 89

Andrew Marvell 93

From *Miscellaneous Poems* (1681) 93
A Dialogue Between the Resolved Soul
  and Created Pleasure 93
On a Drop of Dew 95
The Coronet 96
Eyes and Tears 97
Bermudas 99
A Dialogue Between the Soul and Body 100
The Nymph Complaining for the Death of her Fawn 101
To His Coy Mistress 104
The Definition of Love 105

x · *Contents*

The Picture of Little T. C. in a Prospect of Flowers 106
The Mower Against Gardens 107
Damon the Mower 108
The Mower to the Glowworms 110
The Mower's Song 110
Music's Empire 111
The Garden 112
An Horatian Ode Upon Cromwell's Return
    from Ireland 114
Upon Appleton House 117

Henry Vaughan 139

From *Silex Scintillans*, Part I (1650) 139
Regeneration 139
The Search 142
The Shower 144
Distraction 145
The Pursuit 145
Mount of Olives (I) 146
The Incarnation, and Passion 147
Vanity of Spirit 147
The Retreat 148
[Joy of my life! while left me here] 149
The Morning Watch 150
[Silence, and stealth of days!] 151
Burial 151
[Sure, there's a tie of Bodies!] 152
Peace 153
[And do they so? have they a Sense] 154
Corruption 155
Unprofitablenes 156
Idle Verse 156
Son-days 157
The Dawning 157
Retirement 158
Love, and Discipline 160
The World 160
Mount of Olives (II) 162
Man 163
[I walked the other day . . .] 163
From *Silex Scintillans*, Part II (1655) 165
Ascension Hymn 165
[They are all gone into the world of light!] 166
Cock-crowing 167
The Bird 169

The Timber 170
The Knot 171
The Rainbow 172
The Seed Growing Secretly 173
[As time one day by me did pass] 174
The Dwelling Place 175
The Night 176
The Waterfall 178
Quickness 179
The Book 179

Thomas Traherne 181
From the Dobell Folio 181
The Salutation 181
Wonder 182
Eden 184
Innocence 185
The Preparative 187
The Rapture 189
My Spirit 189
Love 192
From *The Third Century* 193
On News 193
From the Burney Manuscript 195
The Return 195
Shadows In the Water 195
On Leaping Over the Moon 197

Textual Notes 201

Criticism 219
Anthony Low · Metaphysical Poets and Devotional Poets 221
Samuel Taylor Coleridge · [Letters] 232
Aldous Huxley · [The Inner Weather] 233
W. H. Auden · [Anglican George Herbert] 233
T. S. Eliot · [George Herbert as Religious Poet] 236
L. C. Knights · [George Herbert: Resolution
    and Conflict] 242
E. B. Greenwood · [Herbert's "Prayer (I)"] 249
Joseph H. Summers · The Poem as Hieroglyph 255
Douglas Bush · [Crashaw: Single-hearted Worshipper] 270
Helen C. White · [Richard Crashaw: Intellectual Poet] 273
Austin Warren · [Crashaw's Symbolism] 275
Richard Strier · Crashaw's Other Voice 284

xii · *Contents*

Frank Kermode · The Argument of Marvell's "Garden"   295
William Empson · Marvell's 'Garden'   304
M. C. Bradbrook and M. G. Lloyd Thomas ·
  [On "The Nymph Complaining . . ."]   308
Edward S. Le Comte · Marvell's "The Nymph
  Complaining for the Death of Her Fawn"   310
Karina Williamson · Marvell's "The Nymph
  Complaining for the Death of Her Fawn": A Reply   316
Dennis Davison · [Marvell's Religious Poems]   320
Joseph H. Summers · Marvell's "Nature"   326
Robert Ellrodt · [Henry Vaughan]   337
E. C. Pettet · [Henry Vaughan's "Regeneration"]   343
S. Sandbank · Henry Vaughan's Apology for Darkness   354
Robert Ellrodt · [Thomas Traherne]   364
H. M. Margoliouth · [Traherne the Writer]   367
Arthur Clements · [On Traherne's "My Spirit"]   369
Stanley Stewart · [Traherne the Poet]   376

Annotated Bibliography   387

Preface

This volume presents the major work of five poets—George Herbert, Richard Crashaw, Andrew Marvell, Henry Vaughan, and Thomas Traherne. Whether considered with their contemporaries Donne and Milton or not, these five poets created a significant body of religious literature. Each of them is important and impressive in his own right. Herbert and Marvell are regarded, properly, as major poets; Crashaw, Vaughan, and Traherne are poets of real distinction. Remarkably diverse, yet the five also share many familial resemblances, and the differences are less significant than the ways in which they complement or counterpoint each other. These poets are often called "Metaphysical," but that term is misleading even though many find it serviceable. Robert Ellrodt recently referred to these poets as constituting a "school of Herbert." The suggestion is interesting. Not made contentiously, it points to the general orientation: like Elizabethan lyric, seventeenth-century religious verse is a special phenomenon.

For practical reasons—since users of this volume may rely on it as their only text for some or all of these poets—it seems appropriate to include some secular verse by Crashaw and Marvell as well as their religious verse. Herbert and Traherne wrote virtually no secular verse at all; Vaughan's is not distinguished. But Marvell and Crashaw wrote secular poems of great merit, and I have included several here.

In selecting the religious poetry, I have been guided by a broad and accommodating notion of religion. It has not seemed necessary to give particular or peculiar definition, since the seventeenth century was almost embarrassingly rich in religious literature of all kinds and for all tastes. My main concern has been to select poetry of a high order—that is, to use the same standards one would apply in preparing a volume of, say, Elizabethan love lyrics or Victorian poems. Several traps opened up before me—the old prejudice that religion maketh literature, for instance, or the new prejudice that religion and literature do not mix; most people who write about religious poetry either apologize for it or appear to regard the subject as odd, perhaps believing that religion is obviously superior to "mere literature." I hope I have avoided these pitfalls. The imagination is a natural human faculty, not dependent on a man's belief. Since religion was a major element in the ordinary lives of most people in the seventeenth century, and especially of these five poets, any disjunction between religion and other forms of human activity—such as the making of poems—would be quite artificial.

But while I could approach the poetry straightforwardly and without any obtrusive assumptions, the considerations were different in choosing the critical material. Here I have had to be somewhat arbitrary and even inconsistent, in order to achieve different though related aims. My choices were guided by several competing claims, particularly the claims of excellence, usefulness, and diversity. I have not worried much about comprehensiveness, but I have tried to achieve a broad range of critical viewpoints and represent several different approaches or methods. Not a subscriber to any specific critical orthodoxy, I have attempted to bring together critical analyses which exemplify different ways of looking at the poets and their poems. Some of the selections on Marvell, for instance, are organized to form a kind of symposium in which methods and critics clash; the selections dealing with Vaughan and Herbert offer several approaches which are congruent with each other, including commentary by poets whose interests are usually neither scholarly nor critical.

A word about apparatus and format. The texts of the poems are modernized as much as is necessary to facilitate reading. I have, however, resisted the widespread practice of wholesale modernizing —completely changing the punctuation, abolishing capitals or italics which do not conform to a particular manual of style, and otherwise obliterating the individual marks of each poet. Since my procedure involved a number of fine discriminations and caused some inconsistencies, it is described in detail in the Textual Notes. The annotations gloss the poems in the attempt to recover basic meanings of words or images or allusions, or to clarify obscure phrases or constructions. The Annotated Bibliography at the end is selective; the literature on these poets and on seventeenth-century religious poetry generally is so extensive (and so diverse in quality) that only a representative selection can be provided. I have annotated the bibliography somewhat to make it useful both as a guide to the materials and as a supplement to the criticism in this volume.

I am happy to acknowledge some specific, recent, and practical debts. Many librarians were, as usual, helpful and kind, especially librarians at the Bodleian, the British Library, the Cambridge University libraries, and Dr. Williams's Library at the University of London. In the freemasonry of scholarship, Frank Huntley gave wise and generous counsel; Arthur Clements kindly loaned me his copies of the Traherne manuscripts; and Hubert English and Hugh Maclean offered detailed and useful advice on the original proposal. Michael Lynne exercised care and imagination in checking the texts of the poems. Emily Garlin at Norton has seen this volume through with good humor, patience, and dispatch.

All debts begin and end with my wife, Carol Lee, who taught me hope and herself exercised boundless faith and charity.

MARIO A. DI CESARE

The Texts of
The Poems

George Herbert

George Herbert (1593–1633) was the fifth son of Richard and Magdalen Herbert, a distinguished family of the Welsh border. Sir Richard died in 1596; thirteen years later, Lady Magdalen married Sir John Danvers. Herbert studied at Westminster School and Trinity College, Cambridge, with distinction (B.A. 1613, elected Fellow 1616, M.A. 1616), was made Reader in Rhetoric in 1618, and was elected Public Orator to the University (1620–27), a post which permitted powerful contacts and often led to high public office. In 1624 and 1625, Herbert served as member of Parliament for Montgomery, but in 1626 (his high aspirations apparently in decline), Herbert retired from public life. He was already a deacon. In 1629, he married Jane Danvers after a brief courtship; in April 1630 he was presented the rectorship of Bemerton, in Salisbury, and was ordained a priest the following September. During his last years, he suffered ill health, apparently tuberculosis. As priest at Bemerton, he followed the counsels set out in his own treatise, *A Priest to the Temple* (1652). Izaak Walton's *Life* (1670) recounts many edifying tales which, if not strictly true, probably should be. Herbert completed *The Temple* while at Bemerton and sent the poems to his friend Nicholas Ferrar, the founder of the religious community at Little Gidding, in Huntingdonshire. The work was published at Cambridge a few months after Herbert died on March 1, 1633.

From *The Temple* (1633)

The Altar[1]

A broken A L T A R, Lord, thy servant rears,
Made of a heart, and cemented with tears:[2]
Whose parts are as thy hand did frame;
No workman's tool hath touched the same.
           A H E A R T alone   5
           Is such a stone,
           As nothing but
           Thy pow'r doth cut.
           Wherefore each part
           Of my hard heart   10
           Meets in this frame,
           To praise thy name.
That, if I chance to hold my peace,
These stones to praise thee may not cease.[3]
O let thy blessed S A C R I F I C E be mine,   15
And sanctify this A L T A R to be thine.

The Sacrifice[1]

Oh, all ye, who pass by,[2] whose eyes and mind
To worldly things are sharp, but to me blind,
To me, who took eyes[3] that I might you find:
                Was ever grief like mine?

The Princes of my people make a head   5
Against their Maker: they do wish me dead,
Who cannot wish, except I give them bread:
                Was ever grief like mine?

Without me each one, who doth now me brave,
Had to this day been an Egyptian slave.   10
They use that power against me, which I gave:
                Was ever grief like mine?

---

1. See the discussion in Summers, below.
2. See Exodus 20 : 25, "And if thou wilt make me an altar of stone, thou shalt not build it of hewn stone: for if thou lift up thy tool upon it, thou hast polluted it," and Psalms 51 : 7, "A broken and a contrite heart, O God, thou wilt not despise."
3. See Luke 19 : 40, "I tell you, that if these should hold their peace, the stones would immediately cry out."
1. Dramatic monologue; the speaker throughout is Christ. The antitheses derive from the paradoxical nature of Christianity. The form and details come largely from the liturgy for Holy Week, specifically (in the Good Friday liturgy) the *Improperia* or Reproaches, which Christ on the Cross addressed to the ungrateful people. The reader might usefully consult Exodus and the Passion narratives in the Gospels—Matthew 26–27, Mark 14–15, Luke 22–23, and John 18–19.
2. See Jeremiah, Lamentations 1 : 12, "All ye that pass by, behold, and see if there be any sorrow like unto my sorrow."
3. I.e., became man.

Mine own Apostle, who the bag did bear,
Though he had all I had, did not forbear
To sell me also, and to put me there: 15
                    Was ever grief like mine?

For thirty pence he did my death devise,
Who at three hundred did the ointment prize,[4]
Not half so sweet as my sweet sacrifice:
                    Was ever grief, &c.   20

Therefore my soul melts, and my heart's dear treasure
Drops blood (the only beads) my words to measure:
O *let this cup pass, if it be thy pleasure:*[5]
                    Was ever grief, &c.

These drops being tempered with a sinner's tears   25
A balsam are for both the hemispheres:
Curing all wounds, but mine, all, but my fears:
                    Was ever grief, &c.

Yet my Disciples sleep: I cannot gain
One hour of watching, but their drowsy brain   30
Comforts not me, and doth my doctrine stain:
                    Was ever grief, &c.

Arise, arise, they come. Look how they run.
Alas! what haste they make to be undone!
How with their lanterns do they seek the sun!   35
                    Was ever grief, &c.

With clubs and staves they seek me, as a thief,
Who am the way of Truth,[6] the true relief,
Most true to those, who are my greatest grief:
                    Was ever grief, &c.   40

Judas, dost thou betray me with a kiss?
Canst thou find hell about my lips? and miss
Of life, just at the gates of life and bliss?
                    Was ever grief, &c.

See, they lay hold on me, not with the hands   45
Of faith, but fury: yet at their commands
I suffer binding, who have loosed their bands:
                    Was ever grief, &c.

4. Judas, treasurer for the Apostles ("bag did bear"), complained when Mary anointed Christ's feet, that the ointment imght have been "sold for three hundred pence" (see John 12 : 3–6); Judas betrays Christ for thirty pieces of silver (Matthew 26 : 14–16).
5. In the Garden of Gethsemane, Christ feels his "soul sorrowful even unto death," and prays that "this cup"—i.e., the Passion—may "pass" (Matthew 26 : 38 f), and "his sweat was as it were drops of blood" (Luke 22 : 44).
6. See John 14 : 6, "I am the way, the truth, and the life."

All my Disciples fly; fear puts a bar
Betwixt my friends and me. They leave the star,   50
That brought the wise men of the East from far.
                       Was ever grief like mine?

Then from one ruler to another bound
They lead me, urging, that it was not sound
What I taught: Comments[7] would the text confound.   55
                       Was ever grief, &c.

The Priests and rulers all false witness seek[8]
'Gainst him, who seeks not life, but is the meek
And ready Paschal Lamb of this great week:
                       Was ever grief, &c.   60

Then they accuse me of great blasphemy,
That I did thrust into the Deity,
Who never thought that any robbery:[9]
                       Was ever grief, &c.

Some said, that I the Temple to the floor   65
In three days razed, and raised as before.
Why, he that built the world can do much more:
                       Was ever grief, &c.

Then they condemn me all with that same breath,
Which I do give them daily, unto death.   70
Thus *Adam* my first breathing rendereth:[1]
                       Was ever grief, &c.

They bind, and lead me unto *Herod*: he
Sends me to *Pilate*. This makes them agree;
But yet their friendship is my enmity: 75
                       Was ever grief, &c.

Herod and all his bands do set me light,
Who teach all hands to war, fingers to fight,
And only am the Lord of Hosts and might:
                       Was ever grief, &c.   80

Herod in judgement sits while I do stand,
Examines me with a censorious hand:
I him obey, who all things else command:
                       Was ever grief, &c.

7. Christ was accused of misleading teachings which subverted the Mosaic law.
8. See Textual Notes.
9. "Thrust into the Deity . . . robbery" —a difficult passage. It appears to combine Jesus' answer to the inquisitorial priests and their false witnesses, asserting his place as Son of God (Matthew 26 : 59 ff.), with the statement of Philippians 2 : 6, "Who, being in the form of God, thought it not robbery to be equal with God." In the original Greek, the last clause literally means "did not consider equality with God something to be seized"—Paul's point being that the humble Christ, unlike the inferior divinities of various mythologies, does not attempt to seize equality or "thrust into the Deity."
1. Returns or gives back the breath of life. Cf. "Prayer (I)," 2.

The *Jews* accuse me with despitefulness,   85
And vying malice with my gentleness,
Pick quarrels with their only happiness:
   Was ever grief like mine?

I answer nothing, but with patience prove[2]
If stony hearts will melt with gentle love.   90
But who does hawk at eagles with a dove?
   Was ever grief, &c.

My silence rather doth augment their cry;
My dove doth back into my bosom fly,
Because the raging waters still are high:[3]   95
   Was ever grief, &c.

Hark how they cry aloud still, *Crucify*:
It is not fit he live a day, they cry,
Who cannot live less than eternally:
   Was ever grief, &c.   100

Pilate a stranger holdeth off; but they,
Mine own dear people, cry, *Away, away*,
With noises confused frighting the day:
   Was ever grief, &c.

Yet still they shout, and cry, and stop their ears,   105
Putting my life among their sins and fears,
And therefore wish *my blood on them and theirs*:
   Was ever grief, &c.

See how spite cankers things. These words aright
Used, and wished, are the whole world's light: 110
But honey is their gall, brightness their night:
   Was ever grief, &c.

They choose a murderer,[4] and all agree
In him to do themselves a courtesy:
For it was their own cause who killed me: 115
   Was ever grief, &c.

And a seditious murderer he was:
But I the Prince of peace, peace that doth pass
All understanding, more than heav'n doth glass:[5]
   Was ever grief, &c.   120

2. Try to discover.
3. A reference to Noah's dove, which could not alight (Genesis 8 : 9).
4. In keeping with a custom of amnesty at festival time, Pilate offers a choice between Jesus and Barabbas, a seditious murderer (Matthew 27 : 15 ff.; Mark 15 : 7).
5. See I Corinthians 13 : 12, "For now we see through a glass, darkly; but then face to face."

Why, Caesar is their only King, not I:
He clave the stony rock, when they were dry;[6]
But surely not their hearts, as I well try:
      Was ever grief like mine?

Ah! how they scourge me! yet my tenderness   125
Doubles each lash: and yet their bitterness
Winds up my grief to a mysteriousness:
      Was ever grief, &c.

They buffet him, and box him as they list,
Who grasps the earth and heaven with his fist,   130
And never yet, whom he[7] would punish, missed:
      Was ever grief, &c.

Behold, they spit on me in scornful wise,
Who by my spittle[8] gave the blind man eyes,
Leaving his blindness to my enemies: 135
      Was ever grief, &c.

My face they cover, though it be divine.
As *Moses'* face was vailed so is mine,
Lest on their double-dark souls either[9] shine:
      Was ever grief, &c.   140

Servants and abjects flout me; they are witty:
Now prophesy who strikes thee, is their ditty.
So they in me deny themselves all pity:
      Was ever grief, &c.

And now I am delivered unto death,   145
Which each one calls for so with utmost[1] breath,
That he before me well nigh suffereth:
      Was ever grief, &c.

Weep not, dear friends, since I for both have wept
When all my tears were blood, the while you slept: 150

6. *"Caesar . . . dry"*: Like many passages, this is packed with allusions. Moses, a type of Christ, "lifted up his hand and with his rod . . . smote the rock twice: and the water came out abundantly," Exodus 17 : 5–6; and God "smote the stony rock . . . [and] water gushed out," Psalms 78 : 21 (Book of Common Prayer). Despite Christ's goodness, he is rejected; the crowds of Jews cry out, "We have no king but Caesar," John 19 : 15. See also line 170 for "that spiritual Rock (which) was Christ," I Corinthians 10 : 4.
7. In lines 129–131, the 1633 text has "me, me, my, I"; I follow the manuscript readings. The use of the third person here emphasizes the fact that the speaker is not only a suffering man but also God, and thus able to view the whole in the perspective of eternity.
8. John 9 relates the curing of the man born blind; see also Mark 8. There is a pun on *hospital*: see "Thanksgiving," 33.
9. I.e., either Moses' face or Christ's. In Exodus 34 : 29 f., Moses has to cover his face when he talks to the people, because "the skin of his face shone" after his contact with God: Moses embodies the Old Testament or Old Law, while Christ represents the New Testament or New Dispensation.
1. *Utmost* suggests both the vehemence of the outcry and the last (or dying) breath (see line 229).

Your tears for your own fortunes should be kept:
            Was ever grief like mine?

The soldiers lead me to the common hall;
There they deride me, they abuse me all:
Yet for twelve heav'nly legions I could call: 155
            Was ever grief, &c.

Then with a scarlet robe they me array:
Which shows my blood to be the only way,
And cordial left to repair man's decay:
            Was ever grief, &c.   160

Then on my head a crown of thorns I wear:
For these are all the grapes *Sion* doth bear,
Though I my vine planted and watered there:[2]
            Was ever grief, &c.

So sits the earth's great curse[3] in *Adam's* fall   165
Upon my head: so I remove it all
From th' earth unto my brows, and bear the thrall:
            Was ever grief, &c.

Then with the reed they gave to me before,
They strike my head, the rock from whence all store   170
Of heav'nly blessings issue evermore:
            Was ever grief, &c.

They bow their knees to me, and cry, *Hail king*:
Whatever scoffs and scornfulness can bring,
I am the floor, the sink, where they it fling: 175
            Was ever grief, &c.

Yet since man's scepters are as frail as reeds,
And thorny all their crowns, bloody their weeds,[4]
I, who am Truth, turn into truth their deeds:
            Was ever grief, &c.   180

The soldiers also spit upon that face,
Which Angels did desire to have the grace,
And Prophets once to see, but found no place:
            Was ever grief, &c.

Thus trimmed, forth they bring me to the rout,   185
Who *Crucify him*, cry with one strong shout.
God holds his peace at man, and man cries out:
            Was ever grief, &c.

2. Although Christ planted and watered the vine of Sion (House of Israel), this crown of thorns is its only fruit: see Isaiah 5 : 1–7.

3. Genesis 3 : 18, "Thorns also and thistles shall (the earth) bring forth to thee."

4. Clothing.

They lead me in once more, and putting then
Mine own clothes on, they lead me out again.   190
Whom devils fly, thus is he tossed of men:
     Was ever grief like mine?

And now weary of sport, glad to engross[5]
All spite in one, counting my life their loss,
They carry me to my most bitter cross: 195
     Was ever grief, &c.

My cross I bear my self, until I faint:
Then Simon bears it for me by constraint,[6]
The decreed burden of each mortal saint:
     Was ever grief, &c.   200

O all ye who pass by, behold and see;
Man stole the fruit, but I must climb the tree,
The tree of life to all, but only me:[7]
     Was ever grief, &c.

Lo, here I hang, charged with a world of sin,   205
The greater world o'th' two; for that came in
By words, but this by sorrow I must win:
     Was ever grief, &c.

Such sorrow as, if sinful man could feel,
Or feel his part, he would not cease to kneel,   210
Till all were melted, though he were all steel:
     Was ever grief, &c.

But, *O my God, my God!* why leav'st thou me,
The Son, in whom thou dost delight to be?
My God, my God——   215
     Never was grief like mine.

Shame tears my soul, my body many a wound,
Sharp nails pierce this, but sharper that confound,
Reproaches, which are free, while I am bound.
     Was ever grief, &c.   220

Now heal thy self, Physician; now come down.[8]
Alas! I did so, when I left my crown
And father's smile for you, to feel his frown:
     Was ever grief, &c.

---

5. Concentrate, collect.
6. A bystander, Simon of Cyrene, is "compelled to bear his cross" (Matthew 27 : 32) and assist Christ.
7. The tree of the Cross and the tree of Adam's sin (where "Man stole the fruit") are commonly paralleled in Christian literature and art.
8. The proverb "Physician, heal thyself," was quoted by Jesus during his ministry (Luke 4 : 23); on Calvary, he is taunted, "If thou be the Son of God, come down from the cross" (Matthew 27 : 40).

In healing not my self, there doth consist   225
All that salvation, which ye now resist;
Your safety in my sickness doth subsist:
       Was ever grief like mine?

Betwixt two thieves I spend my utmost breath,
As he that for some robbery suffereth.   230
Alas! what have I stolen from you? death:
       Was ever grief, &c.

A King my title is, prefixt on high,
Yet by my subjects am condemned to die
A servile death in servile company: 235
       Was ever grief, &c.

They give me vinegar mingled with gall,
But more with malice: yet, when they did call,
With Manna, Angels' food,[9] I fed them all:
       Was ever grief, &c.   240

They part my garments, and by lot dispose
My coat, the type of love, which once cured[1] those
Who sought for help, never malicious foes:
       Was ever grief, &c.

Nay, after death their spite shall further go   245
For they will pierce my side, I full well know;
That as sin came, so Sacraments[2] might flow:
       Was ever grief, &c.

But now I die; now all is finished.
My woe, man's weal: and now I bow my head.   250
Only let others say, when I am dead,
       Never was grief like mine.

The Thanksgiving

Oh King of grief! (a title strange, yet true,
  To thee of all kings only due)
Oh King of wounds! how shall I grieve for thee,
  Who in all grief preventest[1] me?
Shall I weep blood? Why thou hast wept such store[2]   5
  That all thy body was one door[3]

9. I.e., the Eucharist, the "bread of angels," celebrated in the liturgy of Holy Thursday.
1. See Matthew 14 : 36, "As many as touched [the hem of his garment] were made perfectly whole."
2. Eve came from Adam's side; at the piercing of the second Adam's· side, blood and water flowed (John 19 : 34), signifying the Church and the Sacrament.
1. Anticipate, go before; also, surpass.
2. Abundance.
3. John 10 : 9, "I am the door; by me if any man enter in, he shall be saved." See "The Bag", line 38.

Shall I be scourged, flouted, boxed, sold?
    'Tis but to tell the tale is told.
My God, my God, why dost thou part from me?
    Was such a grief as cannot be.   10
Shall I then sing, skipping thy doleful story,
    And side with thy triumphant glory?
Shall thy strokes be my stroking? thorns, my flower?
    Thy rod, my posy?[4] cross, my bower?
But how then shall I imitate thee, and   15
    Copy thy fair, though bloody hand?
Surely I will revenge me on thy love,
    And try who shall victorious prove.
If thou dost give me wealth, I will restore
    All back unto thee by[5] the poor.   20
If thou dost give me honour, men shall see,
    The honour doth belong to thee.
I will not marry; or, if she be mine,
    She and her children shall be thine.
My bosom friend, if he blaspheme thy name,   25
    I will tear thence his love and fame.
One half of me being gone, the rest I give
    Unto some Chapel, die or live.
As for thy passion—But of that anon,
    When with the other I have done.   30
For thy predestination I'll contrive,
    That three years hence, if I survive,
I'll build a spittle,[6] or mend common ways,
    But mend mine own without delays.
Then I will use the works of thy creation,   35
    As if I used them but for fashion.
The world and I will quarrel; and the year
    Shall not perceive, that I am here.
My music shall find thee, and ev'ry string
    Shall have his attribute to sing;   40
That all together may accord in thee,
    And prove one God, one harmony.
If thou shalt give me wit, it shall appear,
    If thou hast giv'n it me, 'tis here.[7]
Nay, I will read thy book, and never move   45
    Till I have found therein thy love;
Thy art of love, which I'll turn back on thee,
    O my dear Saviour, Victory!
Then for thy passion—I will do for that—
    Alas, my God, I know not what.   50

4. Bunch of flowers or bouquet; a short motto; poetical reproduction (all from *Oxford English Dictionary*).
5. By means of.
6. Hospital.
7. In this book of poems.

The Reprisal

I have considered it, and find
There is no dealing with thy mighty passion:
For though I die for thee, I am behind;
    My sins deserve the condemnation.

O make me innocent, that I   5
May give a disentangled state and free:
And yet thy wounds still my attempts defy,
    For by thy death I die for thee.

Ah! was it not enough that thou
By thy eternal glory didst outgo me?   10
Couldst thou not grief's sad conquests me allow,
    But in all vict'ries overthrow me?

Yet by confession will I come
Into thy conquest: though I can do nought
Against thee, in thee I will overcome   15
    The man, who once against thee fought.

The Agony[1]

Philosophers[2] have measured mountains,
Fathomed the depths of seas, of states, and kings,
Walked with a staff[3] to heav'n, and traced fountains:
    But there are two vast, spacious things,
The which to measure it doth more behove: 5
Yet few there are that sound them; Sin and Love.

Who would know Sin, let him repair
Unto Mount Olivet;[4] there shall he see
A man so wrung with pains, that all his hair,
    His skin, his garments bloody be.   10
Sin is that press and vice, which forceth pain
To hunt his cruel food through ev'ry vein.

Who knows not Love, let him assay
And taste that juice,[5] which on the cross a pike
Did set again abroach;[6] then let him say   15
    If ever he did taste the like.

1. Main metaphor is that of the wine press ("I have trodden the wine press alone" Isaiah 63 : 3), a traditional type of Christ's Passion.
2. Men learned in the sciences.
3. A "Jacob's staff" (Genesis 32 : 10), i.e., a measuring stick as well as a traveler's staff.
4. Place of the Agony and betrayal of Jesus in the Garden of Gethsemane.
5. The wine and blood of the Eucharist.
6. Did open up so that the blood would flow.

Love is that liquor sweet and most divine,
Which my God feels as blood; but I, as wine.

Good Friday

O my chief good,
How shall I measure out thy blood?
How shall I count what thee befell,
And each grief tell?

Shall I thy woes   5
Number according to thy foes?
Or, since one star showed thy first breath,
Shall all thy death?

Or shall each leaf,
Which falls in Autumn, score a grief?   10
Or cannot leaves, but fruit, be sign
Of the true vine?

Then let each hour
Of my whole life one grief devour;
That thy distress through all may run,   15
And be my sun.

Or rather let
My several sins their sorrows get;
That as each beast his cure doth know,
Each sin may so.   20

Since blood is fittest, Lord, to write
Thy sorrows in, and bloody fight;
My heart hath store, write there, where in
One box doth lie both ink and sin:

That when sin spies so many foes,   25
Thy whips, thy nails, thy wounds, thy woes,
All come to lodge there, sin may say,
No room for me, and fly away.

Sin being gone, oh fill the place,
And keep possession with thy grace;   30
Lest sin take courage and return,
And all the writings blot or burn.

Redemption

Having been tenant long to a rich Lord,
Not thriving, I resolved to be bold,

And make a suit unto him, to afford
A new small-rented lease, and cancel th'old.[1]
In heaven at his manor I him sought: 5
    They told me there, that he was lately gone
      About some land, which he had dearly bought
Long since on earth, to take possession.
I straight returned, and knowing his great birth,
    Sought him accordingly in great resorts,   10
      In cities, theatres, gardens, parks, and courts:
At length I heard a ragged noise and mirth
    Of thieves and murderers: there I him espied,
      Who straight, *Your suit is granted*, said, and died.

Sepulchre

O blessed body! Whither art thou thrown?
No lodging for thee, but a cold hard stone?
So many hearts on earth, and yet not one
    Receive thee?

Sure there is room within our hearts good store;   5
For they can lodge transgressions by the score:
Thousands of toys[2] dwell there, yet out of door
    They leave thee.

But that which shows them large, shows them unfit.
What ever sin did this pure rock commit,   10
Which holds thee now? Who hath indicted it
    Of murder?

Where our hard hearts have took up stones[3] to brain thee,
And missing this, most falsely did arraign thee,
Only these stones in quiet entertain thee,   15
    And order.

And as of old, the Law by heav'nly art
Was writ in stone; so thou, which also art
The letter of the word,[4] find'st no fit heart
    To hold thee.   20

Yet do we still persit as we began,
And so should perish, but that nothing can,
Though it be cold, hard, foul, from loving man
    Withhold thee.

1. *New . . . old*: The "Covenant of Grace" whereby God, sending Christ to redeem mankind, canceled the covenant of the Old Law.
2. Trifles.
3. Cf. John 10 : 31, "Then the Jews took stones again to stone him [Christ]."

4. In II Corinthians 3 : 3, Paul describes his readers as "the epistle of Christ . . . written not with ink, but with the Spirit of the living God: not in tables of stone, but in fleshy tables of the heart." Cf. Exodus 31 : 18, for the Mosaic tablets of stone containing the Decalogue.

Easter Wings[1]

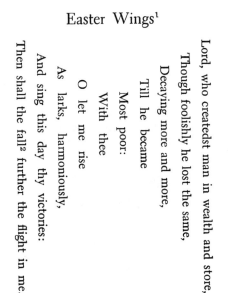

Lord, who createdst man in wealth and store,
Though foolishly he lost the same,
Decaying more and more,
Till he became
Most poor:
With thee
O let me rise
As larks, harmoniously,
And sing this day thy victories:
Then shall the fall[2] further the flight in me.

5

10

1. Printed vertically in the 1633 edition (but horizontally in the manuscripts) the shape of the poem imitates not only the shape of wings and flight of larks, but also the spiritual acts of falling and rising, and the X shape of a cross which made possible the rising.
2. The paradox of the happy fall (*felix culpa*) which brought mankind so great a Redeemer (Saint Augustine, in liturgy for Holy Saturday).

My tender age in sorrow did begin:
And still with sickness and shame
Thou didst so punish sin,
That I became
Most thin.
With thee
Let me combine,
And feel this day thy victory:
For, if I imp[3] my wing on thine,
Affliction shall advance the flight in me.

15

20

3. Graft feathers on a damaged wing so as to make good losses or deficiencies (from falconry).

Easter

Rise heart; thy Lord is risen. Sing his praise
      Without delays,
Who takes thee by the hand, that thou likewise
      With him mayst rise:
That, as his death calcined thee to dust,   5
His life may make thee gold, and much more, just.

Awake, my lute, and struggle for thy part
      With all thy art.
The cross taught all wood to resound his name,
      Who bore the same.   10
His stretched sinews taught all strings, what key
Is best to celebrate this most high day.

Consort both heart and lute, and twist[5] a song
      Pleasant and long:
Or since all music is but three parts vied   15
      And multiplied,
O let thy blessed Spirit bear a part,
And make up our defects with his sweet art.[6]

I got me flowers to straw[7] thy way,
I got me boughs off many a tree: 20
But thou wast up by break of day,
And brought'st thy sweets along with thee.

The Sun arising in the East,
Though he give light, and th' East perfume;
If they should offer to contest   25
With thy arising, they presume.

Can there be any day but this,
Though many suns to shine endeavour?
We count three hundred, but we miss:
There is but one, and that one ever.   30

H. Baptism (I)[1]

As he that sees a dark and shady grove,
      Stays not, but looks beyond it on the sky;
      So when I view my sins, mine eyes remove
More backward still, and to that water fly,

Which is above the heav'ns, whose spring and vent   5
      Is in my dear Redeemer's pierced side.
      O blessed streams! either ye do prevent
And stop our sins from growing thick and wide,

---

5. Weave (e.g., as in polyphonic music).
6. Since all harmony is based on the common triad, the song of heart and lute also needs the Spirit.
7. Strew.
1. "H." = Holy. Roman numerals are added to distinguish poems with similar titles.

Or else give tears to drown them, as they grow.
    In you Redemption measures all my time,   10
    And spreads the plaster equal to the crime.
You taught the *Book of Life*[2] my name, that so

        What ever future sins should me miscall,
        Your first acquaintance might discredit all.

H. Baptism (II)

            Since, Lord, to thee
        A narrow way and little gate[3]
    Is all the passage, on my infancy
        Though didst lay hold, and antedate
            My faith in me.   5

            O let me still
        Write thee great God, and me a child:
    Let me be soft and supple to thy will,
        Small to my self, to others mild,
            Behither[4] ill.   10

            Although by stealth
        My flesh get on, yet let her sister
    My soul bid nothing, but[5] preserve her wealth:
        The growth of flesh is but a blister,
            Childhood is health.   15

Sin (I)[1]

Lord, with what care hast thou begirt us round!
    Parents first season us: then schoolmasters
    Deliver us to laws; they send us bound
To rules of reason, holy messengers,
    Pulpits and Sundays, sorrow dogging sin,   5
    Afflictions sorted, anguish of all sizes,
    Fine nets and stratagems to catch us in,
Bibles laid open, millions of surprises,
Blessings beforehand, ties of gratefulness,
    The sound of glory ringing in our ears: 10
    Without, our shame; within, our consciences;[2]
Angels and grace, eternal hopes and fears.
    Yet all these fences and their whole array
    One cunning bosom-sin blows quite away.

---

2. The heavenly list of the saved; the image is based on the register of citizens common in ancient cities: see Philippians 4 : 3 and Revelation 21 : 27.
3. For the "strait and narrow," see Matthew 7 : 13 f.
4. Short of, except for.
5. *Bid . . . but:* pray for nothing except to.

1. Coleridge (*Biographia Litteraria,* XIX) admired this sonnet "for the purity of the language and the fulness of the sense" and "the simple dignity of the language."
2. On punctuation, see Introduction to Textual Notes.

Affliction (I)

When first thou didst entice to thee my heart,
    I thought the service brave:[3]
So many joys I writ down for my part,
    Besides what I might have
Out of my stock of natural delights,   5
Augmented with thy gracious benefits.

I looked on thy furniture so fine,
    And made it fine to me:
Thy glorious household-stuff did me entwine,
    And 'tice me unto thee.   10
Such stars I counted mine: both heav'n and earth
Paid me my wages in a world of mirth.

What pleasures could I want,[4] whose King I served,
    Where joys my fellows were?
Thus argued into hopes, my thoughts reserved   15
    No place for grief or fear.
Therefore my sudden soul caught at the place,
And made her youth and fierceness seek thy face.

At first thou gav'st me milk and sweetnesses,
    I had my wish and way: 20
My days were strawed with flow'rs and happiness,
    There was no month but May.
But with my years sorrow did twist and grow,
And made a party unawares[5] for woe.

My flesh began[6] unto my soul in pain,   25
    Sicknesses cleave my bones;
Consuming agues dwell in ev'ry vein,
    And tune my breath to groans.
Sorrow was all my soul; I scarce believed,
Till grief did tell me roundly, that I lived.   30

When I got health, thou took'st away my life,
    And more; for my friends die:
My mirth and edge was lost; a blunted knife
    Was of more use[7] than I.
Thus thin and lean without a fence or friend,   35
I was blown through with ev'ry storm and wind.

Whereas my birth and spirit rather took
    The way that takes the town,

---

3. Splendid.
4. Lack
5. Created a faction unwittingly.
6. Remonstrated with, complained to;

lines 26–28 specify the complaints.
7. See below, lines 57 ff.; and see the "Employment" poems on the poet's concern that he be of some use.

Thou didst betray me to a ling'ring book,
        And wrap me in a gown.   40
I was entangled in the world of strife,
Before I had the power to change my life.

Yet, for I threat'ned oft the siege to raise,
        Not simp'ring all mine age,
Thou often didst with Academic praise   45
        Melt and dissolve my rage.
I took thy sweet'ned pill, till I came where
I could not go away, nor persevere.

Yet lest perchance I should too happy be
        In my unhappiness,   50
Turning my purge to food, thou throwest me
        Into more sicknesses.
Thus doth thy power cross-bias me,[8] not making
Thine own gift good, yet me from my ways taking.

Now I am here, what thou wilt do with me   55
        None of my books will show:
I read, and sigh, and wish I were a tree;
        For sure then I should grow
To fruit or shade: at least some bird would trust
Her household to me, and I should be just.   60

Yet, though thou troublest me, I must be meek;
        In weakness must be stout.
Well, I will change the service, and go seek
        Some other master out.
Ah my dear God! though I am clean forgot,   65
Let me not love thee, if I love thee not.[9]

Prayer (I) [1]

Prayer the Church's banquet, Angels' age,
        God's breath in man returning to his birth,
The soul in paraphrase,[2] heart in pilgrimage,
The Christian plummet sounding heav'n and earth;
Engine against th' Almighty,[3] sinners' tower,   5
        Reversed thunder, Christ-side-piercing spear,
        The six-days' world[4] transposing[5] in an hour,
A kind of tune, which all things hear and fear;

---

8. Make me go askew from my aim.
9. Lines 61–66: First, he considers resignation as one answer; then rebellion as
an alternative; then, since neither is satisfactory, he ends in an outcry, a passionate affirmation of the desire and
need for perfect love.
1. See the discussion by E. B. Greenwood, below.
2. Clarifying by expansion.
3. "The Kingdom of Heaven suffereth
violence," Matthew 11:12.
4. The world created in six days; or the
world of the ordinary weekday.
5. Musically.

Softness, and peace, and joy, and love, and bliss,
        Exalted Manna, gladness of the best,   10
        Heaven in ordinary,[6] man well drest,
The milky way, the bird of Paradise,
        Church-bells beyond the stars heard, the soul's blood,
        The land of spices; something understood.

[Prayer (II)][7]

I know it is my sin, which locks thine ears,
             And binds thy hands,
Out-crying my requests, drowning my tears;
Or else the chillness of my faint demands.

But as cold hands are angry[8] with the fire,   5
             And mend it still;
So I do lay the want of my desire,
Not on my sins, or coldness, but thy will.

Yet hear, O God, only for his blood's sake
             Which pleads for me: 10
For though sins plead too, yet like stones[9] they make
His blood's sweet current much more loud to be.

The H. Communion[1]

Not in rich furniture, or fine array,
        Nor in a wedge of gold,
        Thou, who for me wast sold,
        To me dost now thy self convey;
For so thou should'st without me still have been,   5
        Leaving within me sin.

But by the way of nourishment and strength
        Thou creep'st into my breast,
        Making thy way my rest,
        And thy small quantities my length,   10
Which spread their forces into every part,
        Meeting sin's force and art.

Yet can these not get over to my soul,
        Leaping the wall that parts
        Our souls and fleshy hearts;   15
        But as th'outworks, they may control

6. In ordinary, every day setting or dress.
7. Entitled "Church-lock and key" and located after "Church Music" in the 1633 edition; the title used here is from the earliest manuscript. See Textual Notes.
8. In colloquial sense of red, inflamed.
9. As in a brook.
1. See Textual Notes.

My rebel flesh, and carrying thy Name
    Affright both sin and shame.

Only thy grace, which with these elements comes,
    Knoweth the ready way,   20
    And hath the privy key,
Op'ning the soul's most subtle rooms;
While those to spirits refin'd, at door attend
    Dispatches from their friend.

[Church Lock-and-Key][2]

Give me my captive soul, or take
    My body also thither.
Another lift like this will make
    Them both to be together.

Before that[3] sin turned flesh to stone,   5
    And all our lump to leaven,
A fervent sigh might well have blown
    Our innocent earth to heaven.

For sure when Adam did not know
    To sin, or sin to smother,[4]   10
He might to heav'n from Paradise go,
    As from one room t'another.

Thou hast restored us to this ease
    By this thy heav'nly blood,
Which I can go to, when I please,   15
    And leave th'earth to their food.

Love I

Immortal Love, author of this great frame,
    Sprung from that beauty which can never fade;
    How hath man parceled out thy glorious name,
And thrown it on that dust which thou hast made,

While mortal love doth all the title gain!   5
    Which siding with invention, they together
    Bear all the sway, possessing heart and brain,
(Thy workmanship) and give thee share in neither.

Wit fancies beauty, beauty raiseth wit:
    The world is theirs; they two play out the game,   10
    Thou standing by: and though thy glorious name
Wrought our deliverance from th' infernal pit,

2. See Textual Notes.
3. Before.

4. Perhaps also: Sin did not know how to smother man.

Who sings thy praise? only a scarf or glove
Doth warm our hands, and make them write of love.

Love II

Immortal Heat, O let thy greater flame
    Attract the lesser to it: let those fires,
      Which shall consume the world, first make it tame,
And kindle in our hearts such true desires,

As may consume our lusts, and make thee way.[5]   5
    Then shall our hearts pant[6] thee; then shall our brain
      All her invention on thine Altar lay,
And there in hymns send back thy fire again.

Our eyes shall see thee, which before saw dust;
    Dust blown by wit, till that they both were blind: 10
      Thou shalt recover all thy goods in kind,
Who wert disseized[7] by usurping lust:

    All knees shall bow to thee, all wits shall rise,
    And praise him who did make and mend our eyes.

The Temper (I) [1]

How should I praise thee, Lord! how should my rimes
    Gladly engrave thy love in steel,
    If what my soul doth feel sometimes,
      My soul might ever feel!

Although there were some forty heav'ns, or more,   5
    Sometimes I peer above them all;
    Sometimes I hardly reach a score,
      Sometimes to Hell I fall.

O rack me not to such a vast extent;
    Those distances belong to thee: 10
    The world's too little for thy tent,
      A grave too big for me.

Wilt thou meet arms with man, that thou dost stretch
    A crumb of dust from heav'n to hell?
    Will great God measure with[2] a wretch?   15
      Shall he thy stature spell?[3]

5. Make way for you.
6. Pant for.
7. Dispossessed (by force).
1. The title is never used in this poem or the next; "temper" is the unifying concept, suggesting temper of steel, tuning in music, and just proportion.
2. Be compared to, be equalled to, be paired with.
3. Consider, contemplate, scan intently (*Oxford English Dictionary*).

O let me, when thy roof my soul hath hid,
  O let me roost and nestle there:
Then of a sinner thou art rid,
    And I of hope and fear.   20

Yet take thy way; for sure thy way is best:
  Stretch or contract me, thy poor debter:
This is but tuning of my breast,
    To make the music better.

Whether I fly with angels, fall with dust,   25
  Thy hands made both, and I am there:
Thy power and love, my love and trust
    Make one place ev'ry where.

The Temper (II)

It cannot be. Where is that mighty joy,
  Which just now took up all my heart?
  Lord, if thou must needs use thy dart,
Save that,[4] and me; or sin for both destroy.

The grosser world stands to thy word and art;   5
  But thy diviner world of grace
  Thou suddenly dost raise and race,[5]
And ev'ry day a new Creator art.

O fix thy chair of grace, that all my powers
  May also fix their reverence: 10
  For when thou dost depart from hence,
They grow unruly, and sit in thy bowers.

Scatter, or bind them all to bend to thee:
  Though elements change, and heaven move,
  Let not thy higher Court remove,[6]   15
But keep a standing Majesty in me.

Jordan (I)[1]

Who says that fictions only and false hair
Become a verse? Is there in truth no beauty?
Is all good structure in a winding stair?

4. The mighty joy.
5. Raze.
6. The metaphor throughout lines 9–16 is drawn from the royal progress, with its "chair" (throne) usually "fixed" in a "standing Majesty" at the royal palace; the speaker prays that he may serve as a permanent residence.

1. The river Jordan, representing baptismal cleansing and entry to the Promised Land, to Canaan, suggests conversion, salvation, and Christian poetry. Jesus was baptised by John there; in II Kings 5 : 10, Elisha counsels Naaman to "go wash in the Jordan seven times . . . and thou shalt be clean."

May no lines pass, except they do their duty[2]
    Not to a true but painted chair?   5

Is it no verse, except enchanted groves
And sudden arbours shadow coarse-spun lines?[3]
Must purling streams refresh a lover's loves?
Must all be vailed, while he that reads, divines,
    Catching the sense at two removes?   10

Shepherds are honest people, let them sing:
Riddle who list, for me, and pull for Prime:[4]
I envy no man's nightingale or spring
Nor let them punish me with loss of rime
    Who plainly say, *My God, My King.*   15

Employment (I)

If as a flower doth spread and die,
    Thou wouldst extend me to some good,
Before I were by frost's extremity
        Nipt in the bud;

The sweetness and the praise were thine;   5
    But the extension and the room,
Which in thy garland I should fill, were mine
        At thy great doom.

For as thou dost impart thy grace,
    The greater shall our glory be.   10
The measure of our joys is in this place,
        The stuff with thee.

Let me not languish then, and spend
    A life as barren to thy praise,
As is the dust, to which that life doth tend,   15
        But with delays.

All things are busy; only I
    Neither bring honey with the bees,
Nor flowers to make that, nor the husbandry
        To water these.   20

I am no link of thy great chain,[5]
    But all my company is a weed.
Lord place me in thy consort;[6] give one strain
        To my poor reed.

2. Pay reverence to the throne; see "Temper (II)" above, note 6.
3. *Sudden*: appearing unexpectedly; *shadow*: overshadow; make obscure; hide poor workmanship; *coarse-spun lines*: like thread that has been badly spun.
4. *Riddle . . .*: Let anyone who wants to make up (or play at) riddles; *pull for Prime*: draw for a winning hand in the card game "primero" (*Oxford English Dictionary*).
5. The great chain links all creation, from the lowest inanimate objects, complete matter, lacking sense or motion, through the various levels of creation to God, pure animation and pure spirit.
6. Concert; a company or group of musicians.

The H. Scriptures I

Oh Book! infinite sweetness! let my heart
    Suck ev'ry letter, and a honey gain,
    Precious for any grief in any part
To clear the breast, to mollify all pain.
Thou art all health, health thriving till it make   5
    A full eternity: thou art a mass
    Of strange delights, where we may wish and take.
Ladies, look here; this is the thankful glass,
That mends the looker's eyes: this is the well
    That washes what it shows. Who can endear   10
    Thy praise too much? thou art heav'n's Lidger[1] here,
Working against the states of death and hell.
    Thou art joy's handsel:[2] heav'n lies flat in thee,
    Subject to ev'ry mounter's bended knee.

The H. Scriptures II

Oh that I knew how all thy lights combine,
    And the configurations of their glory!
    Seeing not only how each verse doth shine,
But all the constellations of the story.
This verse marks that, and both do make a motion   5
    Unto a third, that ten leaves off doth lie:
    Then as dispersed herbs do watch a potion,[3]
These three make up some Christian's destiny:
Such are thy secrets, which my life makes good,
    And comments on thee: for in ev'ry thing   10
    Thy words do find me out, and parallels bring,
And in another make me understood.
    Stars are poor books, and oftentimes do miss:
    This book of stars lights to eternal bliss.

Whitsunday[4]

Listen sweet Dove unto my song,
And spread thy golden wings in me;
Hatching my tender heart so long,
Till it get wing, and fly away with thee.

Where is that fire which once descended   5
On thy Apostles? thou didst then

---

1. Resident ambassador.
2. First installment.
3. Obscure line. Perhaps "watch a potion" means "expect to be combined in a health-giving potion," just as verses of Scripture relate to (*match?*) one another so that they, in combination, may guide men's lives.
4. The feast of Whitsunday or Pentecost celebrates the descent of the Holy Spirit in "cloven tongues like as of fire" upon the Apostles (Acts 2).

Keep open house, richly attended,
Feasting all comers by twelve chosen men.

Such glorious gifts thou didst bestow,
That th'earth did like a heav'n appear;   10
The stars were coming down to know
If they might mend their wages, and serve here.

The sun, which once did shine alone,
Hung down his head, and wished for night,
When he beheld twelve suns for one   15
Going about the world, and giving light.

But since those pipes of gold,[5] which brought
That cordial water to our ground,
Were cut and martyred by the fault
Of those, who did themselves through their side wound   20

Thou shut'st the door, and keep'st within,
Scarce a good joy creeps through the chink:
And if the braves[6] of conqu'ring sin
Did not excite thee, we should wholly sink.

Lord, though we change, thou art the same;   25
The same sweet God of love and light:
Restore this day for thy great name
Unto his ancient and miraculous right.

Grace

My stock[1] lies dead, and no increase
Doth my dull husbandry improve:
O let thy graces without cease
         Drop from above!

If still the sun should hide his face,   5
Thy house would but a dungeon prove,
Thy works night's captives: O let grace
         Drop from above!

The dew[2] doth ev'ry morning fall,
And shall the dew outstrip thy dove?   10
The dew, for which grass[3] cannot call,
         Drop[4] from above.

5. The Apostles, as channels of grace.
6. Challenges, threats.
1. Tree trunk; cf. Job 14 : 7–9.
2. See Isaiah 45 : 8, "Drop down dew, ye heavens, from above, and let the skies pour down righteousness," used in the Advent liturgy.
3. *Grass* replaces *grace* in this line.
4. *Let* the dew drop from above.

Death is still working like a mole,
And digs my grave at each remove:
Let grace work too, and on my soul   15
      Drop from above.

Sin is still hammering my heart
Unto a hardness, void of love:
Let suppling grace, to cross his art,
      Drop from above.   20

O come! for thou dost know the way:
Or if to me thou wilt not move,
Remove me, where I need not say,
      Drop from above.

Church Monuments[1]

While that my soul repairs to her devotion,
Here I entomb my flesh, that it betimes
May take acquaintance of this heap of dust,
To which the blast of death's incessant motion,
Fed with the exhalation of our crimes,   5
Drives all at last. Therefore I gladly trust

My body to this school, that it may learn
To spell his elements, and find his birth
Written in dusty heraldry and lines;[2]
Which dissolution sure doth best discern,   10
Comparing dust with dust, and earth with earth.
These[3] laugh at Jet and Marble put for signs,

To sever the good fellowship of dust,
And spoil the meeting. What shall point out them,
When they shall bow, and kneel, and fall down flat   15
To kiss those heaps, which now they have in trust?
Dear flesh, while I do pray, learn here thy stem
And true descent: that when thou shalt grow fat,

And wanton in thy cravings, thou mayst know,
That flesh is but the glass,[4] which holds the dust   20
That measures all our time; which also shall
Be crumbled into dust. Mark here below
How tame these ashes are, how free from lust,[5]
That thou mayst fit thy self against thy fall.[6]

1. The extraordinary use of enjambment and the syntax and internal rhymes dissolve the stanza form into a mere skeleton. In the manuscripts, the text is given as one twenty-four line stanza; the 1633 edition has four six-line stanzas.
2. Engraving; genealogy.
3. Dust and earth.

4. Hourglass.
5. Cf. Marvell, "To His Coy Mistress," lines 25–32.
6. *Against*: in preparation for; opposed to; *fall*: physical death; also fall into sin; also tendency to sin because of Adam's fall.

Church Music

Sweetest of sweets, I thank you. When displeasure
    Did through my body wound my mind,
You took me thence, and in your house of pleasure
    A dainty lodging me assigned.

Now I in you without a body move,   5
    Rising and falling with your wings:
We both together sweetly live and love,
    Yet say sometimes, *God help poor Kings.*[7]

Comfort,[8] I'll die; for if you post from me,
    Sure I shall do so, and much more: 10
But if I travel in your company,
    You know the way to heaven's door.

The Windows

Lord, how can man preach thy eternal word?
    He is a brittle crazy glass:
Yet in thy temple thou dost him afford
    This glorious and transcendent place,
    To be a window through thy grace.   5

But when thou dost anneal[9] in glass thy story,
    Making thy life to shine within
The holy Preacher's; then the light and glory
    More rev'rend grows, and more doth win:
    Which else shows wat'rish, bleak, and thin.   10

Doctrine and life, colours and light, in one
    When they combine and mingle, bring
A strong regard and awe: but speech alone
    Doth vanish like a flaring thing,
    And in the ear, not conscience ring.   15

The Quiddity[1]

My God, a verse is not a crown,
No point of honour, or gay suit,
No hawk, or banquet, or renown,
Nor a good sword, nor yet a lute:

7. Presumably, because rapt, happy.
8. Perhaps, "take comfort."
9. To burn in colors upon glass, earthenware, or metal (*Oxford English Dictionary*). Church windows often contain biblical stories.

1. Title in the Williams manuscript is "Poetry." In scholastic philosophy, "quiddity" meant nature or essence of a thing: later, it came to mean overly subtle distinction.

It cannot vault, or dance, or play,   5
It never was in *France* or *Spain;*
Nor can it entertain the day
With a great stable or demain:[2]

It is no office, art, or news,
Nor the Exchange, or busy Hall;   10
But it is that which while I use
I am with thee, and *Most take all.*[3]

The Star

Bright spark, shot from a brighter place,
Where beams surround my Saviour's face,
     Canst thou be any where
     So well as there?

Yet, if thou wilt from thence depart,   5
Take a bad lodging in my heart,
     For thou canst make a debter,
     And make it better.

First with thy fire-work burn to dust
Folly, and worse than folly, lust: 10
     Then with thy light refine,
     And make it shine:

So disengaged from sin and sickness,
Touch it with thy celestial quickness,
     That it may hang and move   15
     After thy love.

Then with our trinity of light,
Motion, and heat, let's take our flight
     Unto the place where thou
     Before didst bow.   20

Get me a standing there, and place
Among the beams, which crown the face
     Of him, who died to part
     Sin and my heart:

That so among the rest I may   25
Glitter, and curl, and wind as they:
     That winding is their fashion
     Of adoration.

Sure thou wilt joy, by gaining me

2. Domain.
3. Winner takes all; the winner here is, finally, God.

To fly home like a laden bee   30
  Unto that hive of beams
  And garland-streams.

Sunday

O day most calm, most bright,
The fruit of this, the next world's bud,
Th' indorsement of supreme delight,
Writ by a friend, and with his blood;
The couch of time; care's balm and bay: 5
The week were dark, but for thy light:
    Thy torch doth show the way.

The other days and thou
Make up one man; whose face thou art,
Knocking at heaven with thy brow: 10
The worky-days are the back-part,
The burden of the week lies there,
Making the whole to stoop and bow,
    Till thy release appear.

Man had straight forward gone   15
To endless death: but thou dost pull
And turn us round to look on one,
Whom, if we were not very dull,
We could not choose but look on still;
Since there is no place so alone,   20
    The which he doth not fill.

Sundays the pillars are,
On which heav'n's palace arched lies:
The other days fill up the spare
And hollow room with vanities.   25
They[4] are the fruitful beds and borders
In God's rich garden: that is bare,[5]
    Which parts their ranks and orders.

The Sundays of man's life,
Threaded together on time's string,   30
Make bracelets to adorn the wife
Of the eternal glorious King.
On Sunday heaven's gate stands ope';
Blessings are plentiful and rife,
    More plentiful than hope.   35

This day my Saviour rose,
And did inclose this light for his:
That, as each beast his manger knows,

4. Sundays.
5. The gaps between Sundays, like the spaces between flower beds, are bare.

Man might not of his fodder miss.
Christ hath took in[6] this piece of ground,   40
And made a garden there for those
    Who want herbs for their wound.[7]

    The rest[8] of our Creation
Our great Redeemer did remove
With the same shake,[9] which at his passion   45
Did th' earth and all things with it move.
As Samson bore the doors away,
Christ's hands, though nailed, wrought our salvation,
    And did unhinge that day.[1]

    The brightness of that day   50
We sullied by our foul offence:
Wherefore that robe we cast away,
Having a new at his expense,
Whose drops of blood paid the full price,[2]
That was required to make us gay,   55
    And fit for Paradise.

    Thou art a day of mirth:
And where the weekdays trail on ground,
Thy flight is higher, as thy birth.
O let me take thee at the bound,   60
Leaping with thee from sev'n to sev'n,
Till that we both, being tossed from earth,
    Fly hand in hand to heav'n!

$$\text{Ana-}\left\{\begin{array}{c}\text{MARY}\\\text{ARMY}\end{array}\right\}\text{-gram}$$

How well her name an *Army* doth present,
In whom the *Lord of Hosts* did pitch his tent!

Employment (II)

He that is weary, let him sit.
    My soul would[1] stir
And trade in courtesies and wit,
    Quitting the fur[2]
To cold complexions[3] needing it.   5

6. Taken into cultivation.
7. Because of the presumed healing power of many kinds of herbs.
8. The day of rest, the seventh day, the old Sabbath ("that day" in line 49).
9. The earthquake at Christ's death (Matthew 27 : 51).
1. Trapped in Gaza, Samson merely "took the doors of the gate of the city . . . and went away with them . . . upon his shoulders" (Judges 16 : 3). "That day" refers perhaps to the Crucifixion, perhaps to the old Sabbath, or both.
2. "These . . . have washed their robes, and made them white in the blood of the Lamb" (Revelation 7 : 14).
1. Wishes to.
2. Academic dress; warm clothing.
3. Constitutions; from theory of humors.

Man is no star, but a quick coal[4]
       Of mortal fire:
Who blows it not, nor doth control
       A faint desire,
Lets his own ashes choke his soul.   10

When the'elements[5] did for place contest
       With him, whose will
Ordained the highest to be best;
       The earth sat still,
And by the others is opprest.   15

Life is a business, not good cheer;
       Ever in wars.[6]
The sun still shineth there or here,
       Whereas the stars
Watch an advantage to appear.   20

Oh that I were an Orange-tree,
       That busy[7] plant!
Then should I ever laden be,
       And never want
Some fruit for him that dressed me.   25

But we are still too young or old;
       The Man is gone,
Before we do our wares unfold:[8]
       So we freeze on,
Until the grave increase our cold.   30

Denial[9]

When my devotions could not pierce
              Thy silent ears;
Then was my heart broken, as was my verse:
       My breast was full of fears
                     And disorder: 5

My bent thoughts, like a brittle bow,
              Did fly asunder:
Each took his way; some would to pleasures go,
       Some to the wars and thunder
                     Of alarms.[1]   10

---

4. A piece of carbon glowing, but without flame (*Oxford English Dictionary*).
5. Earth, air, fire, water. The "highest" element (line 13) is fire, the lowest earth (line 14).
6. See Job 7 : 1.
7. Usefully active; the orange tree bears fruit and blossoms at the same time.

8. We make excuses that we are too young or too old, until suddenly life has slipped by.
9. The main *denial*, including all the others, is the denial of rhythmic fulfilment or harmony or *chiming* (line 29) through the first five stanzas.
1. Calls (trumpet or drums) to arms.

As good go any where, they say,
                    As to benumb
Both knees and heart, in crying night and day,
          Come, come, my God, O come,
                    But no hearing.   15

          O that thou shouldst give dust a tongue
                    To cry to thee,
And then not hear it crying! all day long
          My heart was in my knee,
                    But no hearing.   20

          Therefore my soul lay out of sight,
                    Untuned, unstrung:
My feeble spirit, unable to look right,
          Like a nipt blossom, hung
                    Discontented.   25

          O cheer and tune my heartless breast,
                    Defer no time;
That so thy favours granting my request,
          They and my mind may chime,
                    And mend my rime.   30

Christmas

All after pleasures as I rid[2] one day,
          My horse and I, both tired, body and mind,
          With full cry of affections, quite astray,
I took up[3] in the next inn I could find.
There when I came, whom found I but my dear,   5
          My dearest Lord, expecting[4] till the grief
          Of pleasures brought me to him, ready there
To be all passengers' most sweet relief?
O Thou, whose glorious, yet contracted light,
          Wrapt in night's mantle, stole into a manger;   10
          Since my dark soul and brutish is thy right,
To man of all beasts be not thou a stranger:
          Furnish and deck my soul, that thou mayst have
          A better lodging, than a rack[5] or grave.

The shepherds sing; and shall I silent be?   15
          My God, no hymn for thee?
My soul's a shepherd too; a flock it feeds
          Of thoughts, and words, and deeds.
The pasture is thy word: the streams, thy grace
          Enriching all the place.   20

2. Rode.
3. Settled.
4. Waiting.

5. Place for hay or straw, like Christ's manger.

Shepherd and flock shall sing, and all my powers
     Outsing the daylight hours.
Then we will chide the sun for letting night
     Take up his place and right:
We sing one common Lord; wherefore he should   25
     Himself the candle hold.
I will go searching, till I find a sun
     Shall stay, till we have done;
A willing shiner, that shall shine as gladly,
     As frost-nipt suns look sadly.   30
Then we will sing, and shine all our own day,
     And one another pay:
His beams shall cheer my breast, and both so twine,
Till ev'n his beams sing, and my music shine.

The World

Love built a stately house; where *Fortune* came,
And spinning fancies, she was heard to say,
That her fine cobwebs did support the frame,
Whereas they were supported by the same:
But *Wisdom* quickly swept them all away.   5

Then *Pleasure* came, who, liking not the fashion,
Began to make *Balconies, Terraces,*
Till she had weakened all by alteration:
But rev'rend *laws*, and many a *proclamation*
Reformed all at length with menaces.   10

Then entered *Sin*, and with that Sycamore,[6]
Whose leaves first sheltered man from drought and dew,
Working and winding slily evermore,
The inward walls and sommers[7] cleft and tore:
But *Grace* shored these, and cut that as it grew.   15

Then *Sin* combined with *Death* in a firm band
To raze the building to the very floor:
Which they effected, none could them withstand.
But *Love* and *Grace* took *Glory* by the hand,
And built a braver Palace than before.   20

Vanity (I)

The fleet Astronomer can bore,
And thread the spheres with his quick-piercing mind:
He views their stations, walks from door to door,
     Surveys, as if he had designed

6. The sycamore was thought to be the fig tree of Genesis.
7. Supporting beams, girders.

To make a purchase there: he sees their dances,   5
           And knoweth long before,
Both their full-eyed aspects, and secret glances.

       The nimble Diver with his side
Cuts through the working waves, that he may fetch
His dearly-earned pearl, which God did hide   10
           On purpose from the vent'rous wretch;
That he might save his life, and also hers,
              Who with excessive pride
Her own destruction and his danger wears.

       The subtle Chymick[8] can devest   15
And strip the creature naked, till he find
The callow[9] principles within their nest:
           There he imparts to them his mind,
Admitted to their bed-chamber, before
             They appear trim and drest   20
To ordinary suitors at the door.

       What hath not Man sought out and found,
But his dear God? who yet his glorious law
Embosoms in us, mellowing the ground
           With showers and frosts, with love and awe,   25
So that we need not say, Where's this command?
            Poor Man, thou searchest round
To find out *death*; but missest *life* at hand.

Virtue

    Sweet day, so cool, so calm, so bright,
    The bridal of the earth and sky:
    The dew shall weep thy fall[1] to night;
           For thou must die.

    Sweet rose, whose hue angry[2] and brave[3]   5
    Bids the rash gazer wipe his eye:
    Thy root is ever in its grave,
           And thou must die.

    Sweet spring, full of sweet days and roses,
    A box where sweets[4] compacted lie;   10
    My music shows ye have your closes,[5]
           And all must die.

    Only a sweet and virtuous soul,
    Like seasoned timber, never gives;

8. Chemist in his laboratory.
9. Featherless, stripped, without disguise.
1. In musical terms, the short final line
of each stanza is a "dying fall."

2. Red, with hue of anger.
3. Splendid.
4. Perfumes.
5. Concluding cadences (music).

But though the whole world turn to coal,[6]   15
Then chiefly lives.

The Pearl. Matth. 13. 45[7]

I know the ways of Learning; both the head
And pipes that feed the press, and make it run;[8]
What reason hath from nature borrowed,
Or of it self, like a good housewife, spun
In laws and policy; what the stars conspire,   5
What willing[9] nature speaks, what forced by fire;[1]
Both th'old discoveries, and the new-found seas,
The stock and surplus, cause and history:
All these stand open, or I have the keys:
                              Yet I love thee.   10

I know the ways of Honour, what maintains
The quick returns of courtesy and wit:
In vies of favours whether party gains,[2]
When glory[3] swells the heart, and moldeth it
To all expressions both of hand and eye,   15
Which on the world a true-love-knot may tie,
And bear the bundle,[4] wheresoe'er it goes.
How many drams of spirit there must be
To sell my life unto my friends or foes:
                              Yet I love thee.   20

I know the ways of Pleasure, the sweet strains,
The lullings and the relishes of it;
The propositions of hot blood and brains;[5]
What mirth and music mean; what love and wit
Have done these twenty hundred years, and more: 25
I know the projects of unbridled store:[6]
My stuff is flesh, not brass; my senses live,
And grumble oft, that they have more in me
Than he[7] that curbs them, being but one to five:
                              Yet I love thee.   30

I know all these, and have them in my hand:
Therefore not seeled,[8] but with open eyes

6. Be reduced to a cinder in the general conflagration at the Last Judgment. *Coal*: cinder or ashes.
7. Matthew 13 : 45–46, "Again the kingdom is like unto a merchant man seeking goodly pearls: who when he had found one pearl of great price, went and sold all that he had and bought it."
8. See Zechariah 4 : 12, "Two olive branches which through the two golden pipes empty the golden oil out of themselves . . ." Apparently, the images suggested to Herbert the printing press.
9. Willingly.
1. Of the alchemist.
2. I know which of two parties gains in a contest of favors.
3. Ambition.
4. Of favors, like a servant.
5. *Strains, lullings, relishes, propositions* are all terms of both mirth and music.
6. Wealth.
7. Reason.
8. Eyes sewn like a falcon's in training.

I fly to thee, and fully understand
Both the main sale, and the commodities;[9]
And at what rate and price I have thy love   35
With all the circumstances that may move:
Yet through these labyrinths, not my groveling wit,
But thy silk twist[1] let down from heav'n to me,
Did both conduct and teach me, how by it
      To climb to thee.   40

Affliction (IV)

Broken in pieces all asunder,
  Lord, hunt me not,
  A thing forgot,
Once a poor creature, now a wonder,
  A wonder tortured in the space   5
  Betwixt this world and that of grace.

My thoughts are all a case of knives,
  Wounding my heart
  With scattered smart,
As wat'ring pots give flowers their lives.   10
  Nothing their fury can control,
  While they do wound and pink[2] my soul.

All my attendants are at strife,
  Quitting their place
  Unto my face: 15
Nothing performs the task of life:
  The elements are let loose to fight,
  And while I live, try out their right.

Oh help, my God! let not their plot
  Kill them and me,   20
  And also thee,
Who art my life: dissolve the knot,
  As the sun scatters by his light
  All the rebellions of the night.

Then shall those powers, which work for grief,   25
  Enter thy pay,
  And day by day
Labour[3] thy praise, and my relief;
  With care and courage building me,
  Till I reach heav'n, and much more, thee.   30

9. Advantages.
1. Thread or cord made of plaited fibers of silk; Ariadne gave Theseus a thread to help him find his way out of the labyrinth.
2. Fencing term.
3. Labor for.

Man[4]

My God, I heard this day,
That none doth build a stately habitation,
But he that means to dwell therein.
What house more stately hath there been,
Or can be, than is Man? to[5] whose creation   5
All things are in decay.

For Man is ev'ry thing,
And more: he is a tree, yet bears more fruit;
A beast, yet is, or should be more:
Reason and speech we only bring.   10
Parrots may thank us, if they are not mute,
They go upon the score.[6]

Man is all symmetry,
Full of proportions, one limb to another,
And all to all the world besides: 15
Each part may call the farthest, brother:
For head with foot hath private amity,
And both with moons and tides.[7]

Nothing hath got so far,
But Man hath caught and kept it, as his prey.   20
His eyes dismount[8] the highest star:
He is in little all the sphere.[9]
Herbs gladly cure our flesh; because that they
Find their acquaintance there.

For us the winds do blow,   25
The earth doth rest, heav'n move, and fountains flow.[1]
Nothing we see, but means our good,
As our *delight*, or as our *treasure*:
The whole is, either our cupboard of *food*,
Or cabinet of *pleasure*.   30

The stars have us to bed;
Night draws the curtain, which the sun withdraws;
Music and light attend our head.
All things unto our *flesh* are kind[2]
In their *descent* and *being*; to our *mind*
In their *ascent* and *cause*.   35

4. Underlying this poem is the concept of the Chain of Being (see "Employment [I]," line 21, and note there) and the correlative correspondences between microcosm or the little world of man ("ev'ry thing," line 7) and the macrocosm or universe (line 15).
5. Compared to.
6. They are in man's debt.
7. Alludes to the commonplace notions that the parts of the body mirror the organization of the universe, that these are reciprocally related, and that the bodily members are affected by the actions of "moons and tides."
8. Bring down to earth.
9. The universe.
1. The four elements, air, earth, fire (*heav'n* = sun), water.
2. Akin.

Each thing is full of duty:
Waters united are our navigation;
Distinguished, our habitation;[3]
Below, our drink; above,[4] our meat;   40
Both are our cleanliness. Hath one such beauty?
Then how are all things neat![5]

More servants wait on Man,
Than he'll take notice of: in ev'ry path
He treads down that which doth befriend him,   45
When sickness makes him pale and wan.
Oh mighty love! Man is one world, and hath
Another to attend him.

Since then, my God, thou hast
So brave a Palace built; O dwell in it,   50
That it may dwell with thee at last!
Till then, afford us so much wit,
That, as the world serves us, we may serve thee,
And both thy servants be.

Life

I made a posy, while the day ran by:
Here will I smell my remnant out, and tie
My life within this band.
But time did beckon to the flowers, and they
By noon most cunningly did steal away,   5
And withered in my hand.

My hand was next to them, and then my heart:
I took, without more thinking, in good part
Time's gentle admonition:
Who did so sweetly death's sad taste convey,   10
Making my mind to smell my fatal day;
Yet sug'ring the suspicion.

Farewell dear flowers, sweetly your time ye spent,
Fit, while ye lived, for smell or ornament,
And after death for cures.   15
I follow straight without complaints or grief,
Since if my scent be good, I care not, if
It be as short as yours.

Mortification

How soon doth man decay!
When clothes are taken from a chest of sweets[1]

3. An ellipsis here: when God united the waters (Genesis 1 : 9–10), they were separated ("distinguished") from the land, and so man could find "habitation."
4. As rain contributes to producing food.
5. If "such beauty" exists in just "one" element, what excellence there must be in "all things"!
1. Perfumes.

To swaddle infants, whose young breath
Scarce knows the way;
Those clouts[2] are little winding sheets, 5
Which do consign and send them unto death.

When boys go first to bed,
They step into their voluntary graves,
Sleep binds them fast; only their breath
Makes them not dead. 10
Successive nights like rolling waves,
Convey them quickly, who are bound for[3] death.

When youth is frank and free,
And calls for music, while his veins do swell,
All day exchanging mirth and breath 15
In company;
That music summons to the knell,[4]
Which shall befriend him at the house[5] of death.

When man grows staid and wise,
Getting a house and home, where he may move 20
Within the circle of his breath,
Schooling his eyes;
That dumb inclosure maketh love
Unto the coffin, that attends his death.

When age grows low and weak, 25
Marking his grave, and thawing ev'ry year,
Till all do melt, and drown his breath
When he would speak;
A chair or litter shows the bier,
Which shall convey him to the house of death. 30

Man, ere he is aware,
Hath put together a solemnity,
And drest his hearse, while he has breath
As yet to spare:
Yet Lord, instruct us so to die, 35
That all these dyings may be life in death.[6]

Jordan (II)

When first my lines of heav'nly joys made mention,
Such was their luster, they did so excel,

2. Swaddling clothes.
3. "Both bound up by sleep and jour-
neying toward" death (Summers).
4. The "passing-bell," customarily
sounded while a person was dying.
5. Most editors read *hour*, but *house*
from the 1633 edition seems better, fitting the overt and subtle house imagery
pervading the poem. The final enclosure
or house is the "hearse"; thus, "mortification" not only refers to preparation
for death but also points to the body as
the house of the soul.
6. So that all the symbolical dyings, at
the various stages, may be life preparing
for death, true life being lived here amid
death as a preparation towards true life
after death.

That I sought out quaint words, and trim invention,
My thoughts began to burnish,[7] sprout, and swell,
Curling with metaphors a plain intention,   5
Decking the sense, as if it were to sell.[8]

Thousands of notions in my brain did run,
Off'ring their service, if I were not sped:[9]
I often blotted what I had begun;
This was not quick[1] enough, and that was dead.   10
Nothing could seem too rich to clothe the sun,
Much less those joys which trample on his head.[2]

As flames do work and wind, when they ascend,
So did I weave my self into the sense.
But while I bustled, I might hear a friend   15
Whisper, *How wide[3] is all this long pretence!*
There is in love a sweetness ready penned:
Copy out only that, and save expense.

Obedience

My God, if writings may
Convey[4] a lordship any way
Whither the buyer and the seller please;
Let it not thee displease,
If this poor paper do as much as they.   5

On it my heart doth bleed
As many lines, as there doth need
To pass[5] it self and all it hath to thee.
To which I do agree,
And here present it as my special Deed.   10

If that[6] hereafter Pleasure
Cavil, and claim her part and measure,
As if this passed with a reservation,[7]
Or some such words in fashion;
I here exclude the wrangler from thy treasure.   15

O let thy sacred will
All thy delight in me fulfill!
Let me not think an action mine own way,
But as thy love shall sway,
Resigning up the rudder to thy skill.   20

7. Spread out, grow in vigor.
8. For sale.
9. If I did not meet with success.
1. Alive, lively.
2. Presumably the "joys" are Christ's or heaven's. *His head*: the sun's.
3. Wide of the mark.
4. Transfer by deed (or other legal process).
5. Convey by legal process (lines 13 and 36 also).
6. If.
7. Codicil or rider.

Lord, what is man to thee,[8]
That thou shouldst mind a rotten tree?
Yet since thou canst not choose but see my actions,
So great are thy perfections,
Thou mayst as well my actions guide, as see.   25

Besides, thy death and blood
Showed a strange love to all our good:
Thy sorrows were in earnest; no faint proffer,
Or superficial offer
Of what we might not take, or be withstood.   30

Wherefore I all forego:
To one word only I say, No:
Where in the deed there was an intimation
Of a *gift* or *donation*,
Lord, let it now by way of *purchase* go.   35

He that will pass his land,
As I have mine, may set his hand
And heart unto this deed, when he hath read,
And make the purchase spread
To both our goods, if he to it will stand.   40

How happy were my part,
If some kind man would thrust his heart
Into these lines; till in heav'n's Court of Rolls[9]
They were by winged souls
Entered for both, far above their desert!   45

The British Church

I joy, dear Mother, when I view
Thy perfect lineaments and hue
Both sweet and bright.

Beauty in thee takes up her place,
And dates[1] her letters from thy face,   5
When she doth write.

A fine aspect in fit array,
Neither too mean, not yet too gay,
Shows who is best.

Outlandish[2] looks may not compare: 10

8. Psalms 144 : 3, "Lord what is man, that thou takest knowledge of him?"
9. Where deeds are recorded.
1. March 25 (Feast of the Annunciation, Lady Day) marked the new year in the Anglican calendar.
2. Foreign; the context also suggests "extreme." The Anglican church pursues the middle way between Rome and Geneva in both doctrine and worship.

For all they either painted are,
> Or else undrest.

She on the hills,[3] which wantonly
Allureth all in hope to be
> By her preferred,   15

Hath kissed so long her painted shrines,
That ev'n her face by kissing shines,
> For her reward.

She in the valley[4] is so shy
Of dressing, that her hair doth lie   20
> About her ears:

While she avoids her neighbour's pride,
She wholly goes on th'other side,
> And nothing wears.

But dearest Mother, (what those miss)   25
The mean thy praise and glory is,
> And long may be.

Blessed be God, whose love it was
To double-moat thee with his grace,
> And none but thee.   30

The Quip

The merry world did on a day
With his train-bands[5] and mates agree
To meet together, where I lay,
And all in sport to jeer at me.

First, Beauty crept into a rose,   5
Which when I plucked not, Sir, said she,
Tell me, I pray, Whose hands are those?
But thou shalt answer, Lord, for me.[6]

Then Money came, and chinking still,
What tune is this, poor man? said he: 10
I heard in Music you had skill.
But thou shalt answer, Lord, for me.

Then came brave Glory puffing by
In silks that whistled, who but he?

---

3. Rome; i.e., Catholicism.
4. Geneva; i.e., Calvinism.
5. Trained bands; used for citizen soldiers in London.

6. Psalms 38 : 15, "For in thee, O Lord, have I put my trust: thou shalt answer for me, O Lord my God."

He scarce allowed me half an eye.   15
But thou shalt answer, Lord, for me.

Then came quick Wit-and-Conversation,
And he would needs a comfort be,
And, to be short, make an oration.
But thou shalt answer, Lord, for me.   20

Yet when the hour of thy design
To answer these fine things shall come,
Speak not at large; say, I am thine:[7]
And then they have their answer home.

Iesu

Iesu is in my heart, his sacred name
Is deeply carved there: but th'other week
A great affliction broke the little frame,
Ev'n all to pieces: which I went to seek:
And first I found the corner, where was *I*,   5
After, where *ES*, and next where *U* was graved.
When I had got these parcels, instantly
I sat me down to spell them, and perceived
That to my broken heart he was *I ease you*,
                              And to my whole is *IESU*.   10

Dialogue

Sweetest Saviour, if my soul
          Were but worth the having,
Quickly should I then control
          Any thought of waving.[1]
But when all my care and pains   5
Cannot give the name of gains
To thy wretch so full of stains,
What delight or hope remains?

What (child) is the balance thine,
          Thine the poise and measure?   10
If I say, Thou shalt be mine,
          Finger not my treasure.
What the gains in having thee
Do amount to, only he,
Who for man was sold, can see;   15
That transferred[2] th' accounts to me.

But as I can see no merit,
　　Leading to this favour:
So the way to fit me for it
　　Is beyond my savour.[3]　　　　　　20
As the reason then is thine;
So the way is none of mine:
I disclaim[4] the whole design:
Sin disclaims and I resign.

That[5] *is all, if that I could*　　　　25
　　Get without repining,
And my clay my creature would
　　Follow my resigning.
That as I did freely part
With my glory and desert,[6]　　　　30
Left all joys to feel all smart——
　　Ah! no more: thou break'st my heart.

Dullness

Why do I languish thus drooping and dull,
　　As if I were all earth?
O give me quickness, that I may with mirth
　　　　Praise thee brim-full!

The wanton lover in a curious strain　　5
　　Can praise his fairest fair;
And with quaint metaphors her curled hair
　　　　Curl o'er again.

Thou art my loveliness, my life, my light,
　　Beauty alone to me:　　　　10
Thy bloody death and undeserved, makes thee
　　　　Pure red and white.[7]

When all perfections as but one appear,
　　That those thy form doth show,
The very dust, where thou dost tread and go,　　15
　　　　Makes beauties here.

Where are my lines then? my approaches? views?
　　Where are my window-songs?[8]
Lovers are still pretending,[9] and ev'n wrongs
　　　　Sharpen their Muse:　　20

3. Understanding.
4. Relinquish legal claim.
5. The disclaimer.
6. Pronounced "desart."
7. "Red and white" is commonplace in secular love poetry, but also used in tra- dition of Christ as lover; see Song of Solomon 5 : 10, "My beloved is white and ruddy."
8. Serenades.
9. Always wooing.

But I am lost in flesh, whose sugared lies
        Still mock me, and grow bold:
Sure thou didst put a mind there, if I could
        Find where it lies.

Lord, clear thy gift, that with a constant wit   25
        I may but look towards thee:
Look only; for to *love* thee, who can be,
        What angel fit?

Sin's Round[1]

Sorry I am, my God, sorry I am,
That my offences course it in a ring.
My thoughts are working like a busy flame,
Until their cockatrice[2] they hatch and bring:
And when they once have perfected their draughts,   5
My words take fire from my inflamed thoughts.

My words take fire from my inflamed thoughts,
Which spit it forth like the Sicilian Hill.[3]
They vent[4] the wares, and pass them with their faults,
And by their breathing ventilate[5] the ill.   10
But words suffice not, where are lewd intentions:
My hands do join to finish the inventions:

My hands do join to finish the inventions:
And so my sins ascend three stories high,
As Babel grew, before there were dissensions.   15
Yet ill deeds loiter not: for they supply
New thoughts of sinning: wherefore, to my shame,
Sorry I am, my God, sorry I am.

Peace

Sweet Peace, where dost thou dwell, I humbly crave,
        Let me once know.
    I sought thee in a secret cave,
        And asked if Peace were there.
A hollow wind did seem to answer, No: 5
        Go seek elsewhere.

I did; and going did a rainbow note:
        Surely, thought I,
    This is the lace of Peace's coat:
        I will search out the matter.   10

1. The repetition of lines, as in a "round", reflects the self-perpetuating character of sin.
2. Fabulous creature hatched by a serpent from a cock's egg.
3. The volcanic Mount Etna.
4. Discharge, with secondary meaning of "sell" (the wares).
5. Make the fire burn better.

But while I looked, the clouds immediately
        Did break and scatter.

Then went I to a garden, and did spy
        A gallant flower,
    The Crown Imperial: Sure, said I,   15
        Peace at the root must dwell.
But when I digged, I saw a worm devour
        What showed so well.

At length I met a rev'rend good old man,
        Whom when for Peace   20
    I did demand, he thus began:
        There was a Prince of old[6]
At Salem dwelt, who lived with good increase
        Of flock and fold.

He sweetly lived; yet sweetness did not save   25
        His life from foes.
    But after death out of his grave
        There sprang twelve[7] stalks of wheat:
Which many wond'ring at, got some of those
        To plant and set.   30

It prospered strangely, and did soon disperse
        Through all the earth:
    For they that taste it do rehearse,
        That virtue[8] lies therein,
A secret virtue bringing peace and mirth   35
        By flight of sin.

Take of this grain, which in my garden grows,
        And grows for you;
    Make bread of it: and that repose
        And peace which ev'ry where   40
With so much earnestness you do pursue,
        Is only there.

The Bunch of Grapes[1]

Joy, I did lock thee up. But some bad man
        Hath let thee out again,
And now, me thinks, I am where I began
        Sev'n years ago: one vogue[2] and vein,
        One air of thoughts usurps my brain.   5

6. Melchisedec, "King of Salem, which is, King of peace" (Hebrews 7 : 2), "brought forth bread and wine" (Genesis 14 : 18), prefiguring Christ.
7. The twelve Apostles.
8. Power, potency.
1. On the cluster of Eshcol as a type of Christ, see Summers's essay, below.
2. General tendency.

I did towards Canaan draw, but now I am
Brought back to the Red Sea, the sea of shame.[3]

For as the Jews of old by God's command
      Travelled, and saw no town:
So now each Christian hath his journeys spanned: 10
      Their story pens and sets us down.[4]
      A single deed is small renown.
God's works are wide, and let in future times;
His ancient justice overflows our crimes.

Then have we too our guardian fires and clouds;   15
      Our Scripture-dew drops fast:
We have our sands and serpents, tents and shrouds;[5]
      Alas! our murmurings come not last.
      But where's the cluster? where's the taste
Of mine inheritance? Lord, if I must borrow,   20
Let me as well take up their joy, as sorrow.

But can he want the grape, who hath the wine?
      I have their fruit and more.
Blessed be God, who prospered *Noah's* vine,
      And made it bring forth grapes good store.   25
      But much more him I must adore.
Who of the Law's sour juice sweet wine did make,
Ev'n God himself being pressed for my sake.

The Storm

If as the winds and waters here below
      Do fly and flow,
My sighs and tears as busy were above;
      Sure they would move
And much affect thee, as tempestuous times   5
Amaze poor mortals, and object[6] their crimes.

Stars have their storms,[7] ev'n in a high degree,
      As well as we.
A throbbing conscience spurred by remorse
      Hath a strange force: 10
It quits the earth, and mounting more and more
Dares to assault thee, and besiege thy door.

There it stands knocking, to thy music's wrong,
      And drowns the song.
Glory and honour are set by, till it   15
      An answer get.

3. The journey of the Israelites through the wilderness; because they rebelled near Canaan, God sent them wandering back towards the Red Sea.
4. The Israelites' story is our story.
5. Temporary shelters.
6. Make them conscious of, accuse.
7. Such as meteor showers.

Poets have wronged poor storms: such days are best;
They purge the air without, within the breast.

Paradise

I bless thee, Lord, because I GROW
Among thy trees, which in a ROW
To thee both fruit and order OW.

What open force, or hidden CHARM
Can blast my fruit, or bring me HARM   5
While the inclosure is thine ARM?

Inclose me still for fear I START.
Be to me rather sharp and TART,
Than let me want thy hand and ART.

When thou dost greater judgements SPARE,   10
And with thy knife but prune and PARE,
Ev'n fruitful trees more fruitful ARE.

Such sharpness shows the sweetest FRIEND:
Such cuttings rather heal than REND:
And such beginnings touch their END.   15

The Size[1]

Content thee, greedy heart.
Modest and moderate joys to those, that have
Title to more hereafter when they part,
   Are passing brave.
  Let th'upper springs into the low   5
  Descend and fall, and thou dost flow.

   What though some have a fraught[2]
Of cloves and nutmegs, and in cinnamon sail;
If thou hast wherewithall to spice a draught,
   When griefs prevail,   10
  And for the future time art heir
  To th' Isle of spices? Is't not fair?

   To be in both worlds full
Is more than God was, who was hungry here.
Wouldst thou his laws of fasting disannul?   15
   Enact good cheer?
  Lay out thy joy, yet hope to save it?
  Wouldst thou both eat thy cake, and have it?

1. Status or condition.   2. Freight.

Great joys are all at once;
But little do reserve themselves for more: 20
Those have their hopes; these what they have renounce,
        And live on score:[3]
   Those are at home; these journey still,
   And meet the rest on Sion's hill.

      Thy Saviour sentenced joy,   25
And in the flesh condemned it as unfit,
At least in lump: for such doth oft destroy;
        Whereas a bit
   Doth tice[4] us on to hopes of more,
   And for the present health restore.   30

   A Christian's state and case
Is not a corpulent, but a thin and spare,
Yet active strength: whose long and bony face
        Content and care
   Do seem to equally divide,   35
   Like a pretender,[5] not a bride.

   Wherefore sit down, good heart;
Grasp not at much, for fear thou losest all.
If comforts fell according to desert,[6]
      They would great frosts and snows destroy: 40
   For we should count, since the last joy.

   Then close again the seam,
Which thou hast opened: do not spread thy robe
In hope of great things. Call to mind thy dream,
        An earthly globe,   45
   On whose meridian was engraven,
   These seas are tears, and heav'n the haven.

Artillery

As I one ev'ning sat before my cell,
Me thoughts[1] a star did shoot into my lap.
I rose, and shook my clothes, as knowing well,
That from small fires comes oft no small mishap.
      When suddenly I heard one say,   5
     Do as thou usest,[2] disobey,
     Expel good motions from thy breast,
Which have the face of fire, but end in rest.

I, who had heard of music in the spheres,

---

3. On credit.
4. Entice.
5. Wooer.

6. A four-syllable line is missing after this.
1. It seemed to me.
2. Art accustomed to.

But not of speech in stars, began to muse: 10
But turning to my God, whose ministers
The stars and all things are; If I refuse,
      Dread Lord, said I, so oft my good;
      Then I refuse not ev'n with blood
        To wash away my stubborn thought: 15
For I will do or suffer what I ought.

But I have also stars and shooters[3] too,
Born where thy servants both artilleries use.
My tears and prayers night and day do woo,
And work up to thee; yet thou dost refuse.   20
      Not, but I am (I must say still)
      Much more obliged to do thy will,
        Than thou to grant mine: but because
Thy promise now hath ev'n set thee thy laws.

Then we are shooters both, and thou dost deign   25
To enter combat with us, and contest
With thine own clay. But I would parley fain:
Shun not my arrows, and behold my breast.
      Yet if thou shunnest, I am thine:
      I must be so, if I am mine.   30
        There is no articling[4] with thee:
I am but finite, yet thine infinitely.

The Pilgrimage

I travelled on, seeing the hill, where lay
        My expectation.
     A long it was and weary way.
     The gloomy cave of Desperation
I left on th' one, and on the other side   5
        The rock of Pride.

And so I came to Fancy's meadow strowed
        With many a flower;
     Fain would I here have made abode,
     But I was quickened by my hour.   10
So to Care's copse I came, and there got through
        With much ado.

That led me to the wild of Passion, which
        Some call the wold;[5]
     A wasted place, but sometimes rich.   15
     Here I was robbed of all my gold,

3. Shooting stars, but also those who use   4. Negotiating, arranging by treaty.
artillery.   5. Treeless plain, moorland.

Save one good Angel,[6] which a friend had tied
        Close to my side.

At length I got unto the gladsome hill,
        Where lay my hope,   20
    Where lay my heart; and climbing still,
      When I had gained the brow and top,
A lake of brackish waters on the ground
        Was all I found.

With that abashed and struck with many a sting   25
        Of swarming fears,
    I fell, and cried, Alas my King,
      Can both the way and end be tears?
Yet taking heart I rose, and then perceived
        I was deceived: 30

My hill was further: so I flung away,
        Yet heard a cry
    Just as I went, *None goes that way*
    And lives: If that be all said I,
After so foul a journey death is fair,   35
        And but a chair.[7]

The Bag[1]

Away despair! my gracious Lord doth hear.
      Though winds and waves assault my keel,
      He doth preserve it: he doth steer,
      Ev'n when the boat seems most to reel.
      Storms are the triumph of his art: 5
Well may he close his eyes, but not his heart.[2]

Hast thou not heard, that my Lord JESUS died?
      Then let me tell thee a strange story.
      The God of power, as he did ride
      In his majestic robes of glory,   10
      Resolved to light; and so one day
He did descend, undressing all the way.

The stars his tire[3] of light and rings obtained,
      The cloud his bow, the fire[4] his spear,
      The sky his azure mantle gained.   15
      And when they asked, what he would wear;
      He smiled and said as he did go,
He had new clothes a making here below.

6. A gold coin; also, guardian angel.
7. Place of rest; sedan chair.
1. In *A Reading of George Herbert*, Rosamund Tuve suggests "both a purse and a bag for straining wine through."

2. See Matthew 8 : 24, where Christ sleeps in the boat during the storm on Galilee.
3. Headdress.
4. Lightning.

When he was come, as travellers are wont,
    He did repair unto an inn.   20
    Both then, and after, many a brunt
    He did endure to cancel sin:
    And having giv'n the rest before,
Here he gave up his life to pay our score.

But as he was returning, there came one   25
    That ran upon him with a spear.
    He, who came hither all alone,
    Bringing nor man, nor arms, nor fear,
    Received the blow upon his side,
And straight he turned, and to his brethren cried,   30

If ye have any thing to send or write,
    (I have no bag, but here is room)
    Unto my Father's hands and sight,
    (Believe me) it shall safely come.
    That I shall mind, what you impart;   35
Look, you may put it very near my heart.

Or if hereafter any of my friends
    Will use me in this kind, the door
    Shall still be open; what he sends
    I will present, and somewhat more,   40
    Not to his hurt. Sighs will convey
Any thing to me. Hark, Despair away.

The Collar[5]

  I struck the board,[6] and cried, No more.
     I will abroad.
  What? shall I ever sigh and pine?
My lines and life are free; free as the road,
  Loose as the wind, as large as store.   5
     Shall I be still in suit?[7]

5. The title suggests *choler* (anger), a symbol of discipline, and Christ's yoke or burden: "Take my yoke upon you, and learn of me . . . and ye shall find rest for your souls. For my yoke is easy, and my burden is light" (Matthew 11 : 29–30). Summers calls this poem "one of Herbert's most deliberate ventures in 'hieroglyphic form.' The object of imitation is the disordered life of self-will. . . . Herbert has given a formalized picture of chaos, . . . (especially) in the elaborate anarchy of the patterns of measure and rhyme. The poem contains all the elements of order in violent disorder. No line is unrhymed . . . and each line contains two, three, four, or five poetic feet. . . . The stanzaic norm which is the measure for

that disorder . . . is established, simultaneously with the submission of the rebel, (only) in the final quatrain: 10*a* 4*b* 8*a* 6*b*. The pattern of line lengths and rhyme does not occur until the final four lines; before those lines the elements of the pattern are arranged so as to form almost the mathematical ultimate in lack of periodicity. . . . The poem dramatizes expertly and convincingly the revolt of the heart, and its imitation of colloquial speech almost convinces us of the justice of the cause. But the disorder . . . provides a constant implicit criticism. . . ." (*George Herbert: His Religion and Art* (Cambridge, Mass., 1954), pp. 90–92).
6. Table; communion table, maybe.
7. Petitioner; in attendance; waiting on another (see line 31).

Have I no harvest but a thorn
To let me blood, and not restore
What I have lost with cordial[8] fruit?
         Sure there was wine   10
Before my sighs did dry it: there was corn
      Before my tears did drown it.
Is the year only lost to me?
      Have I no bays to crown it?
No flowers, no garlands gay? all blasted?   15
      All wasted?
Not so, my heart: but there is fruit,
      And thou hast hands.
Recover all thy sigh-blown age
On double pleasures: leave thy cold dispute   20
Of what is fit, and not. Forsake thy cage,
      Thy rope of sands,
Which petty thoughts have made, and made to thee
Good cable, to enforce and draw,
      And be thy law,   25
While thou didst wink and wouldst not see.
      Away; take heed,
      I will abroad.
Call in thy death's head there: tie up thy fears.
      He that forbears   30
To suit and serve his need,
      Deserves his load.
But as I raved and grew more fierce and wild
      At every word,
Me thoughts I heard one calling, *Child:*   35
      And I replied, *My Lord.*

Joseph's Coat[9]

Wounded I sing, tormented I indite,
Thrown down I fall into a bed, and rest:
Sorrow hath changed its note: such is his will,
Who changeth all things, as him pleaseth best.
      For well he knows, if but one grief and smart   5
Among my many had his full career,
Sure it would carry with it ev'n my heart,
And both would run until they found a bier
      To fetch the body; both being due to grief.
But he hath spoiled the race; and giv'n to anguish   10
One of Joy's coats, ticing[1] it with relief
To linger in me, and together languish.
      I live to show his power, who once did bring
      My *joys* to *weep,* and now my *griefs* to *sing.*

8. Invigorating.
9. Genesis 37 : 3, the "coat of many colors" of Joseph; traditionally, Joseph is
paralleled with Christ, his coat with
Christ's humanity at the Crucifixion.
1. Enticing.

The Pulley

When God at first made man,
Having a glass of blessings standing by;
Let us (said he) pour on him all we can:
Let the world's riches, which dispersed lie,
   Contract into a span.   5

   So strength first made a way;
Then beauty flowed, then wisdom, honour, pleasure:
When almost all was out, God made a stay,
Perceiving that alone of all his treasure
   Rest in the bottom lay.   10

   For if I should (said he)
Bestow this jewel also on my creature,
He would adore my gifts instead of me,
And rest in Nature, not the God of Nature:
   So both should losers be.   15

   Yet let him keep the rest,
But keep them with repining restlessness:
Let him be rich and weary, that at least,
If goodness lead him not, yet weariness
   May toss him to my breast.   20

The Search

Whither, O, whither art thou fled,
   My Lord, my Love?
My searches are my daily bread;
   Yet never prove.

My knees pierce th' earth, mine eyes the sky;   5
   And yet the sphere
And centre both to me deny
   That thou art there.

Yet can I mark how herbs below
   Grow green and gay,   10
As if to meet thee they did know,
   While I decay.

Yet can I mark how stars above
   Simper[2] and shine,
As having keys unto thy love,   15
   While poor I pine.

2. Glimmer, twinkle.

I sent a sigh to seek thee out,
   Deep drawn in pain,
Winged like an arrow: but my scout
   Returns in vain.   20

I tuned another (having store)
   Into a groan;
Because the search was dumb before:
   But all was one.[3]

Lord, dost thou some new fabric mould, 25
   Which favour wins,
And keeps thee present, leaving th'old
   Unto their sins?

Where is my God? what hidden place
   Conceals thee still?   30
What covert dare eclipse thy face?
   Is it thy will?

O let not that of any thing;[4]
   Let rather brass,
Or steel, or mountains be thy ring, 35
   And I will pass.

Thy will such an entrenching is,
   As passeth thought:
To it[5] all strength, all subtleties
   Are things of nought.   40

Thy will such a strange distance is,
   As that to it
East and West touch, the poles do kiss,
   And parallels meet.

Since then my grief must be as large, 45
   As is thy space,
Thy distance from me; see my charge,[6]
   Lord, see my case.

O take these bars, these lengths away,
   Turn, and restore me: 50
Be not Almighty, let me say,
   Against, but for me.

When thou dost turn, and wilt be near,
   What edge so keen,
What point so piercing can appear 55
   To come between?

---

3. The result was the same.   5. Compared to it.
4. Above all.   6. Burden.

 For as thy absence doth excell
     All distance known:
So doth thy nearness bear the bell,[7]
     Making two one.   60

The Flower

    How fresh, O Lord, how sweet and clean
Are thy returns! ev'n as the flowers in spring;
    To which, besides their own demean,[1]
The late-past frosts tributes of pleasure bring.
        Grief melts away   5
        Like snow in May,
    As if there were no such cold thing.

    Who would have thought my shriveled heart
Could have recovered greenness? It was gone
    Quite under ground; as flowers depart   10
To see their mother-root, when they have blown;[2]
        Where they together
        All the hard weather,
    Dead to the world, keep house unknown.

    These are thy wonders, *Lord of power*,[3]   15
Killing and quick'ning,[4] bringing down to hell
    And up to heaven in an hour;
Making a chiming of a passing-bell.[5]
        We say amiss,
        This or that is: 20
    Thy word is all, if we could spell.

    O that I once past changing were,
Fast in thy Paradise, where no flower can wither!
    Many a spring I shoot up fair,
Off'ring at[6] heav'n, growing and groaning thither: 25
        Nor doth my flower
        Want a spring-shower,
    My sins and I joining together.[7]

    But while I grow in a straight line,
Still upwards bent, as if heav'n were mine own,   30
    Thy anger comes, and I decline:

7. *Bear the bell*: "To take the first place, to have the foremost rank or position, to be the best. Refers to the bell worn by the leading cow or sheep of a drove or flock" (*Oxford English Dictionary*).
1. Bearing or demeanor; domain, also.
2. Bloomed.

3. See line 43, "Lord of love."
4. Giving life to.
5. At the hour of death, the passing-bell is rung on a single tone, but chiming has pleasing variety.
6. Aiming at.
7. The "spring-shower" is the tears caused by his sins.

What frost to that? what pole is not the zone
Where all things burn,
When thou dost turn
And the least frown of thine is shown?[8]   35

And now in age I bud again,
After so many deaths I live and write,
I once more smell the dew and rain,
And relish versing: O my only light,
It cannot be   40
That I am he
On whom thy tempests fell all night.

These are thy wonders, *Lord of love,*
To make us see we are but flowers that glide:[9]
Which when we once can find and prove,[1]   45
Thou hast a garden for us, where to bide.
Who would be more,
Swelling through store,
Forfeit their Paradise by their pride.

The Son

Let foreign nations of their language boast,
What fine variety each tongue affords:
I like our language, as our men and coast:[2]
Who[3] cannot dress it well, want wit, not words.
How neatly do we give one only name   5
To parent's issue and the sun's bright star!
A son is light and fruit; a fruitful flame
Chasing[4] the father's dimness, carried far
From the first man in th' East, to fresh and new
Western discov'ries of posterity.   10
So in one word our Lord's humility
We turn upon him in a sense most true:
For what Christ once in humbleness began,
We him in glory call, *The Son of Man.*

A True Hymn

My joy, my life, my crown!
My heart was meaning all the day,
Somewhat it fain would say:
And still it runneth mutt'ring up and down
With only this, *My joy, my life, my crown.*   5

8. What frost compares to Your anger?
Arctic and Antarctic seem like the equa-
torial zones when you frown!
9. Slip away unnoticed.

1. Experience.
2. Region, country.
3. Those who.
4. Chasing away, dispelling.

Yet slight not these few words:
If truly said, they may take part
Among the best in art.
The fineness which a hymn or psalm affords,
Is, when the soul unto the lines accords.   10

He who craves all the mind,
And all the soul, and strength, and time,
If the words only rime,
Justly complains, that somewhat is behind[5]
To make his verse, or write a hymn in kind.   15

Whereas if th' heart be moved,
Although the verse be somewhat scant,
God doth supply the want.
As when th' heart says (sighing to be approved)
O, *could I love*! and stops: God writeth, *Loved*.   20

Bitter-sweet

Ah my dear angry Lord,
Since thou dost love, yet strike,
Cast down, yet help afford,
Sure I will do the like.

I will complain, yet praise;   5
I will bewail, approve;
And all my sour-sweet days
I will lament, and love.

Aaron[1]

Holiness on the head,
Light and perfections on the breast,
Harmonious bells below, raising the dead
To lead them unto life and rest.
Thus are true Aarons drest.   5

Profaneness in my head,
Defects and darkness in my breast,
A noise[2] of passions ringing me for dead
Unto a place where is no rest.
Poor priest thus am I drest.   10

Only another head
I have, another heart and breast,

5. Lacking, needed, yet to come.
1. Aaron was the brother of Moses and the chief priest of the Israelites. The stanzas suggest the swelling and dying sound of a bell; the rhymes reiterate the same sound; Aaron's ceremonial gar-ments, divinely prescribed (Exodus 28), represent unchanging ideals to which man must aspire.
2. Musically, a band of musicians; contrasted with "Another music" (line 13).

Another music, making live not dead,
Without whom I could have no rest:
In him I am well drest.   15

Christ is my only head,
My alone only heart and breast,
My only music, striking[3] me ev'n dead,
That to the old man I may rest,
And be in him new drest.[4]   20

So holy in my head,
Perfect and light in my dear breast,
My doctrine tuned by Christ, (who is not dead
But lives in me while I do rest)
Come people; Aaron's drest.   25

The Forerunners

The harbingers[5] are come. See, see their mark,
White is their colour, and behold my head.[6]
But must they have my brain? must they dispark[7]
Those sparkling notions, which therein were bred?
Must dulness turn me to a clod?   5
Yet have they left me, *Thou art still my God.*

Good men ye be, to leave me my best room,
Ev'n all my heart, and what is lodged there:
I pass not,[8] I, what of the rest become,
So *Thou art still my God* be out of fear.   10
He will be pleased with that ditty;
And if I please him, I write fine and witty.

Farewell sweet phrases, lovely metaphors.
But will ye leave me thus? when ye before
Of stews and brothels only knew the doors,   15
Then did I wash you with my tears, and more,
Brought you to Church well drest and clad:
My God must have my best, ev'n all I had.

Lovely enchanting language, sugar-cane,
Honey of roses, whither wilt thou fly?   20
Hath some fond lover ticed thee to thy bane?

3. Includes meaning of striking the bell-clapper.
4. "Seeing that ye have put off the old man with his deeds; And have put on the new man, which is renewed in knowledge after the image of him that created him:" (Colossians 3 : 9–10), and see also Galatians 2 : 20, "I live; yet not I but Christ liveth in me" (see line 24).

5. Messengers in advance of a royal progress who secured lodgings by chalking the doors.
6. His white hairs.
7. Disimpark, to turn deer out of a park; with a play on *dis-spark* (Summers).
8. Care not.

And wilt thou leave the Church, and love a sty?
                Fie, thou wilt soil thy broidered coat,
And hurt thy self, and him that sings thy note.

Let foolish lovers, if they will love dung,   25
With canvas, not with arras⁹ clothe their shame:
Let folly speak in her own native tongue.
True beauty dwells on high: ours is a flame
                But borrowed thence to light us thither.
Beauty and beauteous words should go together.   30

Yet if you go, I pass not; take your way:
For *Thou art still my God* is all that ye
Perhaps with more embellishment can say.
Go birds of spring: let winter have his fee:
                Let a bleak paleness chalk the door,   35
So all within be livelier than before.

Discipline

Throw away thy rod,
Throw away thy wrath:
          O my God,
Take the gentle path.

For my heart's desire   5
Unto thine is bent:
          I aspire
To a full consent.

Not a word or look
I affect to own,   10
          But by book,
And thy book alone.

Though I fail, I weep:
Though I halt in pace,
          Yet I creep   15
To the throne of grace.

Then let wrath remove;
Love will do the deed;
          For with love
Stony hearts will bleed.   20

Love is swift of foot;
Love's a man of war,
          And can shoot,
And can hit from far.

9. Expensive cloth, used for wall hangings or draperies.

Who can scape his bow?   25
That which wrought on thee,
       Brought thee low,
Needs must work on me.

Throw away thy rod;
Though man frailties hath,   30
       Thou art God:
Throw away thy wrath.

The Banquet[1]

Welcome sweet and sacred cheer,
       Welcome dear,
With me, in me, live and dwell:
For thy neatness passeth sight,
       Thy delight   5
Passeth tongue to taste or tell.

O what sweetness from the bowl
       Fills my soul,
Such as is, and makes divine!
Is some star (fled from the sphere)   10
       Melted there,
As we sugar melt in wine?

Or hath sweetness in the bread
       Made a head[2]
To subdue the smell of sin;   15
Flowers, and gums, and powders giving
       All their living,
Lest the enemy should win?

Doubtless, neither star nor flower
       Hath the power   20
Such a sweetness to impart:
Only God, who gives perfumes,
       Flesh assumes,
And with it perfumes my heart.

But as Pomanders and wood   25
       Still are good,
Yet being bruised are better scented:
God, to show how far his love
       Could improve,
Here, as broken, is presented.   30

1. The poem is about the "sacred banquet," i.e., Communion.
2. Opposed.

When I had forgot my birth,
             And on earth
In delights of earth was drowned;
God took blood, and needs would be
             Spilt with me,   35
And so found me on the ground.

Having raised me to look up,
             In a cup
Sweetly he doth meet my taste.
But I still being low and short,   40
             Far from court,
Wine becomes a wing at last.

For with it alone I fly
             To the sky:
Where I wipe mine eyes, and see   45
What I seek, for what I sue;
             Him I view,
Who hath done so much for me.

Let the wonder of this pity
             Be my ditty,   50
And take up my lines and life:
Hearken under pain of death,
             Hands and breath;
Strive in this, and love the strife.

The Elixir[3]

Teach me, my God and King,
In all things thee to see,
And what I do in any thing,
To do it as for thee:

Not rudely as a beast,   5
To run into an action;
But still to make thee prepossest,[4]
And give it his[5] perfection.

A man that looks on glass,
On it may stay his eye;   10
Or if he pleaseth, through it pass,
And then the heav'n espy.

---

3. The philosopher's stone, with which alchemists would transmute metals into gold; also, "essence with property of indefinitely prolonging life" (*Oxford English Dictionary*). See Textual Notes for other version.
4. Always to give you a prior claim.
5. Its.

All may of thee partake:
Nothing can be so mean,
Which with his tincture[6] (for thy sake)   15
Will not grow bright and clean.

A servant with this clause
Makes drudgery divine:
Who sweeps a room, as for thy laws,
Makes that and th'action fine.   20

This is the famous stone[7]
That turneth all to gold:
For that which God doth touch[8] and own
Cannot for less be told.

A Wreath

A wreathed garland of deserved praise,
Of praise deserved, unto thee I give,
I give to thee, who knowest all my ways,
My crooked winding ways, wherein I live,
Wherein I die, not live: for life is straight,   5
Straight as a line, and ever tends to thee,
To thee, who art more far above deceit,
Than deceit seems above simplicity.
Give me simplicity, that I may live,
So live and like, that I may know thy ways,   10
Know them and practise them: then shall I give
For this poor wreath, give thee a crown of praise.

Death

Death, thou wast once an uncouth hideous thing,
                    Nothing but bones,
          The sad effect of sadder groans:
Thy mouth was open, but thou couldst not sing.

For we considered thee as at some six   5
                    Or ten years hence,
          After the loss of life and sense,
Flesh being turned to dust, and bones to sticks.

We look on this side of thee, shooting short,
                    Where we did find   10

6. In alchemy, "principle or . . . substance where character may be infused into material things" (*Oxford English Dictionary*). Here, "for thy sake" is the *true* alchemical principle, the tincture which can purify any action.
7. Elixir or philosopher's stone.

8. "Test the fineness of gold . . . upon a touchstone" (*Oxford English Dictionary*) and also "mark metal . . . with an official stamp after it has been tested" (*Oxford English Dictionary*).
9. The poem makes a wreath by weaving its phrases and words.

The shells of fledge souls left behind,
Dry dust, which sheds no tears, but may extort.

But since our Saviour's death did put some blood
　　　　　　　Into thy face;
　　　Thou art grown fair and full of grace,　　　15
Much in request, much sought for as a good.

For we do now behold thee gay and glad,
　　　　　　　As at Doomsday;
　　　When souls shall wear their new array,
And all thy bones with beauty shall be clad.　　　20

Therefore we can go die as sleep, and trust
　　　　　　　Half that we have
　　　Unto an honest faithful grave;
Making our pillows either down, or dust.

Doomsday

　　　　　　Come away,
　　　　Make no delay.
Summon all the dust to rise,
Till it stir, and rub the eyes;
While this member jogs the other,　　　5
Each one whisp'ring, *Live you brother?*

　　　　　　Come away,
　　　　Make this the day.
Dust, alas, no music feels,
But thy trumpet: then it kneels,　　　10
As peculiar notes and strains
Cure Tarantula's[1] raging pains.

　　　　　　Come away,
　　　　O make no stay!
Let the graves make their confession,　　　15
Lest at length they plead possession:[2]
Flesh's stubbornness may have
Read that lesson to the grave.

　　　　　　Come away,
　　　　Thy flock doth stray.　　　20
Some to winds their body lend,
And in them may drown a friend:

1. It was believed that the hysterical malady Tarantism was caused by a tarantula bite and could be cured by

2. On the grounds that the bodies will wild music and dancing. have been there so long.

Some in noisome vapours grow
To a plague and public woe.[3]

Come away,   25
Help our decay.
Man is out of order hurled,
Parceled out to all the world.
Lord, thy broken consort[4] raise,
And the music shall be praise.   30

Judgement

Almighty Judge, how shall poor wretches brook
        Thy dreadful look,
Able a heart of iron to appall,
        When thou shalt call
    For every man's peculiar book?   5

What others mean to do, I know not well;
        Yet I hear tell,
That some will turn thee to some leaves therein
        So void of sin,
    That they in merit shall excell.   10

But I resolve, when thou shalt call for mine,
        That to decline,
And thrust a Testament into thy hand:
        Let that be scanned.
    There thou shalt find my faults are thine.   15

Heaven

O who will show me those delights on high?
        Echo.   *I.*
Thou Echo, thou art mortal, all men know.
        Echo.   *No.*
Wert thou not born among the trees and leaves?   5
        Echo.   *Leaves.*
And are there any leaves, that still abide?
        Echo.   *Bide.*
What leaves are they? impart the matter wholly.
        Echo.   *Holy.*   10
Are holy leaves the Echo then of bliss?
        Echo.   *Yes.*
Then tell me, what is that supreme delight?
        Echo.   *Light.*

3. "Bodies turning to dust may be scattered by winds which bring mortals to shipwreck, or turning to gases they may spread a pestilence" (F. E. Hutchinson, *The Works of George Herbert* [Oxford, 1941], p. 542).
4. Group of musicians or group of instruments.

Light to the mind: what shall the will enjoy?   15
                    Echo.   *Joy.*
But are there cares and business with the pleasure?
                    Echo.   *Leisure.*
Light, joy, and leisure; but shall they persever?
                    Echo.   *Ever.*   20

Love (III) [1]

Love bade me welcome. Yet my soul drew back
                    Guilty of dust and sin.
But quick-eyed Love, observing me grow slack[2]
                    From my first entrance in,
Drew nearer to me, sweetly questioning,   5
                    If I lacked any thing.

A guest, I answered, worthy to be here:
                    Love said, You shall be he.
I the unkind, ungrateful? Ah my dear,
                    I cannot look on thee.   10
Love took my hand, and smiling did reply,
                    Who made the eyes but I?

Truth Lord, but I have marred them: let my shame
                    Go where it doth deserve.
And know you not, says Love, who bore the blame?   15
                    My dear, then I will serve.
You must sit down, says Love, and taste my meat:
                    So I did sit and eat.

Finis

Glory be to God on high
And on earth peace
Good will towards men.

Sonnets from Walton's *Lives* (1670)[3]

[My God, where is that ancient heat . . .]

My God, where is that ancient heat towards thee,
      Wherewith whole shoals of *Martyrs* once did burn,
      Besides their other flames? Doth Poetry

---

1. "Blessed are those servants, whom the lord when he cometh shall find watching: verily I say unto you, that he shall gird himself, and make them to sit down to meat, and will come forth and serve them" (Luke 13 : 37).
2. Hesitant, reluctant.

3. These two poems are from Izaak Walton's *Lives* (1670) of Donne, Herbert, and others. According to Walton, the two poems were written by Herbert at age seventeen "for a New-years gift" to his mother in 1610.

Wear *Venus'* livery? only serve her turn?
Why are not *Sonnets* made of thee? and lays   5
    Upon thine Altar burnt? Cannot thy love
    Heighten a spirit to sound out thy praise
As well as any she? Cannot thy *Dove*
Outstrip their *Cupid* easily in flight?
    Or, since thy ways are deep, and still the same,   10
    Will not a verse run smooth that bears thy name!
Why doth that fire, which by thy power and might
    Each breast does feel, no braver fuel choose
    Than that, which one day, Worms may chance refuse?

[Sure Lord, there is enough . . .]

Sure Lord, there is enough in thee to dry
    Ocean of *Ink*; for, as the Deluge did
    Cover the Earth, so doth thy Majesty:
Each Cloud distills thy praise, and doth forbid
Poets to turn it to another use.   5
    Roses and Lilies speak thee; and to make
    A pair of Cheeks of them, is thy abuse.
Why should I *Women's eyes* for Crystal take?
Such poor invention burns in their low mind
    Whose fire is wild, and doth not upward go   10
    To praise, and on thee Lord, some *ink* bestow.
Open the bones, and you shall nothing find
    In the best *face* but *filth*, when Lord, in thee
    The *beauty* lies, in the *discovery*.[4]

4. Uncovering or disclosure.

Richard Crashaw

Richard Crashaw (1612/13–1649) was born in London, the only child of a prominent Puritan preacher and virulent anti-Catholic. Both parents died by the time Richard was fourteen. He was educated in London schools, then at the Charterhouse (1629–31), and entered Pembroke College, Cambridge, in 1631; four years later he was elected to a fellowship at Peterhouse, Cambridge—like Pembroke a High-Church college. In 1634, the year of his B.A., he published *Epigrammatum sacrorum liber*, a book of Latin epigrams on scriptural subjects. During the next few years, he taught and pursued poetry, music, and painting, and served in some official capacity at Little Saint Mary's, Cambridge, perhaps as priest; he was also a friend of Nicholas Ferrar and a frequent visitor to the Little Gidding religious community. In any case, he was a "thorough High Churchman" and might have remained so, but in 1643 he left Cambridge, just before being ejected by the Puritans intent on stripping Peterhouse and other colleges of their Laudian trappings. His movements in the next few years are uncertain; he was in Holland for a time, may have returned to Oxford, but in 1646 he had already entered the Roman Catholic church and he was living in Paris with Cowley and other exiles from England, including the Countess of Denbigh and Queen Henrietta Maria. The queen's patronage did not help him in Rome the next year; he died August 21, 1649 at Loreto, where he had a minor post at the cathedral. In 1646, with the help of an English friend, Crashaw's poems were published in a combined volume, *Steps to the Temple and The Delights of the Muses;* there was a much revised and enlarged edition in 1648. The final edition, with revisions and additions, *Carmen Deo Nostro,* was published in Paris in 1652.

From *Steps to the Temple* (1646)

To the Infant Martyrs

Go smiling souls, your new built cages break,
In Heav'n you'll learn to sing ere here to speak,
Nor let the milky fonts that bathe your thirst,
        Be your delay;
The place that calls you hence, is at the worst   5
        Milk all the way.

Upon the Infant Martyrs

To see both blended in one flood
The mothers' milk, the children's blood,
Makes me doubt if Heaven will gather,
Roses hence, or *Lilies* rather.

On the Water of Our Lord's Baptism

Each blest drop, on each blest limb,
Is washed itself in washing him:
'Tis a gem while it stays here,
While it falls hence 'tis a tear.

To Our Lord, Upon the Water Made Wine[1]

Thou water turn'st to wine (fair friend of life);
Thy foe to cross the sweet arts of thy reign
Distills from thence the tears of wrath and strife,
And so turns wine to water back again.

Upon the Ass That Bore Our Saviour[2]

Hath only anger an omnipotence
    In eloquence?
Within the lips of love and joy doth dwell
    No miracle?
Why else had *Baalam's* ass[3] a tongue to chide   5
    His master's pride?
And thou (Heaven-burthened beast) hast ne'er a word
    To praise thy Lord?
That he should find a tongue and vocal thunder,
    Was a great wonder.   10
But oh me thinks 'tis a far greater one
    That thou find'st none.

I Am the Door[4]

And now th'art set wide ope, the spear's sad art,
Lo! hath unlockt thee at the very Heart:
He to himself (I fear the worst)
    And his own hope
Hath *shut* these doors of Heaven, that durst
    Thus set them *ope*.

---

1. At the marriage feast at Cana, John 2.
2. Christ's entry into Jerusalem, Matthew 21 : 7 ff.
3. See Numbers 22 for Baalam's ass.
4. John 10 : 9, "I am the door: by Me if any man enter in, he shall be saved."

Upon Lazarus His Tears

Rich *Lazarus!*[5] richer in those gems, thy tears,
    Than *Dives* in the robes he wears:
He scorns them now, but oh they'll suit full well
    With the purple he must wear in Hell.

Matthew 27: And He Answered Them Nothing

Oh mighty *Nothing!* unto thee,
Nothing, we owe all things that be.
God spake once when he all things made,
He saved all when he *Nothing* said.
The world was made of *Nothing* then;
'Tis made by *Nothing* now again.

Upon Our Saviour's Tomb Wherein Never Man Was Laid

How Life and Death in thee
    Agree!
Thou had'st a virgin Womb
    And Tomb.
A *Joseph*[6] did betroth
    Them both.

On Mr. G. Herbert's Book[7]

Know you fair, on what you look?
Divinest love lies in this book:
Expecting fire from your eyes,
To kindle this his sacrifice.
When your hands untie these strings,[8]   5
Think yo'have an angel by th' wings.
One that gladly will be nigh,
To wait upon each morning sigh.
To flutter in the balmy air,
Of your well perfumed prayer.   10
These white plumes of his he'll lend you,
Which every day to heaven will send you:

5. Lazarus, epitome of suffering poverty, goes to Abraham's bosom after death, but Dives, who "was clothed in purple and fine linen," arrives in hell, where he futilely begs Abraham that "Lazarus . . . dip the tip of his finger in water, and cool my tongue" (Luke 16 : 19–31).
6. Joseph the carpenter and Joseph of Arimathea. The latter, a just man, pro-vided for the dead Jesus "a sepulchre . . . , wherein never man before was laid" (Luke 23 : 50–53).
7. Title: *On Mr. G. Herberts booke intituled the Temple of Sacred Poems, sent to a Gentlewoman.*
8. The ribbons tying together the covers of the book.

To take acquaintance of the sphere,
And all the smooth faced kindred there.
    And though *Herbert's* name do owe[9]   15
    These devotions, fairest; know
    That while I lay them on the shrine
    Of your white hand, they are mine.

From *Delights of the Muses* (1646)

Music's Duel[1]

Now westward *Sol* had spent the richest beams
Of noon's high glory, when hard by the streams
Of *Tiber*, on the scene of a green plat,
Under protection of an oak, there sat
A sweet Lute's-master: in whose gentle airs   5
He lost the day's heat, and his own hot cares.
    Close in the covert of the leaves there stood
A Nightingale, come from the neighboring wood:
(The sweet inhabitant of each glad tree,
Their Muse, their *Siren*, harmless *Siren* she)   10
There stood she listening, and did entertain
The Music's soft report: and mold the same
In her own murmurs, that whatever mood
His curious fingers lent, her voice made good:
The man perceived his rival, and her art,   15
Disposed to give the light-foot Lady sport
Awakes his Lute, and 'gainst the fight to come
Informs it, in a sweet *Praeludium*[2]
Of closer strains, and ere the war begin,
He lightly skirmishes on every string   20
Charged with a flying touch: and straightway she
Carves out her dainty voice as readily,
Into a thousand sweet distinguished tones,
And reckons up in soft divisions,[3]
Quick volumes of wild notes; to let him know   25
By that shrill taste, she could do something too.
    His nimble hands instinct then taught each string
A cap'ring cheerfulness; and made them sing
To their own dance; now negligently rash
He throws his arm, and with a long drawn dash   30
Blends all together; then distinctly trips
From this to that; then quick returning skips

9. Own.
1. Based generally on a popular Latin poem by the Jesuit Famianus Strada (published 1617), the poem is a contest between a nightingale and a lutanist in the traditions of nature versus art. For the text of Strada's poem, see the edition of Crashaw by George Walton Williams (New York, 1970) or the notes in L. C. Martin's Oxford edition (1957).
2. Prelude or introduction.
3. Rapid melodic passages.

And snatches this again, and pauses there.
She measures every measure, every where
Meets art with art; sometimes as if in doubt   35
Not perfect yet, and fearing to be out
Trails her plain[4] ditty in one long-spun note
Through the sleek passage of her open throat:
A clear unwrinkled song, then doth she point it
With tender accents, and severely joint it   40
By short diminutives, that being reared
In controverting warbles evenly shared,
With her sweet self she wrangles; he amazed
That from so small a channel should be raised
The torrent of a voice, whose melody   45
Could melt into such sweet variety,
Strains higher yet; that tickled with rare art
The tattling[5] strings (each breathing in his part)
Most kindly do fall out; the grumbling bass
In surly groans disdains the treble's grace.   50
The high-perched treble chirps at this, and chides,
Until his finger (moderator) hides
And closes the sweet quarrel, rousing all
Hoarse, shrill, at once; as when the trumpets call
Hot Mars to th'harvest of Death's field, and woo   55
Men's hearts into their hands; this lesson too
She gives him back; her supple breast thrills out
Sharp airs, and staggers in a warbling doubt
Of dallying sweetness, hovers o'er her skill,
And folds in waved notes with a trembling bill,   60
The pliant series of her slippery song.
Then starts she suddenly into a throng
Of short thick sobs, whose thundering volleys float,
And roll themselves over her lubric[6] throat
In panting murmurs, stilled[7] out of her breast,   65
That ever-bubbling spring; the sugared nest
Of her delicious soul, that there does lie
Bathing in streams of liquid melody;
Music's best seed-plot, whence in ripened airs
A golden-headed harvest fairly rears   70
His honey-dropping tops, plowed by her breath
Which there reciprocally laboreth
In that sweet soil. It seems a holy choir
Founded to th'name of great *Apollo's*[8] lyre.
Whose silver-roof rings with the sprightly notes   75
Of sweet-lipped Angel-Imps, that swill their throats
In cream of morning *Helicon*,[9] and then

4. Simple melody, without divisions.
5. Prattling.
6. Smooth.
7. Distilled.
8. God of music, poetry, and prophecy, as well as of manly beauty and of the sun.
9. Mountain home of the Muses in Greece; sometimes, the fountains there; also, stringed instrument.

Prefer soft anthems to the ears of men,
To woo them from their beds, still murmuring
That men can sleep while they their Matins sing: 80
(Most divine service) whose so early lay
Prevents[1] the eyelids of the blushing day.
There might you hear her kindle her soft voice,
In the close murmur of a sparkling noise,
And lay the groundwork of her hopeful song,   85
Still keeping in the forward stream, so long
Till a sweet whirlwind (striving to get out)
Heaves her soft bosom, wanders round about,
And makes a pretty earthquake in her breast,
Till the fledged notes at length forsake their nest; 90
Fluttering in wanton shoals, and to the sky
Winged with their own wild echoes prattling fly.
She opes the floodgate, and lets loose a tide
Of streaming sweetness, which in state doth ride
On the waved back of every swelling strain,   95
Rising and falling in a pompous train.
And while she thus discharges a shrill peal
Of flashing airs, she qualifies their zeal
With the cool epode of a graver note,
Thus high, thus low, as if her silver throat   100
Would reach the brazen voice of war's hoarse bird;[2]
Her little soul is ravished: and so poured
Into loose ecstasies, that she is placed
Above herself, Music's *Enthusiast*.
    Shame now and anger mixed a double stain   105
In the Musician's face; yet once again
(Mistress) I come; now reach a strain, my Lute,
Above her mock, or be forever mute.
Or tune a song of victory to me,
Or to thyself sing thine own obsequy;   110
So said, his hands sprightly as fire he flings,
And with a quavering coyness tastes the strings.
The sweet-lipped sisters[3] musically frighted,
Singing their fears are fearfully delighted.
Trembling as when *Apollo's* golden hairs   115
Are fanned and frizzled, in the wanton airs
Of his own breath: which married to his lyre
Doth tune the *Spheres*, and make Heaven's self look higher.
From this to that, from that to this he flies,
Feels Music's pulse in all her arteries,   120
Caught in a net which there *Apollo* spreads,
His fingers struggle with the vocal threads,
Following those little rills, he sinks into

1. Comes before.   3. The Muses.
2. The raven.

A Sea of *Helicon*; his hand does go
Those parts of sweetness, which with *Nectar* drop, 125
Softer than that which pants in *Hebe's* cup.
The humorous strings expound his learned touch
By various glosses; now they seem to grutch[4]
And murmur in a buzzing din, then jingle
In shrill tongued accents: striving to be single. 130
Every smooth turn, every delicious stroke
Gives life to some new Grace; thus doth h'invoke
Sweetness by all her names; thus, bravely thus
(Fraught with a fury so harmonious)
The Lute's light *Genius* now does proudly rise, 135
Heaved on the surges of swollen rhapsodies.
Whose flourish (meteor-like) doth curl the air
With flash of high-borne fancies: here and there
Dancing in lofty measures, and anon
Creeps on the soft touch of a tender tone: 140
Whose trembling murmurs melting in wild airs
Runs to and fro, complaining his sweet cares
Because those precious mysteries that dwell,
In music's ravished soul he dare not tell,
But whisper to the world: thus do they vary 145
Each string his note, as if they meant to carry
Their master's blest soul (snatched out at his ears
By a strong ecstasy) through all the spheres
Of Music's heaven; and seat it there on high
In th' *Empyraeum*[5] of pure harmony. 150
At length (after so long, so loud a strife
Of all the strings, still breathing the best life
Of blest variety attending on
His finger's fairest revolution
In many a sweet rise, many as sweet a fall) 155
A full-mouthed *Diapason*[6] swallows all.
    This done, he lists what she would say to this,
And she although her breath's late exercise
Had dealt too roughly with her tender throat,
Yet summons all her sweet powers for a note 160
Alas! in vain! for while (sweet soul) she tries
To measure all those wild diversities
Of chatt'ring strings, by the small size of one
Poor simple voice, raised in a natural tone,
She fails, and failing grieves, and grieving dies. 165
She dies; and leaves her life the victor's prize,
Falling upon his Lute; o fit to have
(That lived so sweetly) dead, so sweet a Grave!

4. Grumble.   6. Grand burst of harmony.
5. The highest heaven.

From *Carmen Deo Nostro* (1652)

In the Holy Nativity of Our Lord God: A Hymn Sung as by the Shepherds

Chorus.   Come we shepherds whose blest sight
               Hath met love's Noon in Nature's night;
                  Come lift we up our loftier song
               And wake the Sun that lies too long.

               To all our world of well-stol'n joy   5
                  He slept, and dreamt of no such thing,
               While we found out Heav'ns fairer eye,
                  And kissed the cradle of our King.
               Tell him he rises now, too late
               To show us aught worth looking at.   10

               Tell him we now can show him more
                  Than he e'er showed to mortal sight;
               Than he himself e'er saw before;
                  Which to be seen needs not his light.
               Tell him, Tityrus, where th'hast been;   15
               Tell him, Thyrsis, what th'hast seen.

Tityrus.   Gloomy night embraced the place
                  Where the noble Infant lay.
               The Babe looked up and showed his face;
                  In spite of darkness, it was Day.   20
               It was Thy day, Sweet! and did rise
               Not from the East, but from thine Eyes.

                  Chorus. It was Thy day, Sweet

Thyrsis.   Winter chid aloud; and sent
                  The angry North to wage his wars.   25
               The North forgot his fierce intent,
                  And left perfumes instead of scars.
               By those sweet eyes' persuasive pow'rs
               Where he meant frost, he scattered flowers.

                  Chorus. By those sweet eyes'   30

Both.   We saw thee in thy balmy nest,
                  Young dawn for our eternal Day!
               We saw thine eyes break from their East
                  And chase the trembling shades away.
               We saw thee; and we blest the sight;   35
               We saw thee by thine own sweet light.

Tityrus.	Poor World (said I) what wilt thou do
	To entertain this starry Stranger?
	Is this the best thou canst bestow,
	A cold, and not too cleanly, manger?
	Contend, ye powers of heav'n and earth,
	To fit a bed for this huge birth.

Chorus. Contend ye powers

Thyrsis.
Proud world, said I; cease your contest
And let the Mighty Babe alone.
The phoenix builds the phoenix' nest.[7]
Love's architecture is his own.
The Babe whose birth embraces this morn,
Made his own bed e'er he was born.

Chorus. The Babe whose

Tityrus.
I saw the curled drops, soft and slow,
Come hovering o'er the place's head;
Off'ring their whitest sheets of snow
To furnish the fair Infant's bed:
Forbear, said I be not too bold;
Your fleece is white but 'tis too cold.

Chorus. Forbear, said I

Thyrsis.
I saw the obsequious Seraphims
Their rosy fleece of fire bestow.
For well they now can spare their wings
Since Heav'n itself lies here below.
Well done, said I: but are you sure
Your down so warm, will pass for pure?

Chorus. Well done said I

Tityrus.
No, no, your King's not yet to seek
Where to repose his royal Head;
See, see, how soon his new-bloomed Cheek
'Twixt mother's breasts is gone to bed.
Sweet choice, said we! no way but so
Not to lie cold, yet sleep in snow.

Chorus. Sweet choice, said we

Both.
We saw thee in thy balmy nest,
Bright dawn of our eternal day!

40

45

50

55

60

65

70

---

7. The phoenix is a mythological bird, reputedly only one of a kind which lived for five hundred (or a thousand) years, consumed itself in fire, and rose renewed from its own ashes to begin again another long life.

We saw thine eyes break from their East,
    And chase the trembling shades away.   75
We saw thee: and we blest the sight.
We saw thee, by thine own sweet light.

Chorus. We saw thee, &c.

Full Chorus. Welcome, all Wonders in one sight!
    Eternity shut in a span.   80
Summer in Winter. Day in Night.
    Heaven in earth, and God in Man.
Great little one! whose all-embracing birth
Lifts earth to heaven, stoops heav'n to earth.

Welcome. Though nor to gold nor silk,   85
    To more than Caesar's birthright is;
Two sister-seas of Virgin-milk,
    With many a rarely-tempered kiss,
That breathes at once both Maid and Mother,
Warms in the one, cools in the other.   90

Welcome, though not to those gay flies[8]
    Gilded i'th' beams of earthly kings;
Slippery souls in smiling eyes;
    But to poor shepherds, home-spun things:
Whose wealth's their flock; whose wit, to be   95
    Well read in their simplicity.
Yet when young April's husband show'rs
    Shall bless the fruitful Maia's bed,[9]
We'll bring the first-born of her flowers
    To kiss thy Feet and crown thy Head.   100
To thee, dread lamb! whose love must keep
    The shepherds; more than they the sheep.
To Thee, meek Majesty! soft King
    Of simple Graces and sweet Loves.
Each of us his lamb will bring,   105
    Each his pair of silver Doves;
Till burnt at last in fire of Thy fair eyes,
    Our selves become our own best Sacrifice.

Saint Mary Magdalene or The Weeper[1]

Lo where a Wounded Heart with bleeding Eyes conspire,
    Is she a Flaming fountain, or a weeping fire?

8. Parasites.
9. Maia was one of the earliest of the ancient deities, usually described as an earth goddess; the month of May was named for her.
1. The weeper is Mary Magdalene, the notorious sinner, who anointed Christ's feet with her tears and dried them with her hair (Luke 7 : 36 ff.) and later, according to legend, did penance in the desert for thirty years.

1

Hail, sister springs!
Parents of silver-forded rills!
Ever bubbling things!
Thawing crystal! snowy hills,
Still spending, never spent! I mean   5
Thy fair eyes, sweet Magdalene!

2

Heavens thy fair eyes be;
Heav'ns bosom drinks the gentle stream.
'Tis seed-time still with thee,
And stars thou sow'st, whose harvest dares   10
Promise to earth to countershine
Whatever makes heav'n's forehead fine.

3

But we're deceived all.
Stars indeed they are too true;
For they but seem to fall.   15
As Heav'n's other spangles do.
It is not for our earth and us.
To shine in things so precious.

4

Upwards thou dost weep.
Heav'ns bosom drinks the gentle stream.   20
Where the milky rivers creep,
Thine floats above, and is the cream.
Waters above the Heav'ns, what they be
We're taught best by thy Tears and thee.

5

Every morn from hence   25
A brisk Cherub something sips
Whose sacred influence
Adds sweetness to his sweetest lips.
Then to his music. And his song
Tastes of this breakfast all day long.   30

6

Not in the evening's eyes
When they red with weeping are
For the sun that dies,
Sits sorrow with a face so fair,
Nowhere but here did ever meet   35
Sweetness so sad, sadness so sweet.

7

When sorrow would be seen
In her brightest majesty
(For she is a queen)
Then is she drest by none but thee.   40

Then, and only then, she wears
Her proudest pearls; I mean, thy Tears.

8

The dew no more will weep
The primrose's pale cheek to deck,
The dew no more will sleep 45
Nuzzled in the lily's neck;
Much rather would it be thy Tear,
And leave them both to tremble here.

9

There's no need at all
That the balsam-sweating bough 50
So coyly should let fall
His med'cinable tears; for now
Nature hath learnt t'extract a dew
More sovereign and sweet from you.

10

Yet let the poor drops weep 55
(Weeping is the ease of woe)
Softly let them creep,
Sad that they are vanquisht so.
They, though to others no relief,
Balsam may be, for their own grief. 60

11

Such the maiden gem[2]
By the purpling vine put on,
Peeps from her parent stem
And blushes at the bridegroom sun.
This wat'ry blossom of thy eyn, 65
Ripe, will make the richer wine.

12

When some new bright guest
Takes up among the stars a room,
And Heav'n will make a feast,
Angels with crystal vials come 70
And draw from these full eyes of thine
Their master's water: their own wine.

* * *

15

O cheeks! Beds of chaste loves 85
By your own showers seasonably dashed;
Eyes! nests of milky doves
In your own wells decently washed,
O wit of love! that thus could place
Fountain and garden in one face. 90

2. A flower.

16

Oh sweet contest: of woes
With loves, of tears with smiles disputing!
O fair, and friendly foes,
Each other kissing and confuting!
While rain and sunshine, cheeks and eyes   95
Close in kind contrarieties.

17

But can these fair floods be
Friends with the bosom fires that fill thee!
Can so great flames agree
Eternal Tears should thus distill three?   100
O floods, o fires! o suns, o showers!
Mixt and made friends by love's sweet powers.

18

'Twas his well-pointed dart
That digged these wells and drest this vine,
And taught the wounded Heart   105
The way into these weeping eyn.
Vain loves avaunt! bold hands forbear!
The lamb hath dipped his white foot here.

19

And now where'er he strays,
Among the Galilean mountains,   110
Or more unwelcome ways,
He's followed by two faithful fountains;
Two walking baths; two weeping motions;
Portable and compendious oceans.

20

O thou, thy lord's fair store!   115
In thy so rich and rare expenses,
Even when he showed most poor,
He might provoke the wealth of princes.
What prince's wanton'st pride e'er could
Wash with silver, wipe with gold?   120

*   *   *

26

Not, so long she lived,
Shall thy tomb report of thee;
But, so long she grieved,
Thus must we date thy memory.
Others by moments, months, and years   155
Measure their ages; thou, by Tears.

27

So do perfumes expire,
So sigh tormented sweets, oppressed

With proud unpitying fire.
Such Tears the suff'ring rose that's vexed   160
With ungentle flames does shed,
Sweating in a too warm bed.

28

Say, ye bright brothers,
The fugitive sons of those fair eyes
Your fruitful mothers!   165
What make you here? what hopes can 'tice[3]
You to be born? what cause can borrow
You from those nests of noble sorrow?

29

Whither away so fast?
For sure the sordid earth   170
Your sweetness cannot taste
Nor does the dust deserve your birth.
Sweet, whither haste you then? o say
Why you trip so fast away?

30

We go not to seek   175
The darlings of Aurora's bed,[4]
The rose's modest cheek
Nor the violet's humble head,
Though the field's eyes too Weepers be
Because they want[5] such Tears as we.   180

31

Much less mean we to trace
The fortune of inferior gems,
Preferred[6] to some proud face
Or perched upon feared diadems.
Crowned heads are toys.[7] We go to meet   185
A worthy object, our Lord's Feet.

A Hymn to the Name and Honor
of the Admirable Saint Teresa[1]

Love, thou art absolute sole lord
Of Life and Death. To prove the word,
We'll now appeal to none of all

3. Entice.
4. Aurora, bride of Tithonus, was the goddess of the dawn.
5. Lack.
6. Here meaning literally placed before or in front of.
7. Trifles.
1. See Textual Notes. The poem is based on the great *Autobiography* of Saint Teresa of Avila (1515–82), translated into English in 1642 as *The Flaming*

Hart. A mystic as well as a leader of the Counter-Reformation, Teresa was both reformer and head of the Carmelites, an order of ascetic contemplative religious. In the Office for her feast, October 15, the hymn for both matins and lauds uses as theme the contrast between her early desire for martyrdom and her later role as Love's victim.

Those thy old soldiers, great and tall,
Ripe men of martyrdom, that could reach down   5
With strong arms, their triumphant crown;
Such as could with lusty breath
Speak loud into the face of death
Their great Lord's glorious name; to none
Of those whose spacious bosoms spread a throne   10
For Love at large to fill; spare blood and sweat;
And see him take a private seat,
Making his mansion in the mild
And milky soul of a soft child.
    Scarce has she learnt to lisp the name   15
Of martyr; yet she thinks it shame
Life should so long play with that breath
Which spent can buy so brave a death.
She never undertook to know
What death with love should have to do;   20
Nor has she e'er yet understood
Why to show love, she should shed blood.
Yet though she cannot tell you why,
She can Love, and she can Die.
    Scarce has she blood enough to make   25
A guilty sword blush for her sake;
Yet has she 'a Heart dares hope to prove
How much less strong is Death than Love.
    Be love but there; let poor six years
Be posed with maturest fears   30
Man trembles at, you straight shall find
Love knows no nonage,[2] nor the Mind.
'Tis Love, not Years or Limbs that can
Make the martyr, or the man.
    Love touched her Heart, and lo it beats   35
High, and burns with such brave heats;
Such thirsts to die, as dares drink up
A thousand cold deaths in one cup.
Good reason. For she breathes all fire.
Her weak breast heaves with strong desire   40
Of what she may with fruitless wishes
Seek for amongst her Mother's kisses.
    Since 'tis not to be had at home
She'll travail to a martyrdom.
No home for her confesses she   45
But where she may a martyr be.
    She'll to the Moors and trade with them,
For this unvalued[3] diadem.
She'll offer them her dearest breath,
With Christ's Name in't, in change for death.   50

---

2. The time when one is still legally under parents' or guardian's control.
3. Invaluable, priceless.

She'll bargain with them; and will give
Them God; and teach them how to live
In him: or, if they this deny,
For him she'll teach them how to Die.
So shall she leave amongst them sown   55
Her Lord's blood; or at least her own.
   Farewell then, all the world! Adieu.
Teresa is no more for you.
Farewell, all pleasures, sports, and joys,
(Never till now esteemed toys)   60
Farewell what ever dear may be,
Mother's arms or Father's knee;
Farewell house, and farewell home!
She's for the Moors, and Martyrdom.
   Sweet, no so fast! lo thy fair Spouse   65
Whom thou seek'st with so swift vows,
Calls thee back, and bids thee come
T'embrace a milder Martyrdom.
   Blest powers forbid, thy tender life
Should bleed upon a barbarous knife;   70
Or some base hand have power to rase[4]
Thy breast's chaste cabinet, and uncase
A soul kept there so sweet, o no;
Wise heav'n will never have it so.
Thou art love's victim; and must die   75
A death more mystical and high.
Into love's arms thou shalt let fall
A still-surviving funeral
He is the Dart must make the Death
Whose stroke shall taste thy hallowed breath;[5]   80
A dart thrice dipped in that rich flame
Which writes thy spouse's radiant Name
Upon the roof of Heav'n; where aye[6]
It shines, and with a sovereign ray
Beats bright upon the burning faces   85
Of souls which in that name's sweet graces
Find everlasting smiles. So rare,
So spiritual, pure, and fair
Must be th'immortal instrument
Upon whose choice point shall be sent   90
A life so loved; and that there be
Fit executioners for thee,
The fair'st and first-born sons of fire,
Blest Seraphim, shall leave their choir

---

4. Cut, slash.
5. In one of her visions, Teresa saw an angel "of very much beautie" with a "long Dart of gold in his hand" which he "thrust . . . some severall times, through my verie Hart, after such a manner, as that it passed the verie inwards, of my Bowells" and left her "wholy inflamed with a great love of Almightye God" (*The Flaming Hart,* 1642, chapter XXIX). Bernini's great Baroque sculpture of Teresa in ecstasy is based on this passage, as is Crashaw's poem "The Flaming Heart."
6. Forever.

And turn love's soldiers, upon Thee   95
To exercise their archery.
        O how oft shalt thou complain
Of a sweet and subtle Pain.
Of intolerable Joys;
Of a Death, in which who dies   100
Loves his death, and dies again,
And would for ever so be slain.
And lives, and dies; and knows not why
To live, but that he thus may never leave to Die.
        How kindly will thy gentle Heart   105
Kiss the sweetly-killing Dart!
And close in his embraces keep
Those delicious wounds, that weep
Balsam to heal themselves with. Thus
When these thy Deaths, so numerous,   110
Shall all at last die into one,
And melt thy soul's sweet mansion;
Like a soft lump of incense, hasted
By too hot a fire, and wasted
Into perfuming clouds, so fast   115
Shalt thou exhale to Heav'n at last
In a resolving Sigh, and then
O what? Ask not the tongues of men,
Angels cannot tell: suffice,
Thy self shall feel thine own full joys   120
And hold them fast forever. There
So soon as thou shalt first appear,
The moon of maiden stars, thy white
Mistress,[7] attended by such bright
Souls as thy shining self, shall come   125
And in her first ranks make thee room;
Where 'mongst her snowy family
Immortal welcomes wait for thee.
        O what delight, when revealed Life shall stand
And teach thy lips heav'n with his hand;   130
On which thou now may'st to thy wishes
Heap up thy consecrated kisses.
What joys shall seize thy soul, when she
Bending her blessed eyes on thee
(Those second smiles of Heaven) shall dart   135
Her mild rays through thy melting heart!
        Angels, thy old friends, there shall greet thee
Glad at their own home now to meet thee.
        All thy good Works which went before
And waited for thee, at the door,   140
Shall own thee there; and all in one
Weave a constellation
Of Crowns, with which the King thy spouse

7. **Virgin Mary.**

Shall build up thy triumphant brows.
        All thy old woes shall now smile on thee   145
And thy pains sit bright upon thee.
All thy sorrows here shall shine,
All thy Suff'rings be divine.
Tears shall take comfort and turn gems,
And Wrongs repent to diadems.   150
Ev'n thy Deaths shall live; and new
Dress the soul that erst they slew.
Thy wounds shall blush to such bright scars
As keep account of the Lamb's wars.
        Those rare Works where thou shalt leave writ   155
Love's noble history, with wit
Taught thee by none but him, while here
They feed our souls, shall clothe Thine there.
Each heav'nly word by whose hid flame
Our hard hearts shall strike fire, the same   160
Shall flourish on thy brows, and be
Both fire to us and flame to thee;
Whose light shall live bright in thy face
By glory, in our hearts by grace.
        Thou shalt look around about, and see   165
Thousands of crowned souls throng to be
Themselves thy crown. Sons of thy vows,
The virgin-births with which thy sovereign spouse
Made fruitful thy fair soul, go now
And with them all about thee bow   170
To Him, put on (he'll say), put on
(My rosy love) that thy rich zone[8]
Sparkling with sacred flames
Of thousand souls, whose happy names
Heav'n keeps upon thy score. (Thy bright   175
Life brought them first to kiss the light
That kindled them to stars) and so
Thou with the Lamb, thy lord, shalt go;
And wheresoe'er he sets his white
Steps, walk with Him those ways of light   180
Which who in death would live to see,
Must learn in life to die like thee.

From *The Flaming Heart*[9]

    *   *   *

O Heart! the equal poise of love's both parts[1]   75
Big alike with wounds and darts.

---

8. An encircling band (like a girdle), distinct in color or texture from its surroundings.
9. The text is the conclusion of the poem in the 1652 version. See Textual Notes.
1. Refers to active and passive aspects of love, among other things.

Live in these conquering leaves;[2] live all the same;
And walk through all tongues one triumphant Flame.
Live here, great Heart; and love and die and kill;
And bleed and wound, and yield and conquer still.   80
Let this immortal life, where'er it comes.
Walk in a crowd of loves and Martyrdoms.
Let mystic Deaths wait on't; and wise souls be
The love-slain witnesses of this life of thee.
O sweet incendiary! show here thy art,   85
Upon this carcass of a hard, cold heart;
Let all thy scattered shafts of light, that play
Among the leaves of thy large books of day,[3]
Combined against this Breast at once break in
And take away from me my self and sin.   90
This gracious robbery shall thy bounty be;
And my best fortunes such fair spoils of me.
O thou undaunted daughter of desires!
By all thy dow'r of Lights and Fires;
By all the eagle in thee, all the dove;[4]   95
By all thy lives and deaths of love;
By thy large draughts of intellectual day,
And by thy thirsts of love more large than they;
By all thy brim-filled bowls of fierce desire,
By thy last morning's draught of liquid fire;   100
By the full kingdom of that final kiss
That seized thy parting soul, and sealed thee his;
By all the heav'ns thou hast in him,
(Fair sister of the Seraphim!)
By all of Him we have in Thee,   105
Leave nothing of my Self in me!
Let me so read thy life, that I
Unto all life of mine may die!

To the Noblest and Best
of Ladies, The Countess of Denbigh[5]

What heav'n-entreated Heart[6] is this?
Stands trembling at the gate of bliss;
Holds fast the door, yet dares not venture
Fairly to open it, and enter.

---

2. Pages of the *Autobiography*.
3. Light, both spiritual and intellectual (see line 97).
4. *Eagle . . . dove*: complex reference to symbols of fire and light, active and passive, vision and peace, John the Evangelist (the eagle could look at the sun) and the inspiring Holy Spirit.
5. The subtitle reads, "Perswading her to Resolution in Religion, and to render her selfe without further delay into the Communion of the Catholick Church."

There are two versions of the poem (see Textual Notes); this is the earlier. Both poems are parodies of the seduction poem. The countess's husband, the Earl of Denbigh, died in 1643 fighting for King Charles I; later the countess went with Queen Henrietta Maria to Paris, where she did in fact become a Roman Catholic.
6. The poem is preceded by the emblem of a locked heart. See line 34.

Whose Definition is a doubt   5
'Twixt life and death, 'twixt in and out.
Say, lingering fair! why comes the birth
Of your brave soul so slowly forth?
Plead your pretenses (oh you strong
In weakness) why you choose so long   10
In labor of yourself to lie,
Nor daring quite to live nor die?
Ah linger not, loved soul! a slow
And late consent was a long no.
Who grants at last, long time tried   15
And did his best to have denied.
What magic bolts, what mystic bars
Maintain the will in these strange wars!
What fatal, yet fantastic, bands
Keep the free heart from its own hands!   20
So when the year takes cold, we see
Poor waters their own prisoners be.
Fettered, and locked up fast they lie
In a sad self-captivity.
Th'astonished nymphs their flood's strange fate deplore,   25
To see themselves their own severer shore.
Thou that alone canst thaw this cold
And fetch the heart from its stronghold,
Almighty Love! end this long war,
And of a meteor make a star.   30
Oh fix this fair Indefinite.
And 'mongst thy shafts of sovereign light
Choose out that sure decisive dart
Which has the key of this close heart,
Knows all the corners of't, and can control   35
The self-shut cabinet of an unsearched soul.
O let it be at last, love's hour.
Raise this tall trophy of thy power;
Come once the conquering way; not to confute
But kill this rebel-word, *Irresolute*,   40
That so, in spite of all this peevish strength
Of weakness, she may write *Resolved at Length*,
Unfold at length, unfold fair flower
And use the season of love's shower,
Meet his well-meaning wounds, wise heart!   45
And haste to drink the wholesome dart,
That healing shaft, which heav'n till now
Hath in love's quiver hid for you.
Oh, dart of love! arrow of light!
Oh happy you, if it hit right;   50
It must not fall in vain, it must
Not mark the dry regardless dust.
Fair one, it is your fate; and brings

Eternal worlds upon its wings.
Meet it with wide-spread arms; and see   55
Its seat your soul's just center be.
Disband dull fears; give faith the day.
To save your life, kill your delay.
It is love's siege; and sure to be
Your triumph, though his victory.   60
'Tis cowardice that keeps this field
And want of courage not to yield.
Yield then, o yield, that love may win
The fort at last, and let life in.
Yield quickly. Lest perhaps you prove   65
Death's prey, before the prize of love.
This fort of your fair self, if't be not won,
He is repulsed indeed; but you're undone.

Andrew Marvell

Andrew Marvell (1621–1678) was the son of a "Calvinstical" clergyman and schoolmaster at Hull, Yorkshire, and was educated at Hull Grammar School and, from 1633–41, at Trinity College, Cambridge (contemporarily with Crashaw). Though he had a brief fling with Roman Catholicism, his father brought him back to Anglicanism. After his father's accidental death by drowning in 1641, Marvell traveled abroad for some years, tutoring in France for part of the time. From 1651, he served as tutor to Mary Fairfax, daughter of Lord Fairfax, at Nun Appleton House in Yorkshire, to which Fairfax had retired after resigning his command of the Parliamentary armies. He was recommended by John Milton for the position of his assistant as Latin Secretary in 1653, finally received the appointment in 1657; meanwhile he served as tutor to Cromwell's ward, William Dutton. From 1659 to his death, Marvell served as a member of Parliament for Hull, vigorously fighting for constitutional liberties. After the Restoration, he protected Milton from persecution. During this period, he wrote stinging political satires attacking the vices of the time. He died August 18, 1678, in London, apparently as a result of medical incompetence, and was buried in Saint Giles-in-the-Fields. In a pleasant irony, his poetry—none of the great early lyrics had been printed in his lifetime—was published in 1681 by his housekeeper, Mary Palmer, to support her claim to be his "widow" and her title to some £500. Her plan apparently backfired, but at least the poems found their way into print.

From *Miscellaneous Poems* (1681)

A Dialogue Between the Resolved Soul and Created Pleasure

Courage my Soul, now learn to wield
The weight of thine immortal shield.
Close on thy head thy helmet bright.
Balance thy sword[1] against the fight.
See where an army, strong as fair,   5
With silken banners spreads the air.
Now, if thou be'st that thing divine,
In this day's combat let it shine:
And show that Nature wants[2] an Art

---

1. In Ephesians 6 : 11 ff., Saint Paul describes the "whole armor of God," the "shield of faith . . . , the helmet of salvation, and the sword of the Spirit."
2. Lacks.

To conquer one resolved heart.   10

Pleasure   Welcome the Creation's guest,
Lord of Earth, and Heaven's heir.
Lay aside that warlike crest,
And of Nature's banquet share:
Where the souls[3] of fruits and flow'rs   15
Stand prepared to heighten yours.[4]

Soul   I sup above, and cannot stay
To bait[5] so long upon the way.

Pleasure   On these downy pillows lie,
Whose soft plumes will thither fly: 20
On these roses strowed so plain
Lest one leaf thy side should strain.[6]

Soul   My gentler rest is on a thought,
Conscious of doing what I ought.

Pleasure   If thou be'st with perfumes pleased,   25
Such as oft the Gods appeased,
Thou in fragrant clouds shalt show
Like another God below.

Soul   A soul that knows not to presume
Is Heaven's and its own perfume.   30

Pleasure   Every thing does seem to vie
Which should first attract thine eye:
But since none deserves that grace,
In this crystal[7] view *thy* face.

Soul   When the Creator's skill is prized,   35
The rest is all but Earth disguised.

Pleasure   Hark how music then prepares
For thy stay these charming airs;
Which the posting[8] winds recall,
And suspend the river's fall.   40

Soul   Had I but any time to lose,
On this I would it all dispose.
Cease Tempter. None can chain a mind
Whom this sweet chordage[9] cannot bind.

Chorus   *Earth cannot show so brave a sight*   45
As when a single Soul does fence

---

3. Essences.
4. *Your lower soul; Pleasure appeals to the senses in turn, then to beauty, wealth, glory, knowledge.*
5. Take refreshment.
6. *Plain*: flat; *leaf*: petal; *strain*: hurt ("referring to the legend of the Sybarite

who claimed that his comfort was impaired by a single crumpled rose-petal," Frank Kermode, *Selected Poetry of Andrew Marvell* (New York, 1967), p. 50).
7. Mirror
8. Hurrying, rushing.
9. Pun on *chord* and *cord*.

The batteries of alluring Sense
And Heaven views it with delight.
   Then persevere: for still new charges sound:
   And if thou overcom'st thou shalt be crowned.   50

Pleasure   All this fair, and soft, and sweet,
           Which scattering doth shine,
        Shall within one beauty meet,
           And she be only thine.

Soul   If things of sight such Heavens be,   55
        What Heavens are those we cannot see?

Pleasure   Where so e'er thy foot shall go
           The minted gold shall lie;
        Till thou purchase all below,
           And want new words to buy.   60

Soul   Were't not a price[1] who'd value gold?
        And that's worth nought that can be sold.

Pleasure   Wilt thou all the glory have
           That war or peace commend?
        Half the world shall be thy slave   65
           The other half thy friend.

Soul   What friends, if to my self untrue?
        What slaves, unless I captive you?

Pleasure   Thou shalt know each hidden cause;
           And see the future time;   70
        Try what depth the center[2] draws;
           And then to Heaven climb.

Soul   None thither mounts by the degree
        Of knowledge, but humility.[3]

Chorus   *Triumph, triumph, victorious Soul;*   75
        The world has not one pleasure more:
        The rest does lie beyond the Pole,
        And is thine everlasting store.

On a Drop of Dew

See how the orient[4] dew,
   Shed from the bosom of the morn
      Into the blowing[5] roses,
Yet careless of its mansion new,
   For the clear region[6] where 'twas born   5

---

1. Worth money.
2. Of the earth.
3. But rather by humility.
4. Pearllike and born at sunrise (Pierre Legouis, note to Oxford edition of Marvell (1971).
5. Blossoming.
6. Preferring heaven (Legouis suggests that *For* ="because of").

Round in it self incloses:
And in its little globe's extent,
Frames as it can its native element.[7]
How it the purple flow'r does slight,
   Scarce touching where it lies,   10
But gazing back upon the skies,
   Shines with a mournful light;
      Like its own tear,
Because so long divided from the sphere.
Restless it rolls and unsecure,   15
   Trembling lest it grow impure,
Till the warm sun pity its pain,
And to the skies exhale it back again.
   So the Soul, that drop, that ray
Of the clear fountain of Eternal Day,   20
Could it within the human flow'r be seen,
   Rememb'ring still[8] its former height,
   Shuns the sweet leaves and blossoms green;
   And, recollecting[9] its own light,
Does, in its pure and circling thoughts, express   25
The greater Heaven in an Heaven less,[1]
   In how coy[2] a figure wound,
   Every way it turns away:
   So the world excluding round,
   Yet receiving in the Day,   30
   Dark beneath, but bright above:
   Here disdaining, there in love.
How loose and easy hence to go:
How girt and ready to ascend,
   Moving but on a point below,   35
   It all about does upwards bend.
Such did the Manna's sacred dew distill,
White and entire, though congealed and chill,
Congealed on Earth: but does, dissolving, run
Into the glories of th' Almighty Sun.[3]   40

The Coronet

When for[4] the thorns with which I long, too long,
   With many a piercing wound,
   My Saviour's head have crowned,
I seek with garlands to redress that wrong:
   Through every garden, every mead,   5
I gather flow'rs (my fruits are only flow'rs),
   Dismantling all the fragrant tow'rs[5]

7. Heaven (see line 5).
8. Yet; always; in quiet.
9. Collecting again; perhaps, remembering.
1. A lesser heaven.
2. Reserved, contained.
3. For the manna, miraculous food provided the Israelites in the wilderness, see Exodus 16. It covered the ground like dew in the morning; that which was not eaten melted as the sun grew hot.
4. In place of, because of.
5. Tall headdresses.

That once adorned my shepherdess's head.
And now when I have summed up all my store,
   Thinking (so I myself deceive)   10
   So rich a chaplet[6] thence to weave
As never yet the king of Glory wore:
   Alas I find the Serpert old
   That, twining in[7] his speckled breast,
   About the flow'rs disguised does fold,   15
   With wreaths of Fame and Interest.[8]
Ah, foolish Man, that wouldst debase with them,
And mortal glory, Heaven's diadem!
But thou who only could'st the Serpent tame,
   Either his slipp'ry knots at once untie,   20
And disentangle all his winding snare:
Or shatter too with him my curious[9] frame:
And let these wither, so that he may die,
Though set with skill and chosen out with care.
That they, while Thou on both their spoils dost tread,   25
May crown thy Feet, that could not crown thy Head.

Eyes and Tears

1

How wisely Nature did decree,
With the same eyes to weep and see!
That, having viewed the object vain,
They might be ready to complain.

2

And, since the self-deluding Sight,   5
In a false angle takes each height,
These tears which better measure all,
Like wat'ry lines and plummets fall.

3

Two tears, which Sorrow long did weigh
Within the scales of either eye,   10
And then paid out in equal poise,
Are the true price of all my joys.

4

What in the world most fair appears,
Yea even laughter, turns to tears:
And all the jewels which we prize,   15
Melt in these pendants of the eyes.

5

I have through every garden been,
Amongst the red, the white, the green;

---

6. Coronet.
7. Entwining.
8. Self-interest.

9. Elaborately wrought: "curious frame" suggests that *coronet* is also a metaphor for poetry.

And yet, from all the flow'rs I saw,
No honey, but these tears could draw.   20

6

So the all-seeing sun each day
Distills the world with chymic[1] ray;
But finds the essence only showers,
Which straight in pity back he pours.

7

Yet happy they whom Grief doth bless,   25
That weep the more, and see the less;
And, to preserve their sight more true,
Bathe still their eyes in their own dew.

8

So *Magdalen,* in tears more wise
Dissolved those captivating eyes,   30
Whose liquid chains could flowing meet
To fetter her Redeemer's feet.

9

Not full sails hasting loaden home,
Nor the chaste lady's pregnant womb,
Nor *Cynthia* teeming[2] shows so fair,   35
As two eyes swoln with weeping are.

10

The sparkling glance that shoots desire,
Drenched in these waves, does lose its fire.
Yea oft the Thund'rer pity takes
And here the hissing lightning slakes.   40

11

The incense was to Heaven dear,
Not as a perfume, but a tear.
And stars show lovely in the night,
But as they seem the tears of light.

12

Ope then mine eyes your double sluice,   45
And practice so your noblest use.
For others too can see, or sleep;
But only human eyes can weep.

13

Now like two clouds dissolving, drop,
And at each tear in distance stop: 50
Now like two fountains trickle down:
Now like two floods o'erturn and drown.

14

Thus let your streams o'erflow your springs,

1. Alchemical.   2. Full moon.

Till eyes and tears be the same things:
And each the other's difference bears;   55
These weeping eyes, those seeing tears.

Bermudas[3]

Where the remote *Bermudas* ride
In th'ocean's bosom unespied,
From a small boat, that rowed along,
The list'ning winds received this song.
    What should we do but sing his praise   5
That led us through the wat'ry maze,
Unto an isle so long unknown,
And yet far kinder than our own?
Where he the huge sea-monsters wracks,
That lift the deep upon their backs.   10
He lands us on a grassy stage,
Safe from the storms, and prelate's rage.[4]
He gave us this eternal Spring,
Which here enamels every thing;
And sends the fowls to us in care,   15
On daily visits through the air.
He hangs in shades the orange bright,
Like golden lamps in a green night.
And does in the pomegranates close,
Jewels more rich than *Ormus*[5] shows.   20
He makes the figs our mouths to meet,
And throws the melons at our feet.
But apples[6] plants of such a price,
No tree could ever bear them twice.
With cedars, chosen by his hand,   25
From *Lebanon*, he stores the land;
And makes the hollow seas, that roar,
Proclaim the ambergris[7] on shore.
He cast (of which we rather boast)
The Gospel's Pearl[8] upon our coast.   30
And in these rocks for us did frame
A Temple, where to sound his Name.
Oh let our voice his praise exalt,
Till it arrive at Heaven's vault:
Which thence (perhaps) rebounding, may   35
Echo beyond the *Mexique Bay*.[9]

3. In Marvell's time, the Bermudas were a refuge for persecuted Puritans and an image of remoteness, associated with a type of Paradise. The first four and last four lines frame the song.
4. Nicely juxtaposes storms at sea and religious-political persecution.
5. Hormuz, on the Persian Gulf, a center for the pearl and jewel trade.
6. Pineapples.
7. Fragrant substance derived from the sperm whale.
8. Alludes to either, or both, the pearl of great price (Matthew 13 : 45–46) and the pearl cast before swine (Matthew 7 : 6).
9. The Gulf of Mexico. Presumably, their voice is to be heard by the heathen and the Roman Catholics in America.

Thus sung they, in the *English* boat,
An holy and a cheerful note,
And all the way, to guide their chime,
With falling oars they kept the time.   40

A Dialogue Between the Soul and Body[1]

Soul   O who shall, from this dungeon, raise
A Soul enslaved so many ways?
With bolts of bones, that fettered stands
In feet; and manacled in hands.
Here blinded with an eye; and there   5
Deaf with the drumming of an ear.
A Soul hung up, as 'twere, in chains
Of nerves, and arteries, and veins.
Tortured, besides each other part,
In a vain head, and double[2] heart.   10

Body   O who shall me deliver whole,
From bonds of this tyrannic Soul?
Which, stretcht upright, impales me so,
That mine own precipice I go;[3]
And warms and moves this needless[4] frame: 15
(A fever could but do the same),
And, wanting where its spite to try,[5]
Has made me live to let me die,
A Body that could never rest,
Since this ill spirit it possessed.   20

Soul   What magic could me thus confine
Within another's grief to pine?
Where whatsoever it[6] complain,
I feel, that cannot feel, the pain.
And all my care its self employs,   25
That to preserve, which me destroys:
Constrained not only to endure
Diseases, but, what's worse, the cure:
And ready oft the port to gain,
Am shipwrecked into health again.   30

Body   But physic yet could never reach
The maladies thou me dost teach;

1. While the poem turns on Galatians 5 : 17 (" . . . the flesh lusteth against the spirit, and the spirit against the flesh . . ."), it explores the problem in paradoxical terms, playing off mutually restrictive elements of soul and body against each other. In the first two stanzas, both "Soul" and "Body" lay claim, by allusion, to Paul's outcry in Romans 7 (on the relation of the Law and sin, a meditation relevant to this poem), "O wretched man that I am! who shall deliver me from the body of this death?"
2. False, treacherous.
3. Lines 13–14 express both erectness and spiritual pride, both reaching towards heaven and the danger of damnation.
4. I.e., the body does not need it.
5. Make trial of.
6. The body.

Whom first the cramp of hope does tear:
And then the palsy shakes of fear.
The pestilence of love does heat: 35
Or hatred's hidden ulcer eat.
Joy's cheerful madness does perplex:
Or sorrow's other madness vex.
Which knowledge forces me to know;
And memory will not forego.   40
What but a Soul could have the wit
To build me up for sin so fit?
So architects do square and hew,
Green trees that in the forest grew.

The Nymph Complaining for the Death of Her Fawn[7]

The wanton troopers[8] riding by
Have shot my fawn and it will die.
Ungentle men! They cannot thrive
To kill thee. Thou ne'er didst alive[9]
Them any harm; alas nor could   5
Thy death yet do them any good.
I'm sure I never wished them ill;
Nor do I for all this; nor will:
But, if my simple pray'rs may yet
Prevail with Heaven to forget   10
Thy murder, I will join my tears
Rather than fail. But, O my fears!
It cannot die so.[1] Heaven's King
Keeps register of every thing:
And nothing may we use in vain.   15
Ev'n beasts must be with justice slain,
Else men are made their *Deodands*.[2]
Though they should wash their guilty hands
In this warm life blood, which doth part
From thine, and wound me to the heart,   20
Yet could they not be clean: their stain
Is dyed in such a purple grain.
There is not such another in
The world, to offer for their sin.
Unconstant *Sylvio*, when yet   25
I had not found him counterfeit,
One morning (I remember well)
Tied in this silver chain and bell,
Gave it to me; nay and I know

7. Among several points of reference, see the Song of Songs and the story of Silvia's deer killed wantonly by the Trojans (*Aeneid* VII, 475 ff.).
8. Soldiers of the invading Scottish army were called "troopers" (ca. 1640).
9. The syntax suggests that *alive* means "merely by being alive" as well as *while* alive.
1. Unavenged.
2. Personal chattels which are forfeited (literally, *deodandum* means "to be given to God") for causing the death of a human being.

What he said then; I'm sure I do.   30
Said he, look how your huntsman here
Hath taught a fawn to hunt his *dear*.
But *Sylvio* soon had me beguiled.
This waxed tame, while he grew wild,
And quite regardless of my smart,   35
Left me his fawn, but took his heart.[3]
    Thenceforth I set myself to play
My solitary time away,
With this: and very well content,
Could so mine idle life have spent.   40
For it was full of sport; and light
Of foot, and heart; and did invite
Me to its game: it seemed to bless
Its self in me. How could I less
Than love it? O I cannot be   45
Unkind, t' a beast that loveth me.
    Had it lived long, I do not know
Whether it too might have done so
As *Sylvio* did: his gifts might be
Perhaps as false or more than he.   50
But I am sure, for ought that I
Could in so short a time espy,
Thy love was far more better then[4]
The love of false and cruel men.
    With sweetest milk, and sugar, first   55
I it at mine own fingers nurst.
And as it grew, so every day
It waxed more white and sweet than they.
It had so sweet a breath! And oft
I blushed to see its foot more soft,   60
And white (shall I say than my hand?)
Nay, any lady's of the land.
    It is a wond'rous thing, how fleet
'Twas on those little silver feet.
With what a pretty skipping grace,   65
It oft would challenge me the race:
And when 't had left me far away,
'Twould stay, and run again, and stay.
For it was nimbler much than hinds;
And trod, as on the four[5] winds.   70
    I have a garden of my own,
But so with roses overgrown,
And lilies, that you would it guess
To be a little wilderness.
And all the spring time of the year   75
It only loved to be there.

---

3. *Dear,* line 32, is a pun on *deer; heart,*   4. Than.
a pun on *hart.*   5. Pronounced as two syllables.

Among the beds of lilies, I
Have sought it oft, where it should lie;
Yet could not, till it self would rise,
Find it, although before mine eyes.   80
For, in the flaxen lilies' shade,
It like a bank of lilies laid.
Upon the roses it would feed,
Until its lips ev'n seemed to bleed:
And then to me 'twould boldly trip,   85
And print those roses on my lip.
But all its chief delight was still
On roses thus its self to fill:
And its pure virgin limbs to fold
In whitest sheets of lilies cold.   90
Had it lived long, it would have been
Lilies without, roses within.
    O help! O help! I see it faint:
And die as calmly as a saint.
See how it weeps. The tears do come   95
Sad, slowly dropping like a gum.
So weeps the wounded balsam: so
The holy frankincense doth flow.
The brotherless *Heliades*[6]
Melt in such amber tears as these.   100
    I in a golden vial will
Keep these two crystal tears; and fill
It till it do o'erflow with mine;
Then place it in *Diana's* shrine.
    Now my sweet fawn is vanished to   105
Whither the swans and turtles[7] go:
In fair *Elysium* to endure,
With milk-white lambs, and ermines pure.
O do not run too fast: for I
Will but bespeak thy grave, and die.   110
    First my unhappy statue shall
Be cut in marble; and withal,
Let it be weeping too; but there
Th' engraver sure his art may spare;
For I so truly thee bemoan,   115
That I shall weep though I be stone:[8]
Until my tears, still dropping, wear
My breast, themselves engraving there.
There at my feet shalt thou be laid,
Of purest alabaster made: 120
For I would have thine image be
White as I can, though not as thee.

6. Disconsolate at the death of their
brother Phaeton, the three daughters of
Helios were metamorphosed into amber-
dropping trees (poplars, perhaps, or
weeping willows).

7. Turtle doves.
8. Niobe, lamenting the death of the
many children she took such pride in,
was turned to stone.

To His Coy Mistress[9]

Had we but world enough, and time,
This coyness Lady were no crime.
We would sit down, and think which way
To walk, and pass our long love's day.
Thou by the *Indian Ganges'* side   5
Shouldst rubies find: I by the tide
Of *Humber*[1] would complain. I would
Love you ten years before the Flood:
And you should if you please refuse
Till the Conversion of the *Jews*.[2]   10
My vegetable[3] love should grow
Vaster than empires, and more slow.
An hundred years should go to praise
Thine eyes, and on thy forehead gaze.
Two hundred to adore each breast;   15
But thirty thousand to the rest.
An age at least to every part,
And the last age should show your heart.
For Lady you deserve this state;[4]
Nor would I love at lower rate.   20

But at my back I always hear
Time's winged chariot hurrying near:
And yonder all before us lie
Deserts of vast eternity.
Thy beauty shall no more be found;   25
Nor, in thy marble vault, shall sound
My echoing song: then worms shall try
That long preserved virginity:
And your quaint honour[5] turn to dust,
And into ashes all my lust.   30
The grave's a fine and private place,
But none I think do there embrace.

Now therefore, while the youthful hue
Sits on thy skin like morning dew,[6]
And while thy willing soul transpires   35
At every pore with instant[7] fires,
Now let us sport us while we may;
And now, like am'rous birds of prey,
Rather at once our time devour,

9. Using arguments out of the *carpe diem* (literally, "seize the day") tradition, the poem has an apparently logical structure (if ⟶ but ⟶ therefore), its main images turning on the time and space motifs introduced in line 1.
1. The Humber is a river in northern England; it suggests the other end of the world from the Ganges.
2. I.e., from nearly the beginning of time to nearly the end.
3. Like plant life; of the lowest soul, which has only the capacity to grow (and decay).
4. Dignity.
5. Both *quaint* (cf. Middle English "queynte") and *honour* could mean the female genitals.
6. See Textual Note.
7. Urgent, as well as sudden.

Than languish in his slow-chapt[8] pow'r.   40
Let us roll all our strength, and all
Our sweetness, up into one ball:
And tear our pleasures with rough strife,
Thorough[9] the iron gates of life.
Thus, though we cannot make our sun   45
Stand still, yet we will make him run.[1]

The Definition of Love

1

My Love is of a birth as rare
As 'tis for object strange and high:
It was begotten by Despair
Upon Impossibility.

2

Magnanimous Despair alone   5
Could show me so divine a thing,
Where feeble Hope could ne'er have flown
But vainly flapped its tinsel wing.

3

And yet I quickly might arrive
Where my extended Soul is fixt,[2]   10
But Fate does iron wedges drive,
And always crowds it self betwixt.

4

For Fate with jealous eye does see
Two perfect loves; nor lets them close:
Their union would her ruin be,   15
And her tyrannic pow'r depose.

5

And therefore her decrees of steel
Us as the distant Poles have placed,
(Though Love's whole world on us doth wheel)
Not by themselves to be embraced.   20

6

Unless the giddy Heaven fall,
And Earth some new convulsion tear;
And, us to join, the world should all
Be cramped into a *Planisphere*.[3]

8. Slowly devouring; the slow jaws of,
e.g., birds of prey (cf. line 38) or of the
god Kronos (mistakenly identified in the
Renaissance with Time) who, fearing his
children, swallowed them.
9. Through.
1. The three actions in lines 38–46 include imaginative conquest of time and
space (*ball* as "sphere" or "world"),
while recognizing that the "rough strife"
now envisaged (including defloration)
must defy both time and world. The sun
stood still for Joshua (10 : 12) and for
Zeus and Alcmene when they conceived
Hercules.
2. Paradoxically (extension is a property
of matter) gone out of him and attached
to his lady.
3. A flat sphere: a two-dimensional
projection in which the poles are united.

7

As lines so Loves *oblique* may well   25
Themselves in every angle greet:
But ours so truly *parallel,*
Though infinite can never meet.

8

Therefore the Love which us doth bind,
But Fate so enviously debars,   30
Is the Conjunction of the mind,
And Opposition[4] of the stars.

The Picture of Little T. C. in a Prospect of Flowers[5]

1

See with what simplicity
This Nymph begins her golden days!
In the green grass she loves to lie,
And there with her fair aspect tames
The wilder flow'rs, and gives them names:[6]   5
But only with the roses plays;
          And them does tell
What color best becomes them, and what smell.

2

Who can foretell for what high cause
This Darling of the Gods was born!   10
Yet this is she whose chaster laws
The wanton Love shall one day fear,
And, under her command severe,
See his bow broke and ensigns torn.
          Happy, who can   15
Appease this virtuous enemy of man!

3

O then let me in time compound,
And parley with those conquering eyes;
Ere they have tried their force to wound,
Ere, with their glancing wheels, they drive   20
In triumph over hearts that strive,
And them that yield but[7] more despise.
          Let me be laid,
Where I may see thy glories from some shade.

4

Mean time, whilst every verdant thing   25
It self does at thy beauty charm,

---

4. *Conjunction* and *Opposition* are terms from astronomy, indicating spiritual union but opposition between the stars and the lovers.
5. T. C. may be Theophila Cornewall, born 1644; "darling of the gods" (line 10) then would be a pun on her name. *Prospect*: landscape.
6. "A task traditionally attributed to Eve in Eden" (Kermode), though in Genesis God assigns it to Adam.
7. Only.

Reform the errors of the Spring;
Make that the tulips may have share
Of sweetness, seeing they are fair;
And roses of their thorns disarm: 30
               But most procure
That violets may a longer age endure.

5

But O young beauty of the woods,
Whom Nature courts with fruits and flow'rs,
Gather the flow'rs, but spare the buds;   35
Lest *Flora*,[8] angry at thy crime,
To kill her infants in their prime,
Do quickly make th' example yours;
               And, ere we see,
Nip in the blossom all our hopes and thee.   40

The Mower Against Gardens

Luxurious Man, to bring his vice in use,[9]
   Did after him the world seduce;
And from the fields the flow'rs and plants allure,
   Where Nature was most plain and pure.
He first enclosed within the garden's square   5
   A dead and standing pool of air:
And a more luscious earth for them did knead,
   Which stupefied them while it fed.
The pink grew then as double as his mind;
   The nutriment did change the kind.   10
With strange perfumes he did the roses taint,
   And flow'rs themselves were taught to paint.
The tulip, white, did for complexion seek,
   And learned to interline its cheek;
Its onion root they then so high did hold,   15
   That one was for a meadow sold.
Another world was searched, through oceans new,
   To find the *Marvel of Peru*.[1]
And yet these rarities might be allowed,
   To Man, that sov'reign thing and proud,   20
Had he not dealt[2] between the bark and tree,
   Forbidden mixtures there to see.
No plant now knew the stock from which it came;
   He grafts upon the wild the tame:
That the uncertain and adult'rate fruit   25
   Might put the palate in dispute.
His green *Seraglio*[3] has its eunuchs too,
   Lest any tyrant him outdo;
And in the cherry he does Nature vex,

8. Goddess of flowers, wife of Zephyr, the west wind of springtime.
9. *Luxurious*: lustful; *in use*: into common practice.
1. Exotic multicolored imported flower.
2. Intervened.
3. Enclosure; originally, palace of a sultan.

To procreate without a sex.⁴ 30
'Tis all enforced; the fountain and the grot;
  While the sweet fields do lie forgot:
Where willing Nature does to all dispense
  A wild and fragrant innocence;
And *Fauns* and *Fairies* do the meadows till, 35
  More by their presence than their skill.
Their statues, polished by some ancient hand,
  May to adorn the gardens stand;
But howsoe'er the figures do excel,
  The *Gods* themselves with us do dwell. 40

Damon the Mower

1

Hark how the Mower *Damon* sung,
With love of *Juliana* stung!
While ev'ry thing did seem to paint
The scene more fit for his complaint.
Like her fair eyes the day was fair; 5
But scorching like his am'rous care:
Sharp like his scythe his sorrow was,
And withered like his hopes the grass.

2

Oh what unusual heats are here,
Which thus our sunburned meadows sear! 10
The grasshopper its pipe gives o'er;
And hamstringed⁵ frogs can dance no more:
But in the brook the green frog wades,
And grasshoppers seek out the shades.
Only the snake, that kept within, 15
Now glitters in its second skin.

3

This heat the sun could never raise,
Nor Dog Star so inflames the days.
It from an higher beauty grow'th,
Which burns the fields and Mower both: 20
Which mads the Dog, and makes the sun
Hotter than his own *Phaeton*.⁶
Not *July* causeth these extremes,
But *Juliana's* scorching beams.

4

Tell me where I may pass the fires 25
Of the hot day, or hot desires.
To what cool cave shall I descend,
Or to what gelid fountain bend?
Alas! I look for ease in vain,
When remedies themselves complain. 30

4. Propagation by grafting.   6. Charioteer of the sun.
5. Crippled by the heat.

No moisture but my tears do rest,
Nor cold but in her icy breast.

5

How long wilt thou, fair Shepherdess,
Esteem me, and my presents less?
To thee the harmless snake I bring,   35
Disarmed of its teeth and sting.
To thee *chameleons* changing hue,
And oak leaves tipped with honey dew.
Yet thou ungrateful hast not sought
Nor what they are, nor who them brought.   40

6

I am the Mower *Damon*, known
Through all the meadows I have mown.
On me the morn her dew distills
Before her darling daffodils:
And, if at noon my toil me heat,   45
The Sun himself licks off my sweat.
While, going home, the evening sweet
In cowslip-water[7] bathes my feet.

7

What though the piping shepherd stock
The plains with an unnumb'red flock,   50
This scythe of mine discovers wide
More ground than all his sheep do hide.
With this the golden fleece I shear
Of all these closes[8] every year.
And though in wool more poor than they,   55
Yet am I richer far in hay.

8

Nor am I so deformed to sight,
If in my scythe I looked right;
In which I see my picture done,
As in a crescent moon the sun.   60
The deathless fairies take me oft
To lead them in their dances soft;
And, when I tune myself to sing,
About me they contract their ring.

9

How happy might I still have mowed,   65
Had not Love here his thistles sowed!
But now I all the day complain,
Joining my labor to my pain;
And with my scythe cut down the grass,
Yet still my grief is where it was;   70
But, when the iron blunter grows,
Sighing I whet my scythe and woes.

7. Used by ladies as a cleansing agent.   8. Enclosures.

10

While thus he threw his elbow round,
Depopulating all the ground,
And, with his whistling scythe, does cut   75
Each stroke between the earth and root,
The edged steel by careless chance
Did into his own ankle glance;
And there among the grass fell down,
By his own scythe, the Mower mown.   80

11

Alas! said he, these hurts are slight
To those that die by Love's despite.
With shepherd's-purse, and clown's-all-heal,[9]
The blood I staunch, and wound I seal.
Only for him no cure is found,   85
Whom *Juliana's* eyes do wound.
'Tis death alone that this must do:
For Death, thou art a Mower too.

The Mower to the Glowworms

1

Ye living lamps, by whose dear light
The nightingale does sit so late,
And studying all the summer-night,
Her matchless songs does meditate;

2

Ye country comets, that portend   5
No war, nor prince's funeral,
Shining unto no higher end
Than to presage the grass's fall;

3

Ye glowworms, whose officious[1] flame
To wand'ring mowers shows the way,   10
That in the night have lost their aim,
And after foolish fires[2] do stray;

4

Your courteous lights in vain you waste,
Since *Juliana* here is come,
For she my mind hath so displaced   15
That I shall never find my home.

The Mower's Song[3]

1

My mind was once the true survey
Of all these meadows fresh and gay;

9. Herbs used to check bleeding and to heal wounds.
1. Zealous, attentive.
2. Will-o'-the-wisps.
3. This poem has the only "refrain in Marvell's poetry; the rhythm suggests the long regular sweep of the scythe" (H. M. Margoliouth, note to the 1971 Oxford edition of Marvell).

And in the greenness of the grass
Did see its hopes[4] as in a glass;
When *Juliana* came, and she   5
What I do to the grass, does to my thoughts and me.

2

But these, while I with sorrow pine,
Grew more luxuriant still and fine;
That not one blade of grass you spied,
But had a flower on either side;   10
When *Juliana* came, and she
What I do to the grass, does to my thoughts and me.

3

Unthankful meadows, could you so
A fellowship so true forego,
And in your gaudy May-games meet,   15
While I lay trodden under feet?
When *Juliana* came, and she
What I do to the grass, does to my thoughts and me.

4

But what you in compassion ought,
Shall now by my revenge be wrought;   20
And flow'rs, and grass, and I and all,
Will in one common ruin fall.
For *Juliana* comes, and she
What I do to the grass, does to my thoughts and me.

5

And thus, ye meadows, which have been   25
Companions of my thoughts more green,
Shall now the heraldry become
With which I shall adorn my tomb;
For *Juliana* comes, and she
What I do to the grass, does to my thoughts and me.   30

Music's Empire

1

First was the world as one great cymbal made,
Where jarring winds to infant Nature played.
All Music was a solitary sound,
To hollow rocks and murm'ring fountains bound.

2

Jubal[5] first made the wilder notes agree;   5
And *Jubal* tuned Music's *Jubilee*;[6]
He called the *Echoes* from their sullen[7] cell,
And built the organ's city where they dwell.

4. Green is the color of hope.
5. In Genesis 4 : 21, "the father of all such as handle the harp and organ."
6. Hebrew year of emancipation; time of rejoicing; perhaps also the ram's horn which began the year of jubilee, and thus a pun on Jubal (his name means "ram's horn" in Hebrew).
7. Solitary or lonely.

3

Each sought a consort in that lovely place,
And virgin trebles wed the manly bass.   10
From whence the progeny of numbers new
Into harmonious colonies withdrew.

4

Some to the lute, some to the viol went,
And others chose the cornet eloquent.
These practicing the wind, and those the wire,   15
To sing men's triumphs, or in Heaven's choir.

5

Then Music, the mosaic of the air,
Did of all these a solemn noise prepare;
With which she gained the empire of the ear,
Including all between the Earth and Sphere.   20

6

Victorious sounds! yet here your homage do
Unto a gentler conqueror[8] than you;
Who though he flies the Music of his praise,
Would with you Heaven's Hallelujahs raise.

The Garden

1

How vainly men themselves amaze[9]
To win the palm, the oak, or bays;[1]
And their uncessant labors see
Crowned from some single herb or tree,
Whose short and narrow verged[2] shade   5
Does prudently their toils upbraid;
While all flow'rs and all trees do close[3]
To weave the garlands of repose.

2

Fair Quiet, have I found thee here,
And Innocence, thy sister dear!   10
Mistaken long, I sought you then
In busy companies of men.
Your sacred plants, if here below,[4]
Only among the plants will grow.
Society is all but rude,   15
To[5] this delicious solitude.

3

No white nor red[6] was ever seen

---

8. Perhaps Fairfax, of Appleton House: see below.
9. Bewilder: lead into a maze or labyrinth.
1. For military, political, or poetic achievement.
2. Edged.
3. Join, unite.
4. On earth.
5. Compared to.
6. Emblematic of feminine beauty.

So am'rous as this lovely green.[7]
Fond[8] lovers, cruel as their flame,
Cut in these trees their mistress' name.   20
Little, alas, they know, or heed,
How far these beauties hers exceed!
Fair Trees! wheres'e'er your barks I wound,
No names shall but your own be found.

4

When we have run our passions' heat,[9]   25
Love hither makes his best retreat.[1]
The *Gods*, that mortal beauty chase,
Still[2] in a tree did end their race.
Apollo hunted *Daphne* so,
Only that she might laurel grow.   30
And *Pan* did after *Syrinx* speed,
Not as a nymph, but for a reed.[3]

5

What wond'rous life in this I lead!
Ripe apples drop about my head;
The luscious clusters of the vine   35
Upon my mouth do crush their wine;
The nectarine, and curious[4] peach,
Into my hands themselves do reach;
Stumbling on melons, as I pass,
Ensnared with flow'rs, I fall on grass.   40

6

Mean while the mind, from pleasure less,[5]
Withdraws into its happiness:
The mind, that ocean[6] where each kind
Does straight[7] its own resemblance find;
Yet it creates, transcending these,   45
Far other worlds, and other[8] seas;
Annihilating[9] all that's made
To a green thought in a green shade.[1]

7

Here at the fountain's sliding foot,
Or at some fruit-tree's mossy root,   50

7. Of quiet rural solitude.
8. Doting; perhaps also foolish.
9. Race; fervor (with which *run* means "spent").
1. As to a cloister.
2. Always; but also suggesting "in stillness."
3. Apollo pursued Daphne but she turned into a laurel tree (sacred to him as god of poetry) and Pan pursued Syrinx, who turned into a reed, out of which he made pipes to play on.
4. Exquisite.
5. Lesser pleasure.
6. It was commonly thought that the oceans contained counterparts to all earthly creatures.

7. Immediately; compactly ("strait").
8. Because the mind can imagine forms beyond all ordinary reality.
9. Reducing: making the created world seem nothing in comparison to what the mind imagines; reducing the material world to immaterial thought; also, returning to the nothingness (*nihil*) before the Creation.
1. *Green* can mean naive, innocent, fresh, youthful; primarily, it describes the shade cast by foliage, and is contrasted to the red of passion and the white of innocence (see line 17).

Casting the body's vest[2] aside,
My soul into the boughs does glide:
There like a bird it sits, and sings,
Then whets,[3] and combs its silver wings;
And, till prepared for longer flight,[4]   55
Waves in its plumes the various light.[5]

8

Such was that happy Garden-state,
While Man there walked without a mate:
After a place so pure, and sweet,
What other help could yet be meet![6]   60
But 'twas beyond a mortal's share
To wander solitary there:
Two paradises 'twere in one
To live in Paradise alone.

9

How well the skillful gard'ner drew   65
Of flow'rs and herbs this dial[7] new;
Where from above the milder[8] sun
Does through a fragrant zodiac run;
And, as it works, th' industrious bee
Computes its time[9] as well as we.   70
How could such sweet and wholesome hours
Be reckoned but with herbs and flow'rs!

An Horatian Ode Upon Cromwell's Return from Ireland[1]

The forward[2] youth that would appear
Must now forsake his *Muses* dear,
   Nor in the shadows sing
   His numbers languishing.
'Tis time to leave the books in dust,   5
And oil th' unused armour's rust:
   Removing from the wall

2. The body as garment.
3. Preens.
4. Perhaps of soul after death, perhaps of Platonic ascent.
5. Of this world, contrasted to white light of eternity.
6. Genesis 2 : 18, "It is not good that the man should be alone; I will make him an help meet for him."
7. Sundial (the garden itself).
8. Because its rays are tempered by the trees and vegetation.
9. With pun on *thyme*.
1. Oliver Cromwell returned from his Irish conquest in May 1650, not quite eighteen months after the execution of King Charles I; on July 22, 1650, as the new commander of the Parliamentary forces, he invaded Scotland—a task his former superior, General Fairfax, had refused as a matter of principle. The poem apparently was written between these two events. The epithet "Horatian" promises a balanced, even a detached poem, and the work is indeed complicated by dual or ambivalent attitudes, a large number of puns, a cool tone, and the allusions to Lucan—whose unfinished epic on the Roman Civil War, the *Pharsalia,* celebrates as "hero" neither Caesar nor Pompey, either of whom seems obvious, but Liberty and her defender, the Stoic Cato of Utica. The remarkable meter of the poem is probably "Marvell's own invention, but he used it for no other extant poem" (Margoliouth).
2. Ambitious; presumptuous.

The corslet of the hall.[3]
So restless *Cromwell* could not cease[4]
In the inglorious arts of peace, 10
    But through advent'rous war
    Urged his active star:
And, like the three-forked lightning,[5] first
Breaking the clouds where it was nursed,
    Did through his own side 15
    His fiery way divide.[6]
For 'tis all one to courage high
The emulous or enemy;
    And with such to inclose
    Is more than to oppose.[7] 20
Then burning through the air he went,
And palaces and temples rent:
    And *Caesar's* head at last
    Did through his laurels blast.[8]
'Tis madness to resist or blame 25
The force of angry Heaven's flame;
    And, if we would speak true,
    Much to the man is due.
Who, from his private gardens, where
He lived reserved and austere, 30
    As if his highest plot
    To plant the bergamot,[9]
Could by industrious valor climb
To ruin the great work of Time,
    And cast the Kingdom old 35
    Into another mold.
Though Justice against Fate complain,
And plead the ancient rights in vain:
    But those do hold or break
    As men are strong or weak. 40
Nature that hateth emptiness,
Allows of penetration[1] less;
    And therefore must make room
    Where greater spirits come.
What field of all the Civil Wars, 45
Where his were not the deepest scars?
    And *Hampton* shows what part
    He had of wiser art:

3. The poet echoes (perhaps ironically) conventional contemporary views; in fact, he implies, he is *not* making a "personal" statement: as a poet himself, he would not share such views.
4. Rest; "restlessness" was a trait of Lucan's Caesai.
5. Of Zeus.
6. Cromwell early became a leader of the more radical revolutionaries; *side* includes the meaning of "party" or "faction."

7. Kermode suggests, "To pen him in will produce an even more violent reaction than to fight against him."
8. *Caesar* means Charles I, executed despite his "laurels," which are supposed to be immune to lightning. Both Caesar and the lightning wielder are figures of tyranny.
9. A fine species of pear, known as the "pear of kings."
1. I.e., two objects occupying the same place.

Where, twining subtile fears with hope,
He wove a net of such a scope,   50
    That *Charles* himself might chase
    To *Carisbrooke's* narrow case;[2]
That thence the *Royal Actor* borne
The *Tragic Scaffold* might adorn,
    While round the armed bands   55
    Did clap[3] their bloody hands.
He nothing common did or mean
Upon that memorable Scene:
    But with his keener eye
    The axe's edge did try;[4]   60
Nor called the *Gods* with vulgar spite
To vindicate his helpless right,
    But bowed his comely head,
    Down as upon a bed.
This was that memorable hour   65
Which first assured the forced[5] Pow'r.
    So when they did design
    The *Capitol's* first line,
A bleeding head where they begun
Did fright the architects to run;   70
    And yet in that the *State*
    Foresaw its happy fate.[6]
And now the *Irish* are ashamed
To see themselves in one year tamed:[7]
    So much one man can do,   75
    That does both act and know.
They[8] can affirm his praises best,
And have, though overcome, confessed
    How good he is, how just,
    And fit for highest trust: 80
Nor yet grown stiffer with command,
But still in the *Republic's* hand:
    How fit he is to sway
    That can so well obey.
He to the *Commons'* feet presents   85
A *Kingdom,* for his first year's rents;
    And, what he may,[9] forbears
    His fame to make it theirs:

2. King Charles fled to Carisbrooke, which turned out to be a cage ("narrow case") for him. It was rumored that Cromwell had connived at this escape from Hampton Court to prod Parliament into the decision to execute him.
3. Besides continuing the theater metaphor, this may be an allusion to the story that the soldiers were ordered to clap in order to drown out the king's words.
4. *Keener*: than the axe's edge; *try*: test. The Latin *acies* can mean the front line of battle, the sharp edge of a blade, the pupil of the eye, and keen vision.
5. Won by force.
6. The story is told by Livy and Pliny about the digging of the foundations for the Temple of Jupiter in Rome; the omen was taken to mean that Rome would be the head (*caput*) of an empire, so the hill on which the Temple stood was called the Capitoline.
7. Cromwell's Irish campaign—August 1649 to May 1650—was known for ruthlessness.
8. *They*: the Irish. Ironic?
9. So far as he can.

And has his sword and spoils ungirt,
To lay them at the *Public's* skirt.   90
    So when the falcon high
    Falls heavy from the sky,
She, having killed, no more does search.
But on the next green bough to perch;
    Where, when he first does lure,   95
    The falc'ner has her sure.
What may not then our *Isle* presume
While Victory his crest does plume!
    What may not others fear
    If thus he crown each year!   100
A *Caesar* he ere long to *Gaul*,
To *Italy* an *Hannibal*,
    And to all states not free
    Shall *climacteric*[1] be.
The *Pict* no shelter now shall find   105
Within his party-colored mind;
    But from this valour sad
    Shrink underneath the plaid:[2]
Happy if in the tufted brake
The *English hunter* him mistake;[3]   110
    Nor lay his hounds in near
    The *Caledonian*[4] deer.
But thou the Wars' and Fortune's son
March indefatigably on;
    And for the last effect   115
    Still keep thy sword erect:[5]
Besides the force it has to fright
The spirits of the shady Night,
    The same *Arts* that did *gain*
    A *Pow'r* must it *maintain*.   120

Upon Appleton House[1]

To My Lord Fairfax

1

Within this sober frame expect
Work of no foreign *Architect*,
That unto caves the quarries drew,
And forests did to pastures hew;

1. Crucial or critical period.
2. *Pict*: Scot; the Picts painted themselves (Latin *pictus* = "painted") various colors; contemporary Scots were divided by many factions. *Sad*: severe.
3. Because of his colorful camouflage.
4. Scottish.
5. With blade (of power) upraised, not the cross hilt. In ancient myth, the drawn sword has special powers against the spirits of the dead. The Puritans

were hostile to all representations of the Cross.
1. From 1651 to 1653, Marvell served as tutor to Mary Fairfax, daughter of Thomas Fairfax and Ann Vere. Lord Fairfax had been commander in chief of the Parliamentary army, but he opposed the execution of the king (1649) and in June 1650 he resigned in protest against the proposed invasion of Scotland (see "Horatian Ode"). Fairfax then retired

Who of his great design in pain 5
Did for a model vault his brain,[2]
Whose columns should so high be raised
To arch the brows that on them gazed.

2

Why should of all things man unruled
Such unproportioned dwellings build? 10
The beasts are by their dens exprest,
And birds contrive an equal[3] nest;
The low-roofed tortoises do dwell
In cases fit of tortoise-shell:
No creature loves an empty space; 15
Their bodies measure out their place.

3

But he, superfluously spread,
Demands more room alive than dead;
And in his hollow palace goes
Where winds as he themselves may lose. 20
What need of all this marble crust
T' impark the wanton mote of dust,
That thinks by breadth the world t' unite
Though the first builders[4] failed in height?

4

But all things are composed here 25
Like Nature, orderly and near:
In which we the dimensions find
Of what more sober age and mind,
When larger sized men did stoop
To enter at a narrow loop; 30
As practicing, in doors so strait,
To strain themselves through *Heaven's Gate*.

5

And surely when the after age
Shall hither come in *Pilgrimage*,
These sacred places to adore, 35

to his Yorkshire properties, particularly
Appleton House, a large brick mansion
built between 1637 and 1650 on the site
of what had been a Cistercian priory
until the dissolution in 1542.

The poem is loosely organized, and
highly eclectic, without a consistent point
of view or a rigorous structure. The base
is the great-house or topographical
poem; within that, the poet ranges in allusions or points of reference from Christian Platonism and the Church Fathers
to contemporary poets, ruminating about
the active and the contemplative life,
while immersed in (and transcending)
the nature all around him. The framework is a guided tour, beginning with a
description of the house itself (lines 1–
80) which modulates into moralized his-

tory—the story of the nunnery and the attempted seduction of the Fairfax ances-
tress, the "blooming Virgin Thwaites,"
into false and corrupted "religion" (lines
81–280). After this, the grounds are described in various ways: the gardens
(lines 281–368), laid out in military
style; the meadows (369–480), where the
order of the seasons prevails; the woods
(481–624), a major image of the retired
life; the river (625–48). Finally, at evening, returning to the mode of the elaborate compliment, the poet describes
Mary Fairfax, the epitome of the natural
scene, the microcosm of the place, and
the hope of a new and better order.
2. Used his skull as model for the vault.
3. Appropriate.
4. Of the Tower of Babel (Genesis 11).

By *Vere*[5] and *Fairfax* trod before,
Men will dispute how their extent
Within such dwarfish confines went;
And some will smile at this as well
As *Romulus* his bee-like cell.[6]   40

6

Humility alone designs
Those short but admirable lines,
By which, ungirt and unconstrained,
Things greater are in less contained.
Let other vainly strive t'immure   45
Let *circle* in the *quadrature*![7]
These *holy mathematics* can
In ev'ry figure equal man.

7

Yet thus the laden house does sweat,
And scarce endures the *Master* great: 50
But where he comes the swelling hall
Stirs, and the square grows spherical;[8]
More by his magnitude distressed,
Than he is by its straitness pressed;
And too officiously it slights   55
That[9] in it self which him delights.

8

So honor better lowness bears,
Than that unwonted greatness wears.
Height with a certain grace does bend,
But low things clownishly ascend.   60
And yet what needs there here excuse,
Where ev'ry thing does answer use?
Where neatness nothing can condemn,
Nor pride invent what to contemn?

9

A stately frontispiece of poor[1]   65
Adorns without the open door;
Nor less the rooms within commends
Daily new furniture of friends.
The house was built upon the place
Only as for a mark of grace;   70
And for an *Inn* to entertain
Its *Lord* a while, but not remain.

10

Him *Bishops-Hill*, or *Denton* may,
Or *Bilbrough*,[2] better hold than they;

---

5. Ann Vere, Lady Fairfax.
6. The thatched hut of the founder of
Rome resembled a beehive.
7. To square the circle.
8. This refers to the cupola.

9. Its humility.
1. The poor awaiting Fairfax's alms
(with confidence: the "door" is "open")
make a "frontispiece" to the "book."
2. Fairfax estates.

But Nature here hath been so free   75
As if she said, Leave this to me.
Art would more neatly have defaced
What she had laid so sweetly waste;
In fragrant gardens, shady woods,
Deep meadows, and transparent floods.   80

11

While with slow eyes we these survey,
And on each pleasant footstep stay,
We opportunely may relate
The progress of this house's fate.
A *Nunnery* first gave it birth   85
For *Virgin Buildings* oft brought forth.
And all that neighbour-ruin shows
The quarries whence this dwelling rose.

12

Near to this gloomy cloister's gates
There dwelt the blooming virgin *Thwaites*[3]   90
Fair beyond measure, and an heir
Which might deformity make fair.
And oft she spent the summer suns
Discoursing with the subtle nuns;
Whence in these words one to her weaved   95
(As 'twere by chance) thoughts long conceived.

13

"Within this holy leisure we
Live innocently as you see.
These walls restrain the world without,
But hedge our liberty about.   100
These bars inclose that wider den
Of those wild creatures, called men;
The cloister outward shuts its gates,
And, from us, locks on them the grates.

14

"Here we, in shining armor white,   105
Like *Virgin Amazons* do fight:
And our chaste lamps we hourly trim,
Lest the great *Bridegroom* find them dim.[4]
Our orient breaths perfumed are
With incense of incessant pray'r.   110
And holy-water of our tears
Most strangely our complexion clears:

15

"Not tears of grief; but such as those
With which calm pleasure overflows;

3. Isabella Thwaites, Fairfax's ancestor.
4. See Matthew 25 for the parable of the wise and foolish virgins.

Or pity, when we look on you
That live without this happy vow.
How should we grieve that must be seen
Each one a *Spouse*, and each a *Queen*;
And can in *Heaven* hence behold
Our brighter robes and crowns of gold?   120

16

"When we have prayed all our beads,
Some one the holy *Legend* reads;
While all the rest with needles paint
The face and graces of the *Saint*.
But what the linen can't receive   125
They in their lives do interweave.
This work the *Saints* best represents;
That serves for *Altar's ornaments*.

17

"But much it to our work would add
If here your hand, your face we had.   130
By it we would *our Lady* touch;
Yet thus she you resembles much.
Some of your features, as we sewed,
Through every *Shrine* should be bestowed:
And in one beauty we would take   135
Enough a thousand *Saints* to make.

18

"And (for I dare not quench the fire
That me does for your good inspire)
'Twere sacrilege a man t' admit
To holy things, for *Heaven* fit.   140
I see the angels in a crown
On you the lilies show'ring down;
And round about you glory breaks,
That something more than human speaks.

19

"All beauty, when at such a height,   145
Is so already consecrate.
Fairfax I know; and long ere this
Have marked the youth, and what he is.
But can he such a rival seem
For whom you *Heav'n* should disesteem?   150
Ah, no! and 'twould more honour prove
He your *Devoto*[5] were, than *Love*.

20

"Here live beloved, and obeyed,
Each one your sister, each your maid.

5. Devotee.

And, if our Rule seem strictly penned,   155
The Rule itself to you shall bend.
Our *Abbess* too, now far in age,
Doth your succession near presage.
How soft the yoke on us would lie,
Might such fair hands as yours it tie!   160

21

"Your voice, the sweetest of the choir,
Shall draw *Heav'n* nearer, raise us higher:
And your example, if our head,
Will soon us to perfection lead.
Those virtues to us all so dear,   165
Will straight grow sanctity when here:
And that, once sprung, increase so fast
Till miracles it work at last.

22

"Nor is our Order yet so nice,
Delight to banish as a vice.   170
Here pleasure piety doth meet,
One perfecting the other sweet.
So through the mortal fruit we boil
The sugar's uncorrupting oil;
And that which perished while we pull,   175
Is thus preserved clear and full.

23

"For such indeed are all our arts;
Still handling Nature's finest parts.
Flow'rs dress the altars; for the clothes,
The sea-born amber[6] we compose;   180
Balms for the grieved we draw; and pastes
We mold, as baits for curious tastes.
What need is here of man? unless
These as sweet sins we should confess.

24

"Each night among us to your side   185
Appoint a fresh and virgin bride;
Whom if *our Lord* at midnight find,
Yet neither should be left behind.
Where you may lie as chaste in bed,
As pearls together billeted,   190
All night embracing arm in arm,
Like chrystal pure with cotton warm.

25

"But what is this to all the store
Of joys you see, and may make more!

---

6. Ambergris (see "Bermudas"), a fragrant substance derived from the sperm whale.

Try but a while, if you be wise: 195
The trial neither costs, nor ties."
Now *Fairfax* seek her promised faith:
Religion that dispensed hath;
Which she henceforward does begin:[7]
The nun's smooth tongue has sucked her in.   200

26

Oft, though he knew it was in vain,
Yet would he valiantly complain:
"Is this that *Sanctity* so great,
An art by which you finelier cheat?
Hypocrite witches, hence *avant*,   205
Who though in prison yet enchant!
Death only can such thieves make fast,
As rob though in the dungeon cast.

27

"Were there but, when this house was made,
One stone that a just hand had laid,   210
It must have fall'n upon her head
Who first thee from thy faith misled.
And yet, how well soever meant,
With them 'twould soon grow fraudulent:
For like themselves they alter all,   215
And vice infects the very wall.

28

"But sure those buildings last not long,
Founded by folly, kept by wrong.
I know what fruit their gardens yield,
When they it think by night concealed.   220
Fly from their vices. 'Tis thy state,[8]
Not thee, that they would consecrate.
Fly from their ruin. How I fear
Though guiltless lest thou perish there!"

29

What should he do? He would respect   225
Religion, but not Right neglect;
For first Religion taught him Right,
And dazzled not but cleared his sight.
Sometimes resolved his sword he draws,
But reverenceth then the laws: 230
For Justice still that Courage led;
First from a judge, then soldier bred.[9]

30

Small honor would be in the storm.
The Court him grants the lawful form;

7. Unclear. Probably, since religion has
dispensed her from her betrothal, she
now enters the convent.

8. Property, estate.
9. His father was a judge, his maternal
grandfather a heroic soldier.

Which licensed either peace or force,   235
To hinder the unjust divorce.
Yet still the nuns his right debarred,
Standing upon their holy guard.
Ill-counseled women, do you know
Whom you resist, or what you do?   240

31

Is not this he whose offspring fierce
Shall fight through all the *Universe*;
And with successive valor try
France, *Poland*, either *Germany*;
Till one, as long since prophesied,   245
His horse through conquered *Britain* ride?
Yet, against Fate, his spouse they kept,
And the great race would intercept.

32

Some to the breach against their foes
Their *Wooden Saints* in vain oppose.   250
Another bolder stands at push
With their old holy-water brush.
While the disjointed[1] *Abbess* threads
The jingling chain-shot of her beads.
But their loud'st cannon were their lungs;   255
And sharpest weapons were their tongues.

33

But, waving these aside like flies,
Young *Fairfax* through the wall does rise.
Then th' unfrequented vault appeared,
And superstitions vainly feared.   260
The *Relics false* were set to view;
Only the jewels there were true—
But truly bright and holy *Thwaites*
That weeping at the altar waits.

34

But the glad youth away her bears   265
And to the *Nuns* bequeaths her tears:
Who guiltily their prize bemoan,
Like gypsies that a child had stol'n.
Thenceforth (as when th' enchantment ends
The castle vanishes or rends)   270
The wasting cloister with the rest
Was in one instant dispossesed.

35

At the demolishing, this seat
To *Fairfax* fell as by escheat.[2]

---

1. Distracted.
2. Legally, in the absence of an heir, the property reverted to him as lord of the manor.

And what both *Nuns* and *Founders* willed   275
'Tis likely better thus fulfilled:
For if the *Virgin* proved not theirs,
The *Cloister* yet remained hers;
Though many a *Nun* there made her vow,
'Twas no *Religious House* till now.   280

36

From that blest bed the hero came,
Whom *France* and *Poland* yet does fame;
Who, when retired here to peace,
His warlike studies could not cease;
But laid these gardens out in sport   285
In the just figure of a fort;
And with five bastions it did fence,
As aiming one for ev'ry sense.[3]

37

When in the *East* the morning ray
Hangs out the colors of the day,   290
The bee through these known alleys hums,
Beating the *dian*[4] with its drums.
Then flow'rs their drowsy eyelids raise,
Their silken ensigns each displays,
And dries its pan[5] yet dank with dew,   295
And fills its flask[6] with odors new.

38

These, as their *Governor* goes by,
In fragrant volleys they let fly;
And to salute their *Governess*
Again as great a charge they press: 300
None for the *Virgin Nymph*;[7] for she
Seems with the flow'rs a flow'r to be.
And think so still! though not compare[8]
With breath so sweet, or cheek so fair.

39

Well shot ye firemen![9] Oh how sweet,   305
And round your equal fires do meet;
Whose shrill report no ear can tell,
But echoes to the eye and smell.
See how the flow'rs, as at *Parade*,
Under their *Colors* stand displayed: 310
Each *Regiment* in order grows,
That of the tulip, pink, and rose.

---

3. The gardens are laid out in military style.
4. Reveille.
5. The part of the musket lock containing firing powder.
6. Powder flask.

7. Mary Fairfax, Marvell's pupil at Appleton House; at this time, twelve to fourteen years old.
8. *Think . . . compare;* imperatives addressed to the flowers.
9. Men who use firearms.

40

But when the vigilant patrol
Of stars walks round about the Pole,
Their leaves, that to the stalks are curled,   315
Seem to their staves the ensigns furled.
Then in some flow'r's beloved hut
Each bee as sentinel is shut;
And sleeps so too: but, if once stirred,
She runs you through, nor asks the word.[1]   320

41

Oh thou,[2] that dear and happy isle
The garden of the world ere while,
Thou *Paradise* of four[3] seas,
Which *Heaven* planted us to please,
But, to exclude the world, did guard   325
With wat'ry if not flaming sword;
What luckless apple did we taste,
To make us mortal, and thee waste?

42

Unhappy! shall we never more
That sweet *Militia* restore,   330
When gardens only had their tow'rs,
And all the garrisons were flow'rs;
When roses only arms might bear,
And men did rosy garlands wear?
Tulips, in several colours barred,   335
Were then the *Switzers*[4] of our *Guard*.

43

The gardener had the soldier's place,
And his more gentle forts did trace.
The nursery of all things green
Was then the only magazine.   340
The winter quarters were the stoves
Where he the tender plants removes.
But war all this doth overgrow;
We ordnance plant, and power sow.   345

44

And yet there walks one on the sod
Who, had it pleased him and *God*,
Might once have made our gardens spring
Fresh as his own and flourishing.
But he preferred to the *Cinque Ports*[5]   350
These five imaginary forts;

1. Password.
2. England.
3. Pronounced as two syllables.
4. The Papal Swiss Guards and their multicolored uniforms.

5. The "Five Ports," on the southeast coast of England, of which Fairfax was Warden for a time; often used metaphorically (see the "five bastions" of line 287).

And, in those half-dry trenches, spanned[6]
Pow'r which the ocean might command.

45

For he did, with his utmost skill,
Ambition weed, but *Conscience* till.
Conscience, that Heaven-nursed plant,   355
Which most our earthly gardens want.[7]
A prickling leaf it bears, and such
As that which shrinks at every touch;
But flow'rs eternal, and divine,
That in the crowns of saints do shine.   360

46

The sight does from these bastions ply
Th' invisible *Artillery*;
And at proud *Cawood Castle*[8] seems
To point the *Batt'ry* of its beams,
As if it quarreled[9] in the seat   365
Th' ambition of its *Prelate* great;
But o'er the meads below it plays,
Or innocently seems to gaze.

47

And now to the abyss I pass
Of that unfathomable grass,   370
Where men like grasshoppers appear,
But grasshoppers are giants[1] there:
They, in their squeaking laugh, contemn
Us as we walk more low than them:
And, from the precipices tall   375
Of the green spires, to us do call.

48

To see men through this meadow dive,
We wonder how they rise alive;
As, under water, none does know
Whether he fall through it or go;   380
But as the mariners that sound
And show upon their lead the ground,
They bring up flow'rs so to be seen,
And prove they've at the bottom been.

49

No scene that turns with engines strange   385
Does oft'ner than these meadows change:
For when the sun the grass hath vexed,
The tawny mowers enter next;

6. Restrained.
7. Need; lack.
8. Two miles from Appleton House, seat
of the archbishop of York.
9. Quarreled with.

1. See Numbers 13 : 33; "And there we
saw the giants . . . and we were in our
own sight as grasshoppers, and so we
were in their sight."

Who seem like *Israelites* to be
Walking on foot through a green sea.   390
To them the grassy deeps divide,
And crowd a lane to either side.[2]

50

With whistling scythe and elbow strong,
These massacre the grass along:
While one, unknowing, carves the *rail*,[3]   395
Whose yet unfeathered quills her fail.
The edge all bloody from its breast
He draws, and does his stroke detest;
Fearing the flesh untimely mowed
To him a fate as black forebode.   400

51

But bloody *Thestylis*, that waits
To bring the mowing camp their cates,[4]
Greedy as kites has trussed it up,
And forthwith means on it to sup;
When on another quick[5] she lights,   405
And cries, he[6] called us *Israelites*;
But now, to make his saying true,
Rains rain for quails, for manna dew.[7]

52

Unhappy birds! what does it boot
To build below the grasses' root,   410
When lowness is unsafe as height,
And chance o'ertakes what scapeth spite?
And now your orphan parents' call
Sounds your untimely funeral.
Death-trumpets creak in such a note,   415
And 'tis the sourdine[8] in their throat.

53

Or[9] sooner hatch or higher build:
The mower now commands the field;
In whose new traverse[1] seemeth wrought
A camp of battle newly fought: 420
Where, as the meads with hay, the plain
Lies quilted o'er with bodies slain;
The women that with forks it fling,
Do represent the pillaging.

54

And now the careless victors play,   425

2. Form a lane by "crowding" to either side.
3. The corn crake (land rail), a field bird.
4. Food. Thestylis is a camp follower.
5. Alive.
6. The poet (see 389).
7. See Exodus 16 : 13–14 for the "quails" and the "dew" with which the Israelites were miraculously fed after their crossing of the Red Sea.
8. Trumpet.
9. Either.
1. Track.

Dancing the triumphs of the Hay;[2]
Where every mower's wholesome heat
Smells like an *Alexander's sweat*,[3]
Their females fragrant as the mead
Which they in *Fairy Circles* tread: 430
When at their dance's end they kiss,
Their new-made hay not sweeter is.

55

When after this 'tis piled in cocks,
Like a calm sea it shows the rocks:
We wond'ring in the river near   435
How boats among them safely steer.
Or, like the desert *Memphis*[4] sand,
Short *Pyramids* of hay do stand.
And such the Roman camps do rise[5]
In hills for soldiers' obsequies.   440

56

This *Scene*[6] again withdrawing brings
A new and empty face of things;
A leveled space, as smooth and plain
As cloths for *Lely*[7] stretched to stain.
The world when first created sure   445
Was such a *table rase*[8] and pure;
Or rather such is the *toril*
Ere the bulls enter at Madril.[9]

57

For to this naked equal flat,
Which *Levellers*[1] take pattern at,   450
The villagers in common[2] chase
Their cattle, which it closer rase;[3]
And what below the scythe increased[4]
Is pinched yet nearer by the beast.
Such, in the painted world, appeared   455
Davenant with th' Universal Herd.[5]

58

They seem within the polished grass
A landskip drawn in looking glass;[6]
And shrunk in the huge pasture show
As spots, so shaped, on faces do.   460
Such fleas, ere they approach the eye,

2. A country dance (with a pun).
3. Sweet, said Plutarch (cited by Margoliouth in the Oxford edition).
4. A city near the pyramids.
5. Raise.
6. Theater metaphor (see line 385).
7. Canvases for the Dutch portrait painter Sir Peter Lely, who came to England in 1643.
8. Tabula rasa: clean or blank slate.
9. *Toril*: bull ring, *Madril*: Madrid.

1. Faction of the time, which urged social and economic egalitarianism.
2. On the common pasture (also a "level" place).
3. Keep the grass closely cropped.
4. Grew.
5. In *Gondibert*, a contemporary work, Davenant's creation scene includes a "universal herd."
6. A landscape reflected in a mirror would be reduced in size.

In multiplying glasses[7] lie.
They feed so wide, so slowly move,
As *Constellations* do above.

59

Then, to conclude these pleasant Acts,   465
Denton[8] sets ope' its cataracts;
And makes the meadow truly be
(What it but seemed before) a sea.
For, jealous of its *Lord's* long stay,
It tries t' invite him thus away.   470
The river in it self is drowned
And isles th' astonished cattle round.

60

Let others tell the *Paradox*,
How eels now bellow in[9] the ox;
How horses at their tails do kick,   475
Turned as they hang to leeches quick;[1]
How boats can over bridges sail,
And fishes do the stables scale;
How salmons trespassing are found,
And pikes are taken in the pound.   480

61

But I, retiring from the flood,
Take sanctuary in the wood;
And, while it lasts, my self embark
In this yet green, yet growing ark;
Where the first Carpenter[2] might best   485
Fit timber for his keel have pressed;[3]
And where all creatures might have shares,
Although in armies, not in pairs.

62

The double wood of ancient stocks
Linked in so thick an union[4] locks,   490
It like two *Pedigrees*[5] appears,
On one hand *Fairfax*, th' other V*eres*:
Of whom though many fell in war,
Yet more to Heaven shooting are:
And, as they Nature's cradle decked,   495
Will in green age her hearse expect.

63

When first the eye this forest sees
It seems indeed as *Wood* not *Trees*;
As if their neighborhood[6] so old

---

7. Magnifying glasses or microscopes.
8. The river.
9. Because the ox swallowed them.
1. Their tails hanging in the water became live leeches or eels (a popular superstition).

2. Noah (Genesis 6).
3. Obtained.
4. Union is the subject of lines 489–90.
5. Genealogical trees, of the Fairfax and Vere lines.
6. Nearness to each other.

To one great trunk them all did mold.   500
There the huge bulk takes place, as meant
To thrust up a *Fifth Element;*
And stretches still so closely wedged
As if the Night within were hedged.

64
Dark all without it knits; within   505
It opens passable and thin;
And in as loose an order grows
As the Corinthian porticoes.
The arching boughs unite between
The columns of the temple green;   510
And underneath the winged choirs
Echo about their tuned fires.[7]

65
The *Nightingale* does here make choice
To sing the trials of her voice.
Low shrubs she sits in, and adorns   515
With music high the squatted thorns.
But highest oaks stoop down to hear,
And list'ning elders prick the ear.
The thorn, lest it should hurt her, draws
Within the skin its shrunken claws.   520

66
But I have for my music found
A sadder, yet more pleasing sound:
The stock doves, whose fair necks are graced
With nuptial rings, their ensigns chaste;
Yet always, for some cause unknown,   525
Sad pair, unto the elms they moan.
O why should such a couple mourn,
That in so equal flames do burn!

67
Then as I careless on the bed
Of gelid strawberries do tread,   530
And through the hazels thick espy
The hatching throstle's shining eye,
The heron from the ash's top
The eldest of its young lets drop,
As if it stork-like did pretend   535
That tribute to *its Lord* to send.

68
But most the *Hewel's*[8] wonders are,
Who here has the *Holt-felster's*[9] care.
He walks still upright from the root,
Meas'ring the timber with his foot;   540

7. Maybe, love songs.   9. Woodcutter.
8. Green woodpecker.

And all the way, to keep it clean,
Doth from the bark the wood-moths glean.
He, with his beak, examines well
Which fit to stand and which to fell.

69

The good he numbers up, and hacks;   545
As if he marked them with the ax.
But where he, tinkling with his beak,
Does find the hollow oak to speak,
That for his building he designs,
And through the tainted side he mines.   550
Who could have thought the *tallest Oak*
Should fall by such a *feeble stroke!*

70

Nor would it, had the tree not fed
A *Traitor-worm*, within it bred.
(As first our *Flesh* corrupt within   555
Tempts impotent and bashful *Sin*)
And yet that *Worm* triumphs not long,
But serves to feed the *Hewel's* young;
While the oak seems to fall content,
Viewing the treason's punishment.   560

71

Thus I, *easy Philosopher*,
Among the *Birds* and *Trees* confer;
And little now to make me, wants
Or of the *Fowls*, or of the *Plants*.
Give me but wings as they, and I   565
Straight floating on the air shall fly:
Or turn me but, and you shall see
I was but an inverted tree.[1]

72

Already I begin to call
In their most learned original: 570
And where I language want, my signs
The bird upon the bough divines;
And more attentive there doth sit
Than if she were with lime twigs knit.
No leaf does tremble in the wind   575
Which I returning cannot find.

73

Out of these scattered *Sibyl's* Leaves[2]
Strange *Prophecies* my fancy weaves:
And in one history consumes,
Like *Mexique paintings*, all the *Plumes.*[3]   580

---

1. A widely used metaphor in the Renaissance: see A. B. Chambers, *Studies in the Renaissance,* 8 (1961), 291–99.
2. The Sibyl committed her prophecies to leaves; Vergil's Aeneas specifically asks that the Cumaean Sibyl "speak" her prophecy to him (*Aeneid* VI, 77–102), for the leaves might be "scattered."
3. Made of feathers, collagelike.

What *Rome, Greece, Palestine*, ere said
I in this light *Mosaic*[4] read.
Thrice happy he who, not mistook,
Hath read in *Nature's mystic Book*.[5]

74

And see how chance's better wit   585
Could with a mask[6] my studies hit!
The oak-leaves me embroider all,
Between which caterpillars crawl;
And ivy, with familiar trails,
Me licks, and clasps, and curls, and hales.   590
Under this antic cope[7] I move
Like some great *Prelate of the Grove*.

75

Then, languishing with ease, I toss
On pallets swoln of velvet moss;
While the wind, cooling through the boughs,   595
Flatters with air my panting brows.
Thanks for my rest, ye mossy banks,
And unto you, cool Zephyrs, thanks,
Who, as my hair, my thoughts too shed,[8]
And winnow from the chaff my head.   600

76

How safe, methinks, and strong, behind
These trees have I encamped my mind;
Where Beauty, aiming at the heart,
Bends in some tree its useless dart;
And where the world no certain shot   605
Can make, or me it toucheth not.
But I on it securely play,
And gall its horsemen all the day.

77

Bind me ye *Woodbines* in your twines,
Curl me about ye gadding *Vines*,   610
And O so close your circles lace,
That I may never leave this place:
But, lest your fetters prove too weak,
Ere I your silken bondage break,
Do you, O *Brambles*, chain me too,   615
And courteous *Briars*, nail me through.

78

Here in the morning tie my chain,
Where the two woods have made a lane;

4. *Mosaic*: the pattern formed by the light leaves and by the light and shade; also the books of Moses, or the Scriptures, or the allegorical exegesis of them, and thus the poet's new Sibylline leaves.
5. *"Nature's mystic Book"* is the book of the creatures or the book of God's works (distinguished from the "Book of God's words" or Scripture).
6. Disguise, or costume for a masque.
7. Ecclesiastical vestment.
8. Part, separate.

While, like a *Guard* on either side,
The trees before their *Lord* divide;   620
This, like a long and equal thread,
Betwixt two *Labyrinths* does lead.
But, where the floods did lately drown,
There at the evening stake me down.

79

For now the waves are fall'n and dried,   625
And now the meadows fresher dyed;
Whose grass, with moister colour dashed,
Seems as green silks but newly washed.
No *Serpent* new nor *Crocodile*
Remains behind our little *Nile*;[9]   630
Unless it self[1] you will mistake,
Among these meads the only snake.

80

See in what wanton harmless folds
It ev'ry where the meadow holds;
And its yet muddy back doth lick,   635
Till as a crystal mirror slick;
Where all things gaze themselves, and doubt
If they be in it or without.
And for his shade which therein shines,
Narcissus like, the *Sun* too pines.   640

81

Oh what a pleasure 'tis to hedge
My temples here with heavy sedge;
Abandoning my lazy side,
Stretched as a bank unto the tide;
Or to suspend my sliding foot   645
On th' osier's undermined root,
And in its branches tough to hang,
While at my lines the fishes twang!

82

But now away my hooks, my quills,
And angles, idle utensils.   650
The *young Maria*[2] walks tonight:
Hide trifling youth thy pleasures slight.
'Twere shame that such judicious eyes
Should with such toys a man surprise;
She that already is the *Law*   655
Of all her *Sex*, her *Age's Awe*.

83

See how loose Nature, in respect
To her, it self doth recollect;
And everything so whisht[3] and fine,

---

9. It was believed that serpents and crocodiles were bred by spontaneous generation, out of the mud of the Nile.
1. The river, "our little *Nile*."

2. Mary Fairfax, to whom Marvell was tutor.
3. Hushed.

Starts forthwith to its *Bonne Mine*.[4]   660
The *Sun* himself, of *Her* aware,
Seems to descend with greater care;
And lest *She* see him go to bed,
In blushing clouds conceals his head.

84

So when the shadows laid asleep   665
From underneath these banks do creep,
And on the river as it flows
With ebon shuts[5] begin to close;
The modest halcyon[6] comes in sight,
Flying betwixt the day and night;   670
And such an horror calm and dumb,
Admiring Nature does benumb.

85

The viscous air, wheresoe'r she fly,
Follows and sucks her azure dye;
The jellying stream compacts below,   675
If it might fix her shadow so;
The stupid[7] fishes hang, as plain
As flies in crystal overta'en;
And men the silent *Scene* assist,[8]
Charmed with the *Sapphire-winged* Mist.[9]   680

86

Maria such, and so doth hush
The *World*, and through the *Ev'ning* rush.
No new-born *Comet* such a train
Draws through the sky, nor star new-slain.[1]
For straight those giddy rockets fail,   685
Which from the putrid earth exhale,
But by her flames, in *Heaven* tried,
Nature is wholly vitrified.[2]

87

'Tis she that to these gardens gave
That wondrous beauty which they have;   690
She straightness on the woods bestows;
To her the meadow sweetness owes;
Nothing could make the river be
So crystal-pure but only she;
She yet more pure, sweet, straight, and fair,   695
Than gardens, woods, meads, rivers are.

88

Therefore what first she on them spent,
They gratefully again present:

4. Good appearance.
5. Black (ebony) shutters.
6. A bird that was supposed to produce absolute calm on the sea.
7. Stupefied, amazed.

8. Observe, attend.
9. The bird in its flight.
1. Meteor or shooting star.
2. Turned to glass.

The meadow, carpets where to tread;
The garden, flow'rs to crown her head;   700
And for a glass, the limpid brook,
Where she may all her beauties look;
But, since she would not have them seen,
The wood about her draws a screen.

89

For she, to higher beauties raised,   705
Disdains to be for lesser praised.
She counts her beauty to converse
In all the languages as hers;
Nor yet in those her self employs
But for the *Wisdom*, not the *Noise*;   710
Nor yet that *Wisdom* would affect,
But as 'tis *Heaven's Dialect*.

90

Blest Nymph! that couldst so soon prevent
Those trains[3] by youth against thee meant:
Tears (wat'ry shot that pierce the mind)   715
And sighs (Love's cannon charged with wind)
True praise (that breaks through all defense)
And feigned complying innocence;
But knowing where this ambush lay,
She scaped the safe, but roughest way.   720

91

This 'tis to have been from the first
In a domestic heaven nursed,
Under the discipline severe
Of *Fairfax*, and the starry *Vere*;
Where not one object can come nigh   725
But pure, and spotless as the eye;
And goodness doth itself entail
On females, if there want a male.

92

Go now fond sex that on your face
Do all your useless study place,   730
Nor once at vice your brows dare knit
Lest the smooth forehead wrinkled sit;
Yet your own face shall at you grin,
Thorough[4] the black-bag[5] of your skin;
When *knowledge* only could have filled   735
And *Virtue* all those furrows tilled.

93

Hence she with graces more divine
Supplies beyond her sex the line;

3. Artillery.   5. Mask.
4. Through.

And, like a sprig of mistletoe,
On the Fairfacian Oak doth grow;   740
Whence, for some universal good,
The *Priest* shall cut the sacred bud;
While her *glad Parents* most rejoice,
And make their *Destiny* their *Choice.*

94
Mean time ye fields, springs, bushes, flow'rs,   745
Where yet she leads her studious hours
(Till Fate her worthily translates,
And find a *Fairfax* for our *Thwaites*),
Employ the means you have by her,
And in your kind yourselves prefer;[6]   750
That, as all *Virgins* she precedes,
So you all *Woods, Streams, Gardens, Meads.*

95
For you *Thessalian Tempe's*[7] seat
Shall now be scorned as obsolete;
Aranjuez, as less, disdained;   755
The *Bel-Retiro*[8] as constrained;
But name not the *Idalian Grove,*[9]
For 'twas the seat of wanton Love;
Much less the dead's *Elysian Fields,*[1]
Yet nor to them your Beauty yields.   760

96
'Tis not, what once it was, the *World,*
But a rude heap together hurled;
All negligently overthrown,
Gulfs, deserts, precipices, stone.
Your lesser *World*[2] contains the same,   765
But in more decent order tame;
You Heaven's Center, Nature's Lap,
And Paradise's only Map.

97
But now the *Salmon-Fishers* moist
Their *Leathern Boats* begin to hoist;   770
And, like Antipodes in shoes,[3]
Have shod their heads in their canoes.
How *Tortoise-like*, but not so slow,
These rational *Amphibii*[4] go!
Let's in; for the dark *Hemisphere*   775
Does now like one of them appear.

6. Make yourselves the best.
7. The Vale of Tempe, in Greece: a kind of ancient paradise.
8. Spanish palaces noted for their gardens.
9. A favorite place of Aphródite (or Venus), goddess of love, in Cyprus.

1. Habitation of the blessed in the lower world after death (*Aeneid* VI).
2. Appleton House.
3. The men on the other, upside-down, side of the world.
4. Creatures that live on both land and water.

Henry Vaughan

Henry Vaughan (1621/22–1695) was born to Thomas and Denise Vaughan, of an old Welsh family in Breconshire (a county in Wales once inhabited by the Silures—hence the epithet "Silurist"). Along with his twin brother Thomas (who later became a noted Hermetic philosopher), he was educated at Jesus College, Oxford from 1638 to 1640. After two years, Henry left to study law in London, but was called home in 1642 at the outbreak of the Civil War, in which he served committedly on the Royalist side. He was twice married. Though there is no record of a medical degree, he practiced medicine at Newton on the river Usk for most of his life, and wrote and translated medical and medical-alchemical works. He wrote a considerable amount of secular verse, published in his *Poems* (1646), *Olor Iscanus* (*The Swan of Usk*), published 1651, and *Thalia Rediviva* (1678); and he composed and translated various prose works, including essays from Plutarch, a life of Paulinus of Nola, and religious meditations. He died at a ripe age on April 23, 1695. His fame rests primarily on the two volumes of his religious poetry, *Silex Scintillans* (1650 and 1655). There may have been a dramatic religious conversion occasioned by the death of his younger brother William in July 1648, but this was probably just one of many elements that helped to develop his strong religious sense. Another was the influence of the "blessed man, Mr. George Herbert, whose holy *life* and *verse* gained so many pious *Converts* (of whom I am the least)" (Preface to *Silex Scintillans*).

From *Silex Scintillans*, Part I (1650)[1]

Regeneration

1

A Ward, and still in bonds,[2] one day
I stole abroad,
It was high-spring, and all the way

1. *Silex Scintillans: or Sacred Poems and Private Ejaculations* ("Part I" first appeared in 1650, "Part II" in 1655). By his subtitle, Vaughan calls attention to his sense of the impact of Herbert on himself and his work (in the preface, 1655, he calls himself the "least" of many converts gained by the "holy life and verse" of Herbert). *Silex scintillans* means flashing or sparkling flint, imaging the sparks that fly when God strikes the heart. In the Latin "emblem" explicating his title page, Vaughan describes the di-

vine violence and alludes to both the Ezekiel 11 : 19—"I will take the stony heart out of their flesh and will give them an heart of flesh" (and cf. Milton's *Paradise Lost* XI, 3–5)—and to Moses typologically striking the rock and producing water for the Israelites (Exodus 17 : 1–6).

2. The "spirit in bondage"—imprisoned by sin—is contrasted to the "spirit of adoption, whereby we cry, Abba, Father" (see Romans 8 : 14–15).

Primrosed, and hung with shade;
    Yet was it frost within,   5
      And surly winds
Blasted my infant buds, and sin
    Like Clouds eclipsed my mind.

2

Stormed thus; I straight perceived my spring
    Mere stage, and show,   10
My walk a monstrous, mountained thing
    Rough-cast with Rocks, and snow;
    And as a Pilgrim's Eye
      Far from relief,
Measures the melancholy sky   15
    Then drops, and rains for grief,

3

So sighed I upwards still,[3] at last
    'Twixt steps, and falls
I reached the pinnacle, where placed
    I found a pair of scales,   20
    I took them up and laid
      In th' one late pains,
The other smoke, and pleasures weighed
    But proved the heavier grains;

4

With that, some cried, *Away*; straight I   25
    Obeyed, and led
Full East, a fair, fresh field could spy;
    Some called it, *Jacob's Bed*;[4]
    A Virgin-soil, which no
      Rude feet e'er trod,   30
Where (since he stepped there) only go
    Prophets, and friends of God.

5

Here, I reposed; but scarce well set,
    A grove descried
Of stately height, whose branches met   35
    And mixed on every side;
    I entered, and once in
      (Amazed to see't,)
Found all was changed, and a new spring
    Did all my senses greet;   40

6

The unthrift Sun shot vital gold[5]
    A thousand pieces,
And heaven its azure did unfold

---

3. See Textual Notes.
4. Genesis 28 : 11 ff.: the field where Jacob saw, in his sleep, a ladder stretching from heaven and angels ascending and descending.
5. *Unthrift*: prodigal, generous, spendthrift; *vital*: (alchemy) living, life-giving.

Checkered with snowy fleeces,
The air was all in spice   45
And every bush
A garland wore; Thus fed my Eyes
But all the Earth lay hush.

7

Only a little Fountain[6] lent
Some use for Ears,   50
And on the dumb shades language spent
The Music of her tears;
I drew her near, and found
The Cistern full
Of divers stones,[7] some bright, and round   55
Others ill-shaped, and dull.

8

The first (pray mark) as quick as light
Danced through the flood,
But, th'last more heavy than the night
Nailed to the Center stood;   60
I wondered much, but tired
At last with thought,
My restless Eye that still desired
As strange an object brought;

9

It was a bank of flowers, where I descried   65
(Though 'twas mid-day,)
Some fast asleep, others broad-eyed
And taking in the Ray;
Here musing long, I heard
A rushing wind[8]   70
Which still increased, but whence it stirred,[9]
No where I could not find;

10

I turned me round, and to each shade
Dispatched an Eye,
To see, if any leaf had made   75
Least motion, or Reply,
But while I list'ning sought
My mind to ease
By knowing, where 'twas, or where not,
It whispered, *Where I please.*   80

Lord, then said I, *on me one breath,*
And let me die before my death!

---

6. Probably the living water (of baptism), Christ's grace, Christ himself.
7. Thoughts or images; perhaps human souls.
8. Acts 2 : 2, describing "Pentecost: "There came a sound from heaven like the rush of a mighty wind."
9. John 3 : 8, "The wind bloweth where it listeth, and thou hearest the sound thereof, but canst not tell whence it cometh, and whither it goeth: so is every one that is born of the Spirit."

Cant. Cap. 5. ver. 17.[1]
Arise O North, and come thou South-wind, and blow upon my garden, that the spices thereof may flow out.

The Search

'Tis now clear day: I see a Rose
Bud in the bright East, and disclose
The Pilgrim-Sun; all night have I
Spent in a roving Ecstasy[2]
To find my Saviour; I have been   5
As far as *Bethle'm*, and have seen
His Inn, and Cradle; Being there
I met the *Wise-men*, asked them where
He might be found, or what star can
Now point him out, grown up a Man?   10
To *Egypt* hence I fled, ran o'er
All her parched bosom to *Nile's* shore
Her yearly nurse;[3] came back, enquired
Amongst the *Doctors*,[4] and desired
To see the *Temple*, but was shown   15
A little dust, and for the Town
A heap of ashes, where some said
A small bright sparkle was a bed,
Which would one day (beneath the pole,)
Awake, and then refine the whole.[5]   20
    Tired here, I come to *Sychar*; thence
To *Jacob's well*, bequeathed since
Unto his sons, (where often they
In those calm, golden Evenings lay
Wat'ring their flocks, and having spent   25
Those white days, drove home to the Tent
Their *well-fleeced* train;) And here (O fate!)
I sit, where once my Saviour sat;
The angry Spring in bubbles swelled
Which broke in sighs still, as they filled,   30
And whispered, *Jesus had been there*
But Jacob's children would not hear.[6]
Loath hence to part, at last I rise
But with the fountain in my Eyes,

1. This should read, "Song of Solomon 4 : 16."
2. Withdrawal of soul from body.
3. Allusion to annual flooding of the Nile, which "nourishes" Egypt.
4. The learned men with whom the boy Jesus, age twelve, discoursed in the Temple (Luke 2 : 41–50).
5. Lines 15–20 are a complex allusion to the destruction of the Temple by the Romans in 70 A.D. (see the prophecy by Jesus in Luke 21 : 5–6), an act taken by "some" as foreshadowing the final de-

struction of the world by fire, which would "refine the whole"—see the "new heaven and new earth" of Revelation 21. The passage also suggests the resurrection of the body.
6. "Jacob's well" at Sychar is not in Genesis; it is the site, in John 4 : 5–15, of Jesus' revelation to the Samaritan (foreign) woman of his messiahship: "The water I will give . . . shall become . . . a fountain . . . springing up into life everlasting." The well symbolizes the disinheritance of the nonbelieving Jews.

And here a fresh search is decreed   35
He must be found, where he did bleed;
I walk the garden,[7] and there see
Ideas of his Agony,
And moving anguishments that set
His blest face in a bloody sweat;   40
I climbed the Hill, perused the Cross
Hung with my gain, and his great loss,
Never did tree bear fruit like this;
Balsam[8] of Souls, the body's bliss;
But, O his grave! where I saw lent   45
(For he had none,) a Monument,
An undefiled, and new-hewed one,
But there was not the *Corner-stone;*[9]
Sure (then said I,) my Quest is vain,
He'll not be found, where he was slain,   50
So mild a Lamb can never be
'Midst so much blood, and Cruelty;
I'll to the Wilderness, and can
Find beasts more merciful than man,
He lived there safe, 'twas his retreat   55
From the fierce *Jew*, and *Herod's* heat,
And forty days withstood the fell,
And high temptations of hell;
With Seraphins[1] there talked he
His father's flaming ministry,   60
He heav'ned their *walks*, and with his eyes
Made those wild shades a Paradise;
Thus was the desert sanctified
To be the refuge of his bride;[2]
I'll thither then; see, It is day,   65
The Sun's broke through to guide my way.
  But as I urged thus, and writ down
What pleasures should my Journey crown,
What silent paths, what shades, and Cells,
Fair, virgin-flowers, and hallowed *Wells*   70
I should rove in, and rest my head
Where my dear Lord did often tread,
Sug'ring all dangers with success,
Me thought I heard one singing thus;

1

Leave, leave, thy gadding thoughts;   75
Who Pores
and spies

7. The Garden of Gethesemane, where Jesus sweated blood and sought release from the coming Passion.
8. In alchemy, a "healthful preservative essence" (*Oxford English Dictionary*).
9. Joseph of Arimathea provided the tomb of hewn stone (Luke 23 : 53), but Christ, the Corner-stone, arose from the dead (Acts 4 : 10–11, I Peter 2 : 4 ff.).
1. Highest order of angels.
2. The woman of Revelation 12 : 1 f. is commonly interpreted to mean the Church, the Bride of Christ.

Still[3] out of Doors
descries
Within them nought.   80

2

The skin, and shell of things
Though fair,
are not
Thy wish, nor prayer
but got   85
My mere Despair
of wings.

3

To rack old Elements,
or Dust
and say   90
Sure here he must
needs stay
Is not the way,
nor just.
Search well another world; who studies this,   95
Travels in Clouds, seeks *Manna*, where none is.

Acts Cap. 17. ver. 27, 28.
*That they should seek the Lord, if happily they might feel after
him, and find him, though he be not far off from every one of us,
for in him we live, and move, and have our being.*

The Shower

'Twas so, I saw thy birth: That drowsy Lake
From her faint bosom breathed thee, the disease
Of her sick waters, and Infectious Ease.
But, now at Even
Too gross for heaven,   5
Thou fall'st in tears, and weep'st for thy mistake.

2

Ah! it is so with me; oft have I pressed
Heaven with a lazy breath, but fruitless this
Pierced not; Love only can with quick access
Unlock the way,   10
When all else stray
The smoke, and Exhalations of the breast.

3

Yet, if as thou dost melt, and with thy train
Of drops make soft the Earth, my eyes could weep

3. Always.

O'er my hard heart, that's bound up, and asleep,   15
        Perhaps at last
        (Some such showers past,)
My God would give a Sun-shine after rain.

Distraction

O knit me, that am crumbled dust! the heap
        Is all dispersed, and cheap;
      Give for a handfull, but a thought
        And it is bought;
          Hadst thou   5
Made me a star, a pearl, or a rain-bow,
        The beams I then had shot[4]
        My light had lessened not,
         But now
I find my self the less, the more I grow;   10
        The world
Is full of voices; Man is called, and hurled[5]
        By each, he answers all,
        Knows ev'ry note, and call,
         Hence, still   15
Fresh dotage tempts, or old usurps his will.
Yet, hadst thou clipped my wings, when Coffined in
        This quickened[6] mass of sin,
      And saved that light, which freely thou
        Didst then bestow,   20
         I fear
I should have spurned, and said thou didst forbear;
        Or that thy store was less,
        But now since thou didst bless
         So much,   25
I grieve, my God! that thou hast made me such.
        I grieve?
O, yes! thou know'st I do; Come, and relieve
        And tame, and keep down with thy light
        Dust that would rise, and dim my sight,   30
        Lest left alone too long
        Amidst the noise, and throng,
        Oppressed I
Striving to save the whole, by parcels[7] die.

The Pursuit

Lord! what a busy, restless thing
      Hast thou made man?

---

4. Emitted, sent out.
5. Upset, disturbed.
6. Given life.

7. Piece by piece; see "crumbled" (line 1).

Each day, and hour he is on wing,
      Rests not a span;
Then having lost the Sun, and light   5
      By clouds surprised
He keeps a Commerce in the night
      With air disguised;
Hadst thou given to this active dust
      A state untired,   10
The lost Son had not left the husk
      Nor home desired;[8]
That was thy secret, and it is
      Thy mercy too,
For when all fails to bring to bliss,   15
      Then, this must do.
Ah! Lord! and what a Purchase will that be
To take us sick, that sound would not take thee?

Mount of Olives (I) [9]

Sweet, sacred hill! on whose fair brow
My Saviour sat, shall I allow
      Language to love
And Idolize some shade, or grove,
Neglecting thee? such ill-placed wit,   5
Conceit,[1] or call it what you please
      Is the brain's fit,
      And mere disease;

      2
Cotswold, and *Coopers*[2] both have met
With learned swains, and Echo yet   10
      Their pipes, and wit;
But thou sleep'st in a deep neglect
Untouched by any; And what need
The sheep bleat thee a silly Lay
      That heard'st both reed   15
      And sheepward[3] play?

      3
Yet, if Poets mind thee well
They shall find thou art their hill,
      And fountain too,
Their Lord with thee had most to do;   20
He wept once, walked whole nights on thee,
And from thence (his suff'rings ended,)
      Unto glory
      Was attended;

8. The Prodigal Son (Luke 15 : 11 ff.).
9. Compare Herbert's "Jordan" poems. I have added "(I)" to the title. [*Editor.*]
1. Intellectual playing: *conceit* is from the Italian *concetto*, "concept."

2. English hills celebrated in poems, especially pastoral poems, by Jonson, Drayton, Denham, and others.
3. Shepherd.

4

Being there, this spacious ball[4]   25
Is but his narrow footstool all,
    And what we think
Unsearchable, now with one wink[5]
He doth comprise; But in this air
When he did stay to bear our Ill   30
    And sin, this Hill
    Was then his Chair.

The Incarnation, and Passion

Lord! when thou didst thy self undress
Laying by thy robes of glory,
To make us more, thou wouldst be less,
And becam'st a woeful story.

To put on Clouds instead of light,   5
And clothe the morning-star with dust,
Was a translation of such height
As, but in thee, was ne'er expressed;

Brave worms, and Earth! that thus could have
A God Enclosed within your Cell,   10
Your maker pent up in a grave,
Life locked in death, heaven in a shell;

Ah, my dear Lord! what couldst thou spy
In this impure, rebellious clay,
That made thee thus resolve to die   15
For those that kill thee every day?

O what strange wonders could thee move
To slight thy precious blood, and breath!
Sure it was *Love*, my Lord; for *Love*
Is only stronger far than death.   20

Vanity of Spirit

Quite spent with thoughts I left my Cell, and lay
Where a shrill spring tuned to the early day.
    I begged here long, and groaned to know
    Who gave the Clouds so brave[6] a bow,
    Who bent the spheres, and circled in   5
    Corruption with this glorious Ring,[7]
    What is his name, and how I might
    Descry some part of his great light.

4. The world.   7. Eternity: see the "great ring," "The
5. Glance.   World," line 2.
6. Splendid, handsome.

I summon'd nature: pierced through all her store,
Broke up some seals, which none had touched before,   10
    Her womb, her bosom, and her head
    Where all her secrets lay a bed
    I rifled quite, and having passed
    Through all the Creatures, came at last
    To search my self, where I did find   15
    Traces, and sounds of a strange kind.
Here of this mighty spring, I found some drills,[8]
With Echoes beaten from th' eternal hills;
    Weak beams, and fires flashed to my sight,
    Like a young East, or Moonshine night,   20
    Which showed me in a nook cast by
    A piece of much antiquity,
    With Hieroglyphics quite dismembered,
    And broken letters scarce remembered.
I took them up, and (much Joyed,) went about   25
T' unite those pieces, hoping to find out
    The mystery; but this ne'er done,
    That little light I had was gone:
    It grieved me much. At last, said I,
    Since in these veils my Eclipsed Eye   30
    May not approach thee, (for at night
    Who can have commerce with the light?)
    I'll disapparel, and to buy
    But one half glance, most gladly die

The Retreat[9]

    Happy those early days! when I
    Shined in my Angel-infancy.
    Before I understood this place
    Appointed for my second race,[1]
    Or taught my soul to fancy ought   5
    But a white, Celestial thought,
    When yet I had not walked above
    A mile, or two, from my first love,
    And looking back (at that short space)
    Could see a glimpse of his bright-face;   10
    When on some *gilded Cloud*, or *flower*,
    My gazing soul would dwell an hour,
    And in those weaker glories spy
    Some shadows of eternity;
    Before I taught my tongue to wound   15

8. Rills, small streams.
9. Not to be compared to Wordsworth's *Intimations* ode; this poem is about the retreat to childhood from the evils of the world. The poem blends Platonist and Hermetist ideas with Christ's words, "Suffer the little children to come unto me . . . for of such is the kingdom of God. Verily I say unto you, Whosoever shall not receive the kingdom of God as a little child, he shall not enter therein" (Mark 10 : 14–15). The first verse paragraph has a predominantly temporal structure, the second a predominantly spatial structure.
1. "Second race" refers to the preexistence of the soul.

My Conscience with a sinful sound,
Or had the black art to dispense
A sev'ral[2] sin to ev'ry sense,
But felt through all this fleshy dress
Bright *shoots* of everlastingness.[3]   20
   Oh how I long to travel back,
And tread again that ancient track!
That I might once more reach that plain,
Where first I left my glorious train,
From whence th' Enlightened spirit sees   25
That shady City of Palm trees;[4]
But (ah!) my soul with too much stay[5]
Is drunk, and staggers in the way.
Some men a forward motion love,
But I by backward steps would move,   30
And when this dust falls to the urn
In that state I came return.

[Joy of my life! while left me here]

Joy of my life![6] while left me here,
      And still my Love!
How in thy absence thou dost steer
      Me from above!
      A life well lead   5
      This truth commends,
      With quick, or dead
      It never ends.

        2
Stars are of mighty use: The night
      Is dark, and long;   10
The Road foul, and where one goes right,
      Six may go wrong.
      One twinkling ray
      Shot o'er some cloud,
      May clear much way   15
      And guide a crowd.

        3
God's Saints are shining lights: who stays
      Here long must pass
O'er dark hills, swift streams, and steep ways
      As smooth as glass;   20
      But these all night
      Like Candles, shed
      Their beams, and light
      Us into Bed.

2. Different.
3. The soul.
4. Jericho, shown to Moses in the vision of the Promised Land from the top of Mount Pisgah (Deuteronomy 34); here, the Heavenly City.
5. Delay.
6. Believed to be about Vaughan's brother William, or perhaps his first wife, Catherine.

4

They are (indeed,) our Pillar-fires[7]   25
Seen as we go,
They are that City's shining spires
We travel too;
A swordlike gleam[8]
Kept man for sin   30
First *Out*; This beam
Will guide him *In*.

The Morning Watch[9]

O Joys! Infinite sweetness! with what flowers,
And shoots of glory, my soul breaks, and buds!
All the long hours
Of night, and Rest
Through the still shrouds   5
Of sleep, and Clouds,
This Dew[1] fell on my Breast;
O how it *Bloods*,
And *Spirits* all my Earth! hark! In what Rings,
And *Hymning Circulations*[2] the quick world   10
Awakes, and sings;
The rising winds,
And falling springs,
Birds, beasts, all things
Adore him in their kinds.   15
Thus all is hurled
In sacred *Hymns*, and *Order*, The great *Chime*
And *Symphony* of nature. Prayer is
The world in tune
A spirit-voice,   20
And vocal joys
Whose *Echo is* heav'ns bliss.
O let me climb[3]
When I lie down! The Pious soul by night
Is like a clouded star, whose beams though said   25
To shed their light
Under some Cloud
Yet are above,
And shine, and move
Beyond that misty shroud.   30
So in my Bed

7. Cf. the pillar of fire guiding the Israelites (Exodus 13 : 21).
8. Flaming sword guarding east gate of Eden, after Adam and Eve were cast out (Genesis 3 : 24).
9. Morning prayer.
1. Traditional image for grace, divine power, and the coming of Christ.
2. *Bloods, spirits, circulations*: combines old notion of blood creating "spirits"

(highly rarefied substance linking soul and body) and Harvey's new theory of circulation of the blood: "the blood-begotten vital spirits and the circular movement of the blood represent the revitalizing of the poet and the rest of the created world, at dawn" (Joan Bennett, *Five Metaphysical Poets* (Cambridge, 1964, p. 85).
3. Pray

That Curtained grave, though sleep, like ashes, hide
My lamp, and life, both shall in thee abide.

[Silence, and stealth of days!]

Silence, and stealth of days! 'tis now
   Since thou[4] art gone,
Twelve hundred hours, and not a brow
   But Clouds hang on.
As he that in some Cave's thick damp   5
   Locked from the light,
Fixeth a solitary lamp,
   To brave the night,
And walking from his Sun, when past
   That glim'ring Ray   10
Cuts through the heavy mists in haste
   Back to his day,
So o'er fled minutes I retreat
   Unto that hour
Which showed thee last, but did defeat   15
   Thy light, and power
I search, and rack my soul to see
   Those beams again,
But nothing but the snuff[5] to me
   Appeareth plain;   20
That dark and dead sleeps in its known,
   And common urn,
But those, fled to their Maker's throne,
   There shine, and burn;
O could I track them! but souls must   25
   Track one the other,
And now the spirit, not the dust
   Must be thy brother.
Yet I have one *Pearl* by whose light
   All things I see,   30
And in the heart of Earth, and night
   Find Heaven, and thee.

Burial

O Thou! the first fruits of the dead,
   And their dark bed,
When I am cast into that deep
   And senseless sleep
   The wages of my sin,   5
   O then,
Thou great Preserver of all men!
   Watch o'er that loose
   And empty house,
   Which I sometimes lived in.   10

---

4. William Vaughan, d. 1648.   5. The charred part of the candlewick.

2

It is (in truth!) a ruined piece
   Not worth thy Eyes,
And scarce a room but wind, and rain
   Beat through, and stain
    The seats, and Cells within;   15
     Yet thou
Led by thy Love wouldst stoop thus low,
   And in this Cot
   All filth, and spot,
   Didst with thy servant Inn.[6]   20

3

And nothing can, hourly see,
   Drive thee from me,
Thou art the same, faithful, and just
   In life, or Dust;
    Though then (thus crumbed)[7] I stray 25
     In blasts,
Or Exhalations, and wastes
   Beyond all Eyes
   Yet thy love spies
   That Change, and knows thy Clay. 30

4

The world's thy box: how then (there tossed)
   Can I be lost?
But the delay is all; Time now
   Is old, and slow,
    His wings are dull, and sickly;   35
     Yet he
Thy servant is, and waits on thee,
   Cut then the sum,
   Lord haste, Lord come,
   O come Lord *Jesus* quickly!   40

Rom. Cap. 8. ver. 23.

*And not only they, but our selves also, which have the first fruits
of the spirit, even we our selves groan within our selves, waiting for
the adoption, to wit, the redemption of our body.*

[Sure, there's a tie of Bodies!]

Sure, there's a tie of Bodies! and as they
   Dissolve (with it,) to Clay,
Love languisheth, and memory doth rust
   O'er-cast with that cold dust;

6. Dwell.   7. Crumbled, reduced to dust.

For things thus *Centered*, without *Beams*, or *Action*   5
      Nor give, nor take *Contaction*,[8]
And man is such a *Marigold*, these fled,
      That shuts, and hangs the head.

2

Absents within the Line Conspire,[9] and *Sense*
      Things distant doth unite,   10
Herbs sleep unto the *East*, and some fowls thence
      Watch the Returns of light;
But hearts are not so kind:[1] false, short delights
      Tell us the world is brave,[2]
And wrap us in Imaginary flights   15
      Wide of a faithful grave;
Thus *Lazarus* was carried out of town;[3]
      For 'tis our foe's chief art
By distance all good objects first to drown,
      And then besiege the heart.   20
But I will be my own *Deaths-head*; and though
      The flatt'rer say, *I live*,
Because Incertainties we cannot know
      Be sure, not to believe.

Peace

    My Soul, there is a Country
      Far beyond the stars,
  Where stands a winged sentry
      All skillful in the wars,
  There above noise, and danger   5
      Sweet peace sits crowned with smiles,
  And one born in a Manger
      Commands the Beauteous files,
  He is thy gracious friend,
      And (O my Soul awake!)   10
  Did in pure love descend
      To die here for thy sake,
  If thou canst get but thither,
      There grows the flower of peace,
  The Rose that cannot wither,   15
      Thy fortress, and thy ease;
  Leave then thy foolish ranges;
      For none can thee secure,
  But one, who never changes,
      Thy God, thy life, thy Cure.   20

8. In Hermetic thought, dead bodies ("centered" or fixed) lack the "beams" or radiations emanating from all beings and so can neither make nor experience contact with other beings.
9. *Line*: of life; *conspire*: breathe together, i.e., communicate sensations.

1. Natural.
2. Beautiful.
3. Inferred from John 11 : 30, "Jesus was not yet come into the town," and 11 : 38, the fact that Lazarus was buried in a cave.

[And do they so? have they a Sense]

Rom. Cap. 8. ver. 19.
Etenim res Creatae exerto Capite observantes expectant revelati-
onem Filiorum Dei.[4]

And do they so? have they a Sense
    Of ought but Influence?
Can they their heads lift, and expect,[5]
    And groan too?[6] why th'Elect
Can do no more: my volumes said   5
    They were all dull, and dead,
They judged them senseless, and their state
    Wholly Inanimate.
    Go, go; Seal up thy looks,
      And burn thy books.   10

2

I would I were a stone, or tree,
    Or flower by pedigree,
Or some poor high-way herb, or Spring
    To flow, or bird to sing!
Then should I (tied to one sure state,)   15
    All day expect my date;[7]
But I am sadly loose, and stray
    A giddy blast each way;
    O let me not thus range!
      Thou canst not change.   20

3

Sometimes I sit with thee, and tarry
    An hour, or so, then vary.
Thy other Creatures in this Scene
    Thee only aim, and mean;
Some rise to seek thee, and with heads   25
    Erect peep from their beds;
Others, whose birth is in the tomb,
    And cannot quit the womb,
    Sigh there, and groan for thee,
      Their liberty.   30

4

O let not me do less! shall they
    Watch, while I sleep, or play?
Shall I thy mercies still abuse
    With fancies, friends, or news?

4. "For created things, watching with head uplifted, look for the revelation of the Sons of God." The heading is Beza's translation, inaccurately cited, as published by T. Vautrollier (London 1576 and 1582); other editions have completely different renderings. Romans 8 : 19 reads in the King James Version: "For the earnest expectation of the creature waiteth for the manifestation of the Sons of God."
5. Wait, await.
6. Romans 8 : 22: "We know that the whole creation groaneth."
7. Of death.

O brook it not! thy blood is mine,   35
And my soul should be thine;
O brook it not! why wilt thou stop
After whole showers one drop?
Sure, thou wilt joy to see
Thy sheep with thee.   40

Corruption

Sure, It was so. Man in those early days
    Was not all stone, and Earth,
He shined a little, and by those weak Rays
    Had some glimpse of his birth.
He saw Heaven o'er his head, and knew from whence   5
    He came (condemned,) hither,
And, as first Love draws strongest, so from hence
    His mind sure progressed thither.
Things here were strange unto him: Sweat, and till[8]
    All was a thorn, or weed,   10
Nor did those last, but (like himself,) died still
    As soon as they did *Seed*,
They seemed to quarrel with him; for that Act
    That felled him, foiled them all,
He drew the Curse upon the world, and Cracked   15
    The whole frame with his fall.
This made him long for *home*, as loath to stay
    With murmurers, and foes;
He sighed for *Eden*, and would often say
    Ah! what bright days were those!   20
Nor was Heav'n cold unto him; for each day
    The valley, or the Mountain
Afforded visits, and still *Paradise* lay
    In some green shade, or fountain.
Angels lay *Leiger*[9] here; Each Bush, and Cell,   25
    Each Oak, and high-way knew them;
Walk but the fields, or sit down at some *well*,
    And he was sure to view them.
Almighty *Love*! where art thou now? mad man
    Sits down, and freezeth on,   30
He raves, and swears to stir nor fire, nor fan,
    But bids the thread[1] be spun.
I see, thy Curtains are Close-drawn; Thy bow
    Looks dim too in the Cloud,
Sin triumphs still, and man is sunk below   35
    The Center,[2] and his shroud;
All's in deep sleep, and night; Thick darkness lies
    And hatcheth o'er thy people;

8. Tillage, ploughing the ground.
9. Resident ambassador.
1. His fate.

2. Furthest point of world away from God.

But hark! what triumpets that? what Angel cries
    Arise! Thrust in thy sickle.[3]   40

Unprofitableness

How rich, O Lord! how fresh thy visits are!
'Twas but Just now my bleak leaves hopeless hung
    Sullied with dust and mud;
Each snarling blast shot through me, and did shear
Their Youth, and beauty, Cold showers nipped, and wrung   5
    Their spiciness, and blood;
But since thou didst in one sweet glance survey
Their sad decays, I flourish, and once more
    Breathe all perfumes, and spice;
I smell a dew like *Myrrh*, and all the day   10
Wear in my bosom a full Sun; such store
    Hath one beam from thy Eyes.
But, ah, my God! what fruit hast thou of this?
What one poor leaf did ever I yet fall
    To wait upon thy wreath?   15
Thus thou all day a thankless weed dost dress,
And when th' hast done, a stench, or fog is all
    The odour I bequeath.

Idle Verse

Go, go, quaint follies, sugared sin,
    Shadow no more my door;
I will no longer Cobwebs spin,
    I'm too much on the score.[4]

For since amidst my youth, and night,   5
    My great preserver smiles,
We'll make a Match, my only light,
    And Join against their wiles;

Blind, desp'rate *fits*, that study how
    To dress, and trim our shame,   10
That gild rank poison, and allow
    Vice in a fairer name;

The *Purls* of youthful blood, and bowels,[5]
    Lust in the Robes of Love,
The idle talk of fev'rish souls   15
    Sick with a scarf, or glove;
Let it suffice my warmer days
    Simpered, and shined on you,

3. Revelation 14 : 18: "And another angel . . . cried with a loud cry . . . , Thrust in thy sharp sickle, and gather the clusters of the vine of the earth; for her grapes are fully ripe."
4. In debt.
5. *Purls*: swirlings, as of a rill; *bowels*: center of feeling or sensation.

Twist not my Cypress with your Bays,
    Or Roses with my Yew;   20

Go, go, seek out some greener thing,
    It snows, and freezeth here;
Let Nightingales attend the spring,
    Winter is all my year.

Son-days[6]

Bright shadows of true Rest! some shoots of bliss,
              Heaven once a week;
The next world's gladness prepossest in this;
              A day to seek;
Eternity in time; the steps by which   5
We Climb above all ages; Lamps that light
Man through his heap of dark days; and the rich,
And full redemption of the whole week's flight.

2

The Pulleys unto headlong man; time's bower;
             The narrow way;   10
Transplanted Paradise; God's walking hour;
             The Cool o'th' day;[7]
The Creatures' *Jubilee*; God's parle with dust;
Heaven here; Man on those hills of Myrrh, and flowers;
Angels descending; the Returns of Trust;   15
A Gleam of glory, after six-days-showers.

3

The Church's love-feasts; Time's Prerogative,[8]
             And Interest
Deducted from the whole; The Combs, and hive,
             And home of rest.   20
The milky way Chalked out with Suns; a Clue
That guides through erring hours; and in full story
A taste of Heav'n on earth; the pledge, and Cue
Of a full feast: And the Out Courts of glory.

The Dawning[9]

Ah! what time wilt thou come? when shall that cry
    The *Bridegroom's Coming*! fill the sky?
    Shall it in the Evening run
    When our words and works are done?
    Or will thy all-surprising light   5
      Break at midnight?

6. The title puns on *son* and *sun*, as does Herbert's sonnet "The Son," but the poem also closely resembles Herbert's "Prayer" and "Sunday."
7. See Genesis 3 : 8: "And they heard the garden in the cool of the day." the voice of the Lord God walking in

8. As the first day of the week.
9. A meditation on the coming of Christ for the Judgment; the bridegroom image derives from Matthew 25, the parable of the ten virgins or bridesmaids, some of whom are prepared but others not.

When either sleep, or some dark pleasure
Possesseth mad man without measure;
Or shall these early, fragrant hours
     Unlock thy bowers,   10
And with their blush of light descry
Thy locks crown'd with eternity?
Indeed, it is the only time
That with thy glory doth best chime,
All now are stirring, ev'ry field   15
     Full hymns doth yield,
The whole Creation shakes off night,
And for thy shadow looks the light,
Stars now vanish without number,
Sleepy Planets set, and slumber,   20
The pursie[1] Clouds disband, and scatter,
All expect some sudden matter,
Not one beam triumphs, but from far
     That morning star;
O at what time soever thou   25
(Unknown to us,) the heavens wilt bow,
And, with thy Angels in the *Van*,[2]
Descend to Judge poor careless man,
Grant, I may not like puddle lie
In a Corrupt security,   30
Where, if a traveller water crave,
He finds it dead, and in a grave;
But as this restless, vocal *Spring*
All day, and night doth run, and sing,
And though here born, yet is acquainted   35
Elsewhere, and flowing keeps untainted;
So let me all my busy age
In thy free services engage,
And though (while here) of force I must
Have Commerce sometimes with poor dust,   40
And in my flesh, though vile, and low,
As this doth in her Channel, flow,
Yet let my Course, my aim, my Love,
And chief acquaintance be above;
So when that day, and hour shall come   45
In which thy self will be the Sun,
Thou'lt find me drest and on my way,
Watching the Break of thy great day.

Retirement

Who on yon throne of Azure sits,
     Keeping close house

1. Swollen, heavy (*Oxford English Dic-*   2. Vanguard.
tionary, citing this example).

Above the morning star,
Whose meaner shows,
-And outward utensils these glories are   5
That shine and share
Part of his mansion; He one day
When I went quite astray
Out of mere love
By his mild Dove   10
Did show me home, and put me in the way.

2

Let it suffice at length thy fits
And lusts (said he,)
Have had their wish, and way;
Press not to be   15
Still thy own foe, and mine; for to this day
I did delay,
And would not see, but chose to wink,
Nay, at the very brink
And edge of all   20
When thou wouldst fall
My *love-twist*[3] held thee up, my *unseen link*.

3

I know thee well; for I have framed
And hate thee not,
Thy spirit too is mine;   25
I know thy lot,
Extent, and end, for my hands drew the line
Assigned thine;
If then thou wouldst unto my seat,
'Tis not th'applause, and feat   30
Of dust, and clay
Leads to that way,
But from those follies a resolv'd Retreat.

4

Now here below where yet untamed
Thou dost thus rove   35
I have a house as well
As there above,
In it my *Name*, and *honour* both do dwell
And shall until
I make all new;[4] there nothing gay   40
In perfumes, or Array,
Dust lies with dust
And hath but just
The same Respect, and room, with ev'ry clay.

3. See Herbert's "silk twist" ("The Pearl").
4. Revelation 21 : 5: "And he that sat upon the throne said, Behold, I make all things new."

5

A faithful school where thou mayst see   45
In Heraldry
Of stones, and speechless Earth
Thy true descent;
Where dead men preach, who can turn feasts, and mirth
To funerals, and *Lent*.   50
There dust that out of doors might fill
Thy eyes, and blind thee still,
Is fast asleep;
Up then, and keep
Within those doors, (my doors) dost hear? I *will*.   55

Love, and Discipline

Since in a land not barren still
(Because thou dost thy grace distill,)
My lot is fal'n, Blest be thy will!

And since these biting frosts but kill
Some tares in me which choke, or spill   5
That seed thou sow'st, Blest be thy skill!

Blest be thy Dew, and blest thy frost,
And happy I to be so crost,[5]
And cured by Crosses at thy cost.

The Dew doth Cheer what is distrest,   10
The frosts ill weeds nip, and molest,
In both thou work'st unto the best.

Thus while thy sev'ral mercies plot,
And work on me now cold, now hot,
The work goes on, and slacketh not,   15

For as thy hand the weather steers,
So thrive I best, 'twixt joys, and tears,
And all the year have some green Ears.

The World

I saw Eternity the other night
Like a great *Ring*[6] of pure and endless light,
All calm, as it was bright,
And round beneath it, Time in hours, days, years
Driv'n by the spheres   5
Like a vast shadow moved, In which the world
And all her train were hurled;

5. Crossed.
6. Cf. the definition of God as a circle whose center is everywhere but circumference nowhere.

The doting Lover in his quaintest[7] strain
    Did there Complain,
Near him, his Lute, his fancy, and his flights,   10
    Wits sour delights,
With gloves, and knots[8] the silly snares of pleasure
    Yet his dear Treasure
All scattered lay, while he his eyes did pour
    Upon a flow'r.   15

2

The darksome[9] Statesman hung with weights and woe
Like a thick midnight-fog moved there so slow
    He did not stay, nor go;
Condemning thoughts (like sad Eclipses) scowl
    Upon his soul,   20
And Clouds of crying witnesses without
    Pursued him with one shout.
Yet digged the Mole, and lest his ways be found
    Worked under ground,
Where he did Clutch his prey, but one did see   25
    That policy,[1]
Churches and altars fed him, Perjuries
    Were gnats and flies,
It rained about him blood and tears, but he
    Drank them as free.[2]   30

3

The fearful miser on a heap of rust
Sat pining all his life there, did scarce trust
    His own hands with the dust,
Yet would not place[3] one piece above, but lives
    In fear of thieves.[4]   35
Thousands there were as frantic as himself
    And hugged each one his pelf,
The down-right Epicure placed heav'n in sense[5]
    And scorned pretence
While others slipt into a wide Excess   40
    Said little less;
The weaker sort slight, trivial wares Enslave
    Who think them brave,
And poor, despised truth sat Counting by[6]
    Their victory.   45

4

Yet some, who all this while did weep and sing,
And sing, and weep, soared up into the *Ring*,[7]
    But most would use no wing.

7. Most ingenious or clever, most elaborate.
8. Love knots.
9. Gloomy.
1. Strategy or plan.
2. Probably means "as freely as they rained."
3. Invest.
4. See Matthew 6 : 19–20.
5. The senses.

6. Watching, recording.
7. In Hermetic thought, those who escape the world by ascending through the seven spheres sing hymns to the Father in the eighth sphere before entering the substance of God himself. See also the "great multitude" of Revelation 7 and the inhabitants of the New Jerusalem "prepared as a bride adorned for her husband" in Revelation 21.

O fools (said I,) thus to prefer dark night
    Before true light,   50
To live in grots, and caves,[8] and hate the day
    Because it shows the way,
The way which from this dead and dark abode
    Leads up to God,
A way where you might tread the Sun, and be   55
    More bright than he.
But as I did their madness so discuss
    One whispered thus,
This Ring the Bridegroom did for none provide
    But for his bride.[9]   60

John Cap. 2. ver. 16, 17.
All that is in the world, the lust of the flesh, the lust of the Eyes,
and the pride of life, is not of the father, but is of the world.
And the world passeth away, and the lusts thereof, but he that doth
the will of God abideth for ever.

Mount of Olives (II)

When first I saw true beauty, and thy Joys
Active as light, and calm without all noise
Shined on my soul, I felt through all my pow'rs
Such a rich air of sweets,[1] as Evening show'rs
Fanned by a gentle gale Convey and breathe   5
On some parched bank, crowned with a flow'ry wreath;
Odors, and Myrrh, and balm in one rich flood
O'er ran my heart, and spirited my blood,
My thoughts did swim in Comforts, and mine eye
Confessed, *The world did only paint and lie.*   10
And where before I did no safe Course steer
But wandered under tempests all the year,
Went bleak and bare in body as in mind,
And was blown through by ev'ry storm and wind,
I am so warmed now by this glance on me,   15
That, midst all storms I feel a Ray of thee;
So have I known some beauteous *Paisage*[2] rise
In sudden flow'rs and arbours to my Eyes,
And in the depth and dead of winter bring
To my Cold thoughts a lively sense of spring.   20
    Thus fed by thee, who dost all beings nourish,
My withered leafs again look green and flourish,
I shine and shelter underneath thy wing
Where sick with love I strive thy name to sing,
Thy glorious name! which grant I may so do   25
That these may be thy *Praise*, and my *Joy* too.

8. See the Allegory of the Cave in Plato's *Republic*.
9. See Revelation 19 : 7–8 and 19 : 21 on the Marriage of the Lamb.
1. Perfumes, sweet odors.
2. Landscape.

Man

Weighing the steadfastness and state[3]
Of some mean things which here below reside,
Where birds like watchful Clocks the noiseless date
    And Intercourse of times divide,
Where Bees at night get home and hive, and flow'rs   5
        Early, as well as late,
Rise with the Sun, and set in the same bow'rs;

2

    I would (said I) my God would give
The staidness of these things to man! for these
To his divine appointments ever cleave,   10
    And no new business breaks their peace;
The birds nor sow, nor reap, yet sup and dine,
        The flow'rs without clothes live,
Yet *Solomon* was never drest so fine.[4]

3

    Man hath still either toys,[5] or Care,   15
He hath no root, nor to one place is tied,
But ever restless and Irregular
    About this Earth doth run and ride,
He knows he hath a home, but scarce knows where,
        He says it is so far   20
That he hath quite forgot how to go there.

4

    He knocks at all doors, strays and roams,
Nay hath not so much wit as some stones[6] have
Which in the darkest night point to their homes,
    By some hid sense their Maker gave;   25
Man is the shuttle, to whose winding quest
        And passage through these looms
God ordered motion, but ordained no rest.

[I walked the other day . . .]

I walked the other day (to spend my hour,)[7]
        Into a field
Where I sometimes had seen the soil to yield
        A gallant flow'r,
But Winter now had ruffled all the bow'r   5
        And curious store
    I knew there heretofore.

2

Yet I whose search loved not to peep and peer
        I'th' face of things

---

3. *State*: dignity.
4. See the Sermon on the Mount, Matthew 6 : 26–29.
5. Diversions.
6. Loadstones, with magnetic properties.
7. Hour of meditation.

Thought with my self, there might be other springs 10
    Besides this here
Which, like cold friends, sees us but once a year,
    And so the flow'r
    Might have some other bow'r.

3

Then taking up what I could nearest spy 15
    I digged about
That place where I had seen him to grow out,
    And by and by
I saw the warm Recluse alone to lie
    Where fresh and green 20
    He lived of us unseen.

4

Many a question Intricate and rare
    Did I there strow,
But all I could extort was, that he now
    Did there repair 25
Such losses as befell him in this air
    And would e'er long
    Come forth most fair and young.

5

This past, I threw the Clothes quite o'er his head,
    And stung with fear 30
Of my own frailty dropt down many a tear
    Upon his bed,
Then sighing whispered, *Happy are the dead!*
    What peace doth now
    Rock him asleep below? 35

6

And yet, how few believe such doctrine springs
    From a poor root
Which all the Winter sleeps here under foot
    And hath no wings
To raise it to the truth and light of things, 40
    But is still trod
    By ev'ry wand'ring clod.

7

O thou! whose spirit did at first inflame
    And warm the dead,
And by a sacred Incubation[8] fed 45
    With life this frame
Which once had neither being, form, nor name,
    Grant I may so
    Thy steps track here below,

8. Hatching.

8

That in these Masques and shadows I may see   50
    Thy sacred way,
And by those hid ascents climb to that day
    Which breaks from thee
Who art in all things, though invisibly;
    Show me thy peace,   55
    Thy mercy, love, and ease,

9

And from this Care, where dreams and sorrows reign
    Lead me above
Where Light, Joy, Leisure, and true Comforts move
    Without all pain,   60
There, hid in thee, show me his life again
    At whose dumb urn
    Thus all the year I mourn.

From *Silex Scintillans*

Part II (1655)

Ascension Hymn[1]

    Dust and clay
    Man's ancient wear!
    Here you must stay,
    But I elsewhere;
Souls sojourn here, but may not rest;   5
Who will ascend, must be undrest.

    And yet some
    That know to die
    Before death come,
    Walk to the sky   10
Even in this life; but all such can
Leave behind them the old Man.

    If a star
    Should leave the Sphere,
    She must first mar   15
    Her flaming wear,

1. Colossians 3 : 1 ff.: "If ye then be risen with Christ, seek those things which are above. . . . Set your affection on things above, not on things on the earth. For ye are dead and your life is hid with Christ in God. When Christ who is your life shall appear, then shall ye also appear with him in glory. . . . Lie not to one another, seeing that ye have put off the old man with his deeds; And have put on the new man which is renewed in knowledge after the image of him that created him."

And after fall, for in her dress
Of glory, she cannot transgress.

Man of old
Within the line[2]   20
Of *Eden* could
Like the Sun shine
All naked, innocent and bright,
And intimate with Heav'n, as light;

But since he   25
That brightness soiled,
His garments be
All dark and spoiled,
And here are left as nothing worth,
Till the Refiner's fire[3] breaks forth.   30

Then comes he!
Whose mighty light
Made his clothes be
Like Heav'n, all bright;
The Fuller, whose pure blood did flow   35
To make stained man more white than snow.[4]

He alone
And none else can
Bring bone to bone[5]
And rebuild man,   40
And by his all subduing might
Make clay ascend more quick than light.[6]

[They are all gone into the world of light!]

They are all gone into the world of light!
And I alone sit ling'ring here;
Their very memory is fair and bright,
And my sad thoughts doth clear.

It glows and glitters in my cloudy breast   5
Like stars upon some gloomy grove,
Or those faint beams in which this hill is drest,
After the Sun's remove.

2. Boundary.
3. Malachi 3 : 2. "Who may abide the day of his coming? and who shall stand when he appeareth? for he is like a refiner's fire, and like a fuller's soap."
4. *Fuller*: one who beats cloth to cleanse it. See Mark 9 : 3, describing the Transfiguration of Jesus, "And his raiment became shining, exceeding white as snow;
so as no fuller on earth can white them."
5. Ezekiel 37 : 7, "and the bones came together, bone to his bone."
6. Philippians 3 : 21, "Who shall change our vile body . . . like unto his glorious body . . . whereby he is able even to subdue all things unto himself."

I see them walking in an Air of glory,
    Whose light doth trample on my days: 10
My days, which are at best but dull and hoary,
    Mere glimmering and decays.

O holy hope! and high humility,
    High as the Heavens above!
These are your walks, and you have showed them me   15
    To kindle my cold love,

Dear, beauteous death! the Jewel of the Just,
    Shining no where, but in the dark;
What mysteries do lie beyond thy dust;
    Could man outlook that mark!   20

He that hath found some fledged birds nest, may know
    At first sight, if the bird be flown;
But what fair Well, or Grove he sings in now,
    That is to him unknown.

And yet, as Angels in some brighter dreams   25
    Call to the soul, when man doth sleep:
So some strange thoughts transcend our wonted themes,
    And into glory peep.

If a star were confined into a Tomb
    Her captive flames must needs burn there;   30
But when the hand that locked her up, gives room,
    She'll shine through all the sphere.

O Father of eternal life, and all
    Created glories under thee!
Resume thy spirit from this world of thrall[7]   35
    Into true liberty.

Either disperse these mists, which blot and fill
    My perspective[8] (still) as they pass,
Or else remove me hence unto that hill,[9]
    Where I shall need no glass.[1]   40

Cock-crowing

    Father of lights![2] what Sunny seed,
    What glance[3] of day hast thou confined

---

7. Slavery.
8. Telescope; distant vision.
9. Sion (heaven).
1. See also I Corinthians 13 : 12: "For now we see through a glass, darkly; but then, face to face; now I know in part; but then shall I know even as also I am known."

2. "Every good gift and every perfect gift cometh down from the Father of lights" (James 1 : 17).
3. *Seed, glance* (and *grain* in line 8): Hermetical terms for spiritual elements derived from the Father of lights, and providing for the sympathetic attraction between earthly and spiritual things.

Into this bird? To all the breed
This busy Ray thou hast assigned;
      Their magnetism works all night   5
      And dreams of Paradise and light.

Their eyes watch for the morning-hue,
Their little grain[4] expelling night
So shines and sings, as if it knew
The path unto the house of light.   10
      It seems their candle, howe'er done,
      Was tinned[5] and lighted at the sun.

If such a tincture,[6] such a touch,
So firm a longing can empow'r
Shall thy own image think it much   15
To watch for thy appearing hour?
      If a mere blast so fill the sail,
      Shall not the breath of God prevail?

O thou immortal light and heat!
Whose hand so shines through all this frame,[7]   20
That by the beauty of the seat,
We plainly see, who made the same.
      Seeing thy seed abides in me,
      Dwell thou in it, and I in thee.

To sleep without thee, is to die;   25
Yea, 'tis a death partakes of hell:
For where thou dost not close the eye
It never opens, I can tell.
      In such a dark, Egyptian border,[8]
      The shades of death dwell and disorder.   30

If joys, and hopes, and earnest throes,
And hearts, whose Pulse beats still for light
Are given to birds; who, but thee, knows
A love-sick soul's exalted flight?
      Can souls be tracked by any eye   35
      But his, who gave them wings to fly?

Only this Veil which thou hast broke,[9]
And must be broken yet in me,
This veil, I say, is all the cloak

---

4. Dye, tincture.
5. Kindled.
6. Infused quality, spirit or soul of a thing.
7. Universe.
8. The plague of darkness over Egypt (Exodus 10 : 21 ff.).

9. The veil of physical existence hiding the other world from us. See II Corinthians 3 : 14: "Until this day remaineth the same veil untaken away in the reading of the old testament; which veil is done away in Christ. . . ."

And cloud which shadows thee from me.   40
       This veil thy full-eyed love denies,
       And only gleams and fractions spies.

O take it off! make no delay,
But brush me with thy light, that I
May shine unto a perfect day,   45
And warm me at thy glorious Eye!
       O take it off! or till it flee,
       Though with no Lily,[1] stay with me!

The Bird

Hither thou com'st: the busy wind all night
Blew through thy lodging, where thy own warm wing
Thy pillow was. Many a sullen storm
(For which course[2] man seems much the fitter born,)
       Rained on thy bed   5
       And harmless head.

And now as fresh and cheerful as the light
Thy little heart in early hymns doth sing
Unto that *Providence*, whose unseen arm
Curbed them, and clothed thee well and warm.   10
       All things that be, praise him; and had
       Their lesson taught them, when first made.

So hills and valleys into singing break,
And though poor stones have neither speech nor tongue,
While active winds and streams both run and speak,   15
Yet stones are deep in admiration.
Thus Praise and Prayer here beneath the Sun
Make lesser mornings, when the great are done.

For each inclosed Spirit is a star
       Enlight'ning his own little sphere,   20
Whose light, though fetched and borrowed from far,
       Both mornings makes, and evenings there.

But as these Birds of light make a land glad,
Chirping their solemn Matins[3] on each tree:
So in the shades of night some dark fowls be,   25
Whose heavy notes make all that hear them, sad.

       The Turtle[4] then in Palm trees mourns,
       While Owls and Satyrs[5] howl;

---

1. Song of Songs 2 : 16: "My beloved is mine and I am his; he feedeth among the lilies." The lily is the flower of light.
2. Pun on *coarse*.
3. Morning prayer.
4. Turtle dove.
5. Lecherous creatures, half goats, half men, who dwell in deserted or waste places: see Isaiah 13 : 21 and 34 : 12, 14.

The pleasant Land to brimstone turns
And all her streams grow foul.   30

Brightness and mirth, and love and faith, all fly,
Till the Day-spring breaks forth again from high.

The Timber

Sure thou didst flourish once! and many Springs,
Many bright mornings, much dew, many showers
Past o'er thy head: many light *Hearts* and *Wings*
Which now are dead, lodged in thy living bowers.

And still a new succession sings and flies;   5
Fresh Groves grow up, and their green branches shoot
Towards the old and still enduring skies,
While the low *Violet* thrives at their root.

But thou beneath the sad and heavy *Line*
Of death, dost waste all senseless, cold and dark;   10
Where not so much as dreams of light may shine,
Nor any thought of greenness, leaf or bark.

And yet (as if some deep hate and dissent,
Bred in thy growth betwixt high winds and thee,
Were still alive) thou dost great storms resent[6]   15
Before they come, and know'st how near they be.

Else all at rest thou liest, and the fierce breath
Of tempests can no more disturb thy ease;
But this thy strange resentment after death
Means only those, who broke (in life) thy peace.   20

So murdered man, when lovely life is done,
And his blood freezed, keeps in the Center still
Some secret sense, which makes the dead blood run
At his approach, that did the body kill.

And is there any murd'rer worse than sin?   25
Or any storms more foul than a lewd life?
Or what *Resentient*[7] can work more within,
Than true remorse, when with past sins at strife?

He that hath left life's vain joys and vain care,
And truly hates to be detained on earth,   30
Hath got an house where many mansions are,[8]
And keeps his soul unto eternal mirth.

6. Feel, sense, perceive.
7. Stimulus to change of feeling (*Oxford English Dictionary*).
8. John 14 : 2: "In my Father's house there are many mansions."

But though thus dead unto the world, and ceased
From sin, he walks a narrow, private way;
Yet grief and old wounds make him sore displeased,   35
And all his life a rainy, weeping day.

For though he should forsake the world, and live
As mere a stranger, as men long since dead;
Yet joy it self will make a right soul grieve
To think, he should be so long vainly lead.   40

But as shades set off light, so tears and grief
(Though of themselves but a sad blubbered story)
By showing the sin great, show the relief
Far greater, and so speak my Savior's glory.

If my way lies through deserts and wild woods;   45
Where all the Land with scorching heat is curst;
Better, the pools should flow with rain and floods
To fill my bottle, than I die with thirst.[9]

Blest showers they are, and streams sent from above
Begetting *Virgins* where they use to flow;   50
And trees of life no other waters love,
These upper springs and none else make them grow.

But these chaste fountains flow not till we die;
Some drops may fall before, but a clear spring
And ever running, till we leave to fling   55
Dirt in her way, will keep above the sky.[1]

Rom. Cap. 6. ver. 7.
He that is dead, is freed from sin.

The Knot

Bright Queen of Heaven! God's Virgin Spouse!
The glad world's blessed maid!
Whose beauty tied life to thy house,
And brought us saving aid.

Thou art the true Love's-knot; by thee   5
God is made our Ally,
And man's inferior Essence he
With his did dignify.

---

9. See Genesis 21 : 9 f.: Hagar with her son Ishmael, turned out by Sarah and dying of thirst in the wilderness, is led by God to a well "and she went, and filled the bottle with water, and gave the lad drink."

1. Revelation 14 : 3–4, the "hundred and forty and four thousand . . . not defiled with women; for they are virgins," and Revelation 22 : 1–2, the "pure river of water of life," and the tree of life growing on either side of it.

For Coalescent by that Band
  We are his body grown,   10
Nourished with favors from his hand
  Whom for our head we own.

And such a Knot, what arm dares loose,
  What life, what death can sever?
Which us in him, and him in us   15
  United keeps for ever.

The Rainbow

Still young and fine! but what is still in view
We slight as old and soiled, though fresh and new.
How bright wert thou, when *Shem's*[2] admiring eye
Thy burnished, flaming *Arch* did first descry!
When *Terah, Nahor, Haran, Abram, Lot,*[3] 5
The youthful world's gray fathers in one knot,
Did with intentive looks watch every hour
For thy new light, and trembled at each shower!
When thou dost shine darkness looks white and fair,
Storms turn to Music, clouds to smiles and air: 10
Rain gently spends his honey-drops, and pours
Balm on the cleft earth, milk on grass and flowers.
Bright pledge of peace and Sunshine! the sure tie
Of thy Lord's hand, the object of his eye.
When I behold thee, though my light be dim, 15
Distant and low, I can in thine see him,
Who looks upon thee from his glorious throne
And minds the Convenant[4] 'twixt *All* and *One.*
O foul, deceitful men! my God doth keep
His promise still, but we break ours and sleep. 20
After the *Fall,* the first sin was in *Blood,*
And *Drunkenness* quickly did succeed the flood;[5]
But since *Christ* died, (as if we did devise
To lose him too, as well as *Paradise,*)
These two grand sins we join and act together, 25
Though blood and drunkenness make but foul, foul weather.
Water (though both Heaven's windows and the deep,
Full forty days o'er the drowned world did weep,)
Could not reform us, and blood (in despite)
Yea God's own blood we tread upon and slight. 30
So those bad daughters,[6] which God saved from fire,

---

2. A son of Noah (Genesis 9 : 18).
3. See Genesis 11 : 24 ff. for the relationships of these figures.
4. In the 1655 edition, Vaughan has a note to line 14, citing Genesis 9 : 16: "And the bow shall be in the cloud; and I will look upon it, that I may remember the everlasting covenant between

God and every living creature of all flesh that is upon the earth."
5. Cain's murder of Abel (Genesis 4 : 8) and Noah's drunkenness (Genesis 9 : 21).
6. The daughters of Lot (Genesis 19 : 30 ff.).

While *Sodom* yet did smoke, lay with their sire.
Then peaceful, signal bow, but in a cloud
Still lodged, where all thy unseen arrows shroud,
I will on thee, as on a Comet look,   35
A Comet, the sad world's ill-boding book;
Thy light as luctual[7] and stained with woes
I'll judge, where penal flames sit mixt and close.
For though some think, thou shin'st but to restrain
Bold storms, and simply dost attend on rain,   40
Yet I know well, and so our sins require,
Thou dost but Court cold rain, till *Rain* turns *Fire*.

The Seed Growing Secretly

S. *Mark* 4. 26.[8]

If this world's friends might see but once
What some poor man may often feel,
Glory, and gold, and Crowns and Thrones
They would soon quit and learn to kneel.

My dew, my dew! my early love,[9]   5
My soul's bright food, thy absence kills!
Hover not long, eternal Dove!
Life without thee is loose and spills.

Something I had, which long ago
Did learn to suck, and sip, and taste,   10
But now grown sickly, sad and slow,
Doth fret and wrangle, pine and waste.

O spread thy sacred wings and shake
One living drop! one drop life keeps!
If pious griefs Heaven's joy awake,   15
O fill his bottle! thy child weeps![1]

Slowly and sadly doth he grow,
And soon as left, shrinks back to ill;
O feed that life, which makes him blow[2]
And spread and open to thy will!   20

For thy eternal, living wells
None stain'd or withered shall come near:
A fresh, immortal *green* there dwells,
And spotless *white* is all the wear.[3]

7. Sorrowful, mournful.
8. Mark 4 : 26 ff.: "So is the kingdom of God, as if a man should cast seed into the ground . . . and the seed should spring and grow up, he knoweth not how."

9. See "The Retreat," line 8.
1. See "Timber," line 48, note.
2. Bloom.
3. See Revelation 14 and 22, cited in note to "Timber," line 49. *Wear*: fashion.

Dear, secret *Greenness*! nursed below   25
Tempests and winds, and winter-nights,
Vex not, that but one sees thee grow,
That *One* made all these lesser lights.

If those bright joys he singly sheds
On thee, were all met in one Crown,   30
Both Sun and Stars would hide their heads;
And Moons, though full, would get them down.

Let glory be their bait, whose minds
Are all too high for a low Cell:
Though Hawks can prey through storms and winds,   35
The poor Bee in her hive must dwell.

Glory, the Crowd's cheap tinsel still
To what most takes them, is a drudge;
And they too oft take good for ill,
And thriving vice for virtue judge.   40

What needs a Conscience calm and bright
Within it self an outward test?
Who breaks his glass to take more light,
Makes way for storms into his rest.

Then bless thy secret growth, nor catch   45
At noise, but thrive unseen and dumb;
Keep clean, bear fruit, earn life and watch,
Till the white winged Reapers[4] come!

[As time one day by me did pass]

As time one day by me did pass
  Through a large dusky glass[5]
  He held, I chanced to look
  And spied his curious book
Of past days, where sad Heav'n did shed   5
A mourning light upon the dead.

Many disordered lives I saw
  And foul records which thaw
  My kind eyes still, but in
  A fair, white page of thin   10
And ev'n, smooth lines, like the Sun's rays,
Thy name was writ, and all thy days.

O bright and happy Kalendar!

4. Angels, at end of world (Matthew 13 : 39).

5. I Corinthians 13 : 12: "Now we see through a glass, darkly . . ."

Where youth shines like a star
   All pearled with tears, and may   15
   Teach age, *The Holy way*;
Where through thick pangs, high agonies
Faith into life breaks, and death dies.

As some meek *night-piece* which day quails,[6]
   To candle-light unveils: 20
   So by one beamy line
   From thy bright lamp did shine,
In the same page thy humble grave
Set with green herbs, glad hopes and brave.

Here slept my thought's dear mark![7] which dust   25
   Seemed to devour, like rust;
   But dust (I did observe)
   By hiding doth preserve,
As we for long and sure recruits,[8]
Candy with sugar our choice fruits.   30

O calm and sacred bed where lies
   In death's dark mysteries
   A beauty far more bright
   Than the noon's cloudless light;
For whose dry dust green branches bud   35
And robes are bleached in the *Lamb's* blood.[9]

Sleep happy ashes! (blessed sleep!)
   While hapless I still weep;
   Weep that I have out-lived
   My life, and unrelieved   40
Must (soulless shadow!) so live on,
Though life be dead, and my joys gone.

The Dwelling Place

S. John, chap. 1. ver. 38, 39.[1]

What happy, secret fountain,
   Fair shade, or mountain,
Whose undiscovered virgin glory
Boasts it this day, though not in story,
Was then thy dwelling? did some cloud   5
Fixed to a Tent,[2] descend and shroud

---

6. *Night-piece*: picture of a night scene; *quails*: spoils.
7. Object, goal.
8. Supplies.
9. "These are they which . . . have washed their robes, and made them white in the blood of the Lamb" (Revelation 7 : 14).
1. John 1 : 38–39: "They said . . . Rabbi . . . where dwellest thou? He saith, . . . Come and see. They came and saw where He dwelt, and abode with Him that day."
2. During the journey through the wilderness of Sinai, a cloud covers the "tent of the testimony" (Numbers 9 : 15 ff.).

My distressed Lord? or did a star
Beckoned by thee, though high and far,
In sparkling smiles haste gladly down
To lodge light, and increase her own?   10
My dear, dear God! I do not know
What lodged thee then, nor where, nor how;
But I am sure, thou dost now come
Oft to a narrow, homely room,
Where thou too hast but the least part,   15
My God, I mean *my sinful heart.*

The Night

John 2. 3.[3]

Through that pure *Virgin-shrine,*
That sacred veil[4] drawn o'er thy glorious noon
That men might look and live as Glow-worms shine,[5]
          And face the Moon:
Wise *Nicodemus* saw such light   5
As made him know his God by night.

          Most blest believer he!
Who in that land of darkness and blind eyes
Thy long expected healing wings could see,
          When thou didst rise,[6]   10
And what can never more be done,
Did at midnight speak with the Sun!

          O who will tell me, where
He found thee at that dead and silent hour!
What hallowed solitary ground did bear   15
          So rare a flower,
Within whose sacred leafs did lie
The fulness of the Deity.[7]

          No mercy seat of gold,
No dead and dusty *Cherub,* nor carved stone,[8]   20

3. John 2 : 3 should read 3 : 2, the story
of Nicodemus who "came to Jesus by
night, and said unto him, Rabbi, we
know that thou art a teacher come from
God."
4. Christ's flesh (see Hebrews 10 : 20).
5. "There shall no man see Me and
live" (Exodus 33 : 20). "Glow-worms
shine" only under the moon, not the
sun.
6. Matthew 4 : 2: "But unto you that
fear my Name, shall the Sun of righteousness arise with healing in his
wings."

7. Cf. Wisdom 18 : 14–15 (Douay version), "For while all things were in
quiet silence, and the night was in the
midst of her course, thy almighty word
leaped down from heaven from thy royal
throne. . . ." (Incidentally, this is from
the Introit of the Sunday in the octave
of Christmas, and of the eve of the
Epiphany; on the Epiphany itself, the
Lesson is from Isaiah 60 : 1–6, charged
with imagery of light and darkness.)
8. The temple of Solomon, signifying
the Old Law (see Exodus 25 : 17–20).

But his own living works did my Lord hold
    And lodge alone;
  Where *trees* and *herbs* did watch and peep
  And wonder, while the *Jews* did sleep.[9]

    Dear night! this world's defeat;   25
The stop to busy fools; care's check and curb;
The day of Spirits; my soul's calm retreat
    Which none disturb!
  Christ's[1] progress, and his prayer time;
  The hours to which high Heaven doth chime.   30

    God's silent, searching flight:
When my Lord's head is filled with dew, and all
His locks are wet with the clear drops of night;
    His still, soft call;
  His knocking time; The soul's dumb watch,   35
  When Spirits their fair kindred catch.[2]

    Were all my loud, evil days
Calm and unhaunted as is thy dark Tent,
Whose peace but by some *Angel's* wing or voice
    Is seldom rent;   40
  Then I in Heaven all the long year
  Would keep, and never wander here.

    But living where the Sun
Doth all things wake, and where all mix and tire
Themselves and others, I consent and run   45
    To ev'ry mire,
  And by this world's ill-guiding light,
  Err more than I can do by night.

    There is in God (some say)[3]
A deep, but dazzling darkness; As men here   50
Say it is late and dusky, because they
    See not all clear;
  O for that night! where I in him
  Might live invisible and dim.

9. On the Mount of Olives.
1. Vaughan's note in the 1655 edition cites Mark 1 : 35: "And rising very early, going out, (Jesus) went into a desert place and there he prayed," and Luke 21 : 37: "And in the daytime he was teaching in the Temple; but at night going out he abode in the mount that is called Olivet."
2. Song of Songs 5 : 2: "I sleep but my heart waketh: it is the voice of my beloved that knocketh, saying, Open to me my sister my love my dove my undefiled: for my head is filled with dew and my locks with the drops of the night." See also Revelation 3 : 20, "Behold I stand at the door and knock," and I

Kings 19 : 12, God speaking to Elijah in a "still small voice."
3. E.g., Dionysius the Areopagite (also called Pseudo-Dionysius), probably fifth century A.D.; in the *Mystical Theology* he develops concepts of divine darkness, divine ignorance, and unknowing, cited by later writers like Nicholas of Cusa. Dionysius's treatise deals with the "mysteries . . . veiled in the obscurity of the secret Silence, outshining all brilliance with the intensity of their Darkness" and the "Darkness where truly dwells . . . the One who is beyond all" and "the superessential Darkness which is hidden by all the light that is in existing things."

The Waterfall

With what deep murmurs through time's silent stealth
Doth thy transparent, cool and wat'ry wealth
   Here flowing fall,
   And chide, and call,
As if his liquid, loose Retinue stayed   5
Ling'ring, and were of this steep place afraid,
   The common pass
   Where, clear as glass,
   All must descend
   Not to an end: 10
But quick'ned by this deep and rocky grave,
Rise to a longer course more bright and brave.[4]

  Dear stream! dear bank, where often I
  Have sat, and pleased my pensive eye,
  Why, since each drop of thy quick[5] store   15
  Runs thither, whence it flowed before,
  Should poor souls fear a shade or night,
  Who came (sure) from a sea of light?[6]
  Or since those drops are all sent back
  So sure to thee, that none doth lack,   20
  Why should frail flesh doubt any more
  That what God takes, he'll not restore?

  O useful Element and clear!
  My sacred wash and cleanser[7] here,
  My first consigner unto those   25
  Fountains of life, where the Lamb goes![8]
  What sublime truths, and wholesome themes,
  Lodge in thy mystical, deep streams!
  Such as dull man can never find
  Unless that Spirit lead his mind,   30
  Which first upon thy face did move,
  And hatched all with his quick'ning love.[9]

  As this loud brook's incessant fall
  In streaming rings restagnates[1] all,
  Which reach by course the bank, and then **35**

4. Beautiful, resplendent.
5. Living.
6. Sea of light, that is, God, the soul's origin.
7. In baptism.
8. Revelation 7 : 17: "For the Lamb . . . shall lead them unto living fountains of waters."
9. *Hatched*: in Hermetic thought, the act of begetting the world out of creative darkness. See Genesis 1 : 2, "And the spirit of God moved upon the face of the waters," and the opening lines of *Paradise Lost*: "[thou] with mighty wings outspread / Dove-like sat'st brooding on the vast abyss / And madest it pregnant:" (I, 20–22); the Vulgate reading of Genesis 1 : 2 is "incubabat," which is closer to Vaughan's "hatching" and to Milton's "brooding . . . pregnant" than to either the Douay or the King James version.
1. Becomes or remains stagnant.

Are no more seen, just so pass men.
O my invisible estate,
My glorious liberty,[2] still late!
Thou art the Channel my soul seeks,
Not this with Cataracts and Creeks.   40

Quickness

False life! a foil and no more, when
          Wilt thou be gone?
Thou foul deception of all men
That would not have the true come on.

Thou art a Moon-like toil; a blind   5
          Self-posing[3] state;
A dark contest of waves and wind;
A mere tempestuous debate.

Life is a fixed, discerning light,
          A knowing Joy;   10
No chance, or fit: but ever bright,
And calm and full, yet doth not cloy.

'Tis such a blissful thing, that still
          Doth vivify,
And shine and smile, and hath the skill   15
To please without Eternity.

Thou art a toilsome Mole, or less
          A moving mist.
But life is, what none can express,
A *quickness, which my God hath kissed.*   20

The Book

Eternal God! maker of all
That have lived here, since the man's fall;
The Rock of ages! in whose shade
They live unseen, when here they fade.
Thou knew'st this *paper,* when it was   5
Mere *seed,* and after that but *grass*;
Before 'twas *drest* or *spun,* and when
Made *linen,* who did *wear* it then:
What were their lives, their thoughts and deeds
Whether good *corn,* or fruitless *weeds.*   10

Thou knew'st this *Tree,* when a green *shade*

---

2. See Romans 8 : 21, "the glorious lib-   3. Baffling.
erty of the children of God."

Covered it, since a *Cover* made,
And where it flourished, grew and spread,
As if it never should be dead.

Thou knew'st this harmless *beast*, when he   15
Did live and feed by thy decree
On each green thing; then slept (well fed)
Clothed with this *skin*, which now lies spread
A *Covering* o'er this aged book,
Which makes me wisely weep and look   20
On my own dust; mere dust it is,
But not so dry and clean as this.
Thou knew'st and saw'st them all and though
Now scattered thus, dost know them so.

O knowing, glorious spirit! when   25
Thou shalt restore trees, beasts and men,
When thou shalt make all new again,
Destroying only death and pain,
Give him amongst thy works a place,
Who in them loved and sought thy face!   30

Thomas Traherne

Thomas Traherne (1637/38–1674), though born a shoemaker's son in Hereford, was educated at Brasenose College, Oxford (B.A. 1656) thanks to a prosperous relative. He was ordained an Anglican priest in October 1660 and in 1661 was presented (for the second time) to the rectorship at Credenhill in Herefordshire, which he held until his death. He continued at Oxford to M.A. and B.D. (1669). From 1667 on, he was in London as chaplain to Sir Orlando Bridgeman, Keeper of the Great Seal, and later as vicar at Teddington in Middlesex, where he died, in Sir Orlando's house, and was buried October 10, 1674, in his church. Only one prose work was published during his lifetime, the anti-Catholic polemic *Roman Forgeries*; the rambling *Christian Ethics* appeared shortly afterwards (1675), and the *Thanksgivings* in 1699. But the major works—the *Centuries of Meditations* and the poems—had to wait for more than two centuries, until their dramatic discovery in a London bookstall and their identification and publication by Bertram Dobell at the beginning of this century.

From the *Dobell Folio*

The Salutation[1]

1
These little limbs,
These eyes and hands which here I find,
These rosy cheeks wherewith my life begins,
    Where have ye been? Behind
What curtain were ye from me hid so long!   5
Where was, in what abyss, my speaking tongue?

2
When silent I,
So many thousand thousand years,
Beneath the dust did in a chaos lie,
    How could I smiles or tears,   10
Or lips or hands or eyes or ears perceive?
Welcome ye treasures which I now receive.

3
I that so long
Was nothing from eternity,
Did little think such joys as ear or tongue,   15
    To celebrate or see:

1. The first eight poems are from Thomas Traherne's manuscript. See Textual Notes.

181

Such sounds to hear, such hands to feel, such feet,
Beneath the skies, on such a ground to meet.

4

New burnisht joys!
Which yellow gold and pearl excell!   20
Such sacred treasures are the limbs in boys,
In which a soul doth dwell;
Their organized joints, and azure veins
More wealth include, than all the world contains.

5

From dust I rise,   25
And out of nothing now awake,
These brighter regions which salute mine eyes,
A gift from God I take
The earth, the seas, the light, the day, the skies,
The sun and stars are mine; if those I prize.   30

6

Long time before
I in my mother's womb was born,
A God preparing did this glorious store,
The world for me adorn.
Into this Eden so divine and fair,   35
So wide and bright, I come his son and heir.

7

A stranger here
Strange things doth meet, strange glories see;
Strange treasures lodged in this fair world appear,
Strange all, and new to me.   40
But that they mine should be, who nothing was,
That strangest is of all, yet brought to pass.

Wonder

1

How like an Angel came I down!
How bright are all things here!
When first among his works I did appear
O how their Glory me did crown!
The world resembled his *Eternity*,   5
In which my soul did walk;
And ev'ry thing that I did see,
Did with me talk.

2

The skies in their magnificence,
The lively, lovely air;   10
Oh how divine, how soft, how sweet, how fair!
The stars did entertain my sense,[2]

2. Sensory apprehension, especially sight.

And all the works of God so bright and pure,
    So rich and great did seem,
As if they ever must endure,   15
    In my esteem.

3

A native health and innocence
    Within my bones did grow,
And while my God did all his glories shew,
    I felt a vigour in my sense   20
That was all Spirit. I within did flow
    With seas of life, like wine;
    I nothing in the world did know,
    But 'twas divine.

4

Harsh ragged objects were concealed,   25
    Oppressions tears and cries,
Sins, griefs, complaints, dissentions, weeping eyes,
    Were hid: and only things revealed,
Which heav'nly spirits, and the angels prize.
    The state of innocence   30
And bliss, not trades and poverties,
    Did fill my sense.

5

The streets were paved with golden stones,
    The boys and girls were mine,
Oh how did all their lovely faces shine!   35
    The sons of men were holy ones.
Joy, beauty, welfare did appear to me,
    And ev'ry thing which here I found,
    While like an angel I did see,
    Adorned the ground.   40

6

Rich diamond and pearl and gold
    In ev'ry place was seen;
Rare splendors, yellow, blue, red, white and green,
    Mine eyes did ev'rywhere behold,
Great wonders clothed with glory did appear,   45
    Amazement was my bliss.
    That and my wealth was ev'ry where:
    No joy to this![3]

7

Cursed and devised proprieties,[4]
    With envy, avarice   50
And fraud, those fiends that spoil even Paradise,
    Fled from the splendor of mine eyes.

---

3. In comparison to this.
4. *Devised*: legally willed (Louis Martz, suggests, "also, contrived": *English Sev-* *enteenth-Century Verse* (New York, 1973), I, 425) *proprieties*: properties, possessions.

And so did hedges, ditches, limits, bounds,
I dreamed not aught of those,
But wandered over all men's grounds,   55
And found repose.

8

Proprieties themselves were mine,
And hedges ornaments;
Walls, boxes, coffers, and their rich contents
Did not divide my joys, but shine.[5]   60
Clothes, ribbons, jewels, laces, I esteemed
My joys by others worn;
For me they all to wear them seemed
When I was born.

Eden

1

A learned and a happy ignorance[6]
Divided me,
From all vanity,
From all the sloth care pain and sorrow that advance,
The madness and the misery   5
Of men. No error, no distraction I
Saw soil the earth, or overcloud the sky.

2

I knew not that there was a serpent's sting,
Whose poison shed
On men, did overspread   10
The world: nor did I dream of such a thing
As sin; in which mankind lay dead.
They all were brisk and living wights[7] to me,
Yea pure, and full of immortality.

3

Joy, pleasure, beauty, kindness, glory, love,   15
Sleep, day, life, light,
Peace, melody, my sight,
My ears and heart did fill, and freely move.
All that I saw did me delight.
The *Universe* was then a world of treasure,   20
To me an universal world of pleasure.

---

5. In *The Third Century*, Traherne wrote: "I knew no Churlish Proprieties, nor Bounds nor Divisions: but all Proprieties and Divisions were mine: all Treasures and the Possessors of them" (H. M. Margoliouth, Oxford edition of Traherne (1958) vol. I, p. 111).
6. Nicholas of Cusa (ca. 1401–64) wrote *De docta ignorantia* ("Of Learned Ignorance"), a Neoplatonist work of rational speculation and intuition, on God's infinity, the tension of opposites, God's creative activity, and the necessity of thinking of God in analogies and negatives.
7. Persons.

4

Unwelcome penitence was then unknown,
      Vain costly toys,
      Swearing and roaring boys,
Shops, markets, taverns, coaches were unshown;   25
     So all things were that drowned my joys.
No briars choked up my path, nor hid the face
Of bliss and beauty, nor eclipsed the place.

5

Only what Adam in his first estate,
      Did I behold;   30
      Hard silver and dry gold
As yet lay under ground; my blessed fate
     Was more acquainted with the old
And innocent delights, which he did see
In his original simplicity.   35

6

Those things which first his Eden did adorn,
      My infancy
      Did crown. Simplicity
Was my protection when I first was born.
     Mine eyes those treasures first did see   40
Which God first made. The first effects of love
My first enjoyments upon earth did prove;

7

And were so great, and so divine, so pure,
      So fair and sweet,
      So true; when I did meet   45
Them here at first, they did my soul allure,
     And drew away my infant feet
Quite from the works of men; that I might see
The glorious wonders of the Deity.

Innocence

1

But that which most I wonder at, which most
I did esteem my bliss, which most I boast,
And ever shall enjoy, is that within
     I felt no stain, nor spot of sin.

     No darkness then did overshade,   5
     But all within was pure and bright,
     No guilt did crush, nor fear invade
     But all my soul was full of light.

     A joyful sense and purity
      Is all I can remember.   10

The very night to me was bright,
'Twas summer in December.

2

A serious meditation did employ
My soul within, which taken up with joy
Did seem no outward thing to note, but fly   15
    All objects that do feed the eye.

    While it those very objects did
    Admire, and prize, and praise, and love,
    Which in their glory most are hid,
    Which presence only doth remove.   20

    Their constant daily presence I
        Rejoicing at, did see
    And that which takes them from the eye
    Of others, offered them to me.

3

No inward inclination did I feel   25
To avarice or pride: My soul did kneel
In admiration all the day. No lust, nor strife,
    Polluted then my infant life.

    No fraud nor anger in me moved
    No malice jealousy or spite;   30
    All that I saw I truly loved.
    Contentment only and delight

    Were in my soul. O Heav'n! what bliss
        Did I enjoy and feel!
    What powerful delight did this   35
    Inspire! for this I daily kneel.

4

Whether it be that nature is so pure,
And custom only vicious; or that sure
God did by miracle the guilt remove,
    And make my soul to feel his love,   40

    So early: or that 'twas one day,
    Where in this happiness I found;
    Whose strength and brightness so do ray,
    That still it seemeth to surround.

    What e'er it is, it is a light   45
        So endless unto me
    That I a world of true delight
    Did then and to this day do see.

5

That prospect was the gate of Heav'n, that day
The ancient light of Eden did convey   50

Into my soul: I was an Adam there,
    A little Adam in a sphere

    Of joys! O there my ravisht sense
    Was entertained in Paradise,   55
    And had a sight of innocence.
    All was beyond all bound and price.

    An antepast[8] of Heaven sure!
        I on the earth did reign.
    Within, without me, all was pure.
    I must become a child again.[9]   60

The Preparative

1

My body being dead,[1] my limbs unknown;
    Before I skilled[2] to prize
    Those living stars mine eyes,
Before my tongue or cheeks were to me shown,
    Before I knew my hands were mine,   5
Or that my sinews did my members join,
    When neither nostril, foot, nor ear,
As yet was seen, or felt, or did appear;
        I was within
A house I knew not, newly clothed with skin.   10

2

Then was my soul my only all to me,
    A living endless eye,
    Far wider then the sky
Whose power, whose act, whose essence was to see.
    I was an inward *Sphere of Light*,   15
Or an interminable orb of *Sight*,
    An endless and a living day,
A *vital*[3] *Sun* that round about did *ray*
        All life and sense,
A naked simple pure *Intelligence*.   20

3

I then no thirst nor hunger did conceive,
    No dull necessity,
    No want was known to me;
Without disturbance then I did receive
    The fair Ideas[4] of all things,   25
And had the honey even without the stings.
    A meditating inward eye

8. Foretaste.
9. See Matthew 18 : 3, where Jesus says, "Except ye be converted, and become as little children, ye shall not enter into the kingdom of heaven."
1. Inactive. Cf. line 37.

2. Knew how.
3. Life-giving (see line 19).
4. Platonic Ideas (*Republic*), the original and transcendentally existing Forms or archetypes of things.

Gazing at quiet did within me lie,
　　　　And ev'ry thing
Delighted me that was their heav'nly king.　　　　30

4

For *Sight* inherits beauty, *Hearing* sounds,
　　　The *Nostril* sweet perfumes,
　　　All *Tastes* have hidden rooms
Within the *Tongue*; and *Feeling Feeling* wounds
　　　With pleasure and delight: but I　　　　35
Forgot the rest, and was all sight, or eye.
　　　Unbodied and devoid of care,
Just as in Heav'n the holy angels are.
　　　　For simple sense
Is lord of all created excellence.　　　　40

5

Being thus prepared for all felicity,
　　　Not prepossest with dross,
　　　Nor stiffly glued to gross
And dull materials that might ruin me,
　　　Not fettered by an iron fate　　　　45
With vain affections in my earthy state
　　　To any thing that might seduce
My sense, or else bereave it of its use
　　　　I was as free
As if there were nor sin, nor misery.　　　　50

6

Pure empty powers that did nothing loathe,
　　　Did like the fairest glass,
　　　Or spotless polisht brass,
Themselves soon in their objects' image clothe.
　　　Divine impressions when they came,　　　　55
Did quickly enter and my soul inflame.
　　　'Tis not the object, but the light
That maketh Heaven: 'tis a purer sight.
　　　　Felicity
Appears to none but them that purely see.[5]　　　　60

7

A disentangled and a naked sense
　　　A mind that's unpossesst,
　　　A disengaged breast,
An empty and a quick intelligence
　　　Acquainted with the Golden Mean,　　　　65
An even spirit pure and serene,
　　　Is that where beauty, excellence,
And pleasure keep their court of residence.
　　　　My soul retire,
Get free, and so thou shalt even all admire.　　　　70

5. "Traherne, like Wordsworth, be-　not in either 'innate ideas' or a *tabula*
lieves in an active soul with faculties—　*rasa*" (Margoliouth, vol. II, p. 342).

The Rapture

1
Sweet infancy!
O fire of Heaven! O sacred light!
How fair and bright!
How great am I,
Whom all the world doth magnify!   5

2
O heavenly joy!
O great and sacred blessedness,
Which I possess!
So great a joy
Who did into my arms convey!   10

3
From God above
Being sent,[6] the Heavens me enflame,
To praise his Name.
The stars do move![7]
The burning sun doth show his love.   15

4
O how divine
Am I! To all this sacred wealth,
This life and health,
Who raised? Who mine
Did make the same? What hand divine!   20

My Spirit[8]

1
My naked simple life was I.
That act so strongly shined
Upon the earth, the sea, the sky,
That was the substance of my mind.
The sense it self was I.   5
I felt no dross nor matter in my soul,
No brims nor borders, such as in a bowl
We see, my essence was capacity.
That felt all things,
The thought that springs   10
Therefrom's it self. It hath no other wings
To spread abroad, nor eyes to see,
Nor hands distinct to feel,
Nor knees to kneel:

6. The joy (of line 9).
7. Move me to praise.
8. "This is Traherne's most comprehensive poem. It contains the experience of the Infant Eye reflected on in maturity, the mature experience of the Infant Eye regained, the mature man's mystical inner experience, and all three united in an act of the understanding which is it-self a further experience" (Margoliouth, vol. II, p. 349).

But being simple like the Deity 15
  In its own centre is a sphere
  Not shut up here, but ev'ry where.

2

It acts not from a centre to
  Its object as remote,
But present is, when it doth view 20
Being with the being it doth note.
  Whatever it doth do,
It doth not by another engine work,
But by it self; which in the act doth lurk.
Its essence is transformed into a true 25
      And perfect act.
      And so exact
Hath God appeared in this mysterious fact,
  That tis all eye, all act, all sight,
      And what it please can be, 30
      Not only see,
Or do; for tis more voluble⁹ than light:
  Which can put on ten thousand forms,
  Being clothed with what it self adorns.

3

This made me present evermore 35
    With whatso e'er I saw,
  An object, if it were before
  My eye, was by Dame Nature's law,
    Within my soul. Her store
Was all at once within me; all her treasures 40
Were my immediate and internal pleasures,
Substantial joys, which did inform my mind.
    With all she wrought,
    My soul was frought,
And ev'ry object in my soul a thought 45
  Begot, or was; I could not tell,
    Whether the things did there
    Themselves appear,
Which in my spirit *truly* seemed to dwell;
  Or whether my conforming mind 50
  Were not alone even all that shined.

4

But yet of this I was most sure,
    That at the utmost length,
  (So worthy was it to endure)
My soul could best express its strength. 55
    It was so quick and pure,
That all my mind was wholly ev'ry where

9. Protean (see line 33).

What e'er it saw, 'twas ever wholly there;
The sun ten thousand legions[1] off, was nigh:
      The utmost Star,   60
      Tho seen from far,
Was present in the apple of my eye.
    There was my sight, my life, my sense,
      My substance and my mind
        My spirit shined   65
Even there, not by a transient[2] influence.
    The act was immanent, yet there.
    The thing remote, yet felt even here.

5

    O joy! O wonder, and delight!
      O sacred mystery!   70
    My soul a spirit infinite!
    An image of the Deity!
      A pure substantial light!
That being greatest which doth nothing seem!
Why 'twas my all, I nothing did esteem   75
But that alone. A strange mysterious sphere!
      A deep abyss
      That sees and is
The only proper place or Bower of Bliss.
    To its Creator 'tis so near   80
      In love and excellence
      In life and sense,
In greatness worth and nature; and so dear;
      In it, without hyperbole,
    The son and friend of God we see.   85

6

    A strange extended orb of joy,
      Proceeding from within,
    Which did on ev'ry side convey
    It self, and being nigh of kin
      To God did ev'ry way   90
Dilate it self even in an instant, and
Like an indivisible centre stand
At once surrounding all eternity.
      'Twas not a sphere
      Yet did appear   95
One infinite. 'Twas somewhat ev'ry where.
    And tho it had a power to see
      Far more, yet still it shin'd
      And was a mind

---

1. Multitudes, "presumably of miles, though leagues may have had something to do with suggesting the odd but effective use of the word here" (Margoliouth, vol. II, p. 350).

2. *Transient*: the text reads "Transeunt," a spelling used only when the word is opposed to "immanent" (see line 67) rather than to "permanent."

Exerted for it saw infinity   100
    'Twas not a sphere, but 'twas a power
    Invisible, and yet a bower.

7

    O wondrous self! O sphere of light,
        O sphere of joy most fair;
    O act, O power infinite;   105
    O subtle, and unbounded air!
        O living orb of sight!
Thou which within me art, yet me! Thou eye,
And temple of his whole infinity!
O what a world art thou! a world within!   110
        All things appear,
        All objects are
Alive in thee! Supersubstantial, rare,
    Above them selves, and nigh of kin
        To those pure things we find   115
        In his great mind
Who made the world! tho now eclipsed by sin.
    There they are useful and divine,
    Exalted there they ought to shine.

Love

1

    O nectar! O delicious stream!
O ravishing and only pleasure! Where
        Shall such another theme
Inspire my tongue with joys, or please mine ear!
        Abridgement of delights!   5
        And queen of sights!
O mine of rarities! O kingdom wide!
O more! O cause of all! O glorious bride!
        O God! O Bride of God! O King!
        O soul and crown of ev'ry thing!   10

2

    Did not I covet to behold
Some endless monarch, that did always live
        In palaces of gold
Willing all kingdoms realms and crowns to give
        Unto my soul! Whose love   15
        A spring might prove
Of endless glories, honors, friendships, pleasures,
Joys, praises, beauties and celestial treasures!
        Lo, now I see there's such a King,
        The fountain head of ev'ry thing!   20

3

    Did my ambition ever dream

Of such a Lord, of such a love! Did I
      Expect so sweet a stream
As this at any time! Could any eye
      Believe it? Why all power   25
        Is used here
Joys down from Heaven on my head to shower
And Jove beyond the fiction doth appear
      Once more in golden rain to come
      To Danae's pleasing fruitful womb.[3]   30

4

His Ganimede![4] His life! His joy!
Or he comes down to me, or takes me up
      That I might be his boy,
And fill, and taste, and give, and drink the cup.
      But these (though great) are all   35
        Too short and small,
Too weak and feeble pictures to express
The true mysterious depths of blessedness.
      I am his image, and his friend.
      His son, bride, glory, temple, end.   40

From *The Third Century*

On News

1

News from a foreign country came,
As if my treasure and my wealth lay there:
    So much it did my heart enflame!
'Twas wont to call my soul into mine ear.
      Which thither went to meet   5
        The approaching sweet:
    And on the threshold stood,
To entertain[5] the unknown good.
      It hovered there,
      As if 'twould leave mine ear.   10
And was so eager to embrace
The joyful tidings as they came,
'Twould almost leave its dwelling place
    To entertain the same.

3. Jove, in the form of a shower of golden rain, visited Danae in her bronze tower and lay with her; their offspring was Perseus.
4. The shepherd Ganymede was so beautiful that Jupiter fell in love with him and, in the form of an eagle, swooped down, carried him off to Olympus, and made him his cupbearer.
5. Receive.

2

As if the tidings were the things,   15
My very joys themselves, my foreign treasure,
  Or else did bear them on their wings;
With so much joy they came, with so much pleasure.
        My soul stood at the gate
            To recreate[6]   20
        It self with bliss: and to
Be pleased with speed. A fuller view
            It fain would take
        Yet journeys back would make
Unto my heart: as if 'twould fain   25
Go out to meet, yet stay within
To fit a place, to entertain,
        And bring the tidings in.

3

What sacred instinct did inspire
My soul in childhood with a hope so strong?   30
  What secret force moved my desire,
To expect my joys beyond the seas, so young?
        Felicity I knew
            Was out of view:
        And being here alone,   35
I saw that happiness was gone,
        From me! for this,
        I thirsted[7] absent bliss,
And thought that sure beyond the seas,
Or else in some thing near at hand   40
I knew not yet (since nought did please
        I knew) my bliss did stand.

4

But little did the infant dream
That all the treasures of the world were by:
  And that himself was so the cream   45
And crown of all, which round about did lie.
        Yet thus it was. The gem,
            The diadem,
        The ring enclosing all
That stood upon this earthy ball;   50
        The heavenly eye,
        Much wider than the sky.
Where in they all included were
The glorious soul that was the king
Made to possess them, did appear   55
        A small and little thing!

6. Refresh.   7. Thirsted for.

From the *Burney Manuscript*

The Return[8]

To infancy, O Lord, again I come,
    That I my manhood may improve:
    My early tutor is the womb;[9]
        I still my cradle love.
'Tis strange that I should wisest be,   5
When least I could an error see.

Till I gain strength against temptation, I
    Perceive it safest to abide
    An infant still; and therefore fly
        (A lowly state may hide   10
A man from danger) to the womb,
That I may yet new-born become.

My God, thy bounty then did ravish me!
    Before I learned to be poor,
    I always did thy riches see,   15
        And thankfully adore:
Thy glory and thy goodness were
My sweet companions all the year.

Shadows In the Water[1]

In unexperienced infancy
Many a sweet mistake doth lie:
Mistake though false, intending[2] true;
A *Seeming* somewhat more than *View*;
    That doth instruct the mind   5
    In things that lie behind,
And many secrets to us show
Which afterwards we come to know.

Thus did I by the water's brink
Another world beneath me think;   10

8. On this and the following poems, see Textual Notes.
9. (See line 11 also): Margoliouth cites "not Freud, but John 3 : 3–4," where Christ says, "Except a man be born again, he cannot see the kingdom of God," and Nicodemus responds, "How can a man be born when he is old? Can he enter the second time into his mother's womb?"
1. "The reminiscence of childish, and probably also later, intense interest in reflections in water is linked with adult thought of worlds other than the world of our particular sense impressions. But even the child is at least half-consciously exercising his fancy in play (cf. lines 33–40) and so is the adult: the whole is just on the border where fancy and imagination meet" (Margoliouth, vol. II, p. 377).
2. Meaning.

And while the lofty spacious skies
Reversed there abused mine eyes,
    I fancied other feet
    Came mine to touch and meet;
As by some puddle I did play   15
Another world within it lay.

Beneath the water people drowned.
Yet with another Heav'n crowned,
In spacious regions seemed to go
Freely moving to and fro: 20
    In bright and open space
    I saw their very face;
Eyes, hands, and feet they had like mine;
Another sun did with them shine.

'Twas strange that people there should walk,   25
And yet I could not hear them talk:
That through a little wat'ry chink,
Which one dry ox or horse might drink,
    We other worlds should see,
    Yet not admitted be;   30
And other confines there behold
Of light and darkness, heat and cold.

I called them oft, but called in vain;
No speeches we could entertain:
Yet did I there expect to find   35
Some other world, to please my mind.
    I plainly saw by these
    A new *Antipodes*,[3]
Whom, though they were so plainly seen,
A film kept off that stood between.   40

By walking men's reversed feet
I chanced another world to meet;
Though it did not to view exceed
A phantasm, 'tis a world indeed,
    Where skies beneath us shine,   45
    And earth by art divine
Another face presents below,
Where people's feet against ours go.

Within the regions of the air,
Compassed about with Heav'ns fair,   50
Great tracts of land there may be found

3. Those "far distant coasts" (line 54) presumed to be on the other side of the world.

Enriched with fields and fertile ground;
    Where many num'rous hosts,
    In those far distant coasts,
For other great and glorious ends,   55
Inhabit, my yet unknown friends.

Oh ye that stand upon the brink,
Whom I so near me, through the chink,
With wonder see: What faces there,
Whose feet, whose bodies, do ye wear?   60
    I my companions see
    In you, another me.
They seemed others, but are we;
Our second selves those shadows be.

Look how far off those lower skies   65
Extend themselves! scarce with mine eyes
I can them reach. O ye my friends,
What *Secret* borders on those ends?
    Are lofty Heavens hurled
    'Bout your inferior[4] world?   70
Are ye the representatives
Of other peoples' distant lives?

Of all the playmates which I knew
That here I do the image view
In other selves; what can it mean?   75
But that below the purling stream
    Some unknown joys there be
    Laid up in store for me;
To which I shall, when that thin skin
Is broken, be admitted in.   80

On Leaping Over the Moon[5]

I saw new worlds beneath the water lie,
    New people; and another sky,
        And sun, which seen by day
        Might things more clear display.
        Just such another[6]   5
        Of late my brother
Did in his travel see, and saw by night
    A much more strange and wondrous sight:
Nor could the world exhibit such another,
    So great a sight, but in a brother.   10

4. Lower.
5. "The first four stanzas (lines 5–40) relate Philip's youthful adventure and delight. It is pure fancy. The last three (lines 41–70) give it an imaginative application" (Margoliouth, vol. II, p. 378).
6. Another world.

Adventure strange! No such in store we
  New or old, true or feigned, see.
    On earth he seemed to move
    Yet Heaven went above;[7]
      Up in the skies   15
      His body flies
In open, visible, yet magic, sort:
  As he along the way did sport
Like Icarus over the flood he soars
  Without the help of wings or oars.   20

As he went tripping o'er the King's highway,
  A little pearly river lay
    O'er which, without a wing
    Or oar, he dared to swim,
      Swim through the air   25
      On body fair;
He would not use nor trust *Icarian*[8] wings
  Lest they should prove deceitful things;
For had he fall'n, it had been wondrous high,
  Not from, but from above, the sky: 30

He might have dropped through that thin element
  Into a fathomless descent;
    Unto the nether sky
    That did beneath him lie,
      And there might tell   35
      What wonders dwell
On earth above. Yet bold he briskly runs
  And soon the danger overcomes;
Who, as he leapt, with joy related soon
  How *happy he* o'er-leapt the moon.   40

What wondrous things upon the earth are done
  Beneath, and yet above, the sun?
    Deeds all appear again
    In higher spheres; remain
      In clouds as yet: 45
      But there they get
Another light, and in another way
  Themselves to us *above* display,
The skies themselves this earthly globe surround;[9]
  W'are even here within them found.   50

On heav'nly ground within the skies we walk,

---

7. He went above Heaven.
8. With wings fashioned by his father Daedalus, Icarus flew too near the sun, and the wax fastening his wings melted.
9. "On the playful level because above us and also reflected below us, on the scientific level because all round the globe, on the spiritual level because heaven is all about us" (Margoliouth, vol. II, p. 379).

And in this middle center talk:
 Did we but wisely move,
 On earth in Heav'n above,
   We then should be   55
   Exalted high
Above the sky: from whence whoever falls,
 Through a long dismal precipice,
Sinks to the deep abyss where *Satan* crawls
 Where horrid Death and Despair lies.   60

As much as others thought themselves to lie
 Beneath the moon, so much more high
   Himself he thought to fly
   Above the starry sky,
     As *that* he spied   65
     Below the tide.
Thus did he yield me in the shady night
 A wondrous and instructive light,
Which taught me that under our feet there is,
 As o'er our heads, a place of bliss.

Textual Notes

The goal of every editor—a truly satisfactory text—is elusive at best. "A truly satisfactory text" of poetry means many things to many people. For compilers of anthologies, it might mean smoothing over problems and correcting errors and getting the "numbers" right, as in the notorious case of Sir Thomas Wyatt. For some "scientific" editors, it might mean such rigorous fidelity to the original that even unclosed parentheses are not modified. I take it to mean a text as close as possible to the author's intention; for our present purposes, I would add, a text which is communicable.

While a distinction exists between establishing a text and communicating it —the first having to do with determinations of authenticity, reliability, authority, and the second with graphic and other conventions—the two are rooted in the same base: the recovering of the originals. George Herbert's poems exist in numerous seventeenth-century editions as well as in a complete manuscript. The first edition was published within a year of his death. Both the manuscript and the first edition are obviously very close to the author's original, but neither has undisputed authority. For Crashaw's works, we have three major editions—1646, 1648, 1652—two published before his death. In Marvell's case, there is only one, unreliable posthumous edition (1681) of the poems written before 1660. Henry Vaughan presided over two editions of his work, the first part of *Silex Scintillans* in 1650 and a slightly revised edition in 1655 which adds the second part. Vaughan was the only one of our poets whose whole work represented in this book was published during his lifetime. Thomas Traherne left only manuscripts which were not finally published until the beginning of this century.

So far, then, the status of the texts themselves. The problems that arise, both for establishing the text and for normalizing or updating it, are not in exact correlation with this status. Even though, for instance, some of Traherne's text is uniquely corrupt—because of the well-intentioned but wrong-headed ministrations of his brother Philip—large parts of his text are clearly more reliable than the posthumous text of Marvell's poems, which comes to us mainly by way of a fortune hunter who used it to support her claim to be his "widow." We have several texts for many of Crashaw's poems, but there are problems here too. In the first place, the 1646 and 1648 editions were published in London while Crashaw himself was in Paris, with the English court in exile, and then later in Italy (where he died in 1649); the major edition of 1652 was posthumous. Secondly, true to both his poetic strivings and his volatile spiritual temperament, Crashaw's text is rarely stable. Verbally and graphically, his texts fluctuate, sometimes chaotically, so that the existence of different versions of the same poems complicates the editor's task.

To establish my text, I have where feasible (in effect, for all but Crashaw) used the earliest and best originals—the first edition of Herbert and the complete Bodleian manuscript and the Williams manuscript, with consultation of several other seventeenth-century editions (there were eleven, the first four of which are available on microfilm in the STC or *Short-Title Catalogue* series being published by University Microfilms); both editions of Vaughan, and the 1681 edition of Marvell, along with the Bodleian manuscript. For Traherne, I have used photographic copies of the Dobell Folio and the Burney manuscript, generously loaned me by my colleague Arthur Clements. In all cases, I have relied heavily on the magisterial work of modern editors—especially Hutchinson, Margoliouth, Martin, Fogle, and Williams. In this endeavor, I have been aided not only by unfailingly kind and helpful librarians but also by modern technology, whereby more and more texts are being made available, especially in the Scolar facsimiles and the STC and Wing microfilm projects. In the end,

I am most "satisfied" with the texts of Herbert and Vaughan and least with those of Traherne and Crashaw. As for Marvell, in the present state of affairs, we will never have a satisfactory basis for texts of his lyric poems.

Having established my text, the next step was to "normalize" or "update" it, in the interests of communicability. This had its own idiosyncratic problems. To normalize or modernize everything would be simplest, but that means imposing on five diverse bodies of poetry a uniform set of conventions which would, in effect, wipe out both the facts and, in some respects, the very premises of these texts. But because of the widely divergent status of the individual texts, not to normalize completely would result in inconsistency. I have opted for inconsistency. I have modernized the orthography, but I have left virtually all punctuation in its seventeenth-century form and made local decisions about other conventions such as italics and capital letters. As I hope to make clear, little was lost and much gained in modernizing the spelling, but much would have been lost in a wholesale approach. My approach attempts to get the best of both worlds (though at some cost) by making the text completely and undistractingly accessible to the modern reader without reducing it to a bland agglomeration of characters which wipes out the individualities and idiosyncrasies of the authors.

In modernizing the spelling, I have usually: regularized *j, i, u, v,* and *&*; made the appropriate distinctions between *then* and *than*; and reinstated the silent *e* (e.g., in words like *lov'd, veil'd, ador'd*). However, I have retained spellings which are still acceptable alternatives (past participles like *drest* or *slipt*), and I have retained the apostrophe (or even inserted it) where filling out the contraction would interfere with the prosody (e.g., *driv'n, heav'n*). I am satisfied that, generally speaking, such normalization does not violate the author's text.

Spelling, however, is a less deliberate matter than punctuation and other conventions. Often, punctuation serves as a prosodic device that controls or modifies rhythm; italics, capitals, and format affect our sense of emphasis. The reader can, I believe, manage even the vagaries of seventeenth-century punctuation without strain. The degree of deliberateness or purposefulness in these matters varies from author to author; so does the possibility of consistent reproduction.

My format follows the physical layout of the original texts in virtually all cases. So does the punctuation. On occasion, the punctuation of the originals is so erratic as to create a serious distraction, but that is less often the case than one would expect. Modern practice favors much ligher punctuation than was common among our poets, but adopting modern practice wholesale creates its own problems. Here is an example from Vaughan's "The Night." The third stanza (with minor orthographic adjustment of *hallow'd* and *fulness*) reads:

> O who will tell me, where
> He found thee at that dead and silent hour!
> What hallowed solitary ground did bear
>   So rare a flower,
> Within whose sacred leafs did lie
> The fullness of the Deity.

One modern anthology changes both end-stops to question marks. That may be the finally correct interpretation of the text, but it is not an obvious interpretation and may as easily be a violation of the text. It appears to me that Vaughan wrote an exclamation of wonder, of deeply stirred religious feeling, parallel to the two exclamations in the second stanza (which the cited text unaccountably makes into three); the stanza contemplates one of the great mysteries, the silence, darkness, and obscurity of God. But question marks at lines 14 and 18 turn the meditation into rhetorical questions and modify its rhythms subtly but significantly. The slight difficulties which the "unmodern" punctuation may cause are surely well compensated.

Capitals and italics presented their own problems. In the cases of Herbert and Vaughan, the poets whose seventeenth-century texts are probably closest to their own considered intentions, it was "easy" to preserve the originals. Intentionality was clearly involved, and patterns emerge even to the casual viewer.

Crashaw, Marvell, and Traherne are quite different cases. While I did not wish to abandon the possibilities of the originals, consistency would have created an obstacle to the major aim of normalizing—reasonable facility in reading. Traherne uses capitals so frequently—in virtually all nouns and many verbs—that they are seriously distracting; Marvell's printer used them erratically and unpredictably; in Crashaw's text, there is a glittering riot of capitals and italics, in affective but bewildering abundance. In all these, I have made local decisions and spelled them out in the headnotes. In any case, another example from Vaughan may indicate the value of inconsistency. "Mount of Olives (II)," lines 9–10, reads:

> My thoughts did swim in Comforts, and mine eie
> Confest, *The world did only paint and lie.*

One modernized version reads:

> My thoughts did swim in comforts, and mine eye
> Confessed the world did only paint and lie.

I have printed:

> My thoughts did swim in Comforts, and mine eye
> Confessed, *The world did only paint and lie.*

Modernizing "eie" and "Confest" does no damage to the text, but modifying punctuation and italics in line 10 stifles some meanings a sensitive reader would find in the original.

Such then is the compromise I have attempted, in the belief that inconsistency of this sort is preferable to a text which totally obliterates the idiosyncratic and potentially valuable graphics of the originals. If one considers the reader a part of the textual process, a compromise is the best any editor can achieve.

The Textual Notes record significant variants and editorial choices. I have been conservative, but some important modifications were called for; and in some cases I have indicated attractive alternatives which I did not finally choose. Without attempting a census of variants or a comprehensive record of the manuscripts, I have included such useful details as representative revisions from the Williams manuscript in the notes to Herbert; representative titles; and examples of Philip Traherne's meddling in his brother's text. It should be noted that verbal details recorded in the Textual Notes are rendered in old spelling; no other scheme seemed feasible.

GEORGE HERBERT

The principal edition is the Cambridge edition of 1633, *The Temple. Sacred Poems and Private Ejaculations . . . , Printed by Thom. Buck and Roger Daniel, printers to the Universitie;* this edition is now available in a Scolar Press facsimile printed from a copy in the British Museum. This edition (hereafter cited as "1633") was probably seen through the press by Herbert's friend, Nicholas Ferrar of Little Gidding. There are two important manuscripts, the Williams (W) and the Bodleian (B). W, a volume of 120 leaves, includes 69 poems in *The Temple;* now MS Jones B 62 in Dr. Williams's Library, Gordon Square, London, this was probably a slightly earlier version of Herbert's work. The poems sometimes contain substantial variations (some are cited in the Textual Notes, to suggest Herbert's processes of revision), and some of the corrections are in Herbert's hand. The manuscript has been published by Scholars Facsimiles & Reprints (1977) with an introduction by Amy M. Charles. Comparison of the two manuscripts shows that Herbert added about 76 poems between "Obedience" and "The Elixir," but only about 20 within the W poems themselves. B is a folio of 152 leaves, bequeathed to the Bodleian Library, Oxford, by Thomas Tanner (MS Tanner 307). It bears the inscription "The Original of Mr George Herbert's Temple; as it was first Licenced for the presse."

In his Oxford English Text edition (1941), Canon F. E. Hutchinson relied primarily on B for verbal authority and on 1633 for other matters, on the grounds that B represented Herbert's text while 1633 represented the printers' understanding of that text. Hutchinson used W to resolve problems between the 1633 and B. But the B text does not have undoubted authority. Hence, I rely mainly on the 1633 for the texts of the other poems, comparing B and W to this in all cases and consulting the second 1633 edition and several later editions as well, including G. H. Palmer's and, particularly, the careful recent work of Joseph Summers and C. A. Patrides. It must be noted that the differences from Canon Hutchinson's edition are not great; his editorial decisions were usually right. Indeed, while some scholars have questioned his eclectic editorial principles, we all continue in his debt. My own indebtedness I record happily; Hutchinson's volume has been very useful to me for many years now. The 1633 edition appears to me to have somewhat higher authority than B, but none of the evidence adduced thus far demonstrates conclusively its utter and definitive authority. Where the two versions differ significantly, one must examine those differences carefully; in some cases, it seems clear, neither gives a final version.

In my text, I have modernized the spelling, but I have kept as close to the early texts as possible in all other matters—capitalization, italics, punctuation, physical format. My textual notes record significant variations, reasons for my editorial choices, and a number of early readings from W to suggest the processes of revision.

A note on punctuation. The editor of 1633 was remarkably (and sometimes distressingly) consistent in the conventions he adopted and his divergence from the B manuscript (I assume that the B is contemporaneous with, if not actually the copy text used by the 1633 editor); in their excellent recent edition, Lewalski and Sabol argue that the "heavier pointing" of the 1633 does not represent Herbert's intentions as well as does the punctuation of the B manuscript. While still according authority to the 1633 as my main text, I have tried—as all editors must—to outguess the printer of the 1633 as to exactly what Herbert's intentions were, and I find that I have adopted a fair number of punctuation marks from the B manuscript. They occur as a kind of pattern throughout the whole work. The editor of 1633 used semicolons in scores of cases, usually at line endings, where B had a comma or sometimes no punctuation at all; he used colons often where B used periods. In the latter case, the distinction is not great and I have made no changes, but I have modified many of the semicolons.

In the following cases, the comma following certain words (listed here by line) has been adopted from B in place of the 1633 semicolon; in virtually all of these instances, Hutchinson, Summers, and Patrides follow 1633: "The Sacrifice" 2: blind, 27: mine, 30: watching, 38: relief, 54: me, 81: stand, 85: despitefulness, 118: peace, 178: weeds, 202: tree, 217: wound, 218: confound, 233: high, 245: go, / "Redemption" 10: resorts, / "Sepulchre" 14: thee, / "Easter" 19: way, / "H. Baptism (II)" 12: on, 14: blister, / "Affliction (I)" 19: sweetnesses, 21: happiness, 38: town, / "H. Communion" 8: breast, 10: length, / "[Church Lock-and-Key]" 6: leaven, 10: smother, 14: blood, / "Love II" 3: tame, 13: thee, / "Jordan (I)" 11: people, / "Whitsunday" 21: within, / "Grace" 9: fall, / "Church Monuments" 3: dust, / "The Quiddity" 5: play, / "The Star" 6: heart, / "Sunday" 11: back-part, / "Obedience" 23: actions, 38: read, / "The Quip" 22: come, / "Dialogue" 26: *repining,* / "The Size" 10: prevail, / "The Search" 49: near, / "The Flower" 37: write, /"Bitter-Sweet" 2: strike, 3: afford, / "Aaron" 18: dead; / "The Forerunners" 1: mark, / "Death" 9: short, /.

It should also be noted that occasionally the use of punctuation marks in B is heavier than in 1633; in most cases, this amounts to a comma where there is none in 1633. I list a number of examples from B both to indicate another important aspect of this manuscript and to make its readings available—some offer attractive possibilities: "The Agony" 15: say, / "H. Baptism (I)" 1: he, / "Whitsunday" 5: fire, / "Church Monuments" 15: flat, 18: fat, 20: dust, / "Sunday" 2: bud, 19: choose, / "Employment (II)" 18: here: / "Denial" 26: cheer, / "Christmas" 5: I, 14: lodging, rack, / "The World" 15: that, / "Vanity (I)" 14: destruction, / "Virtue" 10: box, / "The Pearl" 29: he, 33: understand, 38: twist, 39: conduct, / "Obedience" 5: much, 10: it, / "The Quip" 9: still, / "Peace" 33: they, it, 35: virtue, / "The Bunch of Grapes" 21: me, / "A True Hymn" 9: fineness, 11: He, / "Aaron" 3: dead, / "The Elixir" 4: it, 5: rudely, 9: man, 23: that, / "Death" 14: face; 21: die, 22: Half, have, /.

ABBREVIATIONS

W	Williams (MS Jones B 62, Dr. Williams's Library)
B	Bodleian (MS Tanner 307)
1633	the first edition (Cambridge 1633)
1633–2d	the second 1633 edition
H	*The Works of George Herbert*, ed. F. E. Hutchinson (Oxford, 1941)
S	*The Selected Poetry* . . . , ed. J. H. Summers (New York, 1967)

The title of Herbert's work is *The Temple*. In this edition, all but two poems are from the main section, *The Church*; the other two are the sonnets from Walton's *Lives*. Where there are several poems with the same name, the conventional numerical distinctions are used. For typographical reasons, "Easter" follows "Easter Wings" (pp. 16–18).

"The Altar"
12 Name. **B** / name **W** / name. **1633**

"The Sacrifice"
1   Oh . . . by **W B** / Partly italicized **1633** / Fully italicized **1633–2d H**
25 tears **W B** / tears, **1633**
38 way of **1633** / way & **W B** / Way and **H S**
57 Priests **W** / Priest **1633 B** (**H** and **S** identify the Priest as Caiaphas [Matthew 26:57], but the context of Herbert's lines clearly evokes Matthew 26:59, "Now the chief priests, and elders, and all the council, sought false witness against Jesus, to put him to death.")
115 cause **B 1633 S** / case **W H** (Summers argues that "they plead for Barabbas to 'do a courtesy' to their own legal *cause* as murderers.")
129–31 him . . . him . . . his . . . he **W B** / me . . . me . . . my . . . I . . . **1633** (There was a similar change in pronouns in 57ff: see note.)
130 grasps **W B** / grasp **1633**
138 vailed **B** / vailed, **1633**
153 common hall **1633** / Common Hall **W B**
171 evermore **B** 1633 / to the poore **W**
177–178 **W** reads:

> Yet since in frailty, cruelty, shrowd turns,
> All Scepters, Reeds: Cloths, Scarlet: Crowns are Thorns:

179 deeds **B** 1633 / scorns **W**
187 **W** reads:

> With stronger blows strike mee as I come out

209 sorrow as, if **H** / Sorrow, as if **W B 1633**
217 **W** reads:

> My soule is full of shame, my flesh of wound:

221 Italicized **H** / Roman type **1633**
237 give **W B** / gave **1633**

"The Thanksgiving"
11 skipping **B** / skipping, **1633** (**W** originally read: "neglecting thy sad story," which makes it clear that the comma in **1633** is wrong.)

"The Reprisal"
Title in **W**: "The Second Thanks-giving"
14 thy **W B** / the **1633**

"Good Friday"
W has an earlier version of 21–32 as a separate poem entitled "The Passion."

See next poem also. In **B** these lines begin a new page but have no title.
21–22 **W** reads:

> Since nothing Lord can bee so good
> To write thy sorrows in, as blood

27 sin **B 1633** / he **W**
29–32 **W** reads:

> Sinn being gone o doe thou fill
> The Place, & keep possession still.
> ffor by the writings all may see
> Thou hast an ancient claime to mee.

"Redemption"
In **W**, has same title as the poem preceding it there, "The Passion." See preceding note.
10-11 **W** reads before correction:

> Sought him in Citties, Theaters, resorts
> In grottos, gardens, Palaces & Courts

"Sepulchre"
Not in **W**. I follow the stanzaic organization of **1633**; **H** and **S** print as eight-line stanzas.
17 old **B H** / eld, **1633**

"Easter Wings"
Though the text is written horizontally in both **W** and **B**, all early editions print the lines vertically.
8 **W** originally had "doe by degree," corrected to "harmoniously"
9 **W** originally had "sacrifice," corrected to "victories"
19 **W** does not have "this day"; as Hutchinson points out, the phrase "assists the parallelism to line 9 but makes line 18 a foot longer than the corresponding line 8."

"H. Baptism (I)"
5 vent **B H** / rent **1633**
12 *Book of Life* **B** / roman type **1633 H S**

"Sin (I)"
1 round! 1633 **H** / round? **B**
7 stratagems **B 1633 H** / casualties **W**
10 ears: 1633 **H** / eares **B**
11 **B** reads: "shame, within our consciences," (Lewalski and Sabol follow this reading, but its sense is difficult to perceive.)

"Affliction (I)"
6 gracious benefits **B 1633** / graces perquisites **W**
7, 8 fine **B 1633** / rich **W**
9–10 entwine, . . . unto thee. **B 1633** / bewitch Into thy familie. **W**
65 God **B 1633** / King **W**

"Prayer (I)"
5 tower **B 1633** / fort **W**

"[Prayer (II)]"
I have made two substantial changes in the order and the titles of the poems here; my revised titles are in brackets. (1) The poem I place here and retitle "[Prayer (II)]" is found in **B** and **1633** as "Church-lock and key," placed between "Church-musick" and "The Windowes." (2) The poem I entitle "[Church Lock-and-Key]" is found in **B** and **1633** as part of "The H. Communion." In making these changes, I have followed the persuasive arguments of Frank Huntley ("A Crux . . . ," *ELH*, VIII (1970), 13–17). In both **W** and **B**, the poems through "H. Baptism" are generally similar in or-

der and text; at this point, the two manuscripts begin to diverge considerably. The **W** poem "The H. Communion" (f. 30v) is not found in **B**; the next six poems in **W**—"Church-Musick," two poems titled "The Christian Temper," and three entitled "Prayer" (ff. 32–35)—are found, revised, in other places in **B**. In **B**, a new poem, "The H. Communion," follows the great sonnet "Prayer (I)." At the end of this poem, the **B** version includes a revision of the second **W** poem "Prayer" (f. 34v), but with a substantial space between the main body of the poem and these four quatrains. The last of the **W** "Prayer" poems (f. 35) reappears, revised, in **B** as "Church-lock and key." Huntley argues that this poem is out of place among the other "ecclesiastical adjuncts," that its title really belongs in the space in **B** between the two parts of the new "H. Communion," and that the poem should be retitled "Prayer" and returned to its proper place. I agree with Huntley's argument and see others. I believe the confusion that Huntley detected arose from either incomplete revision or misunderstanding by the amanuensis or both. The poem I retitle "[Church Lock-and-Key]" is less finished than the other poems—the rhythm is heavy and lines 10 and 16 are particularly awkward. (I believe it is intended as a simple prayer after communion, expressing quiet devotion; the emblematic function of the title which I assign to it seems simple to perceive.) Furthermore, it is clear that the copyist of **B** had some hesitations about the whole matter and that whoever prepared the copy text made revisions, or the printer did, whether justified or not. One important fact bearing on the present problem is this: the anagram poem appears in B (f. 44) just before "Church-lock and key," while in **1633** it comes a dozen or so poems later—in my text, between "Sunday" and "Employment (II)". In the **B** text, the anagram couplet has double lines preceding and following the title—a practice that applies to every other title in the **B** text except for two: "Unkindness" (f. 64v) and "Church-lock and key." I conjecture, then, that the amanuensis of **B** and (if there was a different one) the amanuensis of the copy text for **1633** misunderstood Herbert's revisions and directions in the master copy, or the copy itself may have had incomplete revision.

"The H. Communion"
6   sin. **B** / sinne: **1633 H**
17 Name **B** / name, **1633 H**

"[Church Lock-and-Key]"
13–16 **W** reads:

> But wee are strangers grown, o Lord,
> Lett Prayer help our losses,
> Since thou hast taught us by thy word,
> That wee may gaine by crosses.

"The Temper (I)"
5   some forty **B 1633** / a hundred **W**
25 **W** originally read:
> Whether I Angell it, or fall to dust

"The Temper (II)"
4   **B** reads:
> Save that; and mee, or sin for both destroy.

"Jordan (I)"
5   true **B** / true, **1633**
13 spring **B** / spring; **1633**
14 rime **B** / rime, **1633**

"Employment (I)"
23–24 **W** originally read:

> Lord that I may the Sunns perfection gaine
> Give mee his speed.

"The H. Scriptures I"
2 gain, **1633 H** / gaine; **B**
3 part **B** / part; **1633 H**
11 too much **B 1633** / enough **W**

"The H. Scriptures II"
10 And comments on thee **B 1633** / And more then fancy **W**
14 lights to **B 1633** / can spell **W**

"Church Monuments"
B and **W** write this poem without stanza divisions. However, **W** indents
line 17, after the second of only two full-stopped lines.

"Church Music"
1 you. When **B** / you: when **1633**

"The Windows"
5 window **B** / window, **1633**

"The Quiddity"
Title in **W** is "Poetry."

"The Star"
Indentation pattern follows **B**. **1633** indents second line of each stanza.

"Anagram"
Not in **W**. **B** has it after "Church Music." See note above to "[Prayer (II)]"
and Sister Hanley in *ELN*, IV (1966), 16–19.

"Employment (II)"
21–25 **W** reads:

> O that I had the wing and thigh
>   Of laden Bees;
> Then would I mount up instantly
>   And by degrees
> On men dropp blessings as I fly.

26 still too **B 1633** / ever **W**
29 **W** reads "Thus wee creep on"

"The World"
10 Reformed all at length **B 1633** / Quickly reformed all **W**

"Vanity (I)"
22, 27 Man **B** / man **1633**
22 sought **1633** / wrought **B** (Hutchinson notes that "sought" better fits
the verbal imagery of the poem.)

"Virtue"
2 to night **B 1633 H** (Summers has "tonight" but the prepositional phrase
"to night" is an excellent *modern* reading here.)

"The Pearl . . ."
1 Learning **W B** / learning **1633**
11 Honour **W B** / honour **1633**
21 Pleasure **W B** / pleasure **1633**
32 seeled **W** / sealed **B 1633 H** (The image is from falconry.)
35 love **B** / love; **1633**

"Affliction (IV)"
Title in **W**: "Tentation"
12 pink **W B** / prick **1633**. (Hutchinson argues persuasively for "pink" on
the basis of Herbert's frequent references to fencing and the link to
"Wounding," line 8.)

"Man"
2 none doth build **B 1633** / no man builds **W**

8 more fruit **W** / no fruit **B 1633** (The choice is difficult; Hutchinson, choosing **W**, summarizes at length arguments on both sides.)
26 **W** reads:
> Earth resteth, Heaven moveth, fountains flow

41 **W** reads:
> cleanlines: if one have beauty,

42 neat! **B** / neat? **1633 H**
52 wit, / wit: **B** / wit; **1633 H**

"Mortification"
2 clothes **W 1633 H** / cloths **B**
10 dead. **B** / dead: **1633 H**
18 house **B 1633** / houre **W** (**H** and **S** both choose "houre," but cf. my note in the text.)
30 house **B 1633**; place **W**

"Jordan (II)"
Title in **W**: "Invention"
1 lines **B 1633** / verse **W**
4 sprout **B 1633** / spredd **W**
6 Decking **B 1633** / Praising **W**
14 **W** reads:
> So I bespoke me much insinuation:

18 **W** reads:
> Coppy out that: there needs no alteration.

"Obedience"
15 exclude **B 1633** / shutt out **W**
38 hath read; **B 1633** / doth read **W**

"The British Church"
Stanza organization as in **1633**. **H** and **S** follow **B** in using six-line stanzas.

"The Quip"
The refrain, from Psalms 38:15 (*Book of Common Prayer*), is italicized in **1633–2d**.
18 Wit-and-Conversation **S** (No hyphens in other texts.)

"Iesu"
Title "Jesu" in **1633,** but line 5 necessitates the "I."

"Dullness"
1 thus **B** / thus, 1633 **H**

"Peace"
Format as in **B**, not **1633**
1 dwell, **B** / dwell? **1633**
4 asked **B** / asked, **1633**
21 demand, **B** / demand; **1633**

"The Bunch of Grapes"
1 up. But **B** / up: but **1633 H**
2 again, **B** / again: **1633 H**
6 draw, **B** / draw; **1633 H**

"The Size"
16 Enact **1633** / Exact **B**
39 A line of four syllables is obviously missing after this, but there is no space in **B** or **1633**.

"The Pilgrimage"
14 wold **1633** / would **B**

"The Collar"
The form of this poem has presented problems to every editor since **1633**. I have followed **B** and **1633**, which agree except in line 11 (and that seems a slip); most editors have modified one line or another without explanation—apparently because of the number of feet (the lines vary from dimeter to

pentameter) or syllables, but even in these matters inconsistently. So I prefer the inconsistencies of the early texts, and I print lines 9, 15, and 19 as they are in both **B** and **1633**, and 11 as in **B**.
21 not. Forsake **B** / not forsake **1633** (and many of the other early editions, but it seems clearly a slip)
27 heed, **B** / heed: **1633 H**

"The Flower"
15 Italics added from **B**.
32 zone **B** / zone, **1633**
34 turn **B** / turn, **1633**
37 write, **B** / write; **1633**
43 Italics added from **B**.

"The Son"
6 sun's **1633 H** / sonnes (son's) **B**

"A True Hymn"
49 this **1633** / his **B H**

"Aaron"
4 rest. **B 1633** / rest: **H**
9 rest. **1633** / rest, **B** / rest: **H**
18 dead, **B** / dead; **1633 H**
23 dead **B** / dead, **1633 H**

"The Forerunners"
10 *God* **B** / *God*, **1633 H**

"The Banquet"
2 dear, **B** / dear; **1633**
49 this **1633** / his **B H**

"The Elixir"
   In **W**, the title was first given as "Perfection"; Herbert added "The Elixir" without crossing out the copyist's title. The poem is heavily revised in **W**, the revisions in Herbert's own hand. The significance of the revisions is discussed in White, *The Metaphysical Poets*.
1–4 **W** reads:

> Lord teach mee to referr
> All things I doe to thee
> That I not onely may not erre
> But allso pleasing bee.

W lacks 5–8. Between 12–13, **W** originally had:

> He that does ought for thee,
> Marketh yt deed for thine:
> And when the Divel shakes ye tree,
> Thou saist, this fruit is mine.

21–24 **W** originally had:

> But these are high perfections:
> Happy are they that dare
> Lett in the Light to all their actions
> And show them as they are.

"Death"
14 face, / face; **B 1633 H** / face **W**
16 sought for **B H** / sought for, **1633** / long'd for **W**

"Heaven"
The responses of *Echo* are not italicized in **B** and **W**.
5 trees **B 1633** / woods **W**

"Love (III)"
1 welcome. Yet **B** / welcome: yet **1633 H**
  back **B** / back, **1633 H**
3 Love, **1633 H W** / Love **B**

Glory be . . . Printed here as in **B**. Not in **W**; arranged in two lines in **1633**, which modifies the meaning slightly:

> Glorie be to God on high, and on earth
> peace, good will towards men.

RICHARD CRASHAW

Crashaw's earliest published work was a collection of Latin epigrams, *Epigrammatum sacrorum liber* (1634); many of these were translated for the first English volume, *Steps to the Temple, Sacred Poems, With other Delights of the Muses*, published in 1646 and again, in a much revised and augmented edition, in 1648. *Carmen Deo Nostro* was published at Paris, posthumously, in 1652; this contains many poems from the 1648 edition and several significant additions, especially the first version of "To . . . The Countess of Denbigh." The changes in individual poems from edition to edition are often extensive and sometimes bewildering, and in many cases the versions must simply be described as different versions. There is, for instance, a 1653 version of the poem to the Countess of Denbigh which is in many ways a different poem from the 1652 version. In the Notes, I indicate the main source for each text. Throughout, I have relied heavily, both for interpretation of the principal editions and for notes on the manuscripts, on the magisterial work of L. C. Martin for the Oxford English Text edition, *The Poems English Latin and Greek of Richard Crashaw*, 2nd edition, 1957, and the admirable edition by George Walton Williams, *The Complete Poetry of Richard Crashaw* (New York, 1970), which has in some respects super-ceded Martin's. Williams's edition provides parallel texts of poems extant in two versions—specifically, for our purposes, the Nativity hymn, "The Weeper," and the poem to the Countess of Denbigh.

Because of the variant versions and because Crashaw's practices in matters of orthography and other conventions might be called affective rather than logical, and perhaps because his printer was erratic and inconsistent, Crashaw's texts present particular problems for the editor who must modernize them. Clearly, Crashaw means to use capitals and italics for emphasis, but the practice varies from text to text, so that sometimes it becomes next to impossible to divine his intent. In the face of large inconsistencies between versions or in the texts, I have regretfully not attempted to preserve his patterns of capitalization and italics but have followed instead conservative modern practice. The result may be inconsistent, but that graphic fact mirrors the situation in the seventeenth-century texts. In the notes, I have not attempted to give a detailed rendering of the variant readings or major revisions. My main concern has been to provide a record of editorial choices and emendations.

ABBREVIATIONS

1646	*Steps to the Temple* (1646)
1648	The second edition (1648)
1652	*Carmen Deo Nostro* (1652)
1653	The 1653 revision of "To . . . The Countess of Denbigh"
M	Martin's Oxford edition (1957)
W	Williams's edition

"Steps to the Temple"
Text: **1646**

"Music's Duel"
Text: **1646**. The secular poems have a separate title page—*The Delights of the Muses. Or, Other Poems written on severall occasions* . . .
69   whence **M** (following manuscripts) / when **1646 1648**
99   graver **1648** / grave **1646**
156 full-mouthed **M** (following manuscripts) / full-mouth **1646 1648**

"In the Holy Nativity . . ."
Text: **1652**; substantially revised in **1648** from **1646**.

28   eyes' / eyes **1648** / eye's **1652**
32   Young **1652** / Bright **1648**
41   ye **1648** / the **1652**
43   ye **1648** / the **1652**
47   his own **1652** / all one **1648**
54   bed: **1648** / bed **1652**
56   white, but **1646** / white But **1648 1652**
60   wings **1648** / wing **1652**
69   we **1652** / I **1648**
91   flies **1648** / flyes. **1652**
104 Loves, **1646** / Loves. **1652**

"Saint Mary Magdalene . . ."
Text: **1652**; substantially revised in **1648** from **1646**.
2   silver-forded **1646** / sylver-footed **1652** (**M** merely notes the **1646** read-
     ing; **W** keeps **1652**, arguing that "footed" makes a more relevant image in
     this poem with its emphasis on feet. I agree with Martz that the earlier
     reading "makes an effective image" in the link of rills and fords.)
22   above **1646** / above; **1652**
27   sacred **1652** / soft **1646**
47   tear, **1648** / Tear. **1652**
70   crystal vials **1652** / their Bottles **1646**
91   woes **1648** / woes. **1652**
101 suns, / suns **1652**
159 fire. / fire **1648** / fires **1652**
172 your **1648** / their **1652**

"A Hymn to . . . Saint Teresa"
Text: **1652**. The Pierpont Morgan Library in New York owns a manuscript of this poem with the following title: "A HYMN *to the name and
honour of the renowned* S. TERESIA Foundres of the Reformation of the
Order of barefoote Carmelites; *A Woman for* Angelicall *height of* Contemplation *for* Masculine *courage of* Performance *more then a woman. Who yet
a Child outranne Maturity & durst plott a* Martyrdome; *but was reserved by
God to dy the* living death *of the* life *of his* love. *of whose great impressions
as her noble heart had most high experiment, so hath she in her life most
heroically exprest them, in her Spirituall posterity most fruitfully propagated
them, and in these her heavnly Writings most sublimely, most sweetly taught
them to y*ᵉ *world.*" (Williams's transcription, p. 664, is not quite accurate.)
     The text of the poem does not undergo major changes from version to ver-
sion, but Crashaw added "The Flaming Heart" to this and another Teresa
poem in **1648** and, in **1652,** further added the twenty-four lines that conclude
"The Flaming Heart."
4   great **1652** / stout **1646**
10   spacious bosoms spread **1652** / large breasts built **1646**
44   travail **1652** / travel **1646 1648**
47   trade **1652 1646** / try **1648**
61   (Not in **1652**, supplied from **1648**)
104 he . . . die **1652** / he still may die **1646**
117 resolving **1652** / dissolving **1646**
122 thou shalt first **1648** / you first **1652**
130 his **1652** / her **1646 1648**
175 keeps **1646** / keep **1652**

"The Flaming Heart"
Text: **1652**. The first version, **1648,** was 84 lines long; **1652** adds the last 24
lines (printed here).
Full title: "THE FLAMING HEART UPON THE BOOK AND Picture of
     the seraphicall saint TERESA, (AS SHE IS USUALLY EX-pressed with
     a SERAPHIM biside her.)"
76   wounds **1648** / wound **1652**
     darts. **1652** / darts, **1648**
90   sin. / sin, **1648 1652**

"To . . . The Countess of Denbigh"
Text: **1652**; a greatly revised and expanded version (one-third longer) was published at London in 1653.
10   weakness) / weaknes! **1652**
16   denied. **1653** / deny'd, **1652**
58   delay. / delay **1652**

ANDREW MARVELL

Though more editors have struggled with Marvell's text than with that of any other of our poets, there is no finally definitive edition of his poems. The authority of many of his texts is less certain than of any other of our authors except Traherne. Only a few of Marvell's poems were published in his lifetime. The first edition was the posthumous *Miscellaneous Poems* of 1681 (known as the Folio edition), published by "Mary Marvell" as part of her attempt to pass herself off as Marvell's widow and thus lay claim to his estate. The 1681 provides the only text for most of the poems written before 1660. In many ways more important than 1681 is a volume in the Bodleian Library (MS Engl. poet. d. 49—hereafter referred to as Bodleian)—which contains the 1681 text (with omissions), a hundred manuscript emendations in a hand imitating print, manuscript additions (including three Cromwell poems cancelled from most copies of 1681), and a manuscript appendage of satires. The Bodleian manuscript is apparently the text compiled by Marvell's nephew and friend William Popple for a projected *Complete Poetry*. The Scolar Press has recently published the 1681 folio (the British Museum copy, the best copy available—also, incidentally, published on microfilm by University Microfilms) together with the Bodleian manuscript material.

Many editors of Marvell tamper more or less with the order of the poems, for the order in 1681 is not totally satisfactory. But no reordering has been very satisfactory either. Except for placing the "Horatian Ode" before "Appleton House," I have followed the order of the 1681, which I have used as copy text. Normalizing the text has presented, inevitably, a different set of problems than those incurred elsewhere. The 1681 is erratic in spelling, punctuation, and conventions generally; there are printer's devils such as unclosed parentheses. The Bodleian corrects many small errors, but the basic problem remains. Hence, I have been more conservative than I would have liked in the matter of capitals and punctuation; I have dropped most of the (very numerous) capitals of the 1681, but I have kept most italics and have modified the punctuation only where it seemed absolutely necessary.

ABBREVIATIONS

1681	*Miscellaneous Poems.* By Andrew Marvell, Esq; Late Member of the Honourable House of Commons. London, 1681.
Cooke	*The Works . . . ,* ed. Thomas Cooke. London, 1726.
Bodleian	Bodleian MS Engl. poet. d. 49.
MS	Bodleian MS Don. b. 8.
M (1927)	*The Poems and Letters . . . ,* ed. H. M. Margoliouth. Oxford, 1927.
M	1952, revised edition of the Oxford.
ML	1973, third edition (revised by Pierre Legouis).
Martz	*English Seventeenth-Century Verse,* ed. by Louis L. Martz. New York, 1973.
Lord	*Complete Poetry,* ed. George de Forest Lord. New York, 1968.
Donno	*The Complete Poems,* ed. Elizabeth Story Donno. Baltimore, 1972.

"A Dialogue Between the Resolved . . . ."
51   soft **Bodleian M** / cost **1681. Cooke** conjectures: "All that's costly, fair, and sweet"

"On a Drop of Dew"
4   new, / new; **1681 ML**
5   born **1681 ML** / born, **Cooke**
23 sweet **Bodleian** / sweat **1681** / swart **ML**

"Eyes and Tears"
4   They **1681** / We **Bodleian**
5   And **1681** / Thus **Bodleian**
35 teeming **1681** / seeming **Bodleian**
38 its / it **1681**

"Bermudas"
15 fowls / Fowl's **1681** / Fowle **Bodleian**
37 Paragraphing from **Bodleian**

"A Dialogue . . ."
Bodleian: The amanuensis crossed out the last four lines and wrote "*Desunt multa,*" "Many things are missing." This may have been a guess (if so, a wrong one), or it may have been based on particular knowledge or information or even on a manuscript. Lacking such knowledge or manuscript, we may regard the poem as complete.

"The Nymph Complaining . . ."
119 Legouis suggests that *There* may be a misprint and that *Then* (corresponding to *Until*, 117) would make a better reading.

"To His Coy Mistress"
33 hue 1681 M / glew **Bodleian** / glue **MS Donno**
34 dew **Bodleian Cooke Donno M MS** / lew **M (1927)** / glew **1681 Lord Martz**

This is one of the most famous cruxes in literature. The **1681** read *hue . . . glew*, and many editors have accepted the latter on the grounds that *glew* could be a dialectal variant of *glow* on the analogy *shew : show* and believing that *glew* (meaning "glow") makes better sense in the context than *dew* (see **M, Lord, Martz**). Margoliouth, though he thought that *glew* may have been Marvell's for line 34, found it nonetheless improbable: "The word had its modern sense [of glue] . . . and would therefore be inadmissible in this context"; he emended first to *lew,* "warmth," conjecturing that the *g* was a mistaken repeat of the last letter of the previous word, and then, in the revised edition, to *dew,* the emendation suggested by Cooke in his 1726 edition. (Lewalski and Sabol accept the *lew* reading, without comment.) **Bodleian** emends the **1681** readings, changing *hew* (33) to *glew* and *glew* (34) to *dew*: these readings are followed by **Donno**, who modernizes line 33 to *glue*. In 1970, W. H. Kelleher described another Bodleian manuscript (Don. b. 8), a miscellany in the hand of Sir William Haward, which contains a transcription (1672) of an early version of this poem with the following:

> Now then whil'st ye youthfull Glue
> Stickes on your Cheeke, like Morning Dew,
> *(Notes and Queries*, 215 (1970), 254–56).

In the 3rd Oxford edition, Legouis remarks that "this fact invites us to make Marvell responsible for 'glew,' at least in an earlier version," but Legouis keeps Margoliouth's considered reading, speculating that Marvell "may well not have felt happy about" the word. Margoliouth's original reluctance to accept *glew* as Marvell's final reading seems to me still right.

44 gates **1681** / grates **Bodleian** (**Donno** adopts this reading, but on negative grounds: "the varieties of interpretation . . . indicate a somewhat desperate search for signification.")

"Damon the Mower"
21 mads **Bodleian** / made **1681**
38 dew **Bodleian** / due **1681**
50 unnumb'red / unnumbered **Bodleian** / unnum'red **1681**

"Music's Empire"
5   first **Bodleian** / The word is omitted **1681**

"The Garden"
9   Quiet / quiet **1681**
33   in **1681** / is (conjectured by several editors, beginning with Edward
     Thompson, 1776; the emendation is attractive, but it does not seem
     necessary)
41   pleasure **1681** / pleasures **Bodleian** (adopted by **Donno**, and plausible,
     but not as euphonious as the **1681** reading)

"An Horatian Ode . . ."
This poem was excised from all extant copies of the **1681** except two, the
   British Museum copy and the copy at the Henry Huntington Library.
15   through **1681** / thorough **Bodleian**
25   Kingdom **1681** / kingdoms **Bodleian**
85   *Commons* **Bodleian** / Common **1681**
100   crown **1681** / crowns **Bodleian**

"Upon Appleton House"
22   mote **Bodleian** / Mose **1681**
268   had **Bodleian** / hath **1681**
320   nor **Cooke** / or **1681**
328   thee **Bodleian** / the **1681**
356   earthly **1681** / Earthy **Bodleian**
368   gaze **1681** / graze **Bodleian**
454   beast **Bodleian** / Breast **1681**
472   astonished **Bodleian** / astonish **1681**
609   twines **Bodleian** / 'twines **1681**

HENRY VAUGHAN

The *Silex Scintillans* was first published in 1650, then reissued with the
added second part in 1655. The 1655 edition also includes four reset pages
(Sig. B2 and B3 of the 1650) with substantial variants. Since Vaughan's
major works were printed during his lifetime and under his supervision, his
texts present few problems. In normalizing, I have modified the orthography,
but I have retained the capitalization, italics, and most of the punctuation of
the originals. With only two exceptions, as noted, I have kept the format
of the early editions. Capitalization presented problems, since it seems (and
probably is) erratic, but again and again removing capitals appeared to alter
meaning. Both italics and punctuation are erratic at times, but both contribute
to meaning. I have used the British Museum copy of the 1650 (reproduced
in 1968 by Scholar Press) and the 1655. I have used the excellent modern
editions of L. C. Martin (Oxford, 1957) and French Fogle (New York, 1964;
Norton Library, 1969), but have not attempted to rival them. The notes
record variants but ignore a few obvious errors, which are silently corrected.

ABBREVIATIONS

1650   *Silex Scintillans: or Sacred Poems and Private Ejacula-*
        tions. By Henry Vaughan Silurist. London, 1650.
1655   *Silex Scintillans . . . The second Edition, In two Books; . . .*
        London, 1655.
M   *The Works of Henry Vaughan,* ed. by L. C. Martin. 2nd
        edition, Oxford, 1957.
F   *The Complete Poetry of Henry Vaughan,* ed. by French
        Fogle. New York, 1964.

Silex Scintillans (Part I)

"Regeneration"
17 still (Though there are no great difficulties in interpretation, I suspect that
   Vaughan intended *till*, but that the *s* of *upwards* was accidentally repeated

by the printer. Aurally, *upwards still* and *upwards till* are nearly indistinguishable. The temporal conjunction *till* makes somewhat better sense here, allowing an easier transition to the following clause ["I reach'd"], which is otherwise paratactic—and Vaughan does not seem fond of parataxis. But *still* is not implausible. The fact that *still* occurs twice elsewhere in the poem [lines 1, 63] and that *stillness* is an implicit element supports the original reading.)
48 Earth (emendation suggested by Grosart) / Eare **1650**

"The Search"
89 Dust **1655** / Dust; **1650**

"[Silence and stealth . . .]"
19 snuff (Shawcross and Emma report that the Houghton Library **1650** copy reads "snuft," which they normalize as "snuffed" and interpret as "snuffed beam," i.e., Vaughan's dead brother or the world without spirit. But in my copy the *f* in question looks less like a *t* than like a broken letter. In line 21, they read "unknown," where all other texts read "known.")

"Corruption"
20 *those! / those?* **1650 M F**
26 them; / them, **1650 M F**

"Unprofitableness"
4 shear / share **1650** (It could be a variant spelling of *shear*.)

"The Dawning"
2 *The* / The **1650 M F**
10 bowers, / bowers? **1650 M F**
12 eternity? / eternity; **1650 M F**

"The World"
11 sour / so our **1650**

"Mount of Olives (II)"
Title: "(II)" added

Silex Scintillans (Part II)

"The Timber"
13 if / is **1655**
42 story) / story **1655**

"The Rainbow"
10 Storms / Forms **1655**
26 weather. / weather **1655**

"[As time one day . . .]"
10 Indentation does not follow **1655**.
22 shine, / shine; **1655**
36 blood. / blood **1655**

"The Night"
42 Indentation does not follow **1655**.

"The Waterfall"
16 before, / before. **1655**
26 goes! / goes? **1655 M F**

THOMAS TRAHERNE

Apart from some verses in his prose works, Traherne's poetry was unknown in the seventeenth century. Some poems were discovered and identified by Bertram Dobell at the end of the nineteenth century and first published by Dobell in *The Poetical Works of Thomas Traherne* (London, 1903); the

Dobell Folio is now in the Bodleian (Bodl. MS Engl. Poet. c. 42). A separate collection of poems, including many but not all of the Dobell Folio poems, had been available in Burney MS 392, acquired by the British Museum in 1818 but not noticed until after Dobell's publication. This manuscript, entitled *Poems of Felicity*, was the volume prepared for publication by Philip Traherne, Thomas's brother. In preparing the text, Philip made extensive and usually unfortunate changes; as Margoliouth puts it, "His editing and changing of the text is a disaster" (p. xv). Philip's redaction was published with a misguided introduction by H. I. Bell (Oxford, 1910).

My text follows the manuscript for all but one poem; I have used photocopies kindly loaned me by my colleague Arthur Clements. In all cases, I have checked my own readings against the excellent Oxford English Text edition by H. M. Margoliouth, *Centuries, Poems, and Thanksgivings*, two volumes (1958), with comparison of Anne Ridler's Oxford Standard Authors edition, *Poems, Centuries, and Three Thanksgivings* (1966). Margoliouth includes Philip's versions of the Dobell Folio poems; since he prints these on facing pages, his ordering differs from Miss Ridler's. The editions differ also in choices made when Dobell contains corrections by Thomas of original words: Margoliouth sometimes prefers the original, Miss Ridler rarely does.

I have normalized more extensively than for the other texts. Traherne's conventions, while idiosyncratic, are fairly regular in their idiosyncrasy—e.g., he capitalizes virtually all nouns and many verbs. Rather than guess at levels of emphasis, I have followed modern practice and used lowercase. Perhaps words like *soul* or *eternity* or *nothing* should be capitalized while *diamond* or *ground* are kept in lowercase, but such choices would finally have to be arbitrary. I have capitalized words which Traherne has all in capitals (not a frequent practice), I have not tampered with italicized words, again not frequent, and I have not added capitals. As to punctuation, Traherne's is usually both regular and comprehensible, so few modifications seemed necessary.

In the manuscripts, the orthography is also regular in its idiosyncrasies. Traherne omits final silent *e* most of the time (even, curiously, in words like *celebrate, live, love*)—apparently as part of a deliberate attempt to simplify spelling. (The evidence indicates that the plan was mainly Philip's.) He regularly omits internal silent or elided *e* without signaling the omission (in words like *every, eyes, adorned, seemed*) and usually uses *ie* for *y*, as in *sky* or *vanity*. Thomas's practices are, however, not as regular as Philip's; besides the attempt at simplified spelling (even dropping the final *e* in *true*, for instance), Philip corrects many slips—inserting apostrophes in possessives or emending *ie* to *y* or correcting odd spellings, e.g., *feinds* to *fiends* ("Wonder" 51).

The first eight poems in our text are from the Dobell Folio; the last three are from Philip's manuscript; "On News" is from *The Third Century*. All the poems except "Love" are in Philip's text. In the notes, I have given just a few examples of Philip's meddling. In many cases, Philip apparently first copied Thomas's text, then emended it; wherever possible, incidentally, Margoliouth's edition emended Philip's text and went back to Thomas's. Despite such emendations, however, the texts of the last four poems must be considered suspect.

ABBREVIATIONS

D   Dobell Folio
DT   Thomas's original word(s) in D
F   Philip's manuscript
M   Margoliouth
R   Ridler

"Eden"
13   wights **R** / Weights **D F M**
15–16 **F** reads:

> Joy, Pleasure, Beauty, Kindness, charming Lov,
> Sleep, Life, and Light,

22 **F** reads:

Unwelcom Penitence I then thought not on;

27 briers **DT R** / Thorns **D** (Thomas's correction) **F M**

"The Preparative"

4–8 **F** reads:

Before or Tongue or Cheeks I call'd mine own,
Before I knew these Hands were mine,
Or that my Sinews did my Members join;
When neither Nostril, foot, nor Ear,
As yet could be discern'd, or did appear;

13 Far wider then **DT M** / Just bounded with **D** (Thomas's correction) /
Scarce bounded with **F**

17 **F** reads:

Exceeding that which makes the Days,

21 conceive / perceiv **F**

22 dull / dire **F**

25 fair / tru **F**

26 **F** reads:

The Hony did enjoy without the Stings.

30 **F** reads:

Delighted me that was to be their Heir.

48 els bereave it of **D** (Thomas's correction) / misemploy it from **M**

64 **F** reads:

A quick unprejudic'd Intelligence,

69–70 **F** reads:

My Soul get free,
And then thou may'st possess Felicity.

"My Spirit"

45 soul **DT M** / Heart **D** (Thomas's correction)

51 Were not alone even all that shined. **M** / Were not even all that therein
shind. **D** (Thomas's correction)

54 (So **F** / (so **D M**

56 quick and pure, **D** (Thomas's correction) **F R** / Indivisible, and so
Pure, **DT M**

71 **F** reads:

My Soul a Spirit wide and bright!

79 or Bower of Bliss. **DT M** / of Heavenly Bliss **D** (Thomas's correction)

97–102 **F** reads:

And what it had a Power to see,
On that it always shin'd:
For 'twas a Mind
Exerted, reaching to Infinity:
'Twas not a Sphere; but 'twas a Power
More high and lasting than a Tower.

105 **F** reads:

O Pow'r and Act, *next Infinit,*

"On News"
Text from *The Third Century* (**M**, I, 125–27)

"On Leaping Over the Moon"

3 And / Another (canceled). **M** suggests that Thomas actually wrote:

Another Sun by Day
Did things more clear display.

If so, Philip's change loses the fourfold emphasis (2, 3, 5, 9).

55–56 As first written in **F**; Philip's version:

Then soon should we
Exalted be.

Criticism

ANTHONY LOW

Metaphysical Poets and Devotional Poets

The omission of Donne from this collection offers readers an opportunity to revalue five poets who are often said to belong to his "school" but who were more independent and original than that implies. Two other terms, "Metaphysical" and "devotional," are more immediately helpful.

I

The term "Metaphysical poetry" derives from Dryden's disparaging remark that Donne "affects the metaphysics" with the "fair sex . . . , when he should engage their hearts." Samuel Johnson lent his weight to the phrase in his *Life of Cowley*: "About the beginning of the seventeenth century appeared a race of writers that may be termed the metaphysical poets." Johnson was of two minds about these poets: they were witty and sometimes brilliant, but too often disorderly, perverse, or unclassical. It remained for Grierson and Eliot, early in the twentieth century, to complete the process of recognizing them as a "race" or school and to see them in an almost wholly favorable light.

Recent critics have argued that there is no such thing as a school of Metaphysical poets and that the writers grouped under the name are more different than they are alike. Certainly, each of the writers in this collection has an individual voice. Nonetheless, if we treat "Metaphysical" as a convenient label rather than a strict category, the term can be useful. The major trend in criticism has, in fact, been away from capsule definitions and toward descriptions that elucidate rather than restrict.

One quality often associated with these poets is strength or directness, what some seventeenth-century writers called "masculine expression." Donne's poetry is strong, active, energetic, and concise. He uses a high proportion of verbs and nouns, while keeping adjectives and weaker parts of speech to a minimum. Crashaw often deliberately adapts a passive, receptive role for poetic and devotional reasons of his own, but Herbert, though usually "sweeter" and more lyrical than Donne, is as capable of strength and directness. The powerful conclusion of "Redemption" exemplifies this quality:

> At length I heard a ragged noise and mirth
> Of thieves and murderers: there I him espied,
> Who straight, *Your suit is granted*, said, and died.

Related to "masculine expression" is the abruptness with which Metaphysical poems often begin:

> For Godsake, hold your tongue and let me love.
> (Donne, "The Canonization")

> I struck the board, and cried, No more.
> (Herbert, "The Collar")

> I saw Eternity the other night.
> (Vaughan, "The World")

Crashaw's "Hymn to . . . Saint Teresa" opens more formally—as one would expect from its genre—yet the impact is felt here too:

> Love, thou art absolute sole Lord
> Of life and death.

These openings contribute to the naturalness or familiarity of tone or voice common to Metaphysical poems. Traherne is undramatic but engaging:

> News from a foreign country came.
> ("On News")

Even Crashaw and Marvell, at times the most formal of our poets, can be homely or colloquial:

> The wanton troopers riding by
> Have shot my fawn and it will die.
> (Marvell, "The Nymph Complaining")

Although Herbert consistently views his God as a great king, utterly incommensurable withn his creatures, paradoxically he also writes as if God were his familiar friend, sitting somewhere near the poet's elbow.

T. S. Eliot was among the first to point out how extraordinarly successful the Metaphysical poets were at combining feeling with intellect. Indeed Eliot, followed by more literal-minded disciples, persuaded many people that a "dissociation of sensibility" took place in England later in the seventeenth century, and that ever since that time intellect and feeling have been unhealthily divided. Eliot viewed the Metaphysicals as the last poets (before his time) to write whole poetry out of whole experience. That such a dissociation occurred at any identifiable point in history is now generally doubted; yet Eliot's perception, like the story of a Golden Age in the indefinite past, is useful if one takes it as a critical myth or metaphor. It is certainly true that intellect and feelings have repeatedly tended to dissociate or to become unbalanced in Western literature (and life). Signs of the problem are as evident in Donne's love poetry as anywhere. It is also true that, at their best, the Metaphysicals were able to write a poetry that both thinks and feels, and does so deeply. When Vaughan, for example, evokes the experience or the spiritual vision of childhood innocence in "The Retreat," he bases his poem rigorously on systematic theological concepts and devotional methods. Yet the immediacy of feelings conveyed by the poem has irresistibly reminded readers of Wordsworth's "Ode":

> Happy those early dayes! when I
> Shin'd in my Angell-infancy.
>
> .   .   .   .   .   .
>
> When yet I had not walkt above
> A mile, or two, from my first love,
> And looking back (at that short space,)
> Could see a glimpse of his bright face;
> When on some *gilded Cloud*, or *flowre*
> My gazing soul would dwell an houre,
> And in those weaker glories spy
> Some shadows of eternity. . . .
>
> (lines 1–2, 7–14)

While all the Metaphysical poets emphasize orderly and logical development, most are less likely than Donne to use obtrusive syllogisms or flamboyant sophistries. The logic and the sequential development of Herbert's "Virtue" are impeccable, but also unobtrusive. When, in "The Definition of Love," Marvell's lover speaks like a geometrician, the reader may at least suspect irony. And the syllogism on which "To His Coy Mistress" is based may owe something to Donne's sophistical, insolent, but highly popular tour de force, "The Flea."

Other qualities common in Metaphysical poetry are a sense of drama, a sense of process, and an interest in the inner movements of thoughts and feelings. The poetry of Donne and Marvell especially provided the New Critics of the mid-twentieth century with much material for their view that lyric poetry ought to be read as if it were dramatic. According to this view, one should distinguish between poet and speaker. Thus, when Herbert begins "Denial"

> When my devotions could not pierce
> Thy silent ears;

one should be aware that the speaker is a persona, not necessarily Herbert, and that the poem assumes two audiences: "thou" or God, and the reader. The sense of drama is perhaps strongest in Marvell and Herbert, after Donne:

> Had we but world enough and time,
> This coyness, Lady, were no crime.
>
> (Marvell, "To His Coy Mistress")
>
> When first thou didst entice to thee my heart,
> I thought the service brave.
>
> (Herbert, "Affliction (I)")

But often, the attempt to draw a line between poet and persona becomes an exercise in ingenuity.

Dramatic or not, much Metaphysical poetry is essentially private poetry, that is, poetry that examines and focuses on the inner movements of thought and feeling. The reader sometimes may feel himself an eavesdropper, someone who has accidentally stumbled upon a private scene or overheard a speaker's reflections. In his love poems, Donne insists often that he and his beloved are a microcosm, a little world, from which all else is excluded:

> She is all States, and all Princes, I,
> Nothing else is.
>
> ("The Sun Rising")

Herbert's poems deal mainly with the private relationship of the individual soul to God. According to Izaak Walton, Herbert said that the poems in *The Temple* represent "a picture of the many spiritual conflicts that have past betwixt God and my Soul," and indeed most of his lyrics reflect the complex and subtle processes, changes of attitude, struggles, and surrenders of the inner spiritual life. Crashaw may be less interested in the flux of thought, but his poems typically turn on an inner logic of feelings. Marvell's poetry is perhaps the least private in this sense; nonetheless, in poems as different as "The Garden" and the "Horatian Ode"—the first describing a retreat into the mind, the second a commitment (however reluctant) to political action—Marvell combines objectivity and self-effacement with a pervasive sense of the inner movements and tensions of a complex personality in a way scarcely matched in English poetry until Yeats.

It remains to speak of the most famous attribute of Metaphysical poetry: the conceit. Samuel Johnson spoke of "*discordia concors*" or concordant discord, the "combination of dissimilar images,' and the yoking together by violence of "heterogeneous ideas." George Williamson and others developed Johnson's insights and spoke of two kinds of metaphysical conceit: the extended conceit, comparing two unlike things at great length and with considerable ingenuity, and the telescoped conceit, compressing an unusual combination into a brief space. Donne's comparison of two lovers to a pair of compasses is the standard illustration of the former, and his image of a love token on the skeletal wrist of a defunct lover—"A bracelet of bright haire about the bone"—is an instance of the latter. Few such comparisons are wholly original, however: emblem books, religious iconography, illustrated Bibles, stained-glass windows, and continental literature all provided materials for poets to work with. Yet the successful metaphysical conceit usually gives traditional materials a new twist. Herbert's "The Agony," for example, is based on several iconographic and theological motifs that were widely familiar in his day: the Crucifixion, Christ pictured as a vine or a bunch of grapes, affliction as the wine-press of God, the blood and water from Christ's pierced side as emblems of Holy Communion. What makes "The Agony" a great poem is the way Herbert puts these conventional elements together, freshly and passionately. In particular, the force of the poem derives from his use of the same basic image to embody two opposite abstractions: "Sin" and "Love." This paradox, the basic conceit underlying the poem, is a manifestation of wit but more than mere cleverness, because it underlines a central point in the poem: how closely sin and love are related in this world.

Herbert is known for the often surprising homeliness of his images. "Doomsday" presents us with a picture of the Last Judgment, which at first seems entirely conventional:

> Come away,
> Make no delay.
> Summon all the dust to rise,
> Till it stir, and rub the eyes;
> While this member jogs the other,
> Each one whisp'ring, *Live you brother?*

The scene is based on Ezekiel and the Book of Revelation, though perhaps most familiar to us from Michelangelo's great *Last Judgment* in the Sistine Chapel; but Herbert's tone, his focus, and his poetic insights are all fresh.

The outstanding images in Vaughan's poetry are typically forceful, dynamic, and beautiful. One might think beauty a common characteristic of poetic imagery, but the Metaphysicals tended to use the conventionally beautiful sparingly. On the other hand, Crashaw's images have often been attacked as grotesque or tasteless. Taken out of context they may seem so. The description of Mary Magdalene's tears is a good example:

> Upwards thou dost weep,
> Heavn's bosome drinks the gentle stream.
> Where the milky rivers creep,
> Thine floats above and is the cream.

This is easy to ridicule, yet in its context the image accords perfectly with the poem's affective development. Crashaw's poetry, though firmly underpinned by theology, is essentially a poetry of feeling. Such modern writers as D. H. Lawrence have taught us that Western man might profit if he could feel less inhibitedly. Most Metaphysical poetry encourages the reader both to think and to feel; in Crashaw the thought is subordinated, yet never abandoned.

Marvell is Donne's match as an image maker. He can be brilliant and powerful, as in these famous lines from "To His Coy Mistress":

> But at my back I always hear
> Time's wingèd chariot hurrying near:
> And yonder all before us lie
> Deserts of vast eternity. . . .
> The grave's a fine and private place,
> But none I think do there embrace.

Typically, however, Marvell is cooler and more subtle than Donne. Yet his images are equally memorable. Consider the calm power of these lines, which evoke God's providential care of a paradise amid the waves:

> He gave us this eternal Spring,
> Which here enamels every thing;
> And sends the fowls to us in care,
> On daily visits through the air.
> He hangs in shades the orange bright,
> Like golden lamps in a green night. . . .
> ("Bermudas")

II

Sometimes identifiably "Metaphysical," our five poets are primarily religious—or, more precisely, devotional—poets. Vaughan wrote secular verse which many recent critics admire, but his religious poems are his best and most original work. Crashaw's secular lyrics, such as "Music's Duel," excellent as they are, would hardly be remembered today had he written nothing else. Herbert and Traherne wrote virtually no secular poetry. Like Donne, Marvell created a number of superb secular poems; but, also like Donne, his reputation would be assured had he written only the religious poetry.

Given this predominance of religious poetry, it is striking that these poets should be so consistently popular and influential in our defiantly post-Christian age. Their subject matter, intention, rhetorical strategies, and devotional methods all involve religion. Yet not since the seventeenth century have these poets been so deeply and justly appreciated, so well understood, or so discriminatingly written about as in the last half-century.

The seventeenth century in England saw a great flowering of religious writings of all kinds, from collections of sermons to devotional treatises to polemical tracts. Religious enthusiasm does not, of course, guarantee great poetry, but the climate of the age fostered rapid growth of interest in the methodology of religious devotion. This growth was stimulated by the remarkable outpouring in Europe of great devotional writing: one thinks of Saint Ignatius

Loyola, Teresa of Avila, John of the Cross, and Francis de Sales. In England, the better-known religious writers included Lancelot Andrewes, John Donne, Nicholas Ferrar, Richard Baxter, and Jeremy Taylor. In such a setting, it is no surprise that poets like Herbert, Vaughan, and Traherne should be not only thoroughly learned and technically expert in their craft, but also widely read and deeply literate in theological, religious, and devotional matters. The modern age is likely to think (if it thinks of the matter at all) that devotion should be spontaneous and emotional, but the seventeenth century was apt to think that it should be deliberate and systematic. Until recently, critics of religious poetry were reluctant to recognize that that poetry depends not merely on faith or feeling but also on an elaborate technical system. That is, it requires not just poetic technique but religious and devotional technique.

Among the forms of devotion in use in the seventeenth century, several are of particular interest for the religious poetry: vocal devotion, meditation, and contemplation. Spoken or sung devotion ranged from the liturgical rites of morning and evening prayer and of Holy Communion to cathedral hymnology, and from Latin masses to metrical psalms, which were immensely popular among such groups as the Puritan weavers and other "mechanicks" of London. By nature less introspective than mental prayer, vocal devotion is suited for public use. One might expect for that reason that it would have small influence on the Metaphysical poets, with their obvious bent toward exploring the inner self. Yet such was not the case. Spoken and sung devotions can also be employed privately, and these poets took a considerable interest in the possibility. Donne wrote three hymns, which are among his best and maturest work. Herbert tried his hand at metrical psalmody and composed what appear to be a series of hymns for the church's holy days, which are scattered through *The Temple*. "Easter" is a notable example, whose connections with the musical origins of the hymn form are especially obvious. Vaughan too wrote a series of holy-day hymns, one of the best of which is "Ascension Day." Crashaw wrote a whole series of brilliant hymns, of which the best known is "In the Holy Nativity."

These poems are characterized by an emphasis on sound or on various musical effects. In accordance with the musical theory of the day, going back to Monteverdi but successfully exploited by a succession of major English composers, the "music" of this poetry is in tune with and broadly reinforces the emotional development. Consider, for instance, Vaughan's "The Morning Watch," Marvell's "Bermudas," and Herbert's "Sunday." How such poems might be put to actual use is glimpsed in an incident described by

Izaak Walton, who states that Herbert got up from his sickbed to sing a verse of "Sunday," accompanying himself on the viol. It was the last Sunday of his life.

While vocal devotion is reflected in the sounds or rhythms of many poems, the tradition of meditation is at least as pervasive. Meditation was a highly developed art in the seventeenth century, thanks largely to the numerous treatises which instructed readers. The *Spiritual Exercises* of Ignatius Loyola, though the best known, was only one of many such books. Our understanding of the technical methodology underlying meditation and its relevance for seventeenth-century poetry has been greatly enhanced by Louis Martz in *The Poetry of Meditation* (1954); in this important book, Professor Martz shows how the poetry of Donne, Herbert, Vaughan, and others is influenced by the meditative tradition.

As a form of devotion, meditation involves thought, imagination, and feelings. One meditates by first choosing a topic: a scene from the Bible, for example, such as the Annunciation or the Crucifixion, or an object in nature, or one of the Four Last Things: death, judgment, hell, and heaven. With the aid of the imagination (the faculty of mind that forms and manipulates images) and the reason, this topic is then fleshed out and analyzed. Two of the common methods for doing this were called "composition of place" and "composition by similitude." Composition of place means that a scene is made mentally real by imagining it in detail. For example, to meditate on the Crucifixion, one might picture the hill of Golgotha, Jerusalem in the background, the three crosses, soldiers dicing and cursing, and so on. The meditator may make the scene still more vivid by putting himself in it. All five of the senses might be employed. Composition by similitude means taking an abstraction—death, love, sin—and making it more powerful imaginatively by embodying it in a concrete image or metaphor. Thus a seventeenth-century poet meditates on death, not as an abstraction, but as a skull picked up and touched (*Hamlet*) or a bouquet of flowers that wither in a man's hand even as he admires them (Herbert's "Life"). The end products of meditation are emotions and resolutions, raised up in the course of the exercise: hatred of sin, fear of dying and damnation, resolutions to amend one's life, gratitude and love toward God.

It will already be obvious that, in its combination of reason, imagination, and feelings, meditation is a close cousin of poetry, and especially of Metaphysical poetry. The two cooperate readily. Donne was the greatest of the meditative poets, but Herbert too, when he wished to be, was an accomplished practitioner of the form. "The Agony" is a composition by similitude, which uses the same image to give body and emotional force to two abstractions, sin and love. "The Pilgrimage" is a vivid embodiment of man's spiritual journey through life. "The Collar" captures and actualizes a moment of spiritual conflict. "Death," "Doomsday," and "Judgement" are meditations, in Herbert's inimitable style, on the Last Things: preparations, it would seem, for the soul's entry into heaven that is described in "Love (III)."

Crashaw modifies meditative techniques noticeably. In his logic of the emotions, compositions of place are fragmented and distorted, as if in a Mannerist or a Baroque painting. As Donne seems determined to shock—"Batter my Heart" calls on God to ravish the speaker—so Crashaw seems to play upon our sense of embarrassment or our fear of bad taste. Vaughan was proficient in meditation, but his two poems that employ it most effectively, "The Search" and "Vanity of Spirit," in the end reject it in favor of contemplation, gernerally considered the highest form of devotion and linked to mystical prayer.

Mysticism fell into ill repute in England because the Reformers mistrusted any way of life not directed toward actively doing good in the world. At the same time, the dissolution of the monasteries removed the institutional base of mysticism and furnished political reasons for suspecting it. As a result, while the seventeenth century saw a considerable resurgence of mysticism on the continent, such movements found little support in the Anglican church. Yet several English poets can be fully understood only in the light of the contemplative or mystical traditions.

Briefly, the two primary marks of mystical prayer are direct experience of God and passivity. The individual may prepare himself in various ways for contemplation (for example, by meditating), but the initiative must come from God. Another mark of contemplation is that it is imageless, which differentiates it, in this respect, from meditation. Mystics agree that their prayer is indescribable save in such terms as nothingness, darkness, or unknowing, or by certain traditional systems of indirect metaphor. While a poem may imitate the actual process of meditation, with its twists and turns and developments, contemplation can be described only from the outside and after the fact. The poet is forced to speak of past experience, already completed and difficult to recapture. The dramatic presentation of an ongoing process, so characteristic of poets like Donne and Herbert, necessarily gives way to a more Wordsworthian method. The poet remembers his past, and insofar as he can, recreates it.

From time to time Crashaw appears to soar out of an intense evocation of the senses and feelings into a kind of mystical ecstasy (the word's root meaning is a going-out of the soul). The conclusion of "The Flaming Heart" is a well-known example. But England's chief poet of mysticism is Henry Vaughan. Interpretations of "Regeneration," the important opening poem of *Silex Scintillans*, vary. The poem may be read simply as a theological statement, to the effect that a man cannot earn salvation, which comes to whom God chooses as free gift of his grace. But "Regeneration" is more than theological description. The opening stanzas are a meditation. In a composition by similitude, Vaughan compares the speaker's spiritual progress, in one of his favorite images, to a journey or search. After a hard climb to a mountain peak, from which further progress is impossible, the protagonist discovers he has failed. Suddenly, however, voices intervene from outside, and the speaker is miraculously translated into a new country and a new time of year. Activity yields to passivity. In the last stanzas the poet is led through a series of visions, full of imagery which the mystical tradition had taken from the Song of Songs. The conclusion points toward a mysterious death much like the mystical death Crashaw evokes in the Teresa poems. From the devotional point of view, the poem imitates a transition from meditation to contemplation.

Not all of Vaughan's poems are mystical. Perhaps "The Night" is his most purely contemplative poem, and one of the century's most remarkable poetic achievements. Through nearly all of Vaughan's religious poems, however, there runs some trace of mystical experience. Thus "Cock-crowing," on the theme that man's soul contains a divine spark that corresponds to the eternal day of heaven from which he is exiled, expresses an old philosophical idea, but with such conviction and feeling that experience, not philosophy, seems to energize the poem. And the opening lines of "The World," which contrast the perfect light of eternity with time's dark shadows and insubstantiality, portray eternity so vividly and apparently experientially that critic after critic has been unwilling to leave the first stanza in order to look at the poem as a whole (and it is a carefully crafted whole). Vaughan has often been called a nature mystic, and though this vague term is somewhat suspect, it is also apt. Meditation on the creatures—that is, on God's created nature or natural objects—was a common method of devotion. Herbert uses it in "Life," and Vaughan in "The Waterfall." But as often as not, it would be more accurate to say that Vaughan contemplates the creatures, and in doing so goes beyond them or transcends them, seeing eternity in a grain of sand. The same may be said of Marvell in "On a Drop of Dew."

In the corpus of Marvell's poetry, no distinct line can be drawn between the religious and the secular verse. Unlike Herbert, who repudiates secular poetry in the two "Jordan" poems, or Vaughan, who does the same in his preface to *Silex Scintillans*, Marvell moves comfortably back and forth between the two realms. In this he differs from the usual practice of the Metaphysicals but resembles a friend and contemporary, John Milton. The result of Marvell's inclusiveness is to bring religion into contact with the world, with politics, and with love. His is a sensibility that balances, reconciles, and unifies disparate experience.

Traherne is the most special of these five poets. One might think him the least of the five, yet his poetry has a tremendous attraction for some readers and inspires fierce loyalty among scholars. As a religious Metaphysical poet, Traherne shares many qualities with his fellows (his poems when first discovered were mistaken for Vaughan's), but he is *sui generis*, a unique figure. His "system," like the major metaphors in which he expresses it, is quite different from Vaughan's, as are many of his basic preoccupations.

Traherne's poems assume a traditional Christian view of the history of man as passing through four stages: original innocence, a fall into guilt and sin, redemption through Christ, and (after judgment) glory. There is a corresponding pattern in the individual's life. He begins in a state of innocence and wonder, falls into corruption when he learns to speak, which is an outward sign of reason and volition, but through these same powers has the ability to cooperate with grace in a conversion to a new state of innocence. As in Wordsworth, so in Traherne, the individual's fall from childhood bliss seems partly to involve the loss of a happy unself-consciousness. But it is also due to the corruption of the growing child by society or his parents, who divert him from a true appreciation of God's creation to a preoccupation with toys, baubles, and objects whose value is purely artificial. A selfish desire to possess and to own things exclusively is at the root of this corruption. The mature man is reformed and converted when he learns to recapture his childhood vision of nature, to value things rightly, and to own them not by exclusive possession but by right appreciation. The pattern of innocence-fall-redemption is based on traditional ideas—the same pattern in miniature informs Herbert's "Easter Wings" and Vaughan's "The Retreat"—but Traherne's accomplishment is to portray it in terms of his own personal experience and through his own combinations of imagery.

Complementing this Christian orientation in Traherne's poetry is his overriding concern with what he variously calls pleasure, joy, bliss, happiness, infinite treasure, or felicity. A student of philosophy, he takes with utmost seriousness the ancient philosophical premise that the ultimate end or purpose of man is happiness. The problem, of course, is to determine what makes man truly happy. Traherne's conclusion is that, since man is a creature of infinite desires and wants, only infinite treasures, worlds piled on worlds, with infinite duration, can satisfy him. Traherne's devotional method anticipates Blake. An individual should not suppress his desires, but stir them up, widen and raise them, refuse to accept any limitation on them. Finally, only one thing can satisfy the insatiable soul: an infinite God of infinite generosity. At the heart of Traherne's poetry is a mystical egotism, which obliterates selfishness by giving rein to the self.

III

How far each poet in this collection is Metaphysical or devotional, or what Metaphysical and devotional techniques each employs, are matters which (beyond brief illustration) are best left to the reader. One might say that Herbert as a Metaphysical poet is dramatic, logical, and colloquial, among other things, and as a devotional poet excels in meditation and song; that Crashaw is forceful and unusually ingenious and modifies meditation to favor the emotions; that Vaughan develops process into prosodic dynamism and excels in portraying mystical experience; that Traherne moves privateness toward Romantic self-concern and develops a more personal kind of mysticism; or that Marvell balances Metaphysical with classical and retreats from pure devotion to mixed modes; but there are exceptions to all such rules. As noted earlier, it is preferable not to prescribe: to let each poem speak for itself.

SAMUEL TAYLOR COLERIDGE

[Letters] †

* * * I find more substantial comfort, now, in pious George Herbert's 'Temple,' which I used to read to amuse myself with his quaintness—in short, only to laugh at—than in all the poetry since the poems of Milton. If you have not read Herbert, I can recommend the book to you confidently. The poem entitled 'The Flower,' is especially affecting; and, to me, such a phrase as, 'and relish versing,' expresses a sincerity, a reality, which I would unwillingly exchange for the more dignified, 'and once more love the Muse,' &c. And so with many other of Herbert's homely phrases.

* * *

March 18, 1826

My dear old Friend, Charles Lamb, and I differ widely * * * in our estimation & liking of George Herbert's Sacred Poems. He

---

† From *Collected Letters . . .* , ed. Earl Leslie Griggs (Oxford, 1956—), letters 1159 and 1524. Coleridge owned a copy of the 1674 edition of Herbert's poems, which he annotated; the copy is now at the New York Public Library. In his notebooks, he quotes from *The Temple* often—e.g., "Vanity (I)," "Death," "Doomsday," "Jordan (I)." In a quote from the end of "Employment (II),"— "So we freeze on, / Until the grave increase our cold."—he makes a startling emendation, changing "increase" to "compleat." See volumes III–IV of *The Notebooks of Samuel Taylor Coleridge,* ed. Kathleen Coburn (Princeton, 1973). See also Coleridge's *Biographia Literaria,* chapters 19–20.

greatly prefers Quarles[1]—nay, he *dis*likes Herbert—But if Herbert had only written the two following stanzas[2]—& there are a hundred other that in one mood or other of my mind have impressed me—I should be grateful for the possession of his works—. The stanzas are especially affecting to me, because the folly of over-valuing myself in any reference to my future lot is *not* the sin or danger that besets me—but a tendency to self-contempt, a sense of the utter disproportionateness of all I can call *me*, to the promises of the Gospel— *this* is *my* sorest temptation. The *promises*, I say: not to the *Threats*. For in order to the fulfilment of these, it needs only, that I should be left to myself—to sink into the chaos & lawless productivity of my own still-perishing yet imperishable Nature—Now in this temptation I have received great comfort from the following Dialogue between the Soul & it's Redeemer—* * *

ALDOUS HUXLEY
[The Inner Weather]†

* * *

The climate of the mind is positively English in its variableness and instability. Frost, sunshine, hopeless drought and refreshing rains succeed one another with bewildering rapidity. Herbert is the poet of this inner weather. Accurately, in a score of lyrics unexcelled for flawless purity of diction and appositeness of imagery, he has described its changes and interpreted, in terms of a mystical philosophy, their significance. Within his limits he achieves a real perfection.

* * *

W. H. AUDEN
[Anglican George Herbert]†

* * *

* * * His poetry is the counterpart of Jeremy Taylor's prose:[1] together they are the finest expression we have of Anglican piety at

---

1. Francis Quarles (1592–1644), Herbert's contemporary, best known for his *Emblems*, religious poems accompanying symbolic pictorial representations. [*Editor.*]
2. The text was apparently from Herbert's "Dialogue"; the following page is missing from Coleridge's manuscript. [*Editor.*]
† From *Texts and Pretexts* (New York, 1932), p. 13.

† From *George Herbert: Selected by W. H. Auden* (London, 1973), pp. 10–13.
1. Jeremy Taylor (1613–67), celebrated preacher, chaplain to King Charles I, and bishop; noted for the simplicity, lucidity, vigor, and splendor of his devotional writings, especially *The Rule and Exercise of Holy Living* (1650) and *The Rule . . . of Holy Dying* (1651). [*Editor.*]

its best. Donne, though an Anglican, is, both in his poems and his sermons, much too much of a *prima donna* to be typical.

Comparing the Anglican Church with the Roman Catholic Church on the one hand and the Calvinist on the other, Herbert writes: [Quotes "The British Church," lines 7–24; see pp. 44–45.] Herbert, it will be noticed, says nothing about differences in theological dogma. The Anglican Church has always avoided strict dogmatic definitions. The Thirty-Nine Articles, for example, can be interpreted either in a Calvinist or a non-Calvinist sense, and her Office of Holy Communion can be accepted both by Zwinglians[2] who regard it as a service of Commemoration only, and by those who believe in the Real Presence. Herbert is concerned with liturgical manners and styles of piety. In his day, Catholic piety was typically baroque, both in architecture and in poets like Crashaw. This was too unrestrained for his taste. On the other hand, he found the style of worship practised by the Reformed Churches too severe, too 'inward'. He would have agreed with Launcelot Andrewes[3] who said: 'If we worship God with our hearts only and not also with our hats, something is lacking.' The Reformers, for instance, disapproved of all religious images, but Herbert thought that, on occasions, a stained-glass window could be of more spiritual help than a sermon.

> Doctrine and life, colours and light, in one
> When they combine and mingle, bring
> A strong regard and aw; but speech alone
> Doth vanish like a flaring thing,
> And in the eare, not conscience ring.[4]

Walton tells us that he took enormous pains to explain to his parishioners, most of whom were probably illiterate, the significance of every ritual act in the liturgy, and to instruct them in the meaning of the Church Calendar. He was not a mystic like Vaughan: few Anglicans have been. One might almost say that Anglican piety at its best, as represented by Herbert, is the piety of a gentleman, which means, of course, that at its second best it becomes merely genteel.

As a Christian, he realized that his own style of poetry had its spiritual dangers:

> . . . Is there in truth no beautie?
> Is all good structure in a winding stair?

2. Followers of the Swiss Reformer Ulrich Zwingli (1484–1531), who emphasized a purely symbolic interpretation of the Eucharist, denying every form of the physical presence of Christ in the Eucharist. [*Editor.*]

3. Launcelot Andrewes (1555–1626), famous preacher, bishop of Chichester, Ely, and Winchester, and one of the leaders among the translators who made the King James (or Authorized) Version of the Bible. [*Editor.*]

4. "The Windows." [*Editor.*]

5. "Jordan (I)". [*Editor.*]

But as a poet he knew that he must be true to his sensibility, that all he could do was to wash his sweet phrases and lovely metaphors with his tears and bring them

> to church well drest and clad:
> My God must have my best, even all I had.[6]

He is capable of writing lines of a Dante-esque directness. For example:

> Man stole the fruit, but I must climb the tree,
> The Tree of Life to all but only Me.[7]

But as a rule he is more ingenious, though never, I think, obscure.

> Each thing is full of dutie:
> Waters united are our navigation;
> Distinguished, our habitation;
> Below, our drink; above, our meat;
> Both are our cleanlinesse. Hath one such beautie?
> Then how are all things neat?[8]

He is capable of clever antitheses which remind one of Pope, as when, speaking of a woman's love of pearls for which some diver has risked his life, he says:

> Who with excessive pride
> Her own destruction and his danger wears.[9]

And in a most remarkable sonnet, 'Prayer,' he seems to foreshadow Mallarmé.[1]

> Church-bels beyond the starres heard, the souls bloud,
> The land of spices; something understood.

Wit he had in abundance. Take, for example, 'The Church-Porch'. Its subject matter is a series of moral maxims about social behaviour. One expects to be utterly bored but, thanks to Herbert's wit, one is entertained. Thus, he takes the commonplace maxim, 'Don't monopolize the conversation,' and turns it into:

> If thou be Master-gunner, spend not all
> That thou canst speak, at once; but husband it,
> And give men turns of speech: do not forestall
> By lavishnesse thine own, and others wit,
> As if thou mad'st thy will. A civil guest
> Will no more talk all, then eat all the feast.

A good example of his technical skill is the poem 'Denial'. He was, as we know, a skilled musician, and I am sure he got the idea

6. "The Forerunners." [*Editor.*]
7. "The Sacrifice." [*Editor.*]
8. "Man." [*Editor.*]
9. "Vanity." [*Editor.*]

1. Stephane Mallarmé (1842–1898), leading French Symbolist poet, whose work is often musical, evocative, and obscure.

for the structure of this poem from his musical experience of dis-
cords and resolving them. * * * This poem and many others also
show Herbert's gift for securing musical effects by varying the
length of the lines in a stanza. Of all the so-called 'metaphysical'
poets he has the subtlest ear. As George Macdonald said of him:

> The music of a poem is its meaning in sound as distinguished
> from word . . . The sound of a verse is the harbinger of the truth
> contained in it . . . Herein Herbert excels. It will be found impos-
> sible to separate the music of his words from the music of the
> thought which takes shape in their sound.

And this was Coleridge's estimate:

> George Herbert is a true poet, but a poet *sui generis*,[2] the
> merits of whose poems will never be felt without a sympathy
> with the mind and character of the man.

My own sympathy is unbounded.

T. S. ELIOT

[George Herbert as Religious Poet]†

The poems on which George Herbert's reputation is based are
those constituting the collection called *The Temple*. About *The
Temple* there are two points to be made. The first is that we cannot
date the poems exactly. Some of them may be the product of careful re-writing. We cannot take them as being necessarily in chronological order: they have another order, that in which Herbert wished
them to be read. *The Temple* is in fact, a structure, and one which
may have been worked over and elaborated, perhaps at intervals of
time, before it reached its final form. We cannot judge Herbert, or
savour fully his genius and his art, by any selection to be found in
an anthology; we must study *The Temple* as a whole.

To understand Shakespeare we must acquaint ourselves with all
of his plays; to understand Herbert we must acquaint ourselves with
all of *The Temple*. Herbert is, of course, a much slighter poet than
Shakespeare; nevertheless he may justly be called a major poet. Yet
even in anthologies he has for the most part been underrated. In Sir
Arthur Quiller-Couch's *Oxford Book of English Verse*, which was
for many years unchallenged in its representative character, George
Herbert was allotted five pages—the same number as Bishop King
and much less than Robert Herrick, the latter of whom, most critics

2. Unique, of its own kind. [*Editor.*]   *Their Work* (London, 1962), pp. 15–25.
† From *George Herbert: Writers and*

of to-day would agree, is a poet of very much slighter gifts. For poetic range Herbert was commonly considered more limited than Donne; and for intensity he was compared unfavourably with Crashaw. This is the view even of Professor Grierson, to whom we are greatly indebted for his championship of Donne and those poets whose names are associated with that of Donne.

And here we must exercise caution in our interpretation of the phrase 'the school of Donne'. The present writer once contemplated writing a book under that title; and lately the title has been used by a distinguished younger critic for a study covering the same ground. The phrase is legitimate and useful to designate that generation of men younger than Donne whose work is obviously influenced by him, but we must not take it as implying that those poets who experienced his influence were for that reason lesser poets. (Professor Grierson, indeed, seems to consider Andrew Marvell the greatest, greater even than Donne.) That Herbert learned directly from Donne is self-evident. But to think of 'the school of Donne', otherwise 'the metaphysical poets', as Donne's inferiors, or to try to range them on a scale of greatness, would be to lose our way. What is important is to apprehend the particular virtue, the unique flavour of each one. Comparing them with any other group of poets at any other period, we observe the characteristics which they share: when we compare them with each other, their differences emerge clearly.

Let us compare a poem by Donne with a poem by Herbert; and as Herbert's poetry deals always with religious matter, we shall compare two religious sonnets. First, Donne:

> Batter my heart, three person'd God; for, you
> As yet but knocke, breathe, shine, and seeke to mend;
> That I may rise, and stand, o'erthrow mee', and bend
> Your force, to breake, blowe, burn and make me new.
> I, like an usurpt towne, to'another due,
> Labour to 'admit you, but Oh, to no end,
> Reason your viceroy in mee, mee should defend,
> But is captiv'd, and proves weake or untrue.
> Yet dearely' I love you,' and would be loved faine,
> But am betroth'd unto your enemie:
> Divorce mee, 'untie, or break that knot againe;
> Take mee to you, imprison mee, for I
> Except you 'enthrall mee, never shall be free,
> Nor ever chast, except you ravish mee.

And here is George Herbert: [Quotes "Prayer (I)"; see pp. 21–22.] The difference that I wish to emphasize is not that between the violence of Donne and the gentle imagery of Herbert, but rather a difference between the dominance of intellect over sensibility and the dominance of sensibility over intellect. Both men were highly intellectual, both men had very keen sensibility: but in Donne thought seems in control of feeling, and in Herbert feeling seems in control of thought. Both men were learned, both men were accustomed to preaching—but not to the same type of congregation. In Donne's religious verse, as in his sermons, there is much more of the *orator*: whereas Herbert, for all that he had been successful as Public Orator of Cambridge University, has a much more intimate tone of speech. We do not know what Herbert's sermons were like; but we can conjecture that in addressing his little congregation of rustics, all of whom he knew personally, and many of whom must have received both spiritual and material comfort from him and from his wife, he adopted a more homely style. Donne was accustomed to addressing large congregations (one is tempted to call them 'audiences') out of doors at Paul's Cross, Herbert only the local congregation of a village church.

The difference which I have in mind is indicated even by the last two lines of each sonnet. Donne's

> . . . for I
> Except you 'enthrall me, never shall be free,
> Nor ever chast, unless you ravish mee

is, in the best sense, *wit*. Herbert's

> Church-bels beyond the starres heard, the souls bloud,
> The land of spices; something understood.

is the kind of poetry which, like

> magic casements, opening on the foam
> Of perilous seas, in faery lands forlorn

may be called *magical*.

* * * Herbert, before becoming Rector of Bemerton, had never been a recluse: he had, in his short life, wide acquaintance in the great world, and he enjoyed a happy marriage. Yet it was only in the Faith, in hunger and thirst after godliness, in his self-questioning and his religious meditation, that he was inspired as a poet. If there is another example since his time of a poetic genius so dedicated to God, it is that of Gerard Hopkins. We are certainly justified in presuming that no other subject-matter than that to which he confined himself could have elicited great poetry from George Herbert. Whether we regard this as a limitation, or as the sign of solitary greatness, of a unique contribution to English poetry, will depend upon our sensibility to the themes of which he writes.

It would, however, be a gross error to assume that Herbert's poems are of value only for Christians—or, still more narrowly, only for members of his own church. For the practising Christian, it is true, they may be aids to devotion. When I claim a place for Herbert among those poets whose work every lover of English poetry should read and every student of English poetry should study, irrespective of religious belief or unbelief, I am not thinking primarily of the exquisite craftmanship, the extraordinary metrical virtuosity, or the verbal felicities, but of the *content* of the poems which make up *The Temple*. These poems form a record of spiritual struggle which should touch the feeling, and enlarge the understanding of those readers also who hold no religious belief and find themselves unmoved by religious emotion. * * *[1]

* * * As such, it should be a document of interest to all those who are curious to understand their fellow men; and as such, I regard it as a more important document than all of Donne's *religious* poems taken together.

On the other hand, I find Herbert to be closer in spirit to Donne than is any other of 'the school of Donne'. As the personal bond, through Lady Herbert, was much closer, this seems only natural. Other powerful literary influences formed the manner of Crashaw, the Roman Catholic convert: the Italian poet Marino and the Spanish poet Gongora, and, we are told,[2] the Jesuit poets who wrote in Latin. Vaughan and Traherne were poets of mystical experience: each appears to have experienced early in life some mystical illumination which inspires his poetry. And the other important poet of the 'metaphysical' school, Andrew Marvell, is a master of secular and religious poetry equally. In my attempt to indicate the affinity of Herbert to Donne, and also the difference between them, I have spoken earlier of a 'balance' between the intellect and the sensibility. But equally well (for one has recourse to diverse and even mutually contradictory metaphors and images to express the inexpressible) we can speak of a 'fusion' of intellect and sensibility in different proportions. In the work of a later generation of 'metaphysicals'—notably Cleveland, Benlowes and Cowley[3]—we encounter a kind of emotional drought, and a verbal ingenuity which, having no great depth of feeling to work upon, tends towards cor-

1. Eliot here cites L. C. Knights' comments; see below. [*Editor*.]
2. By Mario Praz, whose *Seicentismo e marinismo in Inghilterra* is essential for the study of Crashaw in particular. [Praz's book, published 1925, studies the impact in England of early seventeenth-century European trends which are sometimes called *baroque*. Two of these are Marinism, named after Giambattista Marino (1569–1625), noted for flamboyant style, extravagant imagery, and conceptual ingenuity, and Gongorism, named after Don Luis de Gongora (1561–1627), who prized affected diction and difficult expression.—*Editor*.]
3. John Cleveland (1613–58); Edward Benlowes (1605–76); Abraham Cowley (1618–67). [*Editor*.]

ruption of language, and merits the censure which Samuel Johnson applies indiscriminately to all the 'school of Donne'.[4]

* * *

I have called upon Mr. Knights's testimony in evidence that Herbert is not a poet whose work is significant only for Christian readers; that *The Temple* is not to be taken as simply a devotional handbook of meditation for the faithful, but as the personal record of a man very conscious of weakness and failure, a man of intellect and sensibility who hungered and thirsted after righteousness. And that by its *content*, as well as because of its technical accomplishment, it is a work of importance for every lover of poetry. This is not, however, to suggest that it is unprofitable for us to study the text for closer understanding, to acquaint ourselves with the liturgy of the Church, with the traditional imagery of the Church, and identify the Biblical allusions. One long poem which has been subjected to close examination is 'The Sacrifice'. There are sixty-three stanzas of three lines each, sixty-one of which have the refrain 'Was ever grief like Mine?' I mention this poem, which is a very fine one, and not so familiar as are some of the shorter and more lyrical pieces, because it has been carefully studied by Professor William Empson in his *Seven Types of Ambiguity*, and by Miss Rosamund Tuve in her *A Reading of George Herbert*. The lines are to be taken as spoken by Christ upon the Cross. We need, of course, enough acquaintance with the New Testament to recognise references to the Passion. But we are also better prepared if we recognise the Lamentations of Jeremiah, and the Reproaches in the Mass of the Presanctified which is celebrated on Good Friday.

> *Celebrant:* I led thee forth out of Egypt, drowning Pharaoh in the Red Sea: and thou hast delivered me up unto the chief priests.
> *Deacon & Subdeacon:* O my people, what have I done unto thee, or wherein have I wearied thee? Testify against me.

It is interesting to note that Mr. Empson and Miss Tuve differ in their interpretation of the following stanza:

> O all ye who passe by, behold and see;
> Man stole the fruit, but I must climbe the tree;
> The tree of life to all, but onely me:
> > Was ever grief like mine?

Mr. Empson comments: 'He climbs the tree to repay what was stolen, as if he were putting the apple back'; and develops this

---

4. In his *Life of Cowley*, Dr. Johnson attacked the "Metaphysical poets" for what he considered their penchant for yoking together, by violence, the "most heterogeneous ideas," for their addiction to extravagant conceits and far-fetched imagery, and for their determination to involve the intellect in poetry. [*Editor.*]

explanation at some length. Upon this interpretation Miss Tuve observes rather tartly: 'All (Mr. Empson's) rabbits roll out of one small hat—the fact that Herbert uses the time honoured 'climb' for the ascent of the Cross, and uses the word 'must', to indicate a far deeper necessity than that which faces a small boy under a big tree.' Certainly, the image of *replacing* the apple which has been plucked is too ludicrous to be entertained for a moment. It is obvious that Christ 'climbs' or is 'lifted' up on the Cross in atonement for the sin of Adam and Eve; the verb 'climb' being used traditionally to indicate the *voluntary* nature of the sacrifice for the sins of the world. Herbert was, assuredly, familiar with the imagery used by the pre-Reformation Church. It is likely also that Donne, learned in the works of the scholastics, and also in the writings of such Roman theologians contemporary with himself as Cardinal Bellarmine, set a standard of scholarship which Herbert followed.

To cite such an instance as this, however, is not to suggest that the lover of poetry needs to prepare himself with theological and liturgical knowledge *before* approaching Herbert's poetry. That would be to put the cart before the horse. With the appreciation of Herbert's poems, as with all poetry, enjoyment is the beginning as well as the end. We must enjoy the poetry before we attempt to penetrate the poet's mind; we must enjoy it before we understand it, if the attempt to understand it is to be worth the trouble. We begin by enjoying poems, and lines in poems, which make an immediate impression; only gradually, as we familiarise ourselves with the whole work, do we appreciate *The Temple* as a coherent sequence of poems setting down the fluctuations of emotion between despair and bliss, between agitation and serenity, and the discipline of suffering which leads to peace of spirit.

The relation of enjoyment to belief—the question whether a poem has more to give us if we share the beliefs of its author, is one which has never been answered satisfactorily: the present writer has made some attempt to contribute to the solution of the problem, and remains dissatisfied with his attempts. But one thing is certain: that even if the reader enjoys a poem more fully when he shares the beliefs of the author, he will miss a great deal of possible enjoyment and of vaulable experience if he does not seek the fullest understanding possible of poetry in reading which he must 'suspend his disbelief'. * * *

* * * The great danger, for the poet who would write religious verse, is that of setting down what he would like to feel rather than be faithful to the expression of what he really feels. Of such pious insincerity Herbert is never guilty. We need not look too narrowly for a steady progress in Herbert's religious life, in an attempt to discover a chronological order. He falls, and rises again. Also, he was

accustomed to working over his poems; they may have circulated in manuscript among his intimates during his lifetime. What we can confidently believe is that every poem in the book is true to the poet's experience. * * *

L. C. KNIGHTS

[George Herbert: Resolution and Conflict] †

The poetry of George Herbert is so intimately bound up with his beliefs as a Christian and his practice as a priest of the Church of England that those who enjoy the poetry without sharing the beliefs may well feel some presumption in attempting to define the human, as distinguished from the specifically Christian, value of his work. The excuse for such an attempt can only be the conviction that there is much more in Herbert's poetry for readers of *all* kinds than is recognized in the common estimate. That his appeal is a wide one is implicit in the accepted claim that he is a poet and not simply a writer of devotional verse; but I think I am right in saying that discussion of him tends to take for granted that admirers are likely to be drawn from a smaller circle than admirers of, say, Donne or Marvell. Even Dr. Hutchinson, whose superbly edited and annotated edition of the complete Works is not likely to be superseded[1]—it would be difficult to imagine a better qualified editor and introducer—even Dr. Hutchinson remarks that, 'if to-day there is a less general sympathy with Herbert's religion, the beauty and sincerity of its expression are appreciated by those who do not share it'. True; but there is also much more than the 'expression' that we appreciate, as I shall try to show. Herbert's poetry is an integral part of the great English tradition.

* * *

Herbert's message to Nicholas Ferrar when, a few weeks before his death, he sent him the manuscript of *The Temple*, is well known.

> Sir, I pray deliver this little book to my dear brother Ferrar, and tell him he shall find in it a picture of the many spiritual conflicts that have passed betwixt God and my soul, before I could subject mine to the will of Jesus my Master; in whose service I have now found perfect freedom; desire him to read it: and then, if he can think it may turn to the advantage of any dejected poor

† From *Explorations* (London, 1946), pp. 112, 121–30.
1. *The Works of George Herbert,* edited with a commentary by F. E. Hutchinson (Oxford University Press). Dr. Hutchinson's essay on Herbert in *Seventeenth-Century Studies Presented to Sir Herbert Grierson* should also be consulted.

soul, let it be made public; if not let him burn it; for I and it are less than the least of God's mercies.

Herbert's poetry was for him very largely a way of working out his conflicts. But it does not, like some religious poetry, simply *express* conflict; it is consciously and steadily directed towards resolution and integration. Dr. Hutchinson rightly describes the poems as 'colloquies of the soul with God or self-communings which seek to bring order into that complex personality of his which he analyses so unsparingly'.

This general account of conflict and resolution as the stuff of Herbert's poetry is, I believe, commonly accepted. But the conflict that gets most—indeed almost exclusive—attention is the struggle between the ambitious man of the world and the priest. Dr. Hutchinson rightly insists that Herbert's conflict of mind was not simply about the priesthood, that his spiritual struggle 'was over the more general issue of his submission to the Divine will' (p. lxviii); but he elsewhere records the opinion that 'his principal temptation, the "one cunning bosome-sin" which is apt to break through all his fences, is ambition'.[2] Now it would certainly be unwise to underestimate Herbert's worldly ambitions, or the severity of the struggle that took place in one 'not exempt from passion and choler', who liked fine clothes and good company, before he could renounce his hopes of courtly preferment and, finally, become a country parson. But it seems to me that if we focus all our attention there, seeing the struggle simply as one between 'ambition' and 'renunciation', we ignore some even more fundamental aspects of Herbert's self-division and at the same time obscure the more general relevance of his experience. Most criticism of the poet tends to suggest that we are simply watching someone else's conflict—sympathetic, no doubt, but not intimately involved ourselves.

Behind the more obvious temptation of 'success' was one more deeply rooted—a dejection of spirit that tended to make him regard his own life, the life he was actually leading, as worthless and unprofitable. Part of the cause was undoubtedly persistent ill-health. 'For my self,' he said, 'I alwaies fear'd sickness more then death, because sickness hath made me unable to perform those Offices for which I came into the world, and must yet be kept in it' (p. 373); and this sense of the frustration of his best purposes through illness is expressed in *The Crosse* and other poems:

> And then when after much delay,
> Much wrastling, many a combate, this deare end,
> So much desir'd, is giv'n, to take away
>   My power to serve thee; to unbend
> All my abilities, my designes confound,
> And lay my threatnings bleeding on the ground

2. *Seventeenth-Century Studies Presented to Sir Herbert Grierson*, p. 154.

It is, however, difficult to resist the impression that his agues and consumption only intensified a more ingrained self-distrust. Commenting on some lines from *The Temper* (i),

> —O let me, when thy roof my soul hath hid,
> O let me roost and nestle there—

Dr. Hutchinson remarks that 'Herbert often shows a fear of unlimited space and loves the shelter of an enclosure'; and his shrinking from the kind of experience that was possible for him shows itself now in the frequently recorded moods of despondency, now in the desire for a simpler and apparently more desirable form of existence:

> My stock lies dead, and no increase
> Doth my dull husbandrie improve.
>
> (*Grace*)

> All things are busie; onely I
> Neither bring hony with the bees,
> Nor flowres to make that, nor the husbandrie
> To water these.

> I am no link of thy great chain,
> But all my companie is a weed. . . .
>
> (*Employment* (i))

> Oh that I were an Orenge-tree,
>   That busie plant!
> Then should I ever laden be,
>   And never want
> Some fruit for him that dressed me.
>
> (*Employment* (ii))

Now this feeling of uselessness and self-distrust has two further consequences: one is a preoccupation with time and death,

> —So we freeze on,
> Untill the grave increase our cold;
>
> (*Employment* (ii))

the other is a sense that life, real life, is going on elsewhere, where he happens not to be himself. It was his weakness, as well as his more positive qualities of 'birth and spirit', that made a career at court seem so intensely desirable: 'the town' was where other people lived active and successful lives. Certainly, then, it was not a small achievement to 'behold the court with an impartial eye, and see plainly that it is made up of fraud, and titles, and flattery, and many other such empty, imaginary, painted pleasures; pleasures that are so empty, as not to satisfy when they are enjoyed.'[3] But it was an even greater achievement to rid himself of the torturing sense of frustration and impotence and to accept the validity of his own

---

3. Herbert to Woodnot, on the night of his induction to Bemerton: recorded by Walton.

experience. His poems come home to us because they give new meanings to 'acceptance'.

The first condition of development was that the disturbing elements in experience should be honestly recognized; and here we see the significance of Herbert's technical achievement, of his realism, of his ability to make his feelings immediately present. In the masterly verse of *Affliction* (i) we have one of the most remarkable records in the language of the achievement of maturity and of the inevitable pains of the process. In the opening stanzas movement and imagery combine to evoke the enchanted world of early manhood, when to follow the immediate dictates of the soul seems both duty and pleasure. [Quotes lines 1–22; see p. 20.] But implicit in the description—as we see from 'entice' and 'entwine'[4] and the phrase, 'argu'd into hopes'—is the admission that there *is* enchantment, an element of illusion in the 'naturall delights', and we are not surprised when the triumphant fourth verse ends with the sudden bleak recognition of ills previously unperceived but inherent in the processes of life:

> But with my yeares sorrow did twist and grow,
> And made a partie unawares for wo.

The three central verses not merely describe the 'woes'—sickness, the death of friends, disappointed hopes—they evoke with painful immediacy the feelings of the sufferer.

> Sorrow was all my soul; I scarce beleeved,
> Till grief did tell me roundly, that I lived.

With characteristic honesty Herbert admits the palliative of 'Academick praise'—something that temporarily 'dissolves' the mounting 'rage'; but the current of feeling is now flowing in a direction completely opposite to that of the opening.

> Whereas my birth and spirit rather took
>   The way that takes the town;
> Thou didst betray me to a lingring book,
>   And wrap me in a gown.
> I was entangled in the world of strife,
> Before I had the power to change my life.

'Betray' and 'entangle' make explicit a sense already present but not openly acknowledged in 'entice' and 'entwine'; and instead of direct spontaneity—'I had my wish and way'—there is division and uncertainty:

> I took thy sweetned pill, till I came where
> I could not go away, nor persevere.

In the eighth stanza the potentialities of emphasis latent in the

4. The earlier reading, in the Williams MS., is more explicit: 'I looked on thy furniture so rich, / And made it rich to me: / Thy glorious household-stuffe did me bewitch / Into thy familie.'

spoken language are used to evoke the full sense of frustration and conflict: [Quotes lines 43–48.] Stanza nine is quieter in tone, bringing into prominence an element in the whole complex attitude of the poet previously expressed only in the quiet control of the verse in which such turbulent feelings have been presented: [Quotes lines 49–54.] The opening lines of the last stanza can be read in two ways according as we bring into prominence the resigned or the rebellious tone:

> Yet, though thou troublest me, I must be meek;
> In weaknesse must be stout . . .

But resignation and rebellion are alike half-measures, and it is here, where the feelings are so subtly poised, that the need for an absolute decision makes itself felt. Return for a moment to the eighth stanza. There the last line, with its strong alliterative emphasis, makes plain that the problem of the will ('*my* wayes') is the central theme of the poem. What we call happiness ('no moneth but May') is the result of events meeting our desires,—'I had my wish and way'; but the universe is not constructed on our plan, and when the will cannot bring itself to accept the cross-bias of existence frustration is inevitable. This commonplace is something that everyone admits in a general way; to accept it fully, in terms of our own personal experience, is another matter. It is because Herbert has faced the issues so honestly and completely that the first alternative that presents itself in the moment of decision has only to be brought into focus to be seen as no real solution at all; and it is because its rejection has behind it the whole weight of the poem that the sudden reversal of feeling is so unforced, the undivided acceptance of the ending so inevitable.

> Yet, though thou troublest me, I must be meek;
> In weaknesse must be stout.
> Well, I will change the service, and go seek
> Some other master out.
> Ah my deare God! though I am clean forgot,
> Let me not love thee, if I love thee not.

In *The Collar* the same problem is approached from a slightly different angle.

> I struck the board, and cry'd, No more.
> I will abroad.
> What? shall I ever sigh and pine?
> My lines and life are free; free as the rode,
> Loose as the winde, as large as store. . . .

> But as I rav'd and grew more fierce and wilde
> At every word,
> Me thoughts I heard one calling, Child!
> And I reply'd, *My Lord*.

At one time I felt that in this well-known ending—a similar sudden 'return' to that of *Affliction* (i)—Herbert was evading the issue by simply throwing up the conflict and relapsing into the naïve simplicity of childhood. But of course I was wrong. The really childish behaviour is the storm of rage in which the tempestuous desires—superbly evoked in the free movement of the verse—are directed towards an undefined 'freedom'. What the poem enforces is that to be 'loose as the wind' is to be as incoherent and purposeless; that freedom is to be found not in some undefined 'abroad', but, in Ben Johnson's phrase, 'here in my bosom, and at home'.

The mature 'acceptance' that one finds in Herbert's poetry has little in common with a mere disillusioned resignation. The effort towards it is positive in direction. Just as Herbert shows no fear of any imposed punishment for sin—of Hell—but only of the inevitable consequences of sin's 'venome',[5] so the recurring stress of his poetry is on life. That 'nothing performs the task of life' is the complaint of *Affliction* (iv);

> O give me quicknesse, that I may with mirth
> Praise thee brim-full,

is his prayer when 'drooping and dull' (*Dulnesse*). And one reason why his religion appears so humane, in a century tending more and more to associate religion with fear and gloom, is that his God is a God of the living.

> Wherefore be cheer'd, and praise him to the full
> Each day, each houre, each moment of the week,
> Who fain would have you be new, tender, quick.
> 			(*Love Unknown*)

It is because he actually did learn from experience to find life 'at hand',[6] life realized in the commonplace details of every day, that so many of his 'homely' metaphors have such freshness and are the opposite of 'stuffy'. But acceptance has a further, final meaning. It involves the recognition not only of one's limited sphere but (the paradox is only apparent) of one's own value. It is this that gives such wide significance to the poem, 'Love bade me welcome: yet my soul drew back' placed deliberately at the end of the poems in 'The Church':

> You must sit down, sayes Love, and taste my meat:
> 		So I did sit and eat.

The achieved attitude—'accepted and accepting'—marks the final release from anxiety.

5. See the second verse of the poem, *Nature*, in which it is not, I think, fanciful to see some resemblance to the far more searching analysis of evil in *Mac-beth*.

6. 'Poore man, thou searchest round / To finde out *death*, but missest *life* at hand.' (*Vanitie* (i).)

With this release not only is significance restored to the present ('Onely the present is thy part and fee . . .'[7]), but death is robbed of its more extreme terrors.[8] The ending of the poem *Death* (which begins, 'Death, thou wast once an uncouth hideous thing') is entirely unforced:

> Therefore we can go die as sleep, and trust
> Half that we have
> Unto an honest faithfull grave;
> Making our pillows either down, or dust.

The integration of attitude thus achieved lies behind the poetry of *Life* ('I made a posie while the day ran by'), and of the well known *Vertue*—a poem that shows in a quite personal way the characteristically Metaphysical 'reconciliation of opposites': the day has lost none of its freshness because its end is freely recognized as implicit in its beginning. But it is in *The Flower* that the sense of new life springing from the resolution of conflict is most beautifully expressed.[9] [Quotes lines 1–14; see p. 59.] He still feels the need for security, for a guaranteed permanence:

> O that I once past changing were,
> Fast in thy Paradise, where no flower can wither.

But in the poem as a whole even the fact that the good hours do not last, that they are bound to alternate with 'frosts' and depression, is accepted without bitterness:

> These are thy wonders, Lord of power,
> Killing and quickning. . . .

As a result the renewed vitality, waited for without fret or fuss, has something of the naturalness and inevitability of the mounting sap. The sixth stanza takes up the spring imagery:

> And now in age I bud again,
> After so many deaths I live and write;
> I once more smell the dew and rain,
> And relish versing: O my onely light,
> It cannot be
> That I am he
> On whom thy tempests fell all night.

The sense of refreshment, conveyed in imagery of extraordinary sensuous delicacy, is as completely realized as the suffering expressed

---

7. *The Discharge.*
8. I should like to refer to D. W. Harding's review of *Little Gidding* in *Scrutiny* (Spring, 1943): 'For the man convinced of spiritual values life is a coherent pattern in which the ending has its due place and, because it is part of a pattern, itself leads into the beginning. An over-strong terror of death is often one expression of the fear of living, for death is one of the life-processes that seem too terrifying to be borne.'
9. I think it should be noticed that in the original order, apparently Herbert's own, *The Flower* is immediately preceded by *The Crosse*, another poem on the theme of acceptance, ending, '*Thy will be done*'.

in the poems of conflict. And like the flower it comes from 'under ground', from the deeper levels of the personality.

The account I have given of the positive direction of Herbert's poetry is not meant to imply that anything like a continuous development can be traced in the poems, few of which can be dated with any precision.[1] In any case, development—when it is of the whole man, not simply of a line of thought—rarely shows the smooth curve that biographers like to imagine. We do know, however, that his life at Bemerton was one of uncommon sweetness and serenity, expressing what Dr. Hutchinson calls 'an achieved character of humility, tenderness, moral sensitiveness, and personal consecration, which he was very far from having attained or even envisaged when he was dazzled by the attractions of the great world'. The poems in which the fluctuating stages of this progress are recorded are important human documents because they handle with honesty and insight questions that, in one form or another, we all have to meet if we wish to come to terms with life.

E. B. GREENWOOD

[Herbert's "Prayer (I)"]†

* * *

Prayer is first of all called 'the Churches banquet'. The phrase has a rich aura of suggestiveness. There are, of course, connotations of sumptuousness and splendour in the word 'banquet' itself in its original meaning, though it must be borne in mind that (as the NED[1] shows) the word had acquired the sense of 'a light repast between meals' by Herbert's time. A banquet involves food and thus the phrase carries the implication that prayer can be viewed as a spiritual food as necessary for the life of the soul as ordinary food is for the life of the body. This 'food' imagery also occurs in l. 10 'Exalted manna', possibly in l. 11 'Heaven in ordinarie' and implicitly in the image of spices in l. 14. The 'love feasts' of the early church may spring to mind. It is, of course, most important not to miss the suggestion of the connection of prayer with the Eucharist, 'La cena, que recrea y enamora' to borrow from the lines of St. John of the Cross * * *.[2] The NED cites Hooker as using the

---

1. A few seem to be early work, some contain references to the priesthood, and poems that appear in the Bodleian, but not in the Williams Manuscript may be assumed to be later than the others: see Dr. Hutchinson's Introduction, pp. l–lvi, and pp. lxvii–lxix. It is worth remarking that *The Pilgrimage, Vertue, Life* and *The Flower* are among the poems found only in the Bodleian MS.

†From "George Herbert's Sonnet 'Prayer': A Stylistic Study," *Essays in Criticism*, XV (1965), 27–45.
1. *New English Dictionary*. [*Editor*.]
2. "The banquet which gladdens and which inspires love." [*Editor*.]

phrase 'this heavenly banquet' to refer to the Eucharist. Herbert's poem 'The Banquet', which is on the subject of the Eucharist, is relevant here. The second metaphor 'Angels age' achieves concentration because of its 'Empsonian ambiguity'. Hutchinson in a note contrasts the phrase with 'Mans age is two hours work, or three:' from the poem 'Repentance' and interprets the phrase as meaning 'prayer acquaints man with the blessed timeless existence of the angels'. Such an insistence on the immortality and infinity of prayer is certainly Herbert's concern in this poem, but as well as having this meaning could not the phrase also carry the implication that prayer is literally as old as the angels because they were the first 'creatures' and were created precisely in order to praise God, praise being easily equatable with prayer? The 'orthodox' view holds that it is the function of the angels to praise God in heaven and of man to praise Him on earth.[3]

The next metaphor takes up a whole line:

'Gods breath in man returning to his birth,'

There is an ambiguity here which centres on the pronoun 'his'. Though by Herbert's time the form 'its' was current colloquially for the neuter, the form 'his' (identical with the masculine) was also still in use. Thus 'his birth' could have man as the antecedent and refer to man's birth, i.e. Adam's creation when God 'formed man of the ground, and breathed into his nostrils the breath of life'. In this case there may be the additional implication that in prayer man is as innocent as Adam before the Fall, indeed at the very moment of his creation. Donne spoke of this innocence in a sermon thus:

'The comfort of being presented to God as innocent as *Adam*, then when God breathed a soule into him, yea as innocent as Christ Jesus himself when he breathed out his soule to God; oh how blessed is that soule that enjoyes it, and how bold that tongue that goes about to express it!'[4]

If we take 'his' as neuter and having 'Prayer' as its antecedent the idea would still involve Adam, since the implication is that in prayer man literally renders breath back to its source God. It is important to note that the metaphor contains the key notion of two-way traffic which I referred to earlier in the essay.

Herbert's next metaphor is taken from the process we have just been practising, namely paraphrase. As Hutchinson points out in his notes the implication is one of expansion. * * * Herbert's own sonnet, like its subject, is an 'expansion' of the soul. Ambiguity is present in the phrase 'The soul in paraphrase'. It could mean 'the

3. I borrow the phrase from Rosemond Tuve, *A Reading of George Herbert*, London, 1952, p. 51.

4. John Donne, *Sermons: Selected Passages with an Essay by Logan Pearsall Smith*, Oxford, 1932, p. 122.

paraphrase of the soul' (genitive) or 'the paraphrase performed by the soul' (instrumental) or even 'the soul in the act of paraphrasing'. Nor is the phonetic nearness of 'phrase' to 'praise' to be forgotten. The 'soul' is man's heavenly part, the 'heart', its companion in the binary structure of this line, is the seat of the earthly affections and emotions. How appropriate, then, that the heart should merely be in 'pilgrimage' towards the heavenly. There is, of course, no need to enlarge on the connotations of the word 'pilgrimage' in a Christian context.

Into the next two lines there enter images of violence. Before considering them let me quote a passage from Donne's sermons on this very topic. It shows how Donne could associate prayer and violence:

'Prayer hath the nature of Impudency; Wee threaten God in Prayer; as *Gregor: Nazi:* adventures to expresse it; He saies, his Sister, in the vehemence of her Prayer, would threaten God, *Et honesta quadam impudentia, egit impudentem;* She came, saies he, to a religious impudency with God, and to threaten him, that she would never depart from his Altar, till she had her Petition granted; and God suffers this Impudency, and more. Prayer hath the nature of Violence; in the publique Prayers of the Congregation, we besiege God, saies *Tertul:* and we take God Prisoner, and bring God to our conditions: and God is glad to be straitned by us in that siege.'

In l. 5:

'Engine against th'Almightie, sinners towre,'

Herbert is, of course, relying on the associations aroused by the most famous 'sinners towre' in the Bible, the tower of Babel described in chapter eleven of Genesis. The men dwelling on the plain in the land of Shinar are proud enough to plan 'a tower whose top may reach unto heaven' and God punishes their pride by scattering them all over the face of the earth and splitting their one universal language into a number of others. In Herbert's use of this allusion there are the elements of one of the favourite figures of metaphysical poetry, paradox or oxymoron. We, like the men of Babel, are sinners, but in using prayer as our 'engine' we may build a tower up to heaven which will be a perfectly legitimate tower, unlike that of our punished forebears. Having taken an example of 'presumption' from sacred scripture, Herbert now makes an allusion to 'profane' literature another example of his fondness for binary sets in this poem. It is well known that Jove's characteristic weapon against presumption was the thunderbolt, hence his name of 'Jupiter Tonans' or 'Jupiter Tonitrualis'. Herbert's metaphor implies that prayer enables us to catch the thunderbolt of the divine wrath as it

hurtles towards us and to reverse its direction, as it were. It would
be a mistake to attempt to 'visualise' the metaphor too closely. Herbert is simply compressing a complex of associations into two words
in order to convey to us poetically prayer's power of averting the
divine wrath. Herbert uses an image of violence but he does not
intend us to view prayer as defiance. We do not hurl the thunderbolt back at Jove, as a 'literal' reading of the figure would suggest.
Nevertheless the fact that there is such a suggestion implicit in the
figure gives it once again the paradoxical quality of an oxymoron.
Implicit too in the figure is the sense of 'two-way' direction I have
commented on earlier as being bound up with Herbert's intention
of emphasising prayer as a sort of Jacob's ladder between earth and
heaven.

The image of the spear, with its striking triple epithet, continues
this train of images of violence. The reference is, of course, to the
incident at the crucifixion recorded in John, XIX, 34, 'But one of
the soldiers with a spear pierced his side, and forthwith came there
out blood and water'. To Herbert and his readers the incident, as
Rosemond Tuve has pointed out, had a traditional typological
interpretation.[5] The 'blood and water' were thought of as figuring
the sacraments which themselves were, of course, a reminder of
man's redemption. As Herbert himself writes in 'The Sacrifice':

> 'For they will pierce my side, I full well know;
> That as sinne came, so Sacraments might flow:'

and in 'The Agonie':

> 'Who knows not Love, let him assay
> And taste that juice, which on the crosse a pike
> Did set again abroach; then let him say
>   If ever he did taste the like.
> Love is that liquor sweet and most divine,
> Which my God feels as bloud; but I, as wine.

In short as in the phrase 'The Churches banquet' Herbert seems
here to be hinting at the close relationship between prayer and the
Eucharist. Here again the idea of two-way traffic is implicit. In
prayer man's spirit ascends to God, in the Eucharist God descends
to man. The next line

> 'The six-daies world transposing in an hour,'

is a kind of contrast to the earlier phrase

> 'The soul in paraphrase,'

in the sense that it figures an immense span of time and space contracted into a mere hour whereas 'The soul in paraphrase' figures, as

5. R. Tuve, op. cit., pp. 54–55.

we have already seen, expansion, the opposite of contraction. No doubt the word 'transposing' suggested the transition to the metaphor of prayer as a music of which all creation stands in awe in the following line. A similar rapid transition to the metaphor of music (an art dear to Herbert as we know from Walton) rendered possible by the suitability of the concepts touched on in one context to a musical context as well can be seen in the poem 'The Temper, I':

> 'Yet take thy way; for sure thy way is best:
> Stretch or contract me, thy poor debter:
> This is but tuning of my breast,
> To make the music better.'

Like so much else in the Old Testament, manna had been given a figurative or typological interpretation of which Herbert could expect his contemporary readers to be aware. It had been connected with the Eucharist. Once again, therefore, Herbert seems to be suggesting the close relationship between prayer and the Eucharist. Once again, too, there is a suggestion of the concept of two-way traffic which we have commented on in connection with the metaphor 'Reversed thunder,' and the line:

> 'God's breath in man returning to his birth.'

The original manna dropped down from heaven to satisfy the Israelites' physical hunger. Prayer, on the contrary, is a spiritual manna which rises up to heaven from earth. The motion of food implicit in 'manna' may have led to the transition to the metaphor 'Heaven in ordinarie', a syntagma modelled no doubt on such phrases as 'chaplain in ordinary'. The word 'ordinarie' had a number of meanings in Herbert's time which would be appropriate to the context here. It could mean 'customary fare', or a place where such fare is taken, or simply 'normal', 'usual', in which case the implication would be that prayer brings heaven into the quotidian. The word 'ordinarie' could also mean the divine service, of course, and the book which contains the divine service. It will be seen that the 'ambiguity' here is partly caused by the fact that the noun 'ordinarie' is not preceded by a determiner (e.g. an article) of any kind. The next phrase 'man well drest,' works in binary contrast with 'Heaven in ordinarie'. Whereas 'Heaven in ordinarie' brings heaven down to earth, so to speak, 'man well drest' takes earth into the presence of heaven. Once again the concept of two-way traffic is present. The implication is that man puts on his spiritual best, so to speak, in order to go into the presence of his Maker. Or, to adapt some words from Shelley's *Defence*, prayer consists of 'the best and happiest moments of the happiest and best minds'.

I have already pointed out the peculiar unity of the final tercet of Herbert's sonnet. In it Herbert seems chiefly concerned to express a sense of the paradisal and to do so turns, not unnaturally, to what he refers to in the poem 'The Foreunners' as:

> 'Lovely enchanting language, sugar-cane,
> Hony of roses.'

The tercet is in fact an example of what Helmut Hatzfeld termed, in connection with the lines from St. John of the Cross quoted earlier, 'a sort of glossolalia, an attempt to transform verbally the experience of love, especially love of God, into a stream of metaphorical designations bearing on intuitively chosen objects of beauty and bliss.[6] We have here beautiful, even 'exotic' connotations. Four out of the five metaphors actually 'figure' paradise. The phrase 'The milkie way' immediately raises our gaze upwards to the beauty of the heavens and the phrase 'the bird of Paradise' is appropriate as a metaphor for prayer (as Hutchinson points out in his notes) because of the bird's 'brilliant colouring' and the fact that it was supposed to reside constantly in the air. Jeremy Taylor has an interesting passage in which he 'moralises' on this piece of seventeenth century natural history:

> 'MANKINDE now taking in his whole constitution, and designe is like the birds of *Paradice* which travellers tell us of in the *Molucco Islands*; born without legs; but by a celestial power they have a recompence made to them for that defect; and they always hover in the air, and feed on the dew of heaven; so are we birds of *Paradice*; but cast out from thence, and born without legs, without strength to walk in the laws of God, or to go to heaven; but by a power from above, we are adopted in our new birth to a celestial conversation, we feed on the dew of heaven.'[7]

The transition in thought from 'milkie way' to 'Paradise' and then to 'starres' is, of course, perfectly easy. The ambiguity of the phrase

> 'Church-bels beyond the starres heard,'

is certainly startling. We have seen that much of the poem's imagery has been concerned with 'two-way traffic', as it were, and this 'two-way' feature is incarnated in the very ambiguity we are considering. For the phrase can, of course, be taken in two ways. It can mean that when we pray we hear the sounds of music coming down to us from heaven beyond the stars. It can also mean that it is the people in heaven who are doing the listening, and that they can hear the music of our prayers ascending to them from earth, from beyond *their* side of the stars. Typical of Herbert is the collocation of the mundane particular 'Church-bels' (metrically he could easily have used a more generic term such as 'music') with 'the

6. Helmut Hatzfeld, 'The Language of the Poet,' *Studies in Philology*, vol. 43, 1946, p. 114.
7. Jeremy Taylor, *The Golden Grove*; *Selected Passages from the Sermons and Writings*, ed. by Logan Pearsall Smith, Oxford, 1930, p. 41.

starres'. Interesting too is Herbert's exploration of the sense of the beauty of music heard in the distance. This is a *motif* which was to become dear to the hearts of many of the Romantic poets because of the *Stimmung*[8] associated with it. The use of the mundane concrete 'Church-bels' differentiates Herbert's effect from such *Stimmung*.

The short metaphor 'the souls blood' is also ambiguous. It could be taken as a telescoped analogy with four terms, i.e. as blood is to the body (namely essential for life) so is prayer to the soul. On the other hand the following passage from Burton's *Anatomy of Melancholy* expressing a view of the blood current in Herbert's time may lead us to another interpretation:

> 'Spirit is a most subtle vapour, which is expressed from the *blood*, and the instrument of the soul to perform all his actions;'.[9]

Herbert's phrase may, then, be interpreted as meaning that as the blood generates the spirits which the soul needs to execute its actions, the blood's relationship to the soul is a perfect analogy to prayer's relationship to it. The next metaphor 'The land of spices' has not only connotations of sensuous beauty, but would have aroused in Herbert's contemporaries associations with that earthly paradise which Milton was to describe so beautifully in *Paradise Lost*, IV, 132–165, an earthly paradise which was traditionally taken as a 'type' of the heavenly paradise. It is at this ecstatic moment that Herbert chooses to make his 'aposiopesis'[1] by means of a phrase which explicitly states what I have tried to show that the very structure of the poem exemplifies, namely that the significance of prayer is infinite, that we can only understand 'something' of it, not everything.

JOSEPH H. SUMMERS

The Poem as Hieroglyph†

Too often Herbert is remembered as the man who possessed the fantastic idea that a poem should resemble its subject in typographical appearance, and who therefore invented the practice of writing poems in shapes such as wings and altars. Herbert, of course, no more invented the pattern poem than he invented 'emblematic

---

8. Evocativeness. [*Editor.*]

9. Robert Burton, *The Anatomy of Melancholy*, ed. by Floyd Dell and Paul Jordan-Smith, New York, 1948, p. 129, i.e. Pt. 1, Sec. 1, Memb. 2, Subs 2. [Burton, 1577–1640, gathered a kind of treasury of miscellaneous contemporary learning in his book; he referred to it fondly as his "rag-bag."—*Editor.*]

1. In rhetorical practice, an abrupt halt designed to suggest that the speaker is too excited to continue. [*Editor.*]

† From chapter VI of *George Herbert: His Religion and Art* (Cambridge, Mass., 1954). Some notes have been slightly abridged.

poetry' or the religious lyric: his originality lies in his achievement
with traditional materials. 'The Altar' and 'Easter-wings,' his two
most famous pattern poems, are not exotic or frivolous oddities;
they are the most obvious examples of Herbert's religious and poetic
concern with what we may call the hieroglyph.

A hieroglyph is 'a figure, device, or sign having some hidden
meaning; a secret or enigmatical symbol; an emblem.[1] In the Renaissance 'hieroglyph,' 'symbol,' 'device,' and 'figure' were often used
interchangeably. Because of special meanings which have become
associated with the other words, 'hieroglyph' seems more useful
than the others today, and even in the seventeenth century it was
often considered the most inclusive term.[2] 'Hieroglyphic,' the older
form of the noun, was derived from the Greek for 'sacred carving,'
and the root usually retained something of its original religious con-
notation. Ralph Cudworth[3] used it in its generally accepted meaning when he said in a sermon, 'The Death of Christ . . . Hieroglyphically instructed us that we ought to take up our Cross likewise,
and follow our crucified Lord and Saviour.'[4] The hieroglyph presented its often manifold meanings in terms of symbolic relationships rather than through realistic representation. * * *

Aside from the metaphorical use of hieroglyphs common to
almost all the poets of the time, the religious lyric poet could most
obviously make his poem a meditation on one of the innumerable
hieroglyphs in nature, art, or the Church, or he could use the hieroglyph as the central image in a meditation on some doctrine or
experience. * * * Most of the poems written for the emblem books
typify the first practice: the moral applications are drawn from the
image point by point. Herbert never wrote a poem quite so crudely.
* * *

* * *

In 'The Bunch of Grapes' Herbert used the hieroglyph in the
second obvious fashion, as the central image in a meditation on a
personal experience. The title of the poem indicates the hieroglyph,
but the 'cluster' is not mentioned until the end of the third stanza.
The subject of meditation is the problem of the absence of joy from
the Christian's life:

> Joy, I did lock thee up: but some bad man
> Hath let thee out again:

1. *NED*, Sb. 2. [*New English Dictionary*, second paragraph.—*Editor*.]
2. In his *Hieroglyphicorum Collectanea,
ex Veteribus et Neotericis Descripta* ('In
hac postrema editione recognita & expur-
gata'; Lvgdvni, 1626), p. 7, Giovanni Pi-
erio Valeriano summarized the general
usage: 'Ad hieroglyphica accedunt em-
blemata, symbola, insignia, quae quamuis
nomine differant, reipsa multis modis
conueniri videntur.' [Hieroglyphs include
emblems, symbols, devices which, while

they have various names, actually correspond with each other in many respects.
—*Editor*.]
3. Ralph Cudworth, 1617–1688, a leader
of the Cambridge Platonists, idealists opposed to Hobbesian materialism and
convinced that reason and religion were
in harmony with each other.
4. Quoted in *NED*, 'Hieroglyphically,' 2,
from 'Sermon I' (1642) in *A Discourse
Concerning the True Notion of the
Lord's Supper* (London, 1670), p. 210.

And now, me thinks, I am where I began
       Sev'n years ago: one vogue and vein,
       One aire of thoughts usurps my brain.
I did towards Canaan draw; but now I am
Brought back to the Red sea, the sea of shame.

Joy, once possessed, has now escaped. Herbert prevents any misunderstanding of the traditional imagery of Canaan and the Red Sea by explaining in the next stanza Paul's teaching that every event during the wandering of the Children of Israel from Egypt to the Promised Land was a type of the Christian's experiences in his journey between the world of sin and heaven:[5] we may discover within the ancient history the heavenly evaluations and solutions for our problems. With the third stanza, Herbert enumerates some of the parallels:

Then have we too our guardian fires and clouds;
       Our Scripture-dew drops fast:
We have our sands and serpents, tents and shrowds;
       Alas! our murmurings come not last.
       But where's the cluster? where's the taste
Of mine inheritance? Lord, if I must borrow,
Let me as well take up their joy, as sorrow.

Joy may not be fully achieved until we reach the Promised Land, but the Christian should at least experience a foretaste of it, such a rich proof of its existence as was the cluster of Eschol to the Children of Israel. But the introduction of Eshcol provides the answer. That 'branch with one cluster of grapes,' which was so large that 'they bore it betweene two vpon a staffe,' had represented a joy which the Israelites refused. To them the bunch of grapes substantiated the report that it was 'a land that eateth vp the inhabitants thereof, and all the people that we saw in it, are men of a great stature. And there we saw the giants, the sonnes of Anak, which come of the giants: and wee were in our owne sight as grashoppers, and so wee were in their sight' (Num. xiii. 23–24). From fear they turned to the rebellion which caused God to decree the wandering of forty years. Of all the adults who saw the grapes, only Caleb and Joshua entered the Promised Land. The image of the bunch of grapes suggests, then, not only the foretastes of Canaan and heaven, but also the immeasurable differences between those foretastes under the Covenant of Works and the Covenant of Grace:

But can he want the grape, who hath the wine?
       I have their fruit and more.
Blessed be God, who prosper'd *Noahs* vine,
       And made it bring forth grapes good store.
       But much more him I must adore,

---

5. I. Cor. x. The marginal reading for 'ensamples,' v. 11, is 'Or, Types.'

Who of the Laws sowre juice sweet wine did make,
Ev'n God himself being pressed for my sake.

The bunch of grapes is a type of Christ and of the Christian's communion. 'I have their fruit and more,' for the grapes, of which the
promise was conditional upon works, have been transformed into
the wine of the New Covenant: 'I' have both the foretaste and the
assurance of its fulfilment. The prospering of 'Noahs vine,' like the
cluster of Eshcol, was a sign of God's blessing. It was a partial fulfilment of 'Bee fruitfull and multiply, and replenish the earth,' and
of God's covenant with all flesh: 'neither shall there any more be a
flood to destroy the earth' (Gen. ix. 1, 11). Yet, as at Eshcol, God's
blessings under the Law could become man's occasion for the
renewal of sin and the curse: Noah's misuse of the vine resulted in
the curse on Ham. The bunch of grapes has furnished the image of
the poet's lost joy, the image of blessings refused or perverted, and
also the image of the Christian's source of joy, ever present if he
will cease his murmurings. The Holy Communion is a constant
reminder of Christ's sacrifice which established the joyful Covenant
of Grace; it is the instrument of present grace; and it foretells the
joy of heavenly communion. The examination of the Christian's
lack of joy has resolved rather than explained the original problem.
The blessing and adoration of the final lines indicate that joy is no
longer lost.

Herbert frequently used a hieroglyph to crystallize, explain, or
resolve the central conflict in a poem. 'Josephs coat,' a strange
sonnet with an unrhymed first line, concerns the mixture of joy and
sorrow in the Christian life, and Joseph is not mentioned in the
text. The conclusion, 'I live to shew his power, who once did bring
My *joyes* to *weep*, and now my *griefs* to *sing*,' is an acknowledgment of God's power, but without the title it might be construed as
an acknowledgment of a powerful and inexplicable Fate. The title,
a reference to a traditional Christian type, gives Herbert's interpretation of the experience of contradictory joys and sorrows. Joseph's
'coat of many colours' was the sign of his father's particular love.[6]
It was also the immediate occasion for his brothers' jealousy and
hatred and for his slavery and suffering; but the presentation of the
coat was, finally, the initial incident in the long chain of causes
which led to the preservation of the Children of Israel in Egypt.
After all the suffering, the sign of Jacob's love ended in beatitude.
The extraordinary mixture of joy and sorrow in the Christian's life
is a particular sign of God's love. Joy has been made 'to *weep*' to

6. George Ryley, 'The Temple explained
and improved' [an eighteenth-century
commentary on Herbert, in a Bodleian
Library manuscript—*Editor*.] pp. 315–16,
summarizes the biblical allusions: 'Joseph's Coat was of *many colours*; very
beautifull; and it was a token of his father's peculiar affection. *Gen.* 37. 3. . . .
This poem speaks the language of the
prophet, *Is.* 61.10, *I will greatly rejoice
in the Lord, &c. for he hath cloathed me
with the garments of salvation*, and of
the Apostle, 2 *Cor.* 6.10, *As sorrowfull,
yet always rejoicing.*'

forestall the self-sufficience which leads to wilful pride, and *'griefs'* have been made 'to *sing*' to preserve the soul and body from despair and death. God's 'Cross-Providences' also lead to beatitude. For Herbert, 'Joyes coat,' with which anguish has been 'ticed' was evidenced by his ability to 'sing,' to compose lyrics even when the subject was grief.

At first reading 'Church-monuments' appears to belong to the group of poems which are explanations of a hieroglyph. For once the modern reader could surmise the title from the contents, for the poem is a considered meditation on 'Church-monuments' in which all their hieroglyphic applications are drawn. [Quotes text; see p. 29.] The first stanza states the purpose of the meditation, that 'my flesh . . . betimes May take acquaintance of this heap of dust.' Most obviously, the monuments form a hieroglyph worthy of the flesh's 'acquaintance' because they contain the dust of formerly living flesh. Yet, with the identification of 'heap of dust' as that 'To which the blast of deaths incessant motion . . . Drives all at last,' the meaning expands to include the dissolution of all earthly things. Through contemplating the monuments the 'bodie' 'may learn To spell his elements.' The ambiguous 'spell' (meaning both to 'divine' the elements and to 'spell out' the inscriptions) introduces as part of the hieroglyph the inscriptions on the monuments. Their 'dustie' physical state (which makes them difficult to decipher) and their intended verbal meaning cause them to serve as intermediate symbols relating the flesh of man and the contents of the tomb. The 'dustie heraldrie and lines' factually tell the genealogies of the deceased and include some conventional version of 'for dust thou art, and vnto dust shalt thou returne.' ('Lines,' associated with 'birth' and 'heraldrie', seems to signify genealogical 'lines' as well as the lines of engraving.) The monuments are an ironic commentary on mortality; their states and messages mock at their composition of 'Jeat and Marble'—too obviously fleshly attempts to deny the dissolution of the bodies which they contain. Can there be monuments to monuments? Can monuments hope for a memorial 'When they shall bow, and kneel' as the body of the meditator is doing, or 'fall down flat' in dissolution, as his body will do and as the bodies within the monuments have already done? The flesh can learn its 'stemme And true descent' both in its origin in dust and in its decline into dust.

The figure of the hour-glass summarizes what 'thou mayst know' from the contemplation of the monuments and further enriches the meaning:

> That flesh is but the glasse, which holds the dust
> That measures all our time; which also shall
> Be crumbled into dust.

It is one of Herbert's most successful condensations, and it is difficult only if we have failed to follow the careful preparation for its introduction. The hour-glass defines the flesh in terms of what has been learned from the monuments. The monuments, like the traditional *memento mori*, have told of more than physical death. It is 'the exhalation of our crimes' which 'feeds' 'the blast of deaths incessant motion'; and the monuments, like the 'grasse' of the Psalmist and Isaiah and the New Testament,[7] have served to exemplify the vain dust of the sin and the 'goodlinesse' and 'glory' of living flesh as well as that of flesh's final dissolution. The function of proud flesh and proud monument is the same: to hold 'the dust That measures all our time,' whether it is the figurative dust of our vain goodliness and glory and sinful wills or the actual dust of our bodies. Dust is the true measure of 'all our time' (not our eternity): the vanity and endurance of our lives and of our ashes provide the sole significances to the flesh and the monument. Finally, the flesh and the monuments, the containers, 'shall Be crumbled into dust,' both symbolic of and undifferentiable from the dust contained. The closing address directs the flesh's attention to the 'ashes' rather than to the monuments:

> Mark here below
> How tame these ashes are, how free from lust,
> That thou mayst fit thy self against thy fall.

The flesh can escape neither its measuring content nor its final goal. The knowledge it has gained may, however, serve as bridle to 'tame' its lust. The flesh may 'fit' itself 'against' its 'fall' in that, in preparation for its known dissolution, it may oppose its 'fall' into pride and lust.[8]

Such an analysis indicates the manner in which Herbert explained the complex meanings of the hieroglyph, but it does not explain 'Church-monuments.' The movement of the words and the lines, of the clauses and the sentences, conveys even without analysis a 'meaning' which makes us recognize the inadequacy of any such prose summary. Yvor Winters has called 'Church-monuments' 'the greatest poem by George Herbert': 'George Herbert's *Church Monuments*, perhaps the most polished and urbane poem of the Metaphysical School and one of the half dozen most profound, is written in an iambic pentameter line so carefully modulated, and with its rhymes so carefully concealed at different and unexpected points in

7. Ps. cii. 11; Isa. xl. 6; I Pet. i. 24.

8. 'Against' and 'fall' are used ambiguously. 'Against' means both 'in preparation for' and 'in opposition to,' and 'fall' means both physical collapse and 'fall' into sin. These ambiguities are characteristic of Herbert's use of the device. Neither is at all recondite: 'against' in the sense of 'in preparation for' often carried something of the meaning of 'in opposition to,' and 'the fall' of man and angels had traditionally equated physical and moral movement.

the syntax, that the poem suggests something of the quiet plainness of excellent prose without losing the organization and variety of verse.'[9] The effect which Winters praised is achieved largely through the extraordinary use of enjambment and the looseness of the syntax. Only three lines of the poem come to a full stop, and nine of the twenty-four lines are followed by no punctuation. Many of the semi-cadences indicated by the punctuation, moreover, prove illusory: the syntax demands no pause, and the commas serve as fairly arbitrary directions for a slight voice rest, obscuring rather than clarifying the simple 'prose' meaning. Winters seems to praise 'Church-monuments' for practices which are found in no other poem in *The Temple*. Herbert characteristically considered his stanzas as inviolable architectural units. Each usually contained a complete thought, representing one unit in the logic of the 'argument,' and the great majority of his stanzas end with full stops.[1] In the form in which it was printed in 1633 'Church-monuments' provides the only example of complete enjambment between stanzas in *The Temple*, and two of the three examples of stanzas in which the final points are commas.[2] When Herbert departs so dramatically from his usual consistent practice, it is advisable to look for the reason. It cannot be found, I believe, in an intent to suggest 'something of the quiet plainness of excellent prose without losing the organization and variety of verse.' These straggling sentences fulfil the criteria for excellence by neither Ciceronian nor Senecan nor Baconian standards of prose. They possess neither the admired periodicity, nor trenchant point, nor ordinary clarity. The series of clauses and participial phrases, each relating to a word in some preceding clause or phrase, threaten to dissolve the sentence structure. The repetitions of 'that' and 'which' give the effect of unplanned prose, a prose which seems to function more by association than by logic.

The poem is a meditation upon a *memento mori*, the hieroglyph of the monuments. One reason for the slowness of the movement and the 'concealed' rhymes might be that the tone of the meditation was intended to correspond to the seriousness of its object. The most important clue, however, is in the manuscripts: in neither the Williams nor the Bodleian MS. is the poem divided into stanzas at all. As F. E. Hutchinson remarked, 'the editor of 1633 recognized that the rhyme-scheme implies a six-line stanza,'[3] and subsequent editors followed the original edition and printed the poem in stanzas. But the manuscript arrangement was not the result of accident

9. *Primitivism and Decadence: A Study of American Experimental Poetry* (New York, 1937), pp. 10, 123.
1. On the rare occasions when a stanza ends with a colon or semicolon, modern usage would often require a period.
2. The third example is st. 5 of 'The

Bag.' Here the comma after line 30, 'And straight he turn'd, and to his brethren cry'd,' is strong, since it precedes the two stanzas of direct quotation.
3. *Works*, p. 499.

or carelessness. In the Williams MS., which Herbert corrected, the non-stanzaic form is emphasized by the indentation of line 17 to indicate a new paragraph.[4] The fact that Herbert established a six-line stanzaic rhyme scheme but did not create stanzas, either formally or typographically, is a minor but a convincing evidence that he intended the poem itself to *be* a *memento mori*, to function formally as a hieroglyph. The dissolution of the body and the monuments is paralleled by the dissolution of the sentences and the stanzas.

The movement and sound of the poem suggest the 'falls' of the flesh and the monuments and the dust in the glass. The fall is not precipitious; it is as slow as the gradual fall of the monuments, as the crumbling of the glass, as the descent of the flesh from Adam into dust. Every cadence is a dying fall. Even the question of stanza 3 contains three commas and ends with the descriptive clause, 'which now they have in trust,' carrying no interrogation. Part of the effect is achieved by obvious 'prose' means. 'Dust' re-echoes seven times in the poem, and the crucial words and phrases describe or suggest the central subject: 'intombe'; 'blast of deaths incessant motion'; 'dissolution'; 'earth with earth'; 'bow, and kneel, and fall down flat'; 'descent'; 'measures'; 'crumbled';[5] 'ashes'; 'fall.' Herbert has also used every means to slow the movement of the neutral words. With the clusters of consonants, it is impossible to read the poem rapidly.[6] The related rhymes, with their internal echoes and repetitions, both give phonetic continuity to the poem and suggest the process of dissolution: 'devotion' and 'motion' are mocked by 'exhalation' and 'dissolution'; 'betimes' and 'crimes' modulate to 'lines' and 'signes' as do 'learn' and 'discern' to 'birth' and 'earth.' 'Trust' and 'lust' are echoed incessantly by 'dust,' and, internally, by 'blast,' and 'last.' Continual internal repetition deprives the end-rhymes of any chime of finality: 'blast-last,' 'earth with earth,' 'bow-now,' 'they-pray,' 'that-that,' 'which-which' disguise and almost dissolve the iambic pentameter line. Three of the six sentences in the poem take up five and a half lines each, but, straggling as they are, each is exhausted before it reaches what should be the end of the stanza. Although the sentences are hardly independent (the many pronominal forms create a complex of interdependent meanings), the expiration of each sentence marks a break which requires a new beginning: after the opening of the poem, each new sentence begins with a long syllable which usually causes a break in the iambic rhythm. The sentences sift down through the rhyme-scheme

4. *Works*, p. 65. In *B* the line begins a new page.
5. The only significant change which Herbert made after the version in *W* was to introduce 'crumbled' in line 22 for the less effective 'broken.'
6. In the twenty-four lines the sound of *t* occurs 59 times; *th* and *th*, 36; *s* and *z*, 51; *sh*, 15; *n*, 35; *d*, 27.

skeleton of the stanzas like the sand through the glass; and the glass itself has already begun to crumble.

'Church-monuments' differs in kind as well as degree from such poems as 'The Church-floore' and 'The Bunch of Grapes.' The natural or religious hieroglyph was an eminently pleasant and profitable subject for a poem, and it could be used either as the object which the poem explained or as the image which explained the poem. Yet Herbert seems to have believed that it was more pleasant and profitable to make the poem itself a hieroglyph. To construct the poem so that its form imaged the subject was to reinforce the message for those who could 'spell'; for the others it would not distract from the statement—and if they read and meditated long enough, surely they would discover the mirroring of the meanings within the form of the poem!

There were fewer readers who could not 'spell' in Herbert's day than in ours. The attempt to make formal structure an integral part of the meaning of a poem assumed a general consciousness of traditional formal conventions. The disturbances of the rhyme schemes in 'Grief' and 'Home,' for example, depend for their effects on the reader's firm expectation of a conventional pattern. Such an expectation could be assumed in readers accustomed to Renaissance English poetry, whether the poetry of the Court or the hymns of the Church or the doggerel of the broadsides. In his hieroglyphs Herbert never attempted to abandon rational control for an 'identity' with a natural object: the poems always embody or assume a firm pattern of logic, rhyme, and rhythm. The formal organization of the subject was imitated by the formal organization of the poem.

The poems in which Herbert's 'imitations' are obvious are those which are likely to draw the fire of strict advocates either of that art which conceals art or of that upwelling inspiration which is oblivious of form. But Herbert often intended the form of a poem to be obvious. The opening stanzas of 'Deniall,' for example, picture the disorder which results when the individual feels that God denies his requests: [Quotes lines 1–10; see p. 34.] The final stanza, with its establishment of the normal pattern of cadence and rhyme, is the symbol of reconstructed order, of the manner in which men (and the poem) function when God grants the request:

> O cheer and tune my heartlesse breast,
> Deferre no time;
> That so thy favours granting my request,
> They and my minde may chime,
> And mend my ryme.

The stanza which had been the symbol of the flying asunder of a 'brittle bow' has become a symbol for the achievement of order.

The form of the final prayer indicates that its request has already been answered. The individual and the poem have moved from fear through open rebellion and 'unstrung' discontent. 'Deniall' is over-come through renewal of prayer: the ordered prayer provides the evidence.

Of Herbert's many other formal hieroglyphs ('Sinnes round,' 'A Wreath,' 'Trinitie Sunday,' etc.) 'Aaron' is one of the most effec-tive. [Quotes poem; see pp. 61–62.] Herbert may have chosen the five stanzas of five'lines each partially because of the five letters in 'Aaron'; if so, the technical problem may have been of importance to the poet, but it does not matter particularly to the reader. Nor does it seem that Herbert primarily intended that each stanza should 'suggest metrically the swelling and dying sound of a bell':[7] the 'bells' and the 'musick' occur only in the third line of each stanza, and the rhymes are hardly bell-like. The central meaning of those identical rhymes and those subtly transformed stanzas[8] is clearly stated in the poem. The profaneness in man's head, the defects and darkness in his heart, the cacophonous passions which destroy him and lead him to a hell of 'repining restlessnesse'[9] *can* be transformed through the imputed righteousness of Christ into the ideal symbolized by Aaron's ceremonial garments.[1] The 'clay'[2] (like the stanzas) retains its outward form, but inwardly all is changed in the divine consumption of the self. As the 'Priest for euer after the order of Melchisedec' 'dresses' the new Aaron with the inward reality for which the first Aaron's garments were but the hieroglyphs, the poem moves with a ritualistic gravity from opposi-tion to a climactic synthesis.

When we have understood Herbert's use of form in these poems, or, say, his extraordinarily formal picture of anarchy in 'The Collar' and his divine numerology in 'Trinitie Sunday' we may see the poems which derive from the Elizabethan acrostics and anagrams in a different light. Aside from the courtiers to whom any exercise in ingenuity was welcome, this type of poem had its serious religious adherents in the seventeenth century. If biblical exegesis demanded the solution of anagrams,[3] and if the good man was truly 'willing to spiritualize everything,' the composition of such poetry was a logical result. With due appreciation of the wit involved, the good man was likely to treat such poetry seriously. The seriousness depended

7. Grierson, *Metaphysical Lyrics*, pp. 231–32.
8. Douglas Bush has remarked that in the first stanza describing the 'type,' the consonants *l*, *m*, and *r* predominate; in the second concerning the 'natural man,' *p*, *st*, *t*, *z*, and *s;* and in the final stanza the two patterns of consonants are united.

9. 'The Pulley.'
1. Hutchinson, *Works*, p. 538, summa-rizes the relevant passages from Exod. xxviii.
2. Cf. 'The Priesthood.'
3. See Kenneth B. Murdock's discussion and quotations in *Handkerchiefs from Paul* (Cambridge, Mass., 1927), pp. liv–lvi.

on a religious subject and on the assumption that the poet would draw 'true' meanings from his word-play. Herbert abided by the rules, and he never repeated the various forms. In *The Temple* there is one true anagram (labelled as such), one echo poem, one 'hidden acrostic,' one poem based on the double interpretation of initials, one based on a syllabic pun, and 'Paradise,' which can only be described as a 'pruning poem.' For his unique example of each type, Herbert usually chose that Christian subject which was most clearly illuminated by the device.

※　＊　＊

In 'The Altar' and 'Easter-wings' Herbert extended the principle of the hieroglyph to a third level. If the natural or religious hiero-glyph was valuable as content (used either as the object which the poem explained or as the image which crystallized the meaning of the poem), and if the poem could be constructed as a formal hiero-glyph which mirrored the structural relationships between the natu-ral hieroglyph, the poem, and the individual's life, it was but a fur-ther step to make the poem a visual hieroglyph, to create it in a shape which formed an immediately apparent image relevant both to content and structure.

Neither the conception of the pattern poem nor the two shapes which Herbert used were at all novel.[4] The Greek Anthology[5] had included six pattern poems (including a pair of wings and two altars), and those patterns were widely imitated in the sixteenth century. Although Thomas Nashe, Gabriel Harvey, and Ben Jonson denounced such poems, the practice flourished.[6] After the appear-ance of *The Temple* patterns were published in profusion. Wither, Quarles,[7] Benlowes, Joseph Beaumont, Herrick, Christopher Harvey, and Traherne were among the practitioners. Both before and after 1633 the literary quality of most of these poems was noto-riously low. The poets seemed usually to consider the shapes as a superficial or frivolous attraction for the reader. As the Renaissance poets and critics never tired of reiterating, pleasure *could* be made a

4. In the discussion which follows I am indebted to Miss Margaret Church's 'The Pattern Poem' (Doctoral thesis, Radcliffe College, 1944), the most useful discus-sion of the history and development of the European pattern poem which I have found. Miss Church's Appendix C, pp. 240–427, 'includes copies of all the pat-tern poems discussed in the text with the exception of several *carmina quadrata* by P. Optatianus Porfirius and Hraban Maur.'

5. A compilation of Greek poetry, mostly on amorous themes, from various anthologies ranging in time from the sev-enth century B.C. to the tenth century A.D. [*Editor.*]

6. Church, p. 161, cites the comments of Nashe, 'Have with you . . .,' *The Works*, ed. R. B. McKerrow (London, 1900), III, 67; Harvey, *Letter-Book*, ed. E. J. L. Scott (Westminster, 1884), pp. 100–01; and Jonson, *The Works*, ed. F. Cunningham (London, 1816), III, 320, 470, 488.

7. Except for one 'lozenge,' 'On God's Law,' in the *Divine Fancies* of 1632, all of Quarles's patterns, like his emblems, were published after 1633. If there was any influence, it was Herbert who influ-enced Quarles.

bait for profit, but a superficial conception of the 'bait' often resulted in very bad poems. Many of the patterns depended largely on wrenched typography, and it was a common practice to compose a poem in ordinary couplets, then chop the lines to fit the pattern.

Herbert's poems are another matter. From his knowledge of both the Greek originals and English practice,[8] Herbert chose the two patterns which could be most clearly related to the purposes of his Christian poetry. His patterns are visual hieroglyphs. The interpretation of them as naïve representations of 'real' objects has resulted in the citation of 'The Altar' as additional proof of Herbert's extreme Anglo-Catholicism. An examination of the poem in the light of its tradition and Herbert's formal practice shows it to be artistically complex and religiously 'low.'[9] [Quotes text; see p. 4.]

When one reads 'The Altar' it is well to remember that the word 'altar' was not applied to the Communion Table in the Book of Common Prayer, and that the canons of Herbert's time directed that the Table should be made of wood rather than stone. Throughout his English writings Herbert always used 'altar' and 'sacrifice' according to the 'orthodox' Protestant tradition of his time: 'altar' is never applied to the Communion Table nor is the Holy Communion ever called a 'sacrifice.'[1] Yet Herbert and his contemporaries cherished the conception of the altar and the sacrifice. The Mosaic sacrifices were considered types of the one true Sacrifice, in which Christ had shed blood for the remission of sins once for all time. To man were left the 'sacrifices' of praise, good works, and 'communication' (Heb. xiii. 15–16). The Hebrew altar which was built of unhewn stones was a type of the heart of man, hewn not by man's efforts but by God alone. The engraving on those stones with which 'all the words of this Law' were written 'very plainly' (Deut. xxvii. 8) was a type of the 'Epistle of Christ,' the message of salva-

8. See Church, pp. 297 ff. English composers of altars before Herbert included Richard Willis (1573), Andrew Willet, and William Browne of Tavistock (in *The Shepherd's Pipe*, 1614). Willet's shapes were printed at the beginning of Sylvester's *Bartas His Devine Weekes & Works* (1605–08). * * *

9. Hutchinson, *Works*, p. 26, notes that in *W* the word 'onely' [line 15—*Editor*] has been corrected to 'blessed.' The change is a poetic improvement, but the original word substantiates my interpretation of the poem.

1. Cf. the references cited by Cameron Mann, *A Concordance to the English Poems of George Herbert* (Boston and New York, 1927). For 'sacrifice,' see 'The Church-porch,' ll. 6, 275; 'The Sacrifice' throughout and especially l. 19; 'Mattens,' l. 3; 'Providence,' l. 14; 'Love unknown,' l. 30. For 'altar' see 'Love

(I),' l. 21 and the first of the 'Sonnets to his Mother,' l. 6. At first reading chapter vi, 'The Parson Praying,' of *A Priest to the Temple* (*Works*, pp. 231–32) seems to provide an exception to Herbert's customary use of 'altar.' After a description of the parson's actions 'when he is to read divine services,' Herbert adds, 'This he doth, first, as being truly touched and amazed with the Majesty of God, before whom he then presents himself; yet not as himself alone, but as presenting with himself the whole Congregation, whose sins he then beares, and brings with his own to the heavenly altar to be bathed, and washed in the sacred Laver of Christs blood.' Despite the familiar imagery, there is no reference here to the Eucharist. The 'altar' and 'the sacred Laver of Christs blood' are truly *in* heaven. * * *

tion engraved on the Christian heart (2 Cor. iii. 3). Herbert's conceptions that the broken and purged heart is the proper basis for the sacrifice of praise and that even stones may participate in and continue that praise were firmly biblical. In his psalm of repentance (Ps. li.) David had stated that the true sacrifices of God are 'a broken and a contrite heart'; Christ had promised that 'the stones' would cry out to testify to Him (Luke xix. 40); and Paul had stated that 'Ye also as liuely stones, are built vp a spirituall house . . . to offer vp spirituall sacrifice' (I Pet. ii. 5).

There is hardly a phrase in 'The Altar' which does not derive from a specific biblical passage. Yet the effect of the poem is simple and fresh. In an important sense this, the first poem within 'The Church' (the central section of *The Temple*), *is* the altar upon which the following poems (Herbert's 'sacrifice of praise') are offered, and it is an explanation of the reason for their composition. God has commanded a continual sacrifice of praise and thanksgiving made from the broken and contrite heart. The condition of mortality as well as the inconstancy of the human heart requires that such a sacrifice be one of those works which 'doe follow them' even when they 'rest from their labours.' For the craftsman and poet, construction of a work of art resulted in that continual sacrifice and introduced the concept of the altar: the poem is a construction upon which others may offer their sacrifices; it is a 'speaking' altar which continually offers up its own sacrifice of praise. The shape of Herbert's poem was intended to hieroglyph the relevance of the old altar to the new Christian altar within the heart. It was fittingly, therefore, a modification of the traditional shape of a classic altar rather than of what Herbert knew as the Communion Table. F. E. Hutchinson's description of the changes in the printing of the poem furnishes a miniature history of progressive misinterpretation.[2] From 1634 to 1667 the shape was outlined merely to draw the reader's attention to its significance. The change in religious temper and vocabulary by 1674 was indicated by 'an engraving of a full-length Christian altar under a classical canopy, with the poem set under the canopy': the assumption was that Herbert had attempted to image a 'Christian altar.' The final liturgical representation of the poem did not, however, occur until the nineteenth century: 'In 1809 there is Gothic panelling and canopy-work behind a modest altar with fringed cloth, fair linen cloth, and the sacred vessels.' Herbert's attempt to use the shape of a classical altar as a hieroglyph of his beliefs concerning the relationships between the heart, the work of art, and the praise of God failed to communicate its meaning to a number of generations. While not one of Herbert's greatest poems, 'The Altar' within its context in *The*

2. *Works*, p. 484.

Temple is still an effective poem if we take the pains to understand it.

'Easter-wings' had been subject to fewer misinterpretations than 'The Altar.' In the last twenty years particularly it has generally been considered a good poem, although there has been little agreement as to the meaning and effectiveness of its pattern. It is the final poem in the group concerning Holy Week, and to read it within its sequence helps to explain some of the difficulties for the modern reader. [Quotes text; see p. 16–17.] The pattern is successful not merely because we 'see' the wings, but because we see how they are made: the process of impoverishment and enrichment, of 'thinning' and expansion which makes 'flight' possible. By that perception and by the rhythmical falling and rising which the shaped lines help to form, we are led to respond fully to the active image and to the poem. The first stanza is a celebration of the *felix culpa*.[3] Man was created in 'wealth and store,' with the capacity for sinlessness. Through Adam's sin Paradise was lost, yet from one point of view the loss was not unhappy: 'where sinne abounded, grace did much more abound' (Rom. v. 20). If man 'rises' in celebration of Christ's victories, the fall will indeed further his flight to God. The second stanza concerns the reduction of the individual by God's punishment for sins. Again, if we 'combine' with Christ 'And feel this day thy victorie,' affliction can prove an advance to flight, for it is through such affliction that souls are led to 'waite vpon the Lord' and 'renew their strength,' and the promise is specific: 'they shall mount vp with wings as Eagles, they shal runne and not be weary, and they shall walke, and not faint' (Isa. xl. 31). The New Testament had related the death and resurrection of the spirit and the body to the germinal cycle of nature, and the favourite English pun on 'son-sun' seemed to acquire a supernatural sanction from Malachi iv. 2: 'But vnto you that feare my Name, shall the Sunne of righteousnesse arise with healing in his wings.' The 'decaying' of the first stanza of Herbert's poem implies the fruitful image of the grain, and the conclusion of that stanza broadens to include the rise of the 'Sun,' the 'harmonious' ascent both of the flight and the song of the larks.[4] The triumphant dichotomies are implied throughout the poem: sickness and health, decay and growth, poverty and wealth, foolishness and wisdom, punishment and reward, defeat and victory, the fall and rise of song and wings and spirit, sin and righteousness, burial and resurrection, death and life. These states are not in polar opposition. The poem and its pattern constantly insist that for man only through the fall is the flight possible; that the

3. "Happy fault," i.e., because Adam's sin "caused" the Redemption. [*Editor.*]

4. See Bennett, *Four Metaphysical Poets*, p. 66.

victory, resurrection, whether in this life or the next, can come only through the death of the old Adam.

The pattern poem is a dangerous form, and its successful practitioners before and after Herbert were few. The conception behind it, however, is neither so naïve nor so dated as some critics have assumed: writing with intentions differing greatly from Herbert's, E. E. Cummings and Dylan Thomas have created successful contemporary pattern poems.[5] For Herbert such poetry was a natural extension of his concern with the hieroglyph. Most of the other poets of his time, whether followers of Spenser, Jonson, or Donne, characteristically used hieroglyphs as the basis for their imagery in either short or extended passages. Herbert's distinction lies in his successful development of the conceptions that the entire poem could be organized around a hieroglyph and that the poem itself could be constructed as a formal hieroglyph.

The hieroglyph represented to Herbert a fusion of the spiritual and material, of the rational and sensuous, in the essential terms of formal relationships. It may have been that his delight in the power and beauty of the hieroglyphic symbol helped to keep his poems from becoming only rational exercises or pious teachings. Yet reason and piety were central, for to Herbert the hieroglyph did not exist as a total mystery or as isolated beauty, but as a beauty and mystery which were decipherable and related to all creation. The message was precise and clear even if complex and subtle. A differing conception of the religious hieroglyph led Crashaw to ecstatic adoration and worship. For Herbert, however, celebration could never be divorced from examination. The hieroglyphs, whether of God's or of man's creation, were to be 'read' rather than adored, and they sent the reader back to God. The chief tool for such reading was the logical use of man's reason.

It was, moreover, delightful as well as edifying for the poet to imitate God in the construction of hieroglyphs. As Sir Philip Sidney had remarked long before, the way in which God had worked in the creation of nature was not so mysterious as marvellous; man could observe and could imitate:

> Neither let it be deemed too saucy a comparison, to balance the highest point of man's wit with the efficacy of nature; but rather give right honour to the heavenly Maker of that maker,

5. As Lloyd Frankenberg has pointed out, *Pleasure Dome: on reading modern poetry* (Boston, 1949), pp. 172–79, Cummings continually writes such poems; the fact that his patterns are based on individual and spontaneous gestures or situations or personalities rather than on symmetrical and abstract forms has disguised the fact from some readers. John L. Sweeney, *The Selected Writings of Dylan Thomas* (New York, 1946), p. xxi, has suggested that the pattern of Thomas's 'Vision and Prayer' may have been inspired by 'Easter-wings.' As Theodore Spencer once remarked, the formal effects of James Joyce's *Ulysses* are directly related to the tradition of George Herbert's poetry.

who having made man to his own likeness, set him beyond and over all the works of that second nature; which in nothing he showeth so much as in poetry; when, with the force of a divine breath, he bringeth things forth surpassing her doings, with no small arguments to the incredulous of that first accursed fall of Adam; since our erected wit maketh us know what perfection is, and yet our infected will keepeth us from reaching unto it.[6]

DOUGLAS BUSH

[Crashaw: Single-hearted Worshipper][†]

* * * Crashaw is the one conspicuous English incarnation of the 'baroque sensibility'. The religio-aesthetic creed and culture of the Counter-Reformation affected all the arts, and indeed aimed at mixing and transcending them, in its effort to make the five senses portals to heaven. The elements of the revival most stimulating to the artistic imagination were the clash and fusion of extremes in the human and divine, the pictorial and the abstract, in the joys and agonies, the spiritual splendour and the mean estate, of Christ, the Virgin, and the pantheon of saints and martyrs. Poetry took on a new and bizarre intricacy of sensuous decoration and symbolic metaphor, a kind of form—or formlessness—which sought a unity deeper and higher than the classical through emotional and impressionistic multiplicity. Aestheticians and literary critics have pursued the elusive concept of baroque as Browne pursued the quincunx,[1] often with equally spacious and elliptical logic, but the simplest definition is 'poetry like Crashaw's'. Its motto might be "Over-ripeness is all'. Crashaw's abundant revision always led to further elaboration and rarely to improvement.

In the *Epigrammatum Sacrorum Liber* of 1634 Crashaw expressly turned away from the traditions of the genre (though not from classical myth) to follow chiefly the Jesuit epigrammatists in treating religious themes while restricting himself to the New Testament. The completely religious character of the volume was only the most obvious sign of the direction its author was to take. We find, not a theologian or thinker, or a troubled soul like Donne or Herbert, but a secure, single-hearted worshipper whose feeling for

6. *The Defence of Poesy, The Miscellaneous Works,* ed. William Gray (Boston, 1860), pp. 69–70.
† From *English Literature in the Earlier Seventeenth Century,* second edition (Oxford, 1962), pp. 147–50.
1. Sir Thomas Browne (1605–82), a physician at Norwich and author of *Religio Medici* (*The Religion of a Physician,* 1643), considered the quincunx —a five-pointed figure—to be the central symbol of the universe and found it everywhere, as he details charmingly in *The Garden of Cyrus* (1658). [*Editor.*]

the central paradoxes of faith does not lessen his sense of the human values in the story of the Son of Mary. And, in spite of the general hard and 'witty' brevity imposed by the form, there are not a few hints of sensuous fancy, the association of gold and purple and roses with the new-born or the crucified Christ, the endless variations on tears, and a version of the popular conceit on the water changed to wine—*Nympha pudica Deum vidit, & erubuit.*[2]

Among the early secular poems in *Steps to the Temple* are sober, half-Jonsonian epitaphs and the more artifical 'Wishes. To his (supposed) Mistress' and 'Love's Horoscope', in which idealism takes a half-cavalier or half-Donnian form. Among translated pieces we might expect two Psalms, if not the *Dies Irae*, to be near Crashaw's heart, and his dilution of such great originals is not altogether insignificant. For all his skill in Latin and Greek verse Crashaw is one of the most unclassical, and erratic, of English poets. The nature of his artistic roots is partly suggested by two re-creations. One is 'Music's Duel' (*ante* 1634?), the uniquely expressionistic and technical elaboration of the Jesuit Strada's popular Latin poem; Crashaw adds religious and symbolic significance to the contrast between the bird's music and the man's. The other, 'Sospetto d'Herode'[3] (1637?), is a highly charged rendering of the first book of Marino's epic on the Slaughter of the Innocents which carries Crashaw's own emphasis on the Christian paradoxes. The Jesuits and perhaps Marino contribute to the famous or notorious 'Weeper' (*ante* 1634?), which offers a severe though not a final test for appreciation of Crashaw and baroque religiosity. A central theme, penitential progress from sin to spiritual perfection, can be extracted, but with difficulty, from the profuse and largely unfocused images. The subject was familiar, even in English, and for the contemporary reader who knew Sidney's *Arcadia* and the sonneteers, Southwell and Giles Fletcher and the emblem-books, there would be little surprise in the individual conceits; but no English poet had produced such a concatenation, or perhaps such grotesque extravagances as some of them—even if playful—are.

Crashaw went far beyond Marinism in power of vision and symbol, yet even in his greater poems he generally hovered between the ideal organic unity of baroque inspiration and a dazzling spray of associated images, and the reader who lacks a special temperament and a knowledge of the symbolic code may be more repelled than attracted. Crashaw's words and details are not vague as modern romantic poetry can be, nor even esoteric, since they grow out of the concrete creed of European Catholicism, but we may be

2. "The chaste nymph saw her God and blushed." [*Editor.*]

3. *The Suspicion of Herod* by Giambattista Marino. [*Editor.*]

unable to find or follow the controlling motive, and at times the poet himself may have lost it. At times, too, he is capable of relatively simple beauty like the opening of 'On the Assumption' or that couplet in 'The Weeper':

> Nowhere but heer did ever meet
> Sweetnesse so sad, sadnes so sweete.

There is some resemblance in 'naïve' conceits between Milton's most Italianate poem, the 'Nativity', and Crashaw's 'Hymn' on the same theme, though their responses to the wonder of the Incarnation are characteristically different; this is one poem of Crashaw's that gained in unity and depth from revision. 'The Glorious Epiphany' is nearer to Milton in part of its substance; here, in a manner very different from the 'Hymn' and of course from Milton, Crashaw develops a threefold contrast, physical, historical, and spiritual, between natural and supernatural light. Another of Crashaw's irregular odes or ecstasies, 'To the Name Above Every Name, the Name of Jesus', is not unlike the 'Epiphany' in symphonic multiplicity, but its devotional passion, 'the witt of love', is more central and typical; and its structure, as Louis Martz has shown, seems to have profited from an ordered model of meditation.

Those who read Crashaw perhaps come back most often to the strong and simple 'Hymn' to St. Teresa, and to the sequel, 'The Flaming Heart', in which cool ingenuity becomes incandescent. The author of the preface of 1646 spoke truly of 'the Quintessence of Phantasie and discourse center'd in Heaven . . . the very Outgoings of the soule'. The 'Poet and Saint' of ascetic life and luxuriant imagination, who seeks fulfilment in the pain and joy of divine annihilation, and freedom from years in Eternity, has little to do with this earth and common experience. He is

> Drest in the glorious madnesse of a Muse,
> Whose feet can walke the milky way;

a beautiful angel beating his luminous wings in a richly coloured Catholic heaven. His nests and spices and wounds and blood, whether we like them or not, have along with their Latin warmth a degree of ritualistic remoteness and abstractness. But the 'strong wine of Love' is a heady drink which, to put to illegitimate use another phrase from the preface, may give birth to the 'prodigious issue of tumorous heats and flashes'. It is almost inevitable that a poet striving to express the inexpressible should seem, at least, not to know the difference between gold and gilt, between spiritual vision and verbal intoxication. One who can soar and burn can also sink and melt. And not merely the uninformed or unsympathetic reader may be embarrassed by the kind of religious emotion that hails the Virgin as 'rosy princesse' and St. Teresa as 'My Rosy Love'. The feeling may not entirely vanish even when, so to speak, Murillo gives way to El Greco:

> By all thy brim-fill'd Bowles of feirce desire
> By thy last Morning's draught of liquid fire;
> By the full kingdome of that finall kisse
> That seiz'd thy parting Soul, & seal'd thee his. . . .

(While the mystic's instinct for erotic imagery has a long tradition behind it, we may be startled to learn that lines 63–117 of 'On a prayer booke sent to Mrs. M. R.' employ a number of images from Carew's 'A Rapture'.) The question whether an indisputable poet is also an indisputable mystic cannot be settled by rule of thumb, and perhaps does not need to be settled. As for the poet, the ordinary reader may feel uneasy when the authentic motives of adoration and self-surrender issue in an undisciplined fervour which has never been rational and never ceases to be sensuous and excited; and he may think that larger and clearer glimpses of the One were granted to the quiet Vaughan.

* * *

HELEN C. WHITE

[Richard Crashaw: Intellectual Poet]†

* * * It is not surprising that a reader fresh from the dazzling speculations of Donne, or from the ordered meditations of Herbert, should feel that Crashaw is so completely absorbed in feeling and image that he seldom or never thinks. Some critics who would not go as far as that would still insist that the intellectual side of Cra-shaw is unimportant or deficient. As a matter of fact, nothing could be farther from the truth. Crashaw was a learned man, trained in the theological disciplines of his tradition and ripely cultivated in the classical literature that was the stock of the humanism of his day. Moreover, as Signor Praz and Mr. Martin have shown, he had a wide acquaintance with the poetry of his own time not only at home but abroad. Indeed, in his own humbler degree Crashaw shares that grace of learned allusion that is one of the charms of Milton's poetry.

But Crashaw is intellectual in another sense to which justice has

† From *The Metaphysical Poets: A Study in Religious Experience* (New York, 1936), pp. 228–30.

hardly been done. The piling up of rhapsodic images in "The Weeper" has blinded readers and even critics to the fact that the great bulk of Crashaw's work is very far from being what Praz so brilliantly described that poem as being, "a rosary of epigrams or madrigals loosely linked together."[1] As a matter of fact, the line of development of the usual Crashaw poem is as firm, basically, as the line of a baroque statue or building, and the logical mass as substantial. The distraction comes from the embellishment, but in general that embellishment is lateral, as it were. It may screen from view the logical advance of the poem; indeed, it often does distract from it, but the forward thrust is always there. Even when the reader feels that he has been swept off his feet by the wind of the poetry, he is being carried steadily to a usually definitive and resonant conclusion. The Nativity hymn and the Teresa poems are superb examples of this.

It is not for nothing that among all the wide range of mystical writers, the mature Crashaw chose for imitation and for praise and for translation two of the most intellectually vigorous, the two who almost more than any other mystics preserve the architectonic power of thought even in the transports of rapture, Teresa of Avila and Thomas Aquinas. For in his own much humbler degree he shows something of the capacity of both for keeping mental control of feeling. Only as with both of these much greater thinkers, there is nothing of the external or the restrictive about this control. It is organic and informative.[2] The thought is the ribbing of the leaf, the spring of the arch that flowers into grace and light.

Indeed, where Crashaw fails from the poetic standpoint, the lapse is usually due to his preoccupation with the thought of the poem at the expense of the image, and so of the feeling. The cherub whose song tasted all day of his breakfast on the Magdalen's tears is an extreme example.[3] The famous "walking baths" of the eyes of the Magdalen that have so effectively distracted generations of critics is another from the same poem.[4] Had Crashaw been a little vaguer in detail or a little less absorbed in the celebration of his theme, neither of these two classic "horrible examples" would have been perpetrated, nor a number of lesser ones. But the important thing to remember is that it is no failure of logical power, of activity or firmness of thinking, that is responsible for the lapses in Crashaw's style.

The substance of the matter is that Crashaw is a man with his eye on the object. His poems are not treatises or descriptions or

1. "Un rosario di epigrammi o di madrigali malamente legati assieme," Mario Praz, *Seicentismo e Marinismo in Inghilterra*, Firenze, 1925, p. 231.
2. Wallerstein, Ruth C., *Richard Crashaw: A Study in Style and Poetic Development*, Madison, 1935, p. 97.
3. "The Weeper," 26–30.
4. Lines 113–114.

analyses or idyls or self-revelations. They are rather emblems, contemplations, hymns, sometimes one of these at a time, more often all together. In so being, they are very much of his time, and can only be understood in terms of the time.

AUSTIN WARREN

[Crashaw's Symbolism]†

Symbolism may be defined as imagery understood to imply a conceptual meaning: such definition is latitudinarian enough to admit the poetry of Mallarmé as well as the ceremonial of the Church. The concept may be a mere overtone, a darkly descried vista, or it may be a category susceptible of prose statement. Some symbolisms are private, founded upon the poet's childhood associations of thing and sentiment; without biographical aid, the reader is likely to find them mere imagism or a congeries of oddly juxtaposed perceptions. Others—like the Christian emblems of dove, lamb, shepherd, cross—are communal. Others must be well-nigh universal, even to men topographically untraveled: the plain, the mountain, the valley, the ocean, the storm, darkness and light, are broadly human.

Parable and allegory may be defined as symbolic narratives in which a conceptual sequence runs parallel to—or, rather, is incarnate in—an imaginative sequence; they are, too, the most explicit forms. Christ parabolically identifies himself with the Good Shepherd; the Word, with the seed; the fig tree, with the unproductive life. Spenser and Bunyan label their persons and places: the Giant Despair, Fidessa, Orgolio, Mr. Worldly Wiseman, Faithful; the Bower of Bliss, the House of Holiness, Doubting Castle, the Delectable Mountains.

The proportion of strength between the image and the concept ranges widely. In eighteenth-century personification, the picture frequently evaporated till but a capital remained; in Mallarmé, the imagery only is presented, though, by its lack of naturalistic congruence, its disjunction, it disturbs the consciousness till the latter evokes some coherent psychological pattern for which all the images are relevant.

Crashaw, sensuous of temperament, wrote a poetry mellifluously musical, lavishly imagistic. At first acquaintance it seems the song of the nightingale hovering over her skill, "bathing in streams of liquid melody"; later, it seems the passage work, the cadenzas, the

† From *Richard Crashaw: A Study in Baroque Sensibility* (Ann Arbor, 1939), pp. 177–93. Footnote references to the poetry are to the edition by L. C. Martin (Oxford, 1957).

glissandi of an endowed and much-schooled virtuoso. Yet his life shows him to have been an ascetic, denying his senses all save their homage to God. In turning to religion and religious poetry, he "changed his object not his passion," as St. Augustine said of the Magdalen:[1] the images of his secular poetry recur in his sacred. He loves his God as he might have loved his "supposed mistress."

Not a preacher or prophet, Crashaw had no "message" to announce. He had suffered and exulted, and exulted in suffering; but his experiences did not tempt him to philosophy or other prose formulation. His was to be a poetry in which the rhythms and images would tell their own tale.

To his symbolism he supplied no chart of prose equivalents. Yet no reader has long studied his poems without feeling that their imagery is more than pageant; that, rather, it is a vocabulary of recurrent motifs.[2]

Nor is this symbolism really undecipherable. In the main it follows traditional Christian lines, drawing on the Bible, ecclesiastical lore, and the books of such mystics as St. Bernard and St. Teresa. Even when it is "private"—as, in some measure, every poet's will be, it yields to persistent and correlating study. Not widely ranging, Crashaw's images reappear in similar contexts, one event elucidating another. No casual reader of his poems, for example, but has been arrested by the recurrence of "nest," usually in rhyming union with "breast"; and, surely, no constant reader has long doubted its psychological import, its equivalence to shelter, refuge, succor.

It need not be maintained—it is, indeed, incredible—that Crashaw constructed a systematic symbolism. It is unlikely, even, that he knew why certain images possessed, for him, particular potence. Obviously much concerned with his technique, given to revision, a lover of the arts, he seems, as a man, ingenuous, free from self-consciousness, imaginatively uncensored.

In his steady movement from secular poetry to an exclusive preoccupation with sacred, from Latin to the vernacular, he relinquished —deliberately, it would seem—the Renaissance decoration of classi-

---

1. "I believe without any levity of conceipt, that hearts wrought into a tendernesse by the lighter flame of nature, are like mettals already running, easilier cast into Devotion then others of a hard and lesse impressive temper, for Saint *Austin* said, *The holy Magdalen changed her object only, not her passion . . .*" (Walter Montagu, *Miscellanea Spiritualia* . . . , 32).
2. Cf. intimations in Osmond, *Mystical Poets*, 118, and Watkin, *The English Way*, 287.

Discussing "Conceits," Kathleen Lea wrote: "In his frequent use of the word 'nest' I do not believe that the image of a bird's nest presented itself to him. . . .

For Crashaw we have an even longer list of words, such as 'womb,' 'tomb,' 'grave,' 'day,' 'death,' and 'fount,' which he used as it were ritualistically and in a colourless sense of his own. While it is proof of his greatness that he had this peculiar idiom of speech, it is also significant of his weakness that this idiom must be re-learned and explained." (*Modern Language Review*, XX [1925], 405.) This was a penetrating insight into the nature of Crashaw's poetic method; and it is the central merit of Miss Wallerstein's *Crashaw* that in some brilliant pages (especially 126-8) it develops and extends this thesis.

cal mythology. As a schoolboy he had written hymns to Venus, poems on Pygmalion, Arion, Apollo and Daphne, Aeneas and Anchises; and in his Latin epigrams, and in "Music's Duel," there occur classical embellishments. From the English sacred poems, however, such apparatus is conspicuously absent. Giles Fletcher, of his English predecessors closest to him in temper and idiom, had compared the ascending Christ to Ganymede, snatched up from earth to attend upon Jupiter;[3] but no such bold correlation of pagan and Christian finds place in Crashaw's poetry. Donne and Herbert, also erudites, had made a similar surrender of their classicism;[4] and to Herbert's example in particular he may have been indebted.

Otherwise, Crashaw makes no attempt to differentiate his sacred from his secular imagery; many characteristic figures and metaphors, "delights of the Muses," are reënlisted in the service of Urania. For example, the familiar paradox of Incarnation, whereby Jesus is at once the son and the father of the Blessed Virgin, is anticipated in the apostrophe to Aeneas carrying Anchises: "Felix! *parentis* qui *pater* diceris esse tui!"[5] The persistent motif of the mystical poems first appears in "Wishes":

> A well tam'd heart
> For whose more noble smart
> Love may bee long chusing a Dart.

Unlike Herbert, Crashaw rarely recollects homely images of market place and fireside; and allusions to the polities and economies of the Stuart world come but seldom. Christ, dying, is called "his own legacy." With the Blessed Virgin, Crashaw, who, too, has set "so deep a share" in Christ's wounds, would draw some "dividend." To these financial metaphors, one may add what at first view seems Herbertian—the angels with their bottles, and the breakfast of the brisk cherub.[6] Yet, though "breakfast" Herbert would surely not have disdained, such intimacy with the habits of cherubs is peculiarly alien to the Anglican spirit of *The Temple*. It is Mary's tears which, having wept upwards, become, at the top of the milky river, the cream upon which the infant angel is fed, adding "sweetnesse to his sweetest lips"; and this context, by its extravagant lusciousness, reduces the blunt word to but a passing grotesquerie.

3. In *Christ's Victory and Triumph in Heaven and Earth* (1610). [*Editor.*]
4. Cf. Warren, "George Herbert," *American Review*, VII, 258 ff.
5. "Fortunate man, you who may be said to be the father of your parent" (Martin, 222–3). [The tale of Aeneas carrying his father Anchises out of burning Troy in flight from the victorious Greeks is found not only in *Aeneid II* but also in numerous Renaissance art works, e.g., by Raphael and Bernini.— *Editor.*]
6. Ibid., 286 (stanza 9); cf. "Charitas Nimia," ibid., 280, and ibid., 309 ("The Weeper," stanza 5).

Some feeling for Nature, especially the dawn and flowers, the young Crashaw undoubtedly had; but even the early poems evince no botanical niceness, no precision of scrutiny. The first of the Herrys poems[7] develops a single metaphor, that of a tree whose blossoms, ravished by a mad wind, never deliver their promised fruit; but unlike Herbert's "orange tree," this is a tree of no specific genus.[8] Crashaw's habitual blossoms are the conventional lily and rose.

These flowers, which appear briefly, in his earliest poems, as outward and visible creatures, do not disappear from his later verse; but they soon turn into a ceremonial and symbolical pair, a liturgical formula, expressive of white and red, tears and blood, purity and love. * * *

If Crashaw's *flora* soon turn symbols, his *fauna* have never owed genuine allegiance to the world of Nature. The worm; the wolf, the lamb; the fly, the bee; the dove, the eagle, the "self-wounding pelican," and the phoenix: all derive their traits and their significance from bestiary or Christian tradition, not from observation; and their symbolism is palpable. In their baseness men are "all-idolizing worms"; in their earthly transience and fickleness and vanity, foolish wanton flies. The bee, a paragon of industry, is still more a creator, preserver, or purveyor of mystic sweetness. The Holy Name of Jesus is adored by angels that throng

> Like diligent Bees, And swarm about it.
> O they are wise;
> And know what *Sweetes* are suck't from out it.
> It is the Hive,
> By which they thrive,
> Where all their Hoard of Hony lyes.[9]

The dove and lamb, of frequent appearance, betoken innocence and purity; they are also meet for votive offering. Sometimes the doves emblemize elect souls, whose eyes should be "Those of turtles, chaste, and true"; sometimes, the Holy Ghost. The *Agnus Dei*, the white lamb slain before the foundation of the world, was Crashaw's favorite symbol for Christ and for him, among all symbols, one of the most affecting.

"By all the Eagle in thee, all the dove": so Crashaw invokes the chaste Teresa, the mystic whose wings carried her high, whose spiritual vision was unflinching and acute.

> Sharpe-sighted as the Eagles eye, that can
> Out-stare the broad-beam'd Dayes Meridian.

7. Four epitaphs in memory of William Herrys, fellow of Pembroke College, Cambridge, who died October 15, 1631. [*Editor.*]

8. Ibid., 167; Herbert, "Employment."
9. "To . . . the Name of Jesus," 153f. [*Editor.*]

Meditating her books, the responsive reader finds his heart "hatcht" into a nest "Of little Eagles, and young loves."[1]

To the phoenix, Crashaw devoted a Latin poem, a "Genethliacon et Epicedion," in which the paradox of a fecund death shows its expected fascination for him. The fragrant, unique, and deathless bird reappears in the Latin epigrams, and in the English poems, both secular and sacred. It occurs twice in the sequence of Herrys elegies; it is belabored at length in the panegyric to Henrietta Maria, "Upon her Numerous Progenie," where it becomes a symbol of supreme worth. In the sacred poems, it assumes its traditional Christian office as sign of the God-man, virgin-born, only-begotten, and immortal.

With most artists, the pleasures of sight are preeminent; with Crashaw, in spite of his interest in pictures and emblems, the fuller-bodied and less sharply defined senses would appear to have afforded richer, more characteristic delight.

His colors are elementary, chiefly conventional, readily symbolic. In his religious poetry, but three occur: red (or purple = *purpureus*), with its traditional relation, through fire and the "Flaming Heart" to love; black; and white. Black is, for him, the sign not of mourning or penitence but of sin and, still more, of finiteness, of mortality: "Dust thou art, and to dust thou shalt return." In his translation of Catullus, men are "dark Sons of Sorrow." Augmented, the phrase reappears in "The Name of Jesus" as "dark Sons of Dust and Sorrow." Elsewhere in the religious poems, man is "Disdainful dust and ashes" or "Darke, dusty Man."

White, perhaps as the synthesis of all colors, perhaps as the symbol of luminous purity, is the most exalting adjective in Crashaw's vocabulary. It occurs in his secular verse, especially in his panegyrics upon the royal family. But it is more frequent in his *carmina sacra*[2] used customarily of the Blessed Virgin or Christ, and most strikingly of Christ as the Lamb.

> Vain loves, avaunt! bold hands forbear!
> The Lamb hath dipp't his white foot here.[3]

The absence from the religious poetry of green, the color of nature, and blue—in the tradition of Christian art, the color of truth and of the Blessed Virgin—is conspicuous; so is the absence of chiaroscuro. By other means, he produces a sensuous luxuriance; but, in respect to the palette, he turns, like the Gospels, to bold antithesis of black and white.

1. On the lore of the eagle, cf. Phipson, *Animal-Lore*, 232–3.
2. Religious poems. [*Editor.*]
3. Cf. "Hymn to St. Teresa": "Thou with the LAMB, thy Lord, shalt goe; / And whereso'ere he setts his white / Stepps, walk with HIM those wayes of light . . ." and the "To the Queen's Majesty": "A Golden harvest of crown'd heads, that meet / And crowd for kisses from the LAMB'S white feet."

For evidence that Crashaw was a lover of music, one need not appeal to "Music's Duel." "On the Name of Jesus," among his four or five masterpieces, calls to celebration all sweet sounds of instrument—

> Be they such
> As sigh with supple wind
> Or answer Artfull Touch. . . .

These flutes, lutes, and harps are the "Soul's most certain wings," Heaven on Earth; indeed, in a moment of quasi-Platonic identification of reality with highest value he equates "All things that Are" with all that are musical. Assuredly, Crashaw intended his own poetry to be—what by virtue of his mastery of vowel and consonant sequences and alliteration it habitually is—sweet to the ear, Lydian. But, for him, it is also true, human music was an initiation into an archetypal music, the harmonious concert of the spheres "which dull mortality more feels than hears." The ears are "tumultous shops of noise" compared with those inner sensibilities which, properly disciplined, may hear, as from afar, the inexpressive nuptial hymn.[4]

Crashaw's favorite adjectives, "sweet" and "delicious," mingle fragrance and taste. His holy odors are chiefly traditional—those of flowers and of spices. "Let my prayer be set forth in Thy sight as the incense," said the Psalmist; but the simile finds its analogy in the ascent of both. The fragrance of spices pervades that manual of the mystics, the *Song of Songs*. To the Infant Jesus, the magi brought frankincense and myrrh. The Magdalen dies as "perfumes expire." The Holy Name is invoked as a "cloud of condensed sweets," bidden to break upon us in balmy and "sense-filling" showers. In his ode on Prayer, the most mystical of his poems, Crashaw bids the lover of God, the virgin soul, to seize the Bridegroom

> All fresh and fragrant as he rises
> Dropping with a baulmy Showr
> A delicious dew of spices. . . .

Sometimes Crashaw's gustatory delights, like those of the

> sweet-lipp'd Angell-Imps, that swill their throats
> In creame of Morning *Helicon* . . .[5]

remain innocently physical. But customarily the pleasure of the palate, too, becomes symbolic, as it is when the Psalmist bids us "taste . . . how good the Lord is." The angels who swarm about the Holy Name are wise because they "know what Sweetes are suck't from out of it." This palatal imagery might be expected to culmi-

4. In my discussion of sensuous correspondences I am indebted to Miss M. A. Ewer's important *Survey of Mystical Symbolism*.
5. "Music's Duel."

nate in apostrophes to the Blessed Sacrament; but not so. For Prot-
estants, the Holy Communion is a symbolic as well as commemora-
tive eating and drinking; to Crashaw, who believed in Transubstantiation, the miraculous feast seemed rather the denial of the senses
than their symbolic employment. His expansive paraphrases of St.
Thomas' Eucharistic hymns are notably sparse in sensuous imagery.
It is not the Blood of Christ on the altar but the redeeming blood
on the cross which prompts him to spiritual inebriation.

Crashaw's liquids are water (tears, penitence); milk (maternal
succor, nutrition); blood (martyrdom on the part of the shedder,
transference of vitality to the recipient); wine (religious inebriation,
ecstasy). Fluid, they are constantly mixing in ways paradoxical or
miraculous. In one of his earliest poems, a metrical version of Psalm
137, blood turns into water. In one of the latest, "Sancta Maria,"
"Her eyes bleed Teares, his wounds weep Blood." From the side of
Christ, crucified, flowed an "amorous flood of Water wedding
Blood." The angels, preparing for a feast, come with crystal phials
to draw from the eyes of the Magdalen "their master's Water: their
own Wine." Milk and blood may mingle, as when maternal love
induces self-sacrifice; water turns to wine when tears of penitence
become the happy token of acceptance and union; wine is transub-
stantiated into blood in the Sacrament; blood becomes wine when,
"drunk of the dear wounds," the apprehender of Christ's redeeming
sacrifice loses control of his faculties in an intoxication of gratitude
and love.

The last of the senses is at once the most sensuous and the least
localized. To it belong the thermal sensations of heat and chill.
Fire, the cause of heat, is, by traditional use, the symbol of love; its
opposites are ordinarily lovelessness and—what is the same—death.
The "flaming Heart" of Christ or of the Blessed Virgin is the heart
afire with love. St. Teresa's ardor renders her insensitive to love's
antonym and opposite, the chill of the grave. Crashaw is likely to
unite the opposites. Since she is both Virgin and Mother, Mary's
kisses may either heat or cool. Lying between her chaste breasts, the
Infant Jesus sleeps in snow, yet warmly.[6]

The supremities of touch, for Crashaw's imagination, are experienced in the mystical "wound of love," in martyrdom, and in nuptial union. In the former states, torment and pleasure mix: the
pains are delicious; the joys, intolerable. In his mystical poems,
Crashaw makes free use of figures drawn from courtship and marriage. Christ is the "Noble Bridegroom, the Spouse of Virgins."
Worthy souls are those who bestow upon His hand their "heaped
up, consecrated Kisses," who store up for Him their "wise
embraces." The soul has its flirtations, its "amorous languish-

---

6. "A Hymne of the Nativity" (Martin, 107): "With many a rarely-temper'd kisse, / That breathes at once both Maid and Mother, / Warmes in the one, cooles in the other."

ments," its "dear and divine annihilations." St. Teresa, love's victim, is sealed as Christ's bride by the "full Kingdom of that final Kiss"; and her mystic marriage has made her the mother of many disciples, many "virgin-births."

In the spirit of St. Ignatius' *Exercitia Spiritualia*, Crashaw performs an "Application of the Senses" upon all the sacred themes of his meditation. God transcends our images as He transcends our reason; but, argues the Counter-Reformation, transcension does not imply abrogation. Puritanism opposes the senses and the imagination to truth and holiness; for Catholicism, the former may be minstering angels. "How daring it is to picture the incorporeal," wrote Nilus Scholasticus in the *Greek Anthology*; "but yet the image leads us up to spiritual recollection of celestial beings."[7] Not *iconoclasts*, some censors would grant that visual imagery, emanating from the "highest" of the senses, may point from the seen to the unseen; there they would halt. Crashaw, like one persistent school of mystics, would boldly appropriate the whole range of sensuous experience as symbolic of the inner life.

Studied case by case, Crashaw's striking imagery will yield its symbolic intent. But its most characteristic feature emerges only when image is collated with image. Poetic symbolism may constantly devise new alliances of sense and concept; indeed, the poet Emerson objected to Swedenborg's "Correspondences"[8] on the precise ground of their fixed and systematic character. With Crashaw, though rigidity is never reached, his metaphors yet form a series of loosely defined analogies and antitheses and cross references, a system of motifs symbolically expressive of themes and emotions persistently his.

Associated images recur like ceremonial formulas. In the secular poems, the lily and the rose have appeared, singly and together. The association continues into the religious poems, but the metaphorical character of the flowers has become explicit. In the epigram on the Holy Innocents, the mother's milk and the children's blood turn, for Crashaw's pious fancy, into lilies and roses. A characteristic later juxtaposition, in the "Hymn for the Circumcision," gives the metamorphosis: "this modest Maiden Lilly, our sinnes have sham'd into a Rose."

A similar ritual coupling is that of the pearl and the ruby. Sometimes these symbols appear singly, sometimes together. In the same

7. *Greek Anthology,* Bk. I, epigram 33. Cf. also epigram 34 (from Agathias Scholasticus): "Greatly daring was the wax that formed the image of the invisible Prince of the Angels, incorporeal in the essence of his form. But yet . . . a man looking at the image directs his mind to a higher contemplation. No longer has he a confused veneration, but imprinting the image in himself, he fears him as if he were present. The eyes stir up the depths of the spirit, and Art can convey by colours the prayers of the soul." [See note above, to Summers, p. 265.—*Editor.*]

8. Emmanual Swedenborg (1688–1722), philosopher, scientist, commentator on Scripture, and mystic, who emphasized "correspondences" between the world of nature and that of spirit. [*Editor.*]

"Hymn for the Circumcision" Crashaw sees Christ's drops of blood as rubies. The tears of the Magdalen are Sorrow's "richest Pearles." They are united in the eighteenth stanza of "Wishes." Still united, they reappear in the religious poetry: When men weep over the bloody wounds of Christ,

> The debt is paid in *Ruby*-teares,
> Which thou in Pearles did'st lend.[9]

Another frequent union—and this not of contrasts but of contradictories—couples fire and water, an oxymoron of images. Already, in an early poem, the sun is represented as paying back to the sea in tears what, as fire, it borrowed. When the Magdalen washes Christ's feet with tears, wiping them with her hair,

> Her eyes flood lickes his feets faire staine,
> Her haires flame lickes up that againe.
> This flame thus quench't hath brighter beames:
> This flood thus stained fairer streames.[1]

The Blessed Virgin is the "noblest nest Both of love's fires and floods." The tears of contrition or of sorrow, so far from extinguishing the fire of love, make it burn more ardently.

But one cannot thus far have surveyed Crashaw's imagery without perceiving how the whole forms a vaguely defined but persistently felt series of interrelations. There are things red—fire, blood, rubies, roses, wine—and things white—tears, lilies, pearls, diamonds: symbols of love and passion; symbols of contrition, purity, innocence.

On its sensuous surface, his imagination sparkles with constant metamorphosis: tears turn into soft and fluid things like milk, cream, wine, dew; into hard things like stars, pearls, and diamonds. Beneath, the same experiences engage poet and poem.

All things flow. Crashaw's imagery runs in streams; the streams run together; image turns into image. His metaphors are sometimes so rapidly juxtaposed as to mix—they occur, that is, in a succession so swift as to prevent the reader from focusing separately upon each. The effect is often that of phantasmagoria. For Crashaw, the world of the senses was evidently enticing; yet it was a world of appearances only—shifting, restless appearances. By temperament and conviction, he was a believer in the miraculous; and his aesthetic method may be interpreted as a genuine equivalent of his belief, as its translation into a rhetoric of metamorphosis. If, in the Gospels, water changes to wine and wine to blood, Crashaw was but imaginatively extending this principle when he turned tears into pearls, pearls into lilies, lilies into pure Innocents.

Style must incarnate spirit. Oxymoron, paradox, and hyperbole

9. "On the Wounds of Our Crucified Lord" (Martin, 99).   1. English epigram (Martin, 97).

are figures necessary to the articulation of the Catholic faith. Crashaw's *concetti*,[2] by their infidelity to nature, claim allegiance to the supernatural; his baroque imagery, engaging the senses, intimates a world which transcends them.

RICHARD STRIER

Crashaw's Other Voice[†]

Richard Crashaw's religious poetry, while filled with deep humility, is strikingly free of self-consciousness. "May we guess his heart / By what his lipps bring forth, his only part / Is God and godly thoughts" wrote his friend Thomas Car.[1] His conversion to Roman Catholicism set Crashaw free of the painstaking diagnosis of emotions and states of mind which Protestant eschatology stimulated.[2] For Crashaw, as for Empedocles,[3] there are but two great principles, love and strife. But for Crashaw, the match is not equal: love is "Absolute sole lord / Of Life and Death," an ultimate truth; strife is a lesser truth, relative and human. Love moves all things; only in man is there strife and tension. The symbols and rituals of the Church dominate Crashaw's imagination: the Cross, the name of Christ, the Incarnation, the Eucharist, the life of the saint or the death of the martyr—the objects of Love. The voice in which Crashaw celebrates the mystery and joy of his holy love is Crashaw's characteristic voice; it is a voice which is exultant and assured, vibrant with the richness of satisfied religious ardor.

In certain of the *Carmen Deo Nostro*, however, strife is present. There is no prolonged introspection in Crashaw's poetry, but in this handful of poems there is the kind of tension, concern, and doubt associated with introspection and the kind of language associated with this tension. These are the poems written *to other people*. These poems cannot have the note of attainment. For himself, Crashaw could be sure, for others he could not. Human concern acted upon Crashaw's poetic language the way introspection acted upon the language of Donne or Herbert, forcing him to work out an idiom capable of expressing psychological complexity. The poem of Crashaw's closest in manner and spirit to Donne or Herbert's religious poetry is the 1652 version of "To the Noblest and Best of

2. Conceits. [*Editor*.]

† From *Studies in English Literature 1500–1900*, IX (1969), 135–48. With minor changes by the author. Slightly abridged.

1. Thomas Car, "Crashaw The Anagramme" in *The Poems of Richard Crashaw*, ed. L. C. Martin (Oxford, 1957),

p. 133.

2. See Herbert Grierson on this. "Introduction," *Metaphysical Lyrics and Poems of the Seventeenth Century* (New York, 1959), pp. xlvi–xlvii.

3. Greek philosopher, fifth century B.C. [*Editor*.]

Ladies, the Countess of Denbigh."[4] The verse of this poem is aus-
terely controlled; it does not burst with poetic and spiritual fire-
works but reverberates with the pressure of passion on argument. Its
music is not the soaring of Hosannah but the echoing of profound
human concern. The "motive" of the poem, the impulse which
prompts and impels it, is not the religion but the compassion of a
deeply religious man: Batter *her* heart three person'd God. This is
Crashaw's other voice.

The first part of the poem's subtitle, "Persuading her to Resolution in Religion," suggests a fundamental commitment to the metaphysical method, for persuasion involves some degree of logical
coherence and force as well as passionate conviction. Moreover, the
peom is not merely intended to persuade but to convert: the
Countess is to "render herself without further delay into the Communion of the Catholic Church." The reasoned discourse of his
message must express the poet's emotional distress at the Countess's
spiritual condition. The poem must simultaneously analyze and
evoke. Crashaw must attempt to create in the Countess a "direct
sensuous apprehension" of his thought. He must systematically
refuse to exploit to its full potential the logic of metaphor that it
may remain tractable to the logic of discourse. The radiant spirit is
faced with a sobering task: he must point the Way to a troubled
soul. Pope complained of Crashaw's lack of exactness, and although
conceding he was "none of the worst versificators," warned that
"the lines and Life of the picture are not to be inspected too
narrowly."[5] The lines and life of Crashaw's persuasion "to resolution in religion" *must* be capable of withstanding inspection.

The poem begins with what seems a powerful visual image:

> What heav'n-intreated Heart is This
> Stands trembling at the gate of blisse;
> Holds fast the door; yet dares not venture
> Fairly to open it, and enter.

The word "trembling" dominates the emotional coloration of these
lines. We see the figure entreated and yet acutely self-conscious;
caught between fear and longing, its trembling indecision has prepared for its lack of daring, its inability to cross the threshold. The
feminine rime and the comma before "and" in the second couplet
enhance the effect. But in all this we have confused the affective
power of this opening evocation with its actual content; we have
immediately filled in the synechdoche and supplied a denotative
level where Crashaw has employed only abstractions. There is no
visual image, for it is the Heart, a metaphor for a particular aspect

4. The 1653 version, far more characteristic of Crashaw, is an inferior and far
less interesting poem.

5. *The Correspondence of Alexander
Pope*, ed. George Sherburn, (Oxford,
1956), vol. I, p. 110.

of the human personality, which is heaven-entreated. A spiritual state is being described in mock-physical terms. The figure which had seemed so concrete is wholly metaphorical.[6] But even after we recognize our "mistake," the situation presented remains strangely concrete; the vividness of the emotional response these lines evoke stays on even after we have made the necessary intellectual readjustment. All the verbs describe common, simple, physical actions; they are all present and active and the movement from a past to a present participle adds to the sense of immediacy and produces a sense of entering *in medias res.* The experience of halting at a doorstep is so familiar and basic an image of irresolution as to be an essentially charged situation. The gate is the gate of bliss: an immediately recognizable human situation embodies a theological dilemma. This is actually neither allegory nor personification, but rather the purposeful confusion of the tenor and vehicle of a metaphor. A subtle and apt poetic device, it affirms the fact that the human and the theological concerns of the poem are identical and inseparable.

Crashaw proceeds from this "mixed" metaphor to an abstract formulation, simply making clear what has already been presented; this is a Heart "Whose Definition is a Doubt / Twixt Life & Death, twixt In & Out." Thus far the poem has been impersonal evocation and description; now the internal scene presented is explicitly identified as the Countess's spiritual condition, and the poet addresses her directly: "Say, lingring fair! why comes the birth / Of your brave soul so slowly forth?" The "your" comes almost as a revelation. The image of birth in these lines takes on—following as it does immediately upon "Twixt Life & Death, twixt In & Out"—a literal, almost graphic quality. Relying on a sublimated strongly physical image, Crashaw evokes and defines a spiritual state. The Countess is in limbo: to dare is "to love," to be born; to remain passive, paralyzed by irresolution, is spiritual death. The Countess enters the poem in person, so to speak, at this point, and the poet's voice takes on a distinctive tone. The initial spondee is sharp and peremptory. Albeit gently, the poet is demanding an explanation, for—and this note is sustained throughout the poem—he professes an inability to understand her hesitation, the lingering slowness of this birth. He cannot understand and he will not sympathize. He must be cruel only to be kind. Crashaw seems, momentarily, to forget himself:

> Plead your pretences (o you strong
> In weakness!) why you choose so long
> In labor of your selfe to ly,
> Not daring quite to live nor dy?

Placing an exclamatory statement in parenthesis, the poet

6. Compare Austin Warren, "Interlude: Baroque Art and the Emblem," in *Richard*   *Crashaw: A Study in Baroque Sensibility* (Louisiana, 1939).

expresses his muted rage. That the Countess's soul was "brave" had served to increase the poet's painful amazement, but her strength angers him, for she is "strong in weakness." A new element enters —that of choice. In the opening lines there was no great sympathy for the trembling Heart, but a kind of spiritual cowardice or meekness seemed the reason this heart was "defined by" doubt. Now wilfullness is seen as the reason. The Countess is "pleading her pretenses," thinking too precisely upon the event, rationalizing and deluding herself, falling into what Crashaw elsewhere calls Reason's "dark and knotty snares." The poet for whom "Keep close, my soul's inquiring eye!" was a fervent prayer could not stand quietly by and allow this fall to occur. Failure to dare is lack of faith. "Seek, and ye shall find," said Christ; "knock, and it shall be opened unto you." The Countess's heart is "heav'n-*intreated*." Her fault is deeper than lassitude in seeking. Heaven has made the first move and the Countess is stubbornly and incomprehensibly refusing to heed the Call which has come to her. Instead she chooses "In labor of [her] selfe to ly." The pun on "labor" here is surely intentional: the Countess is prolonging the rebirth pains of her soul. For Crashaw, the self is something to be transcended. By choosing to leave the gate of bliss unopened and unentered, the Countess is clinging to her worldly identity, refusing to reject the limitations of her self. Crashaw presents the Countess's movement toward Catholicism as equivalent to a novice's movement toward mystical initiation.

As if repenting of the harsh almost strident tone of his outburst, as if afraid of having further disturbed rather than fortified the trembling heart, Crashaw's next words to the Countess are gentle, quietly and tenderly reasonable: "Ah linger not, lov'd soul! a slow / And late consent was a long No. . . ." He is not condemning and scolding but entreating; the pace of the verse slows down a bit. The "lingring fair" is beseeched to linger not. As the poem progresses, Crashaw becomes more and more explicit, creating the effect that he is speaking out more and more openly as his sense of urgency intensifies. He speaks as one who has attained inner peace; nowhere does he hint that surrender of the self had been a similar agony for him. Crashaw dramatizes the steady mounting of his amazement at the tragic paradox of the divided will. He will not acknowledge the reality, much less the necessity, of the Countess's dilemma. His compassion cannot admit of its own existence because to do so would affirm the reality of its object. Pity alone can be admitted to. Crashaw will not acknowledge the Hound of Heaven type of religious experience.[7] By indirection, saying one thing and meaning another, he expresses his attitude: "What magick bolts,

7. See Francis Thompson's poem, "The Hound of Heaven," which represents the soul in flight, being pursued by God. [*Editor.*]

what mystick Barres / Maintain the will in these strange warres!"
The words "magick" and "mystick" do not refer to the actual spiritual situation of the Countess; rather they express the poet's pro-
fessed inability to account for her situation—there is something
unnatural at work in it, something "strange." "Mystick," when
Crashaw uses it elsewhere, is always a joyous word, but there is
nothing "mystical and high" about the Countess's dilemma. Birth
too is normally for Crashaw an image of joy—"Unfold thy fair
Conceptions; And display / The Birth of our Bright Joys." In this
anxious poem, however, Crashaw must consciously pervert and dis-
locate the whole system of intrinsic values normally implicit in his
poetic language. This reversal of the poetic values of recurrent
words from their "natural" order in his poetry—from joy to pain—
expresses the poignance and severity which Crashaw perceives in the
Countess's inner strife. Clinging to paradox-ridden mortality is
unnatural; it breaks the bond of joy. The poet's language itself is
crying out for redress. A vocabulary pre-eminently suited to Love is
being used in a poem dominated by the image of war. And the
Countess is fleeing Him down the labyrinthine ways of her own
mind.

Crashaw allows his intellectual outrage to express the outrage of
his whole being. He treats the *bellum intestinum*[8] as no more than
a whim, an illusion. The thought is elaborated as the emotion
accretes: "What fatall, yet fantastick, bands, / Keep the free Heart
from it's own hands!" The bands are "fantastick"—self-created,
unreal. But these bands of illusion can be "fatall," for this is the
most dangerous inner state possible. A psychological reality can
block the way to ultimate Reality. Without minimizing the possible
consequences of the Countess's spiritual condition, Crashaw insist-
ently points up the terrible absurdity of it. This explains the com-
passionate yet almost hysterical tone of these lines: exclamation
points have replaced question marks as the poet's protest against the
continuance of this strange war within the will. The free Heart is
being kept from its own hands, selfhood is hindering the operation
of grace. Crashaw's "image" is a subtle and affecting one; again an
abstraction becomes largely emotional and intuitive in its appeal.
He relies for his effect on the associations of his words—"free,"
restraining "bands." Again we respond to the sublimated image.
We assent intellectually to the image which our emotions have
already constructed. The heart already had its metaphorical
"hands" in order to have held fast the door of bliss. Crashaw retains
a subtle control of the emotional quality and connotative flow in his
language. The mock-physicality of his imagery keeps us anchored in
the actuality of the situation. The heart which should be offering
itself is defending itself; the Countess is clinging to illusion, linger-

8. Civil war. [*Editor.*]

ing in mortality by pleading her pretenses, and this, as we know, is a matter of Life or death. Our selves should become our own best sacrifice.[9]

Crashaw's analysis recalls Milton's "Sufficient to have stood, though free to fall." The poem's first twenty lines suggest a generalized pattern of the proper workings of the inner world in relation to which the exact condition of the Countess's inner mechanism is being diagnosed. It is the Heart which is capable of receiving grace; from the heart, with the help of the will, the soul is seen as emerging. The soul is not "born" until the heart is free from the self (lines 7–8 and 11). Selfhood keeps the heart "from its own hands," the soul. The Will must reject the self in favor of the soul. Once "born"—freed from selfhood by a proper choice—the soul becomes the hands with which the Heart grasps bliss. The heart united with God, the human personality is unified, the all-too-human inner war is supplanted by the peace that passeth understanding. Conversion, like mystical ecstasy, is brought about by a union of wills.[1] The soul on the one hand and the self on the other are defined phenomena: the Will alone is undefined and can swing the inner balance by how it allies itself. For Crashaw, the resolution of the human personality is not the establishment of an ordered hierarchy so much as consummation of the whole being in the soul as the soul attains consummation in God.

Crashaw is using reason to persuade to the renunciation of reason. He is presenting an either/or. This explains the strangely stern character of the poem beneath its initial hesitancy and its strained but careful modulation. The first section of the poem is the section of definition and analysis, yet the lines expand and constrict with the flow of the poet's emotion. There is a compelling mixture of precise denotative language with conceptually vague but emotionally precise imagery in these lines. The poet's astonishment is made to correspond to the objective reality: this condition *is* a thing to be wondered at. The intellectual rigor of Crashaw's sermonizing is muted and informed by the direct flow of his emotion from "What heav'n-intreated Heart" to "Say, lingring fair" to "Ah linger not." We never forget, never cease to feel, that the poet is writing to a loved soul, and that the poem is an act of love.

From the semi-allegorical Heart and its hands, Crashaw leaps to an emotionally equivalent semi-naturalistic image:

> So when the year takes cold, we see
> Poor waters their owne prisoners be.
> Fetter'd, and lockt up fast they ly
> In a sad selfe-captivity.

9. Crashaw, "In the Holy Nativity of Our Lord God," *Poems*, p. 251.
1. Saint John of the Cross writes: "The supernatural union comes about when the two wills—that of the soul and that of God—are conformed in one." *The Dark Night of the Soul*, trans. by Kurt F. Reinhardt (New York, 1957), p. 91.

The grammatical stress on the reflexive is sustained and empha-sized. The martial imagery and the imagery of restraint are subtly united. The slow, heavy rhythm, the half-rhyme in the second coup-let, enhance the haunting quality of these lines. Crashaw linger-ingly teases all its emotional potential out of his conceit. This is by no means a wholly "objective" correlative, for Crashaw explicitly includes in his use of the natural image the subjective adjectives which are implicit within it. The Pathetic Fallacy is necessary here; Crashaw has no desire to make a sharp distinction between the thing and his perception of it. Expanding on the suggestion of the "fetter'd" waters, Crashaw makes the image more cogent and pre-cise by adding consciousness of itself to the river's plight, personify-ing the freezing waters as nymphs trapped in their own substance —their own selves: "The astonisht nymphs their flood's strange fate deplore / To see themselves their own severer shore." Through these lines, another self-contained flat sentence enclosed within the couplet, the *pathos* is exquisitely, lingeringly extended by the shift from tetrameter into pentameter. The implication of these lines is that the Countess's whole being—if she would but attend to it—is just as astonished by the failure of her will as the nymphs are at their situation—or as the poet is at the Countess's. To strengthen the equivalence between the Countess and the nymphs, Crashaw establishes a linguistic identity between their dilemmas by using the same adjective to describe them. The nymphs see the strangeness of their "strange fate" but the Countess does not seem to sense the strangeness of her "strange warres." The whole tone of the poem has changed. It has moved from the horror to "the pity of it." These images cling. Question and exclamation have yielded to flat statement. The shift in tone results from a shift in Crashaw's emphasis from the Countess's power of choice to her helplessness. Crashaw is attempting to resolve the problem of his own sympathy, for throughout the poem he has been struggling for detachment, for a height from which to pity. He achieves a certain detachment here, but the palpability of the grief in the nymph image betrays him. His pity remains tinged with compassion. The poet remains in the realm Keats marks off as "Here, where men sit and hear each other groan." But there will be no more outbursts; he will set himself wholly to the task of coherent and powerful persuasion.

For Crashaw, love is both love of God and God's Love. Against the passivity we have just seen and the pity we have just felt, grace is balanced. The Empedoclean dualism is made explicit. The warmth of Love is juxtaposed against the terrible coldness of self-captivity; Love can end the inner war:

> Thou that alone canst thaw this cold,
> And fetch the heart from its strong Hold;
> Allmighty Love! end this long warr.

"Thou," another opening stress, is powerfully abrupt after the very casual elaboration of the "captive waters" metaphor. The briskness of this diction comes as a relief after the almost extreme purity of diction of the preceding lines—the verse itself is warmer. The next line of the poem presents a single perfect image. Although perhaps not elaborate enough to be a true conceit, it functions like the metaphysical conceit at its best: as a focal point where an emotion and an abstract conception are perceived as an integral unit within a sharply defined sensory image. In this single image, the humane and religious impulse behind the entire poem crystallizes. Love will end "the warr," "And of a meteor make a starr." The meteor is an archetypal metaphor of tragedy, of momentary brilliance and inevitable descent. A star is the emblem of the permanence and serenity which grace bestows; it is a still-point, not subject to change and not, as Crashaw wrote elsewhere, "by alternate shreds of light / Sordidly shifting hands with shades and night." Crashaw would do this for the loved soul of the Countess; Love would do this for her: transmute her flux into stillness. For precision and concentrated suggestiveness, there is little even in Herbert to surpass this careful heartfelt image of Crashaw's, at once passionate and abstract.

The poet continues to address Love, enumerating its powers:

> O fix this fair Indefinite.
> And mongst thy shafts of soveraign light
> Choose out that sure decisive dart
> Which has the Key of this close heart,
> Knowes all the corners of't, and can controul
> The self-shut cabinet of an unsearcht soul.

This language is very calm and assured; Crashaw is in perfect intellectual control. Fixing the fair indefinite is explication of the meteor-star image. Crashaw's emphasis is all on the sureness and decisiveness of Love as contrasted with the hesitation and doubt of spiritual strife. Love chooses and controls; the soul seems passive. Crashaw prays that it may be at last "love's hour." He has fully prepared the context for the uncompromising and absolute nature of his vision; Love must "Come once the conquering way; not to confute / But kill this rebel word, Irresolute." All this prayer and declaration has been that the Countess may "write Resolv'd at Length." The poet evinces no compassion whatever at this point for the Countess's strength in weakness—he calls it "peevish." As long as and whenever the poem's emphasis is upon the soul's passivity, Crashaw can maintain his detachment intact.

But this one-sided activism of Love is misleading. Thoroughly anti-Calvinist, the poem is consistent in its denial of determinism, including the determinism of grace freely given. The Countess's soul is unsearched because she has not sought. She must allow Love to heal her self-tormented soul. She must meet heaven half way; there must be a *conjunction* of *eros* and *agape*:[2]

> Unfold at length, unfold fair flowre
> And use the season of love's showre,
> Meet his well-meaning Wounds, wise heart!

The image of Christ's wounds ties in, subtly and potently, with the dominant war imagery, and marks the transformation of strife into Love which has taken place in the imagery of the poem. If the Countess does not open her heart to the joy of spring but chooses to remain in the *pathos* of spiritual winter, she is betraying Christ and His sacrifice. There is extraordinary restraint in the gingerness and lack of poetic fanfare with which Crashaw introduces into the poem and then quickly moves off from the unspeakable condemnation of spiritual cowardice implicit in the appeal to Christ's sacrifice. Crashaw viewed his life as "one long debt / Of Love" to Christ.[3] It is sufficient that he allude to, without directly mentioning, the Name Above Every Name. A second feminine rime occurs —"shower" and "flower"—serving to further buffer and soften the impact. It is perhaps because Crashaw's language is so rigidly controlled here that "the current of his feeling" fails to carry his mixed metaphor—"And hast to drink the wholsome dart."[4]

In the next four lines of the poem, Crashaw abandons the steady level he had maintained since "O fix this fair indefinite," and the verse again expands and constricts with the flow of his emotion, moving from a personal sense of joy to an impersonal sense of the possibility of despair. This rapid crescendo-diminuendo produces an effect of remarkable power:

> O Dart of love! arrow of light!
> O happy you, if it hitt right,
> It must not fall in vain, it must
> Not mark the dry regardless dust.

The full stop after the ecstatic first couplet is long and audible and painful; we feel the poet forcing himself to conceive what is for him truly inconceivable. The second couplet is a "dying fall." In its repetition of "must not," in its dull monotonality and slow, halting rhythm, in the exact metrical equivalence of its two lines, in the heavy monosyllables which emphasize the polysyllabic "regardless," in the thudding alliteration of the d's, there is a haunting and terrible sense of waste and needless desolation. The Countess can be healed only by letting herself be wounded.

---

2. *Eros*: human love, based on passionate attraction ("erotic love"); *agape*: the love of benevolence, friendship; spiritual or idealized love. [*Editor*.]

3. "Vexilla Regis," *Poems*, p. 277.

4. I think that Crashaw's poetic lapses are in general lapses of feeling. His imagery is best when he is caught up in it emotionally, not when he is intellectually toying with it or working it out.

Yet immediately after this warning, Crashaw reaffirms his faith in the determined outcome of the Countess's spiritual strife:

> Fair one, it is your fate; and brings
> Eternal worlds upon its wings.
> Meet it with wide-spread arms; and see
> It's seat your soul's just center be.

By using the resources of poetry, Crashaw can have it both ways. He presents the Countess's present situation as unbearable and conjures vivid images of what it would mean to choose wrong while at the same time attempting to deny the reality of her choice by presenting the preferable alternative as inevitable. He does not want to intensify her dilemma. This playing upon the naturalness and inevitability of her conversion is an efficacious device, for it presents her choice as the poet sees it—between illusion and reality. This is truly poetry of persuasion. Illusion is pain and entrapment in the self; renunciation would be *easy* and joyous. The ease of the false dilemma's solution, of conversion, is central to the tonality of the poem. The seat of the dart would become the "just center" of the soul, or it would find its way to the soul's already existing center—there is an ambiguity in the line—but Crashaw's emphasis on the naturalness of this state is clear. Strife is absurd, all he is asking is that the Countess assent to the inevitable. Yet at the same time the poet expresses a sustained awareness of the implications of not assenting. The transmutation of the *bellum intestinum* into the triumph of Love (signalled in the poem's imagery by the dart of Love and Christ's well-meaning wounds) produces a carefully wrought, paradoxical affirmation:

> Disband dull fears; give faith the day.
> To save your life, kill your delay.
> It is love's seege; and sure to be
> Your triumph, though his victory.
> 'Tis cowardice that keeps this feild
> And want of courage not to yeild.

After the passivity of "and see / It's seat your soul's just center be," the poem again shifts to the active and hortatory—"disband," "give," "kill." Crashaw openly attacks spiritual cowardice. Defiance is weakness, acceptance strength; daring is humility, hesitation pride: a total reversal of secular values has been successfully effected.

Crashaw further elaborates the military conceit in terms of love: "Yield then o yield, that love may win / The Fort at last, and let life in." Spenser describes Sansloy's attempt on Una thus:

> So when he saw his flatt'ring arts to fayle,
> And subtile engines bet from batteree,

> With greedy force he gan the fort assayle.
> Whereof he weend possessed soone to bee,
> And win rich spoile of ransackt chastetee.
>
> (FQ I. vi. 5)

The sexuality of "yielding the fort" to love is explicit. Earlier, Crashaw described the wholesome dart of love's light as: "That healing shaft which heav'n till now / Hath in love's quiver hid for you." The shaft which will soothe the frenzy of doubt and calm the tormented heart has been hidden in "love's quiver." In *Delights of the Muses*—"though of a more humane mixture as sweet as they are innocent"[5]—Crashaw wrote in "Song Out of the Italian":

> O deliver
> Love his Quiver
> From thy Eyes he shoot: his Arrows,
> Where Apollo
> Cannot follow:
> Feather'd with his Mother's Sparrows.

The same image—in identical words—describes the Anacreontic Cupid[6] in a woman's eyes and the possibility of grace. "Do not be afraid, loved soul, relax, dare; it is yielding which requires true integrity"—suddenly we realize what Crashaw has been saying. He is persuading the Countess to gather her spiritual rosebuds while she may. Recall "Unfold at length, unfold fair flowre, / And use the season of love's showre." The urgency of the poem comes because there is not world enough or time, because "late consent was a long no." "By fleeting nuances of language, he suggests an anterior mode of poetic expression and hence of experience, and in a context which is new to it."[7]

The poet's final words are direct and menacing address to the coy mistress of this poem:

> Yeild quickly. Lest perhaps you prove
> Death's prey before the prize of love.
> The fort of your faire selfe, if't be not won,
> He is repulst indeed; But you are undone.

Crashaw's God only knocks, breathes and shines, does not ravish but waits for "the awful daring of a moment's surrender" to bestow the ultimate gift. Crashaw has attempted to mitigate the starkness of the Countess's choice and the awfulness of her situation, but he must in the end leave the Countess with a clear awareness of them. He blunts and dulls the emotional vibrance of the poem that he

---

5. Thomas Car, "Preface to the Reader" of *Steps to the Temple, Poems,* p. 76.

6. Anacreon was a Greek lyric poet (sixth-century B.C.) who celebrated love and wine. [*Editor.*]

7. Yvor Winters, *In Defense of Reason* (New York, 1947), p. 133. William Empson makes similar and related points in *Seven Types of Ambiguity* (New York, 1961), Chapt. 7.

may present its intellectual content with greater and greater force and openness. The poem ends on a final paradox, the last couplet again stretching out into pentameter: if the fair woman does *not* yield her fort, maintains her human selfhood and self-sufficiency— her too long preserved spiritual virginity—*then* she is undone. Human realities demand paradox; grace presents itself to mortality in paradoxical terms, but grace, like death, ends the paradoxes of mortality. The Countess's is a tortured mind and troubled human heart; Crashaw suits his language to his subject. There is, in this poem to the Countess of Denbigh, a great deal of "tough reasonableness beneath the slight lyric grace."[8]

* * *

FRANK KERMODE

The Argument of Marvell's "Garden"†

* * *

The garden is a rich emblem, and this is not the place to explore it in any detail; indeed I shall say nothing of the symbolic gardens of the Middle Ages which were still alive in the consciousness of the seventeenth century. The gardens to which Marvell most directly alludes in his poem are the Garden of Eden, the Earthly Paradise, and that garden to which both Stoic and Epicurean, as well as Platonist, retire for solace or meditation. The first two are in many respects one and the same; the third is the garden of Montaigne, of Lipsius, and of Cowley. I shall not refer to the *hortus conclusus*,[1] though at one point in my explication of Marvell's poem I allude to a Catholic emblem-writer. Doubtless the notion of Nature as God's book affects the poetic tradition; it certainly occurs in poems about solitude at this period. But I think it is misleading to dwell on the history of the idea.

Of the complexity of the Earthly Paradise, with all its associated images and ideas, it is not necessary to say much: it is of course a staple of pastoral poetry and drama, and the quality of Marvell's allusions to it will emerge in my explication. But a word is needed about the garden of the solitary thinker, which Marvell uses in his argument against the libertine garden of innocent sexuality.

It is to be remembered that we are not dealing with the innocence of Tasso's Golden Age, where there is a perfect concord between appetite and reason, or with the garden of innocent love

8. T. S. Eliot, "Andrew Marvell," *Selected Essays* (New York, 1950), p. 252. † From *Essays in Criticism*, II (1952), 225–41. Slightly abridged. 1. Garden enclosed. [*Editor.*]

that Spenser sketches in *Faerie Queen,* IV, x, where 'thousand payres of louers walkt, Praysing their god, and yeelding him great thankes', and 'did sport Their spotlesse pleasures, and sweet loues content'. The libertines use the argument of the innocence of sense to exalt sensuality and to propose the abolition of the tyrant Honour, meaning merely female chastity. This is the situation of the *Jouissance*[2] poetry which was fashionable in France, and of which Saint-Amant's well-known example, excellently translated by Stanley, is typical. It is equally the situation of Randolph's 'Upon Love Fondly Refused' and his 'Pastoral Courtship', Carew's 'Rapture' and Lovelace's 'Love Made in the first Age'.[3] In Randolph's Paradise there is no serpent—'Nothing that wears a sting, but I'[4] —and in Lovelace's

> No Serpent kiss poyson'd the Tast
> Each touch was naturally Chast,
> And their mere Sense a Miracle.[5]

And so it is throughout the libertine versions of sensual innocence. The garden, the place of unfallen innocence, is identified with a naturalist glorification of sensuality. The garden which is formally opposed to this one by Marvell is the garden where sense is controlled by reason and the intellect can contemplate not beauty but heavenly beauty.

It was Montaigne, this time in his Stoic role, who gave wide currency to the pleasures of *Solitary* seclusion. The relevant ideas and attitudes were developed into a poetic genre. Many poets certainly known to Marvell practised this genre, among them Fane and Fairfax and the French poets, notably Saint-Amant, whose *Solitude* demonstrates how easily he moved in this, the antithesis of the *Jouissance* mode. This famous poem was translated by Fairfax and by Katharine Phillips.[6] This is the poetry of the meditative garden, whether the meditation be pseudo-Dionysian, or Ciceronian, or merely pleasantly Epicurean, like Cowley's. There is, of course, a play of the senses in which woman has no necessary part, though the equation of all appetite with the sexual appetite in the libertines tends to ignore it; this unamorous sensuality is firmly castigated by Lipsius in his treatment of gardens. If the garden is treated merely as a resort of pleasure, for the 'inward tickling and delight of the senses' it becomes 'a verie sepulchre of slothfulnes'. The true end of the garden is 'quietnes, withdrawing from the world, medita-

---

2. Enjoyment. [*Editor.*]
3. Thomas Stanley (1625–78), historian, scholar, translator, and lyric poet; Antoine-Girard de Saint-Amant (1594–1661), courtier, soldier, poet; Thomas Randolph (1605–1635), dramatist and poet. [*Editor.*]

4. *Poems*, ed. G. Thorn-Drury, 1929, p. 110.
5. *Poems*, ed. C. H. Wilkinson, 1930, p. 147.
6. Katharine Phillips (1631–64), known also as "Orinda," was perhaps the first woman poet in England. [*Editor.*]

tion', the subjection of the distressed mind to right reason.[7] The true ecstasy is in being rapt by intellect, not by sex.

Retirement; the study of right reason; the denial of the sovereignty of sense; the proper use of created nature; these are the themes of Marvell's poem laboriously and misleadingly translated into prose. As poetry the work can only be studied in relation to its genre, though that genre may be related to ethical debates. To the naturalist *Jouissance* Marvell opposes the meditative *Solitude*. The fact that both these opposed conceptions are treated in the work of one poet, Saint-Amant, and a little less explicitly in Théophile[8] and Randolph also, should warn against the mistaking of seriousness for directness of reference to ethical propositions. 'The Garden' uses and revalues the 'norms' of the genre: it is not a contribution to philosophy, and not the direct account of a contemplative act.

IV

Henry Hawkins, the author of the emblem-book *Partheneia Sacra*, adopts a plan which enables him, in treating the emblematic qualities of a garden, to direct the attention of the pious reader away from the delights of the sense offered by the plants to a consideration of their higher significance. As in Marvell, sensual pleasure has to give way to meditation.[9] We now proceed to the explication of Marvell's poem, with a glance at Hawkins's wise disclaimer: 'I will not take upon me to tel al; for so of a Garden of flowers, should I make a Labyrinth of discourse, and should never be able to get forth' (p. 8).

The poem begins by establishing that of all the possible gardens it is dealing with that of retirement, with the garden of the contemplative man who shuns action. The retired life is preferred to the active life in a witty simplification: if the two ways of life are appraised in terms of the vegetable solace they provide it will be seen that the retired life is quantitatively superior. The joke is in the substitution of the emblem of victory for its substance. If you then appraise action in terms of plants you get single plants, whereas retirement offers you the solace of not one but *all* plants. This is a typical 'metaphysical' use of the figure called by Puttenham[1] the Disabler. The first stanza, then, is a witty dispraise of the active life, though it has nothing to distinguish it sharply from other kinds of garden-poetry such as libertine or Epicurean— except possibly the hint of a secondary meaning 'celibate' in the

7. *De Constantia, Of Constancie,* translated by Sir J. Stradling, ed. R. Kirk and C. M. Hall, 1939, pp. 132ff.
8. Théophile de Viau (1590–1626), "libertine" poet. [*Editor.*]
9. *Partheneia Sacra,* ed. Iain Fletcher, 1950 (reprint of 1633), p. 2. [In Greek, *partheneia* can mean either the *virgin* or, in the neuter plural, *songs sung to a*

maiden. Hawkins's subtitle is: "The Mysterious and Delicious Garden of the Sacred Parthenes . . . , to the honour of the Incomparable Virgin Mary . . ."— *Editor.*]
1. George Puttenham (d. 1590), critic of poetry and author of the important *Art of English Poesy* (1589). [*Editor.*]

word *single* and a parallel sexual pun on *close*,[2] which go very well with the leading idea that woman has no place in this garden.

The Innocence of the second stanza cannot itself divide the poem from other garden-poems; for Innocence of a sort is a feature of the libertine paradise, as well as of the Epicurean garden of Cowley and indeed most gardens.

> Your sacred Plants, if here below,
> Only among the Plants will grow—

lines which are certainly a much more complicated statement than that of *Hortus*—seem to have stimulated Mr. Klonsky to astonishing feats. But the idea is not as difficult as all that. Compare 'Upon Appleton House'—

> For he did, with his utmost Skill,
> *Ambition* weed, but *Conscience* till,
> *Conscience*, that Heaven-nursed Plant,
> Which most our Earthly Gardens want.
>
> (XLV)

Your sacred plants, he says, addressing Quiet and Innocence, are unlike the palm, the oak and the bays in that if you find them anywhere on earth it will be among the plants of the garden. The others you can find 'in busie Companies'. The joke here is to give Quiet and her sister plant-emblems like those of the active life, and to clash the emblematic and the vegetable plants together. The inference is that Innocence may be found only in the green shade (*concolor Umbra* occurs at this point in the Latin version). Society (with its ordinary connotations of 'polish' and 'company') is in fact all but rude (unpolished) by comparison with Solitude, which at first appears to be lacking in the virtues Society possesses, but which possesses them, if the truth were known, in greater measure (the Ciceronian-Stoic 'never less alone than when alone' became so trite that Cowley, in his essay 'Of Solitude', apologized for referring to it).

We are now ready for a clearer rejection of libertine innocence. Female beauty is reduced to its emblematic colours, red and white (a commonplace, but incidentally one found in the libertine poets) and unfavourably compared with the green of the garden as a dispenser of sensual delight. This is to reject Saint-Amant's 'crime innocent, à quoi la Nature consent'.[3] A foolish failure to understand the superiority of green causes lovers to insult trees (themselves the worthier object of love) by carving on them the names of women. (This happens in Saint-Amant's *Jouissance*.) Since it is the green garden, and not women that the poet chooses to regard as

2. Proposed by A. H. King, *English Studies*, XX (1938), 118–21.

3. *OEuvres Complètes*, ed. Ch-L. Livet, 1855, I, 119.

amorous, it would be farcically logical for him to carve on the trees their own names. The garden is not to have women or their names or their love in it. It is natural (green) and amorous (green—a 'norm' of the poem) in quite a different way from the libertine garden.

Love enters this garden, but only when the pursuit of the white and red is done, and we are without appetite. (Love is here indiscriminately the pursued and the pursuer. Weary with the race and exertion (*heat*) it 'makes a retreat' in the garden; hard-pressed by pursuers it carries out a military retreat.) The place of retreat has therefore Love, but not women: they are metamorphosed into trees. The gods, who might be expected to know, have been misunderstood; they pursued women not as women but as potential trees, for the green and not for the red and white. Marvell, in this witty version of the metamorphoses, continues to 'disable' the idea of sexual love. Here one needs quite firmly to delimit the reference, because it is confusing to think of *laurel* and *reed* as having symbolic significations. It is interesting that this comic metamorphosis (which has affinities with the fashionable mock-heroic) was practised for their own ends by the libertine poets; for example, in Saint-Amant's 'La Metamorphose de Lyrian et de Sylvie', in Stanley's Marinesque 'Apollo and Daphne', in Carew's 'Rapture', where Lucrece[4] and other types of chastity become sensualists in the libertine paradise, and very notably in Lovelace. Thus, in 'Against the Love of Great Ones':

> Ixion[5] willingly doth feele
> The Gyre of his eternal wheele,
> Nor would he now exchange his paine
> For Cloudes and Goddesses againe.
>
> (*Poems*, p. 75)

The sensuous appeal of this garden is, then, not sexual, as it is in the libertines. It has, none the less, all the enchantment of the Earthly Paradise, and all its innocence: this is the topic of the fifth stanza. The trees and plants press their fruit upon him, and their gifts are in strong contrast to those of the libertine garden,

> Love then unstinted, Love did sip,
> And Cherries pluck'd fresh from the Lip,
> On Cheeks and Roses free he fed;
> Lasses like *Autumne* Plums did drop,
> And Lads, indifferently did crop
> A Flower, and a Maiden-head.
>
> (*Poems*, p. 146)

---

4. Raped by Sextus, the son of King Tarquin of Rome, Lucrece was so offended by the violation of her virtue that she took her own life. [*Editor.*]

5. When Ixion tried to seduce Hera, Zeus tricked him with a cloud, by which he fathered the Centaurs; Ixion's punishment was to be bound on a perpetually turning wheel of fire. [*Editor.*]

The fruits of green, not of red and white, are offered in primeval abundance, as they are in the Fortunate Islands or in any paradise. Everything is by nature lush and fertile; the difference between this and a paradise containing a woman is that here a Fall is of light consequence, and without tragic significance. ('Insnar'd with *flowers, I* fall on grass.') In the same way, Marvell had in 'Upon Appleton House (LXXVII) bound himself with the entanglements not of wanton limbs, in the libertine manner of Carew, Randolph and Stanley, but of woodbine, briar and bramble. * * *

In this garden both man and nature are unfallen; it is therefore, for all its richness, not a trap for virtue but a paradise of perfect innocence. Even the fall is innocent; the sensuous allurements of the trees are harmless, and there is no need to 'fence The Batteries of alluring Sense'. It is evident that Empson and King were quite right to find here a direct allusion to the Fall.

Modern commentators all agree that the sixth stanza, central to the poem, is a witty Platonism, and of course this is so. The danger is that the Platonism can be made to appear doctrinal and even recherché, when in fact it is reasonably modest, and directly related to genre treatments of love in gardens. There is, however, a famous ambiguity in the first two lines: how are we to take 'from pleasure less'? It can mean simply (1) reduced by pleasure, or (2) that the mind retires because it experiences less pleasure than the senses, or (3) that it retires from the lesser pleasure to the greater. The first of these might be related to the doctrine of the creation in *Paradise Lost*, VIII, 168f.—'I am who fill Infinitude, nor vacuous the space. Though I uncircumscrib'd myself retire, And put not forth my goodness . . .' This would be consistent with the analogy later drawn between the human and divine minds. But the second is more likely to be the dominant meaning, with a proper distinction between mind and sense which is obviously relevant to the theme ('None can chain a mind Whom this sweet Chordage cannot bind'). The third meaning is easily associated with this interpretation. The mind withdraws from the sensual gratification offered in order to enjoy a happiness of the imagination. * * * The metaphor is not unfamiliar—'Some have affirm'd that what on earth we find The sea can parallel for shape and kind'—and the idea is that the forms exist in the mind of man as they do in the mind of God. By virtue of the imagination the mind can create worlds and seas too which have nothing to do with the world which is reported by the senses. This is the passage which seems to have caused such trouble to commentators, who look to learned originals like Plotinus and Ficino for the explanation: but in fact the Platonism here is dilute and current.

It is a commonplace of Renaissance poetic that God is a poet, and that the poet has the honour of this comparison only because of the creative force of fancy or imagination. Nor is the power exclusive to poets. The mind, which 'all effects into their causes brings'[6] can through the imagination alone devise new and rare things: as Puttenham says, 'the phantasticall part of man (if it be not disordered) is a representer of the best, most comely and bewtifull images or appearances of thinges to the soule and according to their very truth' (p. 19). Puttenham shuns 'disordered phantasies . . . monstruous imaginations or conceits' as being alien to the truth of imagination, but it is conceivable that Marvell, in his suggestion of the mind's ability to create, refers to a more modern psychology and poetic, with its roots in the Renaissance, but with a new emphasis. * * * The mental activity which Marvell is describing is clear; it is the working of the imagination, which, psychologically, follows sense and precedes intellection, and is therefore the means of rejecting the voluptuous suggestions of sense; and which 'performs its function when the sensible object is rejected or even removed'.[7] The mind's newly created worlds are, in the strict sense, phantasms, and without susbstance: and since they have the same mental status as the created world, it is fair to say that 'all that's made' is being annihilated, reduced to a thought.

But a green thought? This is a great bogey; but surely the thought is green because the solitude is green, which means that it is also the antithesis of voluptuousness? Here the normative signification of green in the poem is in accord with what is after all a common enough notion—green for innocence. Thus, in 'Aramantha' Lovelace asks:

> Can trees be green, and to the Ay'r
> Thus prostitute their flowing Hayr?
> *(Poems,* p. 112)

But I cannot think the green has any more extensive symbolic intention. Green is still opposed to red and white; all this is possible only when women are absent and the senses innocently engaged.

The stanza thus alludes to the favourable conditions which enable the mind to apply itself to contemplation. The process is wittily described, and the psychology requires no explanation in terms of any doctrinaire Platonism, whether pseudo-Dionysian, Plotinian, or Florentine.

The seventh stanza is also subject to much ingenious comment. The poet allows his mind to contemplate the ideas, and his soul begins a Platonic ascent. Here there are obvious parallels in the English mystics, in Plotinus, in medieval and Florentine Platonism;

6. Sir John Davies, *Nosce Teipsum* ('The Intellectual Powers of the Soul,' stanza 5).

7. Gianfrancesco Pico della Mirandola, *De Imaginatione*, edited and translated by H. Caplan, 1930, p. 29.

but we must see this stanza as we see the rest of the poem, in relation to the genre. Failing to do this we shall be involved in an endless strife between rival symbolisms, as we are if we try to find an
external significance for *green*. As it is, there is no need to be over-
curious about the fountain; its obvious symbolic quality may have
an interesting history, but it is primarily an easily accessible emblem
of purity. As for the use of the bird as an emblem of the soul, that
is an image popularized by Castiglione,[8] and used by Spenser of the
early stages of the ascent:

> Beginning then below, with th'easie vew
> Of this base world, subiect to fleshly eye,
> From thence to mount aloft by order dew,
> To contemplation of th'immortall sky,
> Of that soare faulcon so I learne to fly,
> That flags awhile her fluttering wings beneath,
> Till she her selfe for stronger flight can breath.
> *(Hymne of Heavenly Beauty*, pp. 22–8)

Spenser has just passed from the consideration of woman's love and
beauty to the heavenly love and beauty. The bird which prepares
its wings for flight is evidently a symbol with as settled a meaning
as the dew, which Marvell also shared with many other poets.

The hungry soul, deceived with false beauties, may have 'after
vain deceiptfull shadowes sought'—but at last it looks 'up to that
soveraine light, From whose pure beams al perfect beauty springs'
(*H.H.B.*, 291, 295). Marvell's bird 'Waves in its Plumes the various Light.' * * * Note how this same image is used in literature
more closely related to Marvell.

> Les oyseaux, d'un joyeux ramage,
> En chantant semblent adorer
> La lumière qui vient dorer
> Leur cabinet et leur plumage—[9]

Thus Théophile, in his Ode, 'Le Matin'.[1] In *Partheneia Sacra*
Hawkins uses the dove as other poets use the dew or the rainbow—

> Being of what coulour soever, her neck being opposed to the Sun
> wil diversify into a thousand coulours, more various then the Iris
> it-self, or that Bird of *Juno* in al her pride; as scarlet, cerulean,
> flame-coulour, and yealding a flash like the Carbuncle, with ver-
> milion, ash-coulour, and manie others besides. . . .

> (p. 202)

8. *The Book of the Courtier,* translated
by Thomas Hoby, Everyman Edition, p.
338. [Baldassare Castiglione's *Cortegiano*
was originally published in 1528; Hoby's
translation appeared in 1562. An elegant,
widely-read dialogue setting out all the
characteristics of the ideal courtier, the
book concludes with a long Platonist discourse on the nature of love.—*Editor.*]
9. [With their joyous noise, the birds as
they sing seem to adore the light which
comes to gild their little house and their
plumage—*Editor.*]
1. *OEuvres Complètes,* ed. M. Alleaume,
1856, I, 174–5.

Marvell's use of the Platonic light-symbolism is therefore not technical, as it might be in Chapman, but generalized, as in Quarles or Vaughan, and affected by imagery associated with the garden genres. We are thus reminded that the point about the ascent towards the pure source of light is not that it can be achieved, but that it can be a product of *Solitude* rather than of *Jouissance* and that it is an alternative to libertine behaviour in gardens. It is the ecstasy not of beauty but of heavenly beauty.

The eighth stanza at last makes this theme explicit. This is a special solitude, which can only exist in the absence of women, the agents of the most powerful voluptuous temptation. This has been implied throughout, but it is now wittily stated in the first clear reference to Eden. The notion that Adam would have been happy without a mate is not, of course, novel; St. Ambrose believed it. Here it is another way of putting the case that woman offers the wrong beauty, the wrong love, the red and white instead of the green. Eve deprived Adam of solitude, and gave him instead an inferior joy. Indeed she was his punishment for being mortal (rather than pure Intelligence?). Her absence would be equivalent to the gift of a paradise (since her presence means the loss of the only one there is). This is easy enough, and a good example of how naturally we read references to the more familiar conceptions of theology and philosophy as part of the play of wit within the limited range of a genre.

In the last stanza the temperate quiet of the garden is once more asserted, by way of conclusion. (The Earthly Paradise is always in the temperate zone.) The time, for us as for the bee (a pun on 'thyme') is sweet and rewarding; hours of innocence are told by a dial of pure herbs and flowers. The sun is 'milder' because in this zodiac of flowers fragrance is substituted for heat; Miss Bradbrook and Miss Lloyd Thomas have some good observations here. The time computed is likewise spent in fragrant rather than hot pursuits. This is the *Solitude*, not the *Jouissance*; the garden of the *solitaire* whose soul rises towards divine beauty, not that of the voluptuary who voluntarily surrenders to the delights of the senses.

This ends the attempt to read 'The Garden' as a poem of a definite historical kind and to explore its delicate allusions to a genre of which the 'norms' are within limits ascertainable. Although it is very improbable that such an attempt can avoid errors of both sophistication and simplification, one may reasonably claim for it that in substituting poetry for metaphysics it does no violence to the richness and subtlety of its subject.

WILLIAM EMPSON

Marvell's 'Garden'†

The chief point of the poem is to contrast and reconcile conscious and unconscious states, intuitive and intellectual modes of apprehension; and yet that distinction is never made, perhaps could not have been made; his thought is implied by his metaphors. There is something very Far-Eastern about this; I was reminded of it by Mr. Richard's discussion, in a recent *Psyche*, of a philosophical argument out of Mencius. The Oxford edition notes bring out a crucial double meaning (so this at least is not my own fancy) in the most analytical statement of the poem, about the Mind:—

> Annihilating all that's made
> To a green Thought in a green shade.

'Either "reducing the whole material world to nothing material, i.e., to a green thought," or "considering the material world as of no value compared to a green thought"'; either contemplating everything or shutting everything out. This combines the idea of the conscious mind, including everything because understanding it, and that of the unconscious animal nature, including everything because in harmony with it. Evidently the object of such a fundamental contradiction (seen in the etymology: turning all *ad nihil*, *to* nothing, and *to* a thought) is to deny its reality; the point is not that these two are essentially different but that they must cease to be different so far as either is to be known. So far as he has achieved his state of ecstasy he combines them, he is 'neither conscious nor not conscious,' like the seventh Buddhist stage of enlightenment. (It is by implying something like this, I think, that the puns in Donne's *Extasie* too become more than a simple Freudian giveaway). But once you accept this note you may as well apply it to the whole verse.

> Meanwhile the Mind, from pleasure less,
> Withdraws into its happiness;
> The Mind, that Ocean where each kind
> Does streight its own resemblance find;
> Yet it creates, transcending these,
> Far other Worlds, and other Seas;
> Annihilating . . .

From pleasure less. Either 'from the lessening of pleasure'—'we are quiet in the country, but our dullness gives a sober and self-knowing happiness, more intellectual than that of the overstimulated pleasures of the town' or 'made less by this pleasure'—'The pleasures of the country give a repose and emotional release which make me feel less intellectual, make my mind less worrying and introspective.' This is the same opposition; the ambiguity gives two meanings to pleasure, corresponding to his Puritan ambivalence about it, and to the opposition between pleasure and happiness. *Happiness*, again, names a conscious state, and yet involves the idea of things falling right, happening so, not being ordered by an anxiety of the conscious reason. (So that as a rule it is a weak word; it is by seeming to look at it hard and bring out its implications that the verse here makes it act as a strong one).

This same doubt gives all their grandeur to the next lines. The sea if calm reflects everything near it; the mind as knower is a conscious mirror. Somewhere in the sea are sea-lions and -horses and everything else, though they are different from land ones; the unconscious is unplumbed and pathless, and there is no instinct so strange among the beasts that it lacks its fantastic echo in the mind. In the first version thoughts are shadows, in the second (like the *green thought*) they are as solid as what they image; and yet they still correspond to something in the outer world, so that the poet's intuition is comparable to pure knowledge. (Keats may have been quoting the sixth verse, by the way, when he said that if he saw a sparrow on the path he pecked about on the gravel.) This metaphor may reflect back so that *withdraws* means the tide going down; the *mind* is *less* now, but will return, and it is now that one can see the rock-pools. On the Freudian view of an Ocean, *withdraws* would make this repose in nature a return to the womb; anyway it may mean either 'withdraws into self-contemplation' or 'withdraws altogether, into its mysterious processes of digestion.' *Streight* may mean 'packed together,' in the microcosm, or 'at once'; the beasts see their reflection (perhaps the root word of the metaphor) as soon as they look for it; the calm of nature gives the poet an immediate self-knowledge. But we have already had two entrancingly witty verses about the sublimation of sexual desire into a taste for Nature, and the *kinds* look for their *resemblance*, in practice, out of a desire for *creation*; in the mind, at this fertile time for the poet, they can do so 'at once,' being 'packed together.' This profound transition, from the correspondences of thought with fact to those of thought with thought, to *find* which is to be *creative*, leads on to the next couplet, in which not only does the *mind* *transcend* the world it mirrors, but a sea, by a similar transition, transcends both land and sea too, which implies self-consciousness and all the antinomies of philosophy. And it is true that the sea reflects the *other worlds* of the stars. Yet even here the double meaning is not lost; all land-beasts have their sea-beasts, but the sea also has the kraken; in the depths as well as the transcendence of the mind are things stranger than all the kinds of the world.

Green takes on great weight here, as Miss Sackville West pointed out, because it has been a pet word of Marvell's before; to list the uses before the satires may seem a trivial affectation of scholarship, but at least shows how often he used the word. In the Oxford text; pages 12, l. 23: 17, l. 18: 25, l. 11: 27, l. 4: 31, l. 27: 38, l. 3: 45, l. 3: 70, l. 376: 71, l. 390: 74, l. 510: 122, l. 2. Less important, 15, l. 18: 30, l. 55: 42, l. 14: 69, l. 386: 74, l. 484: 85, l. 82: 89, l. 94. It is connected here with grass, buds, children, and an as yet virginal prospect of sexuality,[1] a power of thought as yet only latent in sensibility, and the peasant stock from which the great families emerge. The 'unfathomable' grass both shows and makes a soil fertile; it is the humble, permanent, undeveloped nature which sustains everything, and to which everything must return; children are connected with this both as buds, because of their contact with Nature (as in Wordsworth) and unique fitness for Heaven (as in the Gospels).

> The tawny mowers enter next,
> Who seem like Israelites to be
> Walking on foot through a green sea[2]

connects greenness with oceans and gives it a magical security; though one must drown in it.

> And in the greenness of the grass
> Did see my hopes as in a glass[3]

connects greenness with mirrors and the partial knowledge of the mind. The complex of ideas he concentrates into this passage, in fact, had been worked out separately already.

To nineteenth century taste the only really poetical verse of the poem is the central fifth of the nine; I have been discussing the sixth, whose dramatic position is an illustration of its very penetrating theory. The first four are a crescendo of wit, on the themes 'success or failure is not important, only the repose that follows the exercise of one's powers' and 'women, I am pleased to say, are no longer interesting to me, because nature is more beautiful.' One effect of the wit is to admit, and so make charming, the impertinence of the second of these, which indeed the first puts in its place; it is only for a time, and after effort among human beings, that he can enjoy solitude. The value of these moments made it fitting to pretend they were eternal; and yet the lightness of his

1. Cf. 'giving a green gown' 16th century; 'having a bit of green' 20th century.

2. "Appleton House," stanza 49. [*Editor.*]
3. "The Mower's Song." [*Editor.*]

expression of their sense of power is more intelligent, and so more convincing, than Wordsworth's solemnity on the same theme, because it does not forget the opposing forces.

> When we have run our Passions heat,
> Love hither makes his best retreat.
> The *Gods*, that mortal beauty chase,
> Still in a Tree did end their race.
> *Apollo* hunted *Daphne* so,
> Only that she might Laurel grow,
> And *Pan* did after *Syrinx* speed,
> Not as a Nymph, but for a Reed.

The energy and delight of the conceit has been sharpened or keyed up here till it seems to burst and transform itself; it dissolves in the next verse into the style of Keats. So his observation of the garden might mount to an ecstasy which disregarded it; he seems in this next verse to imitate the process he has described, to enjoy in a receptive state the exhilaration which an exercise of wit has achieved. But striking as the change of style is, it is unfair to empty the verse of thought and treat it as random description; what happens is that he steps back from overt classical conceits to a rich and intuitive use of Christian imagery. When people treat it as the one good 'bit' of the poem one does not know whether they have recognised that the Alpha and Omega of the verse are the Apple and the Fall.

> What wond'rous Life is this I lead!
> Ripe Apples drop about my head;
> The Luscious Clusters of the Vine
> Upon my Mouth do crush their Wine;
> The Nectaren, and curious Peach,
> Into my hands themselves do reach;
> Stumbling on Melons, as I pass,
> Insnar'd with Flow'rs, I fall on Grass.

Melon, again, is the Greek for apple; 'all flesh is *grass*,' and its own *flowers* here are the snakes in it that stopped Eurydice.[4] Mere grapes are at once the primitive and the innocent wine; the *nectar* of Eden, and yet the blood of sacrifice. *Curious* could mean 'rich and strange' (nature), 'improved by care' (art) or 'inquisitive' (feeling towards me, since nature is a mirror, as I do towards her). All these eatable beauties give themselves so as to lose themselves, like a lover, with a forceful generosity; like a lover they *ensnare* him. It is the triumph of his attempt to impose a sexual interest upon nature; there need be no more Puritanism in this use of sacri-

---

4. The wife of Orpheus, she died of the bite of a serpent. [*Editor.*]

ficial ideas than is already inherent in the praise of solitude; and it is because his repose in the orchard hints at such a variety of emotions that he is contemplating *all that's made*. Sensibility here repeats what wit said in the verse before; he tosses into the fantastic treasure-chest of the poem's thought all the pathos and dignity that Milton was to feel in his more celebrated Garden; and it is while this is going on, we are told in the next verse, that the mind performs its ambiguous and memorable *withdrawal*. For each of the three central verses he gives a twist to the screw of the microscope and is living in another world.

M. C. BRADBROOK and M. G. LLOYD THOMAS

[On "The Nymph Complaining . . ."]†

The Nymph complaining for the death of her Faun opens with straightforward and charming naturalism; it ends by drawing largely on *The Song of Solomon* and its identification of the fawn with Christ. The nymph is at once amusing and touching and aesthetically delightful (rather like Henry James' young girls).[1] She is firm in her pious conviction that the wanton troopers who have shot her fawn will be punished:

> Ev'n Beasts must be with justice slain;
> Else Men are made their *Deodands*.[2]

(A deodand is itself a beast or quite inanimate: thus men may be degraded below the beasts: the force of the technical ecclesiastical term as used by the little nymph can only be appreciated later.)

In the opening part of the poem the fawn is a substitute for Sylvio, the unconstant lover whose present it was:

> Said He, look how your Huntsman here
> Hath taught a Faun to hunt his *Dear*.
> But *Sylvio* soon had me beguil'd.
> This waxed tame; while he grew wild,
> And quite regardless of my Smart,
> Left me his Faun, but took his Heart[3]

It is not certain whether the nymph is meant to see the puns or not; they certainly give the effect of rallying her upon this grief. But her simplicity becomes a religious purity when she comes directly to the subject of the fawn:

† From *Andrew Marvell* (Cambridge, England, 1940), pp. 47–50.
1. Cf. *Upon Appleton House*, L–LIII.
2. Lines 16–17.
3. Lines 31–6.

> Among the beds of Lillyes, I
> Have sought it oft, where it should lye; . . .
> For, in the flaxen Lillies shade,
> It like a bank of Lillies laid.
> Upon the Roses it would feed,
> Until its Lips ev'n seem'd to bleed. . . .
> Had it liv'd long, it would have been
> Lillies without, Roses within[4]

My beloved is mine, and I am his: he feedeth among the lillies.
Untill the day breake, and the shadowes flee away: turne my beloved and be thou like a Roe, or a yong Hart, upon the mountaines of Bether. . . .
Thy two breasts, like two yong Roes, that are twinnes, which feed among the lillies.
Untill the day breake, and the shadowes flee away, I will get mee to the mountaines of myrrhe, and to the hill of frankincense. . . .
My beloved is gone downe into his garden, to the beds of spices, to feede in the gardens, and to gather lillies.
I am my beloveds, & my beloved is mine: he feedeth among the lillies. . . .
I am the rose of Sharon, and the lillie of the valleys.[5]

The whiteness of the fawn is insisted on throughout the poem: as well as being stressed in *The Song of Solomon* it is of course symbolic of the Agnus Dei. It is this identification which allows the transition to martyrdom:

> O help! O help! I see it faint:
> And dye as calmely as a Saint.
> See how it weeps. The Tears do come
> Sad, slowly dropping like a Gumme.
> So weeps the wounded Balsome: so
> The holy Frankincense doth flow.[6]

It would be difficult to do this now without being blasphemous: it is a very complete example of a hierarchy of love, but to relate is not to obliterate differences: Marvell's very nicety of control of the transitions has impressed on the reader the need for making fine distinctions. It is equally implied that the two ends of the scale *are* related. The love of the girl for her fawn is taken to be a reflection of the love of the Church for Christ.

4. Lines 77 ff.
5. *The Song of Solomon*, II, 16–17; IV, 5–6; VI, 2–3; II, 1.
6. Lines 93–8. Cf. the earlier lines, referring to the troopers, who now seem to have slain that which would have redeemed them: 'There is not such another in The World, to offer for their Sin' (lines 23–4). The whole poem may be related to the death and metamorphosis of Fida's hind in William Browne's *Britannia's Pastorals* (Bk. I, Songs 4 and 5). Browne's nymph represents religious Faith and the hind, Truth. The new connections with such poets as Browne and Giles Fletcher are important and will be discussed in the next chapter.

EDWARD S. Le COMTE

Marvell's "The Nymph Complaining for the Death of Her Fawn"†

To all appearances, "The Nymph Complaining for the Death of Her Fawn" is a pastoral delineating with "a pretty skipping grace" and many *concetti* a girl's tender relation with and mourning for her pet that "wanton Troopers riding by / Have shot." The poem, a favorite with anthologists even before Palgrave added a portion of it to *The Golden Treasury* in 1883, undoubtedly has had a good number of appreciators, and, of these, none (including T. S. Eliot, who certainly cannot be accused of lack of sensitivity in these matters) had taken it other than literally until the appearance of *Andrew Marvell* by M. C. Bradbrook and M. G. Lloyd Thomas (Cambridge, 1940). These ladies advanced (pp. 47 ff.) the startling thesis that the poem is an allegory on the Crucifixion. In the critics' own words, " 'The Nymph complaining for the death of her Fawn' opens with straightforward and charming naturalism; it ends by drawing largely on *The Song of Solomon* and its identification of the fawn with Christ." No formal protest having been registered against this view, there is some danger that the silence of more than a decade may be interpreted as signifying universal consent. In fact, Marvell's standard editor, Professor H. M. Margoliouth, was favorably disposed, in his review: "I am not convinced that they are wrong. If they are right, the poem takes on altogether new color and significance" (*RES*, XVII, 221; compare Ruth Wallerstein, who takes a middle position, *Studies in Seventeenth-Century Poetic* [Madison, 1950], pp. 335–36). It may not be belaboring the obvious, then, to argue that the poem is *not* about the Crucifixion and to show incidentally what, in so far as the poem has a traceable background, that background is. On the positive side, this paper will offer more than one reason for believing that the poem is what Émile Legouis (in Legouis and Cazamian's *History of English Literature*) calls it, "semi-mythological."

The Bradbrook-Thomas interpretation comes in the form of an *aperçu*, we being mostly left to work out the details as best we can. And, contrary to the implication of the sentence quoted above, it appears to be the first paragraph of the poem, not the last, which holds out the best prospect for such an interpretation. [Quotes lines 1–24] Here are blood, prayers, sin, Heaven's King, and sacrifice. In a Christian poet the combination is certainly provocative,

† From *Modern Philology*, L (1952), 97–101. A revised and expanded version of this essay appears in Edward S. Le Comte's *Poet's Riddles: Essays in Seventeenth Century Explication* (Port Washington, N.Y.: Kennikat Press), pp. 161–79.

and, if the poem continued in this strain, we should have a right to suspect allegory. It is true that there are already grave theological problems, in such a case. Allowing that the "wanton Troopers" are the slayers of the Savior, can it be said, "nor cou'd Thy death yet do them any good"? But the main point is that 24 lines in a poem of 122 lines do not make it an allegory, and even the last couplet quoted above (the most provocative of all) fits into place as part of the poem's pattern of hyperbole and conceit, half-Italianate, half-metaphysical, whereby the fawn is magnified, at mankind's—and particularly womankind's—expense. Marvell, whose Eden in "The Garden" is conspicuous for barring Eve, is being beguilingly anti-feminine in his insistence on how much whiter the fawn is than the nymph:

> And oft
> I blusht to see its foot more soft,
> And white, (shall I say then my hand?)
> NAY any Ladies of the Land.

He is reacting against the Petrarchan tradition by removing woman from the pedestal, substituting a fawn, and making the woman the wooer. Whereas poets going back to Horace (*Car.* i. 23) and Ovid (*Met.* xi. 771 f.) and including Wyatt (the poem commencing, "They flee from me") had maidens flee men like fawns, Marvell's fawn—and what a sweet revenge it is!—literally as well as figuratively leaves Marvell's nymph far behind (ll. 63–70). The poem, like any good poem, has overtones, but these are not religious: rather they have to do, as in other of Marvell's poems, with the Eden (or nature) versus civilization issue.

The second verse paragraph deals, one would think, the death-blow to the Bradbrook-Thomas thesis:

> Unconstant *Sylvio*, when yet
> I had not found him counterfeit,
> One morning (I remember well)
> Ty'd in this silver Chain and Bell,
> Gave it to me: nay and I know
> What he said then; I'me sure I do.
> Said He, look how your Huntsman here
> Hath taught a Faun to hunt his *Dear.*
> But *Sylvio* soon had me beguil'd.
> This waxed tame, while he grew wild,
> And quite regardless of my Smart,
> Left me his Faun, but took his Heart.

In all common sense—however unfashionable that has become in criticism—does this tone, do these undoctrinal puns, permit us still to believe that the fawn is Christ? And who is Sylvio? The name suggests nothing except a figure in a pastoral poem. Is Sylvio a pagan lover from whom the nymph turned to Christ? In the first place, the two influences were side by side for a time. In the second place, how can Sylvio be said to have been the giver of the fawn ("Ty'd in this silver Chain and Bell"!), if the fawn is Christ? It does not work out. It will not bear a moment's thought.

And in the fourth verse paragraph, this is said:

> Had it liv'd long, I do not know
> Whether it too might have done so
> As *Sylvio* did: his Gifts might be
> Perhaps as false or more than he.

How can this be said of the Savior? How can this be said, even if— the only possibility—it is meant to indicate lapse of faith on the part of the church, the nun, the Virgin Mary, or whoever the nymph is supposed to be according to the Misses Bradbrook and Thomas? Quoting lines 93–98, these critics grant, "It would be difficult to do this now without being blasphemous." But the above inversion is still more dangerous.

Let us grant what must be granted. There is a deer here and a deer in the Song of Solomon: "My beloved is like a roe or a young hart" (2 : 9). In both works the deer skips (2 : 8), as young deer are wont to do. Also there are lilies common to both: the biblical "beloved . . . feedeth among" them (2 : 16); Marvell's does something similar. [Quotes lines 77–92] Where is the crown of thorns here?

It is most confusing to say that "the whitness of the fawn . . . is of course symbolic of the Agnus Dei." It is true, a lamb is mentioned:

> Now my Sweet Faun is vanish'd to
> Whether the Swans and Turtles go:
> In fair *Elizium* to endure,
> With milk-white Lambs, and Ermins pure.

But who are the ermines? One imagines that, if Marvell had wished to be so understood, he would have used a lamb instead of a fawn, or if, like Dryden in *The Hind and the Panther*, he had intended something allegorical by his deer, he would have found ways of consistently intimating as much. Instead, he ends, as he began, with a series of conceits. [Quotes lines 111–122] What parting shot of doctrine is here? One can discern, at most, an amalgamation of Cyparissus, the youth who so notably grieved for his accidentally slain pet deer (Ovid *Met.* x. 106 ff.; Spenser, *The Faerie Queene*, I, vi, 17), and Niobe. As for white deer, they can be found outside the Song of Solomon. Petrarch himself has one (meaning by it Laura), *Rime*, No. CXC, the sonnet beginning, "Una candida cerva sopra l'erba."[1] The white roebuck is a commonplace in folklore (a fact which Robert Graves has lately publicized in *The White Goddess*). Life itself still furnishes albinistic fallow deer. Marvell could have got both fact and legend from the section on deer in Pliny's *Natural History*: "Sunt aliquando et candido colore, qualem fuisse traditur Q. Sertorii cervam, quam esse fatidicam Hispaniae gentibus persuaserat" (viii. 117).[2] (Lines 66–68, quoted below, reproduce accurately viii. 113: "semper in fuga adquiescunt stant-esque respiciunt, cum prope ventum est, rursus fugae praesidia repe-tentes.")[3] Plutarch in his life of that general tells more about the famous white hind of Sertorius, how he feigned it was given him by the goddess Diana and communicated to him divine messages. It is possible that among the "300 head of deer" (Augustine Birrell, *Andrew Marvell* [New York, 1905], p. 31) in the park at Nunap-pleton was a white fawn. But this is to oppose the extreme of mysti-cism with the extreme of literalism. Let us say Marvell's fawn is white in sign of beauty, superiority, and innocence. The color and everything else about the fawn are amply accounted for without resort to biblical allegory; on the other hand, there is much, too much, in the poem that mocks any attempt at a theological reading.

Note that it is "troopers" who shot the fawn—which connotes, then as now, soldiers. The *Oxford English Dictionary*, recording no appearance of the word before 1640, states: "The term was used in connexion with the Covenanting Army which invaded England in 1640." If allegory is our game, why may we not say that the fawn stands for Merry England, mortally wounded in the Civil War?

> For it was full of sport; and light
> Of foot, and heart; and did invite,
> Me to its game: . . .
>   It is a wond'rous thing, how fleet
> 'Twas on those little silver feet.
> With what a pretty skipping grace,
> It oft would challenge me the Race:
> And when 'thad left me far away,
> 'Twould stand, and run again, and stay.
> For it was nimbler much than Hindes;
> And trod, as on the four Winds.

Things will never be again what they were in Marvell's youth, not to push further back to the Elizabethans (who got their culture through Italy—Sylvio is an Italian name). This is Marvell's "Fare-well, Rewards and Fairies."

1. "A white doe amid the grass." [*Editor*.]
2. "Sometimes the stags are of the same white color as that hind of Q. Sertorius's was supposed to have been—that hind which, he convinced the Spanish tribes, had the gift of prophecy." [*Editor*.]
3. "Always during their flight, they pause and stand, and look back, and when someone comes near, they seek again the safety of flight. [*Editor*.]

Two—or, rather, three—can easily play at this game of letting our thoughts wander. It is not even to be denied, considering the fact of the Civil War and the fact of Marvell's (or any seventeenth-century Puritan's) intimacy with the Bible, that the poet's thoughts *could* have wandered in both these directions, at times, as he wrote. But this is mere psychobiographical conjecture—or autobiographical woolgathering—rather than defensible interpretation of a poem whose lines are straight and clear, however much fun the frivolity of trying to twist them. Not every fancy or free association that may dart into a reader's head is fair. One reader who was questioned as to the meaning of the poem replied without hesitation that it represented a girl's lamentation for her lost virginity. The reader went on to substantiate this view in painful detail, beginning with the word "wanton"!

Let us freely admit, without straining grotesquely for Christian "color and significance," that "The Nymph Complaining for the Death of Her Fawn" is less pious than, say, *The White Doe of Rylstone*. It does not follow, as night the day, that Wordsworth's is the better poem. Heaviness is not all. Poe, in singling out Marvell's poem on the occasion of its appearance in S. C. Hall's *The Book of Gems* in 1836, flatly took issue with the editor by denominating it "poetry of the *very loftiest order*" (*Complete Works*, ed. James A. Harrison [New York, 1902], IX, 102). And for Poe the poem was lighter than for other readers, since he strangely and characteristically, ignoring Sylvio and the tone of the opening lines, insisted on calling the nymph a "child," "the little maiden."

To come back to those opening lines, the part to which it is proposed to sacrifice the whole, they admit of a pagan interpretation—and that is more what the rest of the poem seems to require. In line 104 "*Diana's* Shrine" is mentioned. The nymph has turned away from men, become a practitioner of chastity and lover of deer, like Diana. Marvell is not likely to be using the word "nymph" just casually to mean girl. Diana was *the* nymph, *nympha nympharum*, and her followers were nymphs. In connection with the opening suggestion of recompense for a slain fawn, one is probably supposed to remember, if anything, not Christ, but the sacred stag which Agamemnon and his party slew (*they* were troopers, on the way to the Trojan War) while hunting in the grove of Artemis at Aulis, and on account of which the goddess exacted the sacrifice of Iphigenia. That such an exchange would be worth while in the present case is denied by Marvell's nymph:

> There is not such another in
> The World, to offer for their Sin.

The attitude in the first verse paragraph is, as Grosart noted, similar to Blake's in "Auguries of Innocence": "A Robin Red breast in a

Cage / Puts all Heaven in a Rage" and "A Horse misus'd upon the Road / Calls to Heaven for Human Blood," etc. Pity for the stricken deer is shown by Shakespeare (*As You Like It*, II, 1, 33 ff.), Drayton (*Poly-Olbion*, XIII, 147 ff.), and Montaigne (*Essais*, II, 11), and the antivenery literature includes More's *Utopia* (II, 6), Erasmus' *Encomium Moriae* (19), Plutarch's *De solertia animalium* (i–ii), and goes back to Pythagoras and the Pythagoreans (see Ovid *Met.* xv. 75 ff.).

What set the Misses Bradbrook and Thomas off in an allegorical direction? Was it, perhaps, *another* poem? It was, judging by the footnote on page 49: "The whole poem may be related to the death and metamorphosis of Fida's hind in William Browne's *Britannia's Pastorals* (Book I, Songs 4 and 5). Browne's nymph represents religious Faith and the hind, Truth." This suggestion is not original with these critics—it goes back to the edition of Margoliouth, who, in turn, is repeating Robert Poscher (*Andrew Marvells poetische Werke* [Vienna, 1908], p. 30). The only proposal that has so far been offered for a source for Marvell's poem,[4] it is not very cogent. The nearest that Browne's hind comes to being shot by hunters is that a shepherd's dog barks at it; thereupon, without fear, it walks up to Fida in a friendly way (Song 3), only to be later (Song 4) devoured by the man-monster Riot: on which occasion we are given, not Fida's implorations, but the hind's. The happy ending has it that from the mangled remains springs up the maiden Aletheia (observe that Browne, like Dryden, makes unmistakable *his* allegories).

If we must have a source for the simple situation in Marvell's poem, we can do better by turning to a more famous poet than Browne—Virgil. In the seventh book of the *Aeneid*, lines 475 ff., we are told how the Fury Allecto stirred up war between the Rutulians and the Trojans in Italy by causing Ascanius, while out hunting with his men, to wound mortally, with his arrow, the pet stag of— the name is not without interest—Silvia. We are provided with details (Browne offers none) of what this pet, stolen from its mother's udder, meant to the girl, how she had tamed it and adorned its antlers with garlands, and was wont to comb and bathe it. It became accustomed to its mistress' table, "mensaeque adsuetus erili," inspiration enough for Marvell's couplet,

> With sweetest milk, and sugar, first
> I it at mine own fingers nurst.

Moaning and with the blood flowing, the stag finds its way back to its mistress, who reacts as one would expect.

4. It has been thought best, for the purposes of fuller exposition, to leave this article as written before Kenneth Muir anticipated one of its points in his note, "A Virgilian Echo in Marvell," *N & Q*, CXCVI (March 17, 1951), 115.

> Silvia prima soror palmis percussa lacertos
> Auxilium vocat et duros conclamat agrestis,[5]

says Virgil, "O help! O help!" cries Marvell's nymph, whose name, if she is to be assigned one, is Silvia rather than Pietà.

KARINA WILLIAMSON

Marvell's "The Nymph Complaining for the Death of Her Fawn": A Reply[†]

In his article in 1952,[1] Professor Le Comte was right to expose the flaws in Miss Bradbrook and Miss Lloyd Thomas' theory of the religious significance of Marvell's poem; but neither his objections nor his alternative explanations seem to me to justify his assertion that "the poem, like any good poem, has overtones, but these are not religious," or his suggestion that the recognition of any religious associations is a frivolous distortion of the "straight and clear" lines of the poem. His remark, "Not every fancy or free association that may dart into a reader's head is fair," raises the crucial point; if the biblical associations with Miss Bradbrook and Miss Lloyd Thomas claimed to detect were as "free" and unwarranted as Professor Le Comte suggests, their interpretation would indeed be indefensible; but in my view there is enough evidence to show that the poem certainly has "religious overtones," even if they are not sufficient to justify a cohesive religious interpretation.

In any case, Professor Le Comte misrepresents Miss Bradbrook and Miss Lloyd Thomas when he attributes to them the thesis that "the poem is an allegory on the Crucifixion"; their interpretation is not so circumscribed. Their suggestion is that the poem presents "a very complete hierarchy of love," in which "the love of the girl for her fawn is taken to be a reflection of the love of the Church for Christ"; they even enter a caveat, warning that "to relate is not to obliterate differences. Marvell's very nicety of control of the transitions has impressed on the reader the need for making distinctions" (pp. 49–50). The only justification for Professor Le Comte's reading of their theory is the footnote on page 49 referring to lines 93–98, with which they compare the earlier lines about the troopers, "who now seem to have slain that which would have redeemed them."

5. Now the girl Silvia, beating her arms, called out for help and aroused the tough farmers. [*Editor.*]

† *Modern Philology*, LI (1954), 268–71.

1. Edward S. Le Comte, "Marvell's 'The Nymph Complaining for the Death of Her Fawn.' " *MP, L* (1952), 97–101, referring to M. C. Bradbrook and M. G. Lloyd Thomas, *Andrew Marvell* (Cambridge, 1940), pp. 47 ff.

The cardinal reason for supposing that the poem is intended to have religious associations is that the central passage seems so clearly to draw on the Song of Solomon. Professor Le Comte makes light of this point, but it cannot be dismissed so readily; the parallels are very striking, even more than is shown in the quotations given by Miss Bradbrook and Miss Lloyd Thomas (probably they thought it already obvious), so I give an expanded version. Compare with lines 71–92 [quotes] the Song of Solomon:

> The voice of my beloved! behold, he cometh leaping upon the mountains, skipping upon the hills [cf. Marvell, l. 65].
> My beloved is like a roe or a young hart . . . [Song of Sol., 2 : 8–9].
> My beloved is mine and I am his: he feedeth among the lilies.
> Until the day break and the shadows flee away, turn, my beloved, and be thou like a roe or a young hart upon the mountains of Bether [2 : 16–17].
> I am come into my garden, my sister, my spouse: . . . I have eaten my honeycomb with my honey; I have drunk my wine with my milk [5 : 1; cf. Marvell, l. 55].
> My beloved is white and ruddy. . . . His cheeks are as beds of spices, as sweet flowers: his lips like sweet lilies, dropping sweet myrrh. . . . His mouth is most sweet [5 : 10, 13, 16; cf. Marvell, ll. 58–59].
> My beloved is gone down into his garden, to the beds of spices, to feed in the gardens, and to gather lilies.
> I am my beloved's and my beloved is mine: he feedeth among the lilies [6 : 2–3].
> By night on my bed I sought him whom my soul loveth: I sought him but I found him not [3 : 1].

Possibly, also, the fawn's "Chain and Bell," which Professor Le Comte finds so ludicrous in a religious context, may have been suggested by the "chains of gold" around the neck of the lover (1:10). I am not trying to suggest that the parallels are logically exact—the lover's lips are like lilies, while the fawn's are rose-stained[2]—but that the verbal similarities are too frequent and striking to be accidental. It is difficult to believe that an educated reader of Marvell's time could have missed these associations when we remember how familiar the Song of Solomon would have been to him. Besides the many commentaries and expositions on it published in the sixteenth and seventeenth centuries, numerous metrical versions testify to its popularity in literary circles. I have found mention of seventeen printed versions between 1549 and 1659, including ones by Quarles, George Sandys, Drayton, and a lost version by Spenser (if

2. But see P. Carey's "Crucifixus pro nobis," *Seventeenth century lyrics*, ed. Ault (2d ed.; London, 1950), p. 262, referring to Christ in the cradle, "His lips are blue / (Where roses grew)."

his printer is to be relied upon). In addition to these, there are in the Bodleian alone five MS translations or paraphrases in verse, of the seventeenth century, including one by Marvell's friend, Lord Fairfax; while the use made of the Song in seventeenth-century emblem books and poetry in general is incalculable. It was conventional to address Christ, or speak of him, in terms of the Song of Solomon, as in Herrick's carol for Christmas, "The Star-Song":

> Tell us, thou cleere and heavenly Tongue
> Where is the Babe but lately sprung?
> Lies He the Lillie-banks among? [ll. 1–3],[3]

and in Vaughan's "Dressing":

> O thou that lovest a pure and whitend soul!
> That feedst among the Lillies 'till the day
> Break, and the shadows flee . . . [ll. 1–3],[4]

which is just a paraphrase of the Song, 2:16–17. Professor Le Comte's comment after lines 91–92—"Where is the crown of thorns here?"—is irrelevant. It is the relationship between the church and Christ (or the Virgin and Christ in Roman Catholic interpretations), not the suffering of Christ, that is supposed to be prefigured in the Song of Solomon.

Of course, use of the Song language is no guaranty that a religious allusion is intended (the passage in Chaucer's tale of January and May[5] is a famous example of the exploitation of it for secular purposes), but that would be the normal deduction; and here there has already been a certain direction of associations into religious channels through the use of terms with a specifically religious denotation: "prayers," "heaven" and "Heaven's King," "saint," "holy frankincense," "deodand" ("the Priest-craft Word," according to Hickering [1705], quoted by OED).

Moreover, an awareness of the poem's religious resources makes other phrases two-edged. The fawn treading "as on the four Winds" becomes reminiscent of the Psalmist's vision of God, "who walketh upon the wings of the wind" (104 : 3; cf. also 18 : 10), an image which found its way into the Sarum Missal; the comparison of the fawn's tears to "the wounded Balsome" may be connected with the idea of the wounded Christ as the "Balsam of Soules" (Vaughan, "The Search," l. 44),[6] "Whose brest weepes Balm for wounded man" (Crashaw, "The Hymn of Sainte Thomas," l. 46).[7]

3. *Poetical Works*, ed. Moorman (Oxford, 1915), p. 367.
4. *Works*, ed. Martin (Oxford, 1914), p. 455.
5. *Complete Works*, ed. Robinson (Oxford, 1933), p. 149, ll. 2138 ff.
6. *Works*, p. 406.

7. *Poems*, ed. Martin (Oxford, 1927), p. 293. Curiously enough, in "The Weeper" Mary Magdalene's tears, like the fawn's, are likened both to the Balsam (stanza 12) and to "the Amber-weeping Tree" (stanza 8).

With the whole passage in Marvell, compare Herbert's "The Sacrifice":

> Therefore my soul melts, and my hearts dear treasure
> Drops bloud. . . .
> These drops being temper'd with a sinners tears
> A Balsome are for both the Hemispheres
>
> [ll. 21–22, 25–26].[8]

Professor Le Comte finds in the nymph's renunciation of human love (ll. 37–40, 53–54, 109 ff.) a likeness to Diana: "The nymph has turned away from men, become a practitioner of chastity and lover of deer, like Diana. Marvell is not likely to be using the word 'nymph' just casually to mean girl. Diana was *the* nymph, *nympha nympharum*, and her followers were nymphs." A nymph, whether divine or human, was essentially virginal; "A Virgine, a faire young Maide" is the definition in Bullokar's dictionary (1616), and "Nymphs of the Woods" are defined as "Virgin-Goddesses" by Coles (1676). The conception of virginity is as appropriate to the "undefiled" bride of the Song of Solomon (see 4 : 12; 5 : 2; 6 : 9) and to subsequent "brides of Christ" as to Diana and her followers. I do not see that the two sets of associations are incompatible.

Professor Le Comte asks "who are the ermines?" Unlike the swans, turtles (often merely a synonym for doves), and lambs, they have no precise connections with religion (the swan is the type of Christ and of Mary in Roman Catholic literature),[9] but their appropriateness is surely obvious: they were noted for their whiteness, like the fawn itself, and a legend for purity. The legend found its way into Dyche's dictionary in the eighteenth century: "The Animal is milk white, and so far from Spots, that 'tis reported that he will rather die or be taken than sully its Whiteness" (1735); but it was already well known in the seventeenth (see John Hall's "The Ermine").

Others of the issues which Professor Le Comte raises are more serious. If we admit the connection between the fawn of the poem and the roe (= Christ) of the Song of Solomon and recognize the possibility of other religious associations being present, as in lines 23–24, which could have obvious Christian implications, we ultimately have to face the question of how far the analogies are meant to stretch. And here some of Professor Le Comte's objections to a complete identification of the fable with the story of the Crucifixion seem to me unanswerable. The most important are the dubious theology of lines 5–6 (though it is arguable that this applies only to

8. *Works*, ed. Hutchinson (Oxford, 1941), p. 27.
9. Cf. Crashaw, "Upon Our Lords Last Comfortable Discourse with His Disci- ples." *Poems*, p. 95; and Henry Hawkins, *Partheneia sacra* (1633), p. 27, where the swan is an emblem of the Virgin.

the murderers); the impossibility of fitting the passage relating to Sylvio (ll. 25–36) into any reasonable interpretation on Christian lines; and, indeed, the total lack of specific allusions (other than the actual slaying of the fawn) to the events of the Passion. The suggestion of a possible source in the story of Sylvia's stag in the *Aeneid*, on the other hand, though very likely correct, does not explain away the religious allusions. What, then, is their function? My view is that the poem certainly has "religious overtones" but that they are intended as overtones, not as a ground bass. In other words, they are not meant to supply another level of significance parallel to, or expressed through, the literal surface meaning but to intensify that "meaning." One is reminded of Empson's remark in connection with the Heliades image: "one expects a simile with reserves of meaning",[1] part of the power of this poem lies in its reserves; they help to give to an apparently slight story that effect of seriousness which T. S. Eliot noticed.[2] They are part of the "wit" of the poem, a "wit" involving "probably, a recognition, implicit in the expression of every experience, of other kinds of experience which are possible."[3] Lines such as

> There is not such another in
> The World, to offer for their Sin.

are effective, not for their "hyperbole and conceit" in Professor Le Comte's phrase, but because, within the poem, they seem so true. The experience manifested in the poem is felt to belong to the total order of human experience.

DENNIS DAVISON

[Marvell's Religious Poems]†

Truly, to Marvell, fashionably dressed, addicted somewhat to drinking sack, a poet and a music-lover, Puritanism was neither an ascetic discipline nor a rigid theological dogma, but the penetration of his being by forces of moral seriousness and resolute reasonableness. He had little contact with the popular militant Puritanism of the London proletariat or the Leveller[1] elements, impregnated as it was with social revolutionary ideas: his cultural background and his identification with Cromwell did not encourage him to extend any

---

1. *Seven Types of Ambiguity* (2d ed.; London, 1949), p. 168.
2. "Andrew Marvell," *Selected Essays* (2d ed.; London, 1949), p. 300.
3. Ibid., p. 303.

† From *Andrew Marvell: Selected Poetry and Prose* (New York, 1952), Introduction, pp. 43–50.
1. On the Levellers, see the note to "Appleton House," line 450. [*Editor.*]

sympathy, for instance, to hawkers and peddlers. "I hope the country will not long be infested with those people," he wrote in 1677. Nor does his religious poetry, unlike, for example, that of Blake, reveal a sensitivity to social ills. Again, as in his love poetry, Marvell accepts current fashions in religious poetry; yet, characteristically, pastiche gives way to a distinctive personal utterance.

In *Eyes and Tears*, not explicitly religious perhaps, we see the mingling of sensual and religious moods, that lachrymose eroticism cultivated by Crashaw:

> So *Magdalen*, in Tears more wise
> Dissolv'd those captivating Eyes,
> Whose liquid Chaines could flowing meet
> To fetter her Redeemers feet.

Superficially analogous to this type of poem is *On a Drop of Dew*, where the drop is inevitably compared to a tear. The religious sentiments involve the expression of divine purity trembling in a sinful world. This is not a theological poem but an emblematic description, in neat similes, enfolding most delicately intimations of purity as precarious and as tense as the surface-tension of the drop of dew. The idiom is Crashaw's, strengthened and purified by impersonal geometrical imagery:

> Moving but on a point below,
> It all about does upwards bend.

The abstract intellectual appeal of mathematical forms, traditional both in Platonic and scholastic thought, is fused with a sensuous appreciation of the dewy ball, which:

> Does, in its pure and circling thoughts, express
> The greater Heaven in an Heaven less.

Nevertheless, the dominant thought is religious in its awareness of and insistence on the concept of purity shunning imperfection, and the final lines:

> . . . but does, dissolving, run
> Into the Glories of th'Almighty Sun,

suggest not only the Heavenward aspirations of the soul but also the Platonic concept, recently revived by Kepler, of the sun as the residence of God.

In *The Coronet* the Puritan scorn of profane ornament, even when offered to God, is applied to the poet's art, which must be sacrificed at the feet of Christ in order to avoid the temptations of ambition. Compared with the first sonnet in Donne's *La Corona*, where the poet asks God to accept a crown of prayer and praise, or with Herbert's *Easter*, in which the offering of "flowers to strew

Thy way" is superfluous but not polluted, Marvell's renunciation of poetry is more strictly Puritan. His early poems are denounced fiercely as:

> . . . the Thorns with which I long, too long,
>   With many a piercing wound,
>   My Saviours head have crown'd.

Yet there was never a more regretful:

> Dismantling all the fragrant Towers
>   That once adorn'd my Shepherdesses head.

And this leads Marvell to soften his rejection of poetry. He does not imply that the beauty of the verse is itself evil, but there is always the danger of the Serpent with its "wreaths of Fame and Interest" (or, as Milton said, "Fame is the spur . . ."). In contrast to this suspicious attitude to poetry, Marvell speaks of his art as "my curious frame" that is "set with Skill and chosen out with Care." The two aspect of poetry have thus been presented; Marvell poses the alternative—God must either destroy the Serpent or his poetry. Only if he is unable to purify his verse does Marvell need to make the sacrifice; even then he makes of the sacrifice a gesture of positive strength. The garland "May crown thy Feet, that could not crown thy Head." This poem illustrates the sanity of Marvell's Puritanism. He balances honest regret at "Dismantling all the fragrant Towers" with a recognition of the Serpent's snares: the alternatives are given, and the hypothetical sacrifice is gracefully made.

The theme of renunciation is more clearly sounded in *A Dialogue between the Resolved Soul and Created Pleasure*. The soul's enemy is Nature—that is, the world, mother of all temptations: these are described with the wistful sympathy of one who has really felt their troubling charm. "Nature's banquet" invites with its fruits and flowers, its luxurious perfumed bed, strewn with roses, and, most exquisite of all temptations, music. Woman next tempts him (and the stanza reminds us of the terms used to describe Celia in *The Match*). Finally, after Gold has vainly pleaded, Pleasure offers the supreme bait to intellectual curiosity. The poet resists the *libido sciendi*[2] as he resists the lures of the flesh, sacrificing to God not only beauty but human knowledge, or at least the pride it engenders. The poem shows Marvell's moods of Puritan intolerance at its most extreme, but the effect is again softened, partly by the sympathetic evocation of the various temptations, the scarcely concealed regret at the renunciation, and partly by the positive nature of that renunciation. The soul does not reject temptation for a state of tortured asceticism or a mystical annihilation of the personality: the

2. Lust to know. [*Editor.*]

emphasis is on the soul functioning, but in a purer fashion. Instead of the idle bed of roses, there is the mental assurance of:

> My gentler Rest is on a Thought,
> Conscious of doing what I ought.

The rejection of false power leads instead to a truer conception of personal friendship that proceeds by honest conduct and control over ambitious thoughts:

> What Friends, if to my self untrue?
> What Slaves, unless I captive you?

Personal piety, as with Herbert, was for Marvell a way of conducting a useful life, administering to the needs of others, whether in Parliament or country parish. Thus although Marvell approaches the sterner Puritan attitudes of rejection, there is the compensating impression that his motives are not cold prudishness but the earnest desire to purify his way of life. Marvell was preparing himself, if not in the way that we might do to-day, for an arduous life as civil servant and M.P., where there would be many temptations in the form of bribery or the misuse of power.

The same allegorical framework characterizes A *Dialogue between the Soul and Body*, but there is here no operatic chorus, and the assured victory of the soul gives way to a painful, and more complex, recognition of the dual claims of body and soul, and their inevitable antagonism. This old theological problem of soul and body, raised each time science attempts to establish links between mind and matter, expressed itself outwardly in the battle of Hobbes and the divines, and the only notable synthesis was achieved by Spinoza; Descartes was responsible for a particularly artificial type of dualism.[3]

Donne had expressed a mistrust of the senses in *The Second Anniversary*:

> Thou shalt not peep through lattices of eyes,
> Nor hear through labyrinths of ears. . . .

Marvell has the same conception of the imprisoning, not informing, senses:

> Here blinded with an Eye; and there
> Deaf with the drumming of an Ear.

The interdependence of soul and body, however, does not result in

---

3. Thomas Hobbes (1588–1679) emphasized rationalism and materialism in his philosophical works, especially *Leviathan* (1651); Baruch Spinoza (1632–77) unified the world by way of pantheism; Rene Descartes (1596–1650) based philosophical reasoning on mathematical principle and founded philosophy on self-consciousness—*Cogito ergo sum*: "I think, therefore I am." [*Editor*.]

a Spinozan renewal of confidence, but in the agonized torture that each applies to each. The soul complains:

> O who shall, from this Dungeon, raise
> A Soul inslav'd so many wayes?
> With bolts of Bones, that fetter'd stands
> In Feet; and manacled in Hands.

The body, on the other hand, feels equally unfree:

> O who shall me deliver whole,
> From bonds of this Tyrannic Soul?

The dominant theme of the inescapable interaction of body and soul, in which both are antagonistic, provides some kind of philosophical unity, but it is a tragic, not a happy, one. The last lines of the poem sum this up concisely:

> So Architects do square and hew,
> Green Trees that in the Forest grew.

The architect-soul can only discipline the body-tree with cruelty, and destructive blows, and natural beauty is sacrificed, yet a new beauty is created. (It is almost Yeats's concept—"A terrible beauty is born.") I do not think that it is illegitimate to see that what in this poem is for Marvell a theological problem may also be a religious parallel for that painful problem he also grappled with in the political sphere. The "Kingdome old," equated with the admired personality of the King, had also been squared and hewn by the "forced Pow'r" of the new architect Cromwell (Cromwell is called the "Architect" in *The First Anniversary*.)

Two other religious dialogues are enframed in a pastoral setting. *Clorinda and Damon*, an exchange of brief phrases, has a certain gauche rapidity which reminds us of the words of a song without the musical setting—and perhaps it is. The theme is that of pagan sensuality vanquished by Christian purity: the retorts of the newly converted shepherd are brutally apposite. Although the Puritan rejection is harsh enough, the curious use of the pastoral idiom, with Pan for Christ, and a "slender Oate" to play on, lends an incongruous air, charmingly idyllic, to excessively prudish sentiments. A *Dialogue between Thyrsis and Dorinda* reveals mystical aspirations of an unusual nature, expressed with the innocuous simplicity of the pastoral mode. A certain subdued wit is still present, and in the naïve picture of Elysium a hint about a more egalitarian society is inserted:

> Shepheards there, bear equal sway,
> And every Nimph's a Queen of *May*.

But the strongest note is the dreamy, pensive 'mysticism' of Dorinda:

> O sweet! oh sweet! How I my future state
> By silent thinking, Antidate.

Is this merely reverie, not too seriously intended, or does Marvell suggest those rare states of the thinking soul when it glimpses Heaven, as Whichcote[4] believed? Certainly the later mention of suicide seems serious enough, and that a Puritan should make such a suggestion is most curious.

G. H. Palmer has said, "The religious lyric is the cry of the individual heart to God." Though this is true to some extent of Herbert or Donne, it is significant that Marvell avoids the personal lyric form and prefers the dialogue. In Donne a main conflict is between his deep sense of sin and his desire for forgiveness and eternal life:

> Swear by thyself that at my death, thy son
> Shall shine as he shines now, and heretofore.

Herbert is more particularly torn by a sense of frustration, of the futility of his life, and by a fear that he has lost contact with God:

> All things are busy; only I
> Neither bring honey with the bees . . .

Marvell's concern, expressed in impersonal terms, is almost entirely with that conflict between the temptations of pleasure and the resolute life devoted to the glory of God. This is portrayed in terms of soul and body, or of luxurious idleness contrasted with the arduous pilgrimage of the soul, or of the worldly distractions of poetry and music when the mind should be fixed on heaven. The idiom and the attitudes may roughly be called Puritan, but the underlying conflict is a moral and practical one. It is the reflection of the actual alternative offered to Marvell and his contemporaries (in the same social stratum)—the alternative of a life of comparative ease at Court, university, in bishop's palace, or in country house, or that of a life of activity in the armies, the lower ministry, the civil service, diplomacy, commerce, or Parliament. As a tutor Marvell was balanced between the alternatives of ease and activity in a way that could only emphasize the conflicts in his mind. Since his religious poetry reflects this outer conflict of different ways of life he might follow, it is full of complex and sometimes unresolved problems. The final impression is one of honesty of self-analysis; yet although the poems present certain doubts, there is the overriding suggestion that some sacrifice of pleasure must be made for the health of the

4. Benjamin Whichcote (1609–83), a leader of the Cambridge Platonists, exalted man as reasonable being, against the pessimistic view of human nature prevailing among contemporary Puritans. [*Editor.*]

soul. The positive faith that the purified soul will rise to new victories lends an air of confidence to these religious poems. This emphasis on a purer soul, this *Puritanism* in a literal sense, which means in practice the decision to lead a good, useful life, shows that Marvell's religious impulse is closely bound up with his conception of man's rôle in society. This identity of much of Puritan moral sentiments with the needs of individualistic commercialism has been very well illustrated by Tawney, in his *Religion and the Rise of Capitalism*. We may also note that Marvell's essentially practical and rational interest in religion is akin to the attitudes encouraged by the work of the Cambridge Platonists.

JOSEPH H. SUMMERS

Marvell's "Nature"†

The similarities between the verse of Marvell and that of many modern poets are seductive. A number of Marvell's poems have been cited as evidence to support the critical assumption, based largely on modern poetic practice, that the most mature and rich works of literature are necessarily ironical. One can disagree with the assumption and still recognize that irony, not of a paralyzing variety, is central to most of Marvell's poems. Marvell's surfaces, moreover, are close to one modern ideal. The tones of the typical modern *personae* echo the sensuous richness of Marvell more often than the logical violence of Donne—that poet who wrote "To Mr. Samuel Brooke," boastfully yet accurately, "I sing not Siren like to tempt; for I / Am harsh." The "speakers" of Marvell's poems are farther removed from immediate embroilment in action than are Donne's. They approach their situations from some distance, with a wider and a clearer view. Their speech is closer to that of meditation or of a quiet colloquy in a garden than to the raised voice, the immediate and passionate argument. And the verse which they speak shows a concern for euphony, a delicate manipulation of sound patterns suggesting Campion's[1] songs—or much of the verse of Eliot and MacLeish and many younger poets.

The differences between Marvell and the moderns, however, are equally noteworthy, and failure to perceive them has resulted in strange readings of a number of Marvell's poems. To prevent misreadings, to define any specific poem, we need to achieve some sense of the body of Marvell's work. And here is the difficulty, for

† From *ELH*, XX (1953), 121–35.
1. Thomas Campion (1567–1620), musician and poet, composer of several books of airs, i.e., lyrics written for solo performance accompanied by lute or bass viol. [*Editor.*]

our sense of that work is likely to be an impression of dazzling frag-
ments, each brilliant and disparate. The reader may feel that the
sixth stanza of "The Gallery," the poem in which the poet invites
Chlora to view her portraits in his soul as "an inhumane murther-
ess," Aurora, "an enchantress," Venus, and "a tender shepherdess,"
applies more justly to the poet than to Chlora:

> These Pictures and a thousand more,
> Of Thee, my Gallery do store;
> In all the Forms thou can'st invent
> Either to please me, or torment.

Yet the poem assures us that Chlora is one, however numerous her
pictures; and the poet who could take various and even contradictory positions on the claims of the active and contemplative lives, of
the body and the soul, of the time-honored plea to "seize the day,"
of gardens ("These Pictures and a thousand more") is equally one
poet. The attempts to bring intellectual order out of the apparent
confusion by means of a hypothetical biographical development of
the poet have been unconvincing. The development or rather break
in his poetic practice after 1660 is clear. Before that time, the single
poem "Upon Appelton House" indicates that Marvell was an
extraordinarily sophisticated poet, capable of employing numerous
traditions and multiple attitudes as occasions or moments
demanded. Among the few attitudes which I have been unable to
discover in Marvell's poetry, however, are those expressed in two of
the modern poems which owe most to Marvell. Archibald Mac-
Leish's "You, Andrew Marvell' concludes with the lines,

> And here face downward in the sun
> To feel how swift how secretly
> The shadow of the night comes on . . .

Robert Penn Warren's "Bearded Oaks" includes the following
stanza:

> Upon the floor of light, and time,
> Unmurmuring, of polyp made,
> We rest; we are, as light withdraws,
> Twin atolls on a shelf of shade.

In Marvell's verse man is neither an atoll nor an island, and if night
is anticipated, so is light.

An examination of Marvell's uses of "Nature," the world of the
flowers and fruits and the green grass, provides a sketch not only of
the virtuosity and multiple intellectual and moral stances within the
poems, but also of the central vision which occurs most frequently
in the most successful poems. Occasionally Marvell used nature as
an image of classical order, an artfully contrived realization of the

mean which man is to imitate—or, more properly, which a specific
man has imitated. Jonson had shown in his ode "To the Memory of
Sir Lucius Cary and Sir Henry Morison" that nature conceived as
an ordered mean was a most effective source of hyperbolical compliment. In "Upon the Hill and Grove at Bill-borow," Fairfax too is
at one with nature. After his active life (in which he had "thunder'd" "Through Groves of Pikes," "And Mountains rais'd of dying
Men"), Fairfax has returned to the retirement of the hill and grove;
the humanized landscape is both his ward and his image:

> See how the arched Earth does here
> Rise in a perfect Hemisphere!
> The stiffest Compass could not strike
> A Line more circular and like;
> Nor softest Pensel draw a Brow
> So equal as this Hill does bow.
> It seems as for a Model laid,
> And that the World by it was made.
>
> (st. i)
>
> ———
>
> See what a soft access and wide
> Lyes open to its grassy side;
> Nor with the rugged path deterrs
> The feet of breathless Travellers.
> See then how courteous it ascends,
> And all the way it rises bends;
> Nor for it self the height does gain,
> But only strives to raise the Plain.
>
> (st. iii)

After this delightfully artificial description of landscape as Republi-
can gentleman, we are not surprised that these Roman oaks should
speak oracles of praise for Fairfax. In the opening lines of "Upon
Appelton House," an ordered and properly proportioned nature is
again the symbol for Fairfax and his dwelling, particularly in contrast to the "unproportion'd dwellings" which the ambitious have
constructed with the aid of "Forrain" architects: "But all things are
composed here, / Like Nature, orderly and near." Nature is also
near and extraordinarily "orderly" when a natural object. "A Drop
of Dew" for example, is examined as an emblem. Here we are close
to Herbert, but in Marvell we are chiefly compelled by the ingenuity with which the natural is made to reflect the conceptual.

More often nature is nearer if not so orderly when it is conceived
as the lost garden, whether Eden or the Hesperides or England:

> O Thou, that dear and happy Isle
> The Garden of the World ere while,
> Thou *Paradise* of four Seas,
> Which *Heaven* planted us to please,
> But, to exclude the World, did guard

With watry if not flaming Sword;
What luckless Apple did we tast,
To make us Mortal, and The Wast?
>   ("Upon Appelton House," st. xli)

The lost garden represents not measure but perfect fulfillment; its memory is an occasion for ecstasy:

And Ivy, with familiar trails,
Me licks, and clasps, and curles, and hales.
Under this *antick Cope* I move
Like some great *Prelate of the Grove*,

Then, Languishing with ease, I toss
On Pallets swoln of Velvet Moss.
>   ("Upon Appelton House," st. lxxiv–lxxv)

What wond'rous Life in this I lead!
Ripe Apples drop about my head;
The Luscious Clusters of the Vine
Upon my Mouth do crush their Wine;
The Nectaren, and curious Peach,
Into my hands themselves do reach;
Stumbling on Melons, as I pass,
Insnar'd with Flow'rs, I fall on Grass.
>   ("The Garden," st. v)

It is in this vein that Marvell occasionally gives a sensuous particularity to his descriptions of natural objects which may remind us of Vaughan's "those faint beams in which this hill is drest, / After the Sun's remove" ("They are all gone into the world of light!"), and which has led some readers to consider him a romantic born too early. And yet the "gelid *Strawberryes*" and "The hatching *Thrastles* shining Eye" of "Upon Appelton House" contribute to a complicated vision of nature which is finally unlike the nineteenth-century's; the "*Hewel's* wonders" (the activities of the woodpecker) teach the "*easie Philospher*" who "Hath read in *Natures mystick Book*" the just relationships between sin and death:

Who could have thought the *tallest Oak*
Should fall by such a *feeble Strok*'!

Nor would it, had the Tree not fed
A *Traitor-worm*, within it bred.
(As first our *Flesh* corrupt within
Tempts impotent and bashful *Sin*.)
And yet that *Worm* triumphs not long,
But serves to feed the *Hewels young*.
While the Oake seems to fall content,
Viewing the Treason's Punishment.
>   ("Upon Appelton House," st. lxix–lxx)

In "The Garden," too, identification with nature is neither complete nor simple. The famous fifth stanza which I have quoted above, expertly "imitates" the bodily ecstasy, and the following stanzas systematically portray the higher ecstasies of the mind and the soul; all, moreover, are framed with witty and civilized reversals of the ordinary civilized values, of classic myth, of the biblical account of the creation of woman, and of the idea that sexual relations are "natural." To read "The Garden" and "The Mower Against Gardens" in succession is to realize that in Marvell's poetry the man-made garden and the "natural" meadows are significant not intrinsically but instrumentally. Both poems are ultimately concerned with lost perfection. "The Garden" presents a fictional and momentary attempt to recapture what has been lost. In "The Mower Against Gardens," the garden itself is an image of the sophisticated corruption responsible for the loss of "A wild and fragrant Innocence." Marvell's image of the lost garden is as much an occasion for the recognition of man's alienation from nature as it is for remembered ecstasy.

The degree to which Marvell both followed and modified conventional practice can be seen most clearly in the "pastoral" poems in which he substituted the mower for the traditional shepherd. The life of the shepherds had imaged the pre-agricultural golden age, the paradisiacal simplicity ideally if not actually associated with the simple country life, away from cities and civilizations, wars and corruptions. When love was concerned, the passion was usually direct, uncontaminated by worldly considerations, and not much affected by age, even if the lover was unhappy or the mistress proved untrue. The good shepherd and his sheep could imply the ideal political relation between the ruler and the ruled, and the Christian poets explored the rich possibilities of the Good Shepherd and his flock and the large pastoral inheritance of the Psalms. Milton, who retained the shepherd image in "Lycidas," kept the humanist emphasis on higher man (the poet, the pastor) as the guide of less perceptive humanity through the labyrinth of nature to an ultimate goal. The shepherd followed Christ, and he also led his own sheep into the true fold. Marvell used some of this material in a direct if not very distinguished fashion in "Clorinda and Damon," and although the participants are oarsmen rather than shepherds, the spirit of the tradition is present in "Bermudas." He gave up most of these associations, however, when he chose the figure of the mower as his central image. That figure, of course, had its own traditions. As "Damon the Mower" mentions, the mower's craft had long served to picture man's greatest mystery and fear:

> Only for him no Cure is found,
> Whom *Julianas* Eyes do wound.
> 'Tis death alone that this must do:
> For Death thou art a Mower too.

The mower who cut down the living grass was a natural symbol for death. Because of the seasonal nature of his activities, he was also a symbol for time. Marvell's mower does not lead; he destroys. However simple his character or sincere his love, he cuts down for human ends what nature has produced. He symbolizes man's alienation from nature:

> With whistling Sithe, and Elbow strong,
> These Massacre the Grass along:
> While one, unknowing, carves the *Rail*,
> Whose yet unfeather'd Quils her fail.
> The Edge all bloody from its Breast
> He draws, and does his stroke detest;
> Fearing the Flesh untimely mow'd
> To him a Fate as black forebode.
>
> ("Upon Appelton House," st. 1)

"The Mower's Song" is a playful and elaborately artificial lament of a lover, but it is more than that. The refrain insists that the mower-lover's relation to nature exactly parallels his cruel mistress's relation to him:

> For *Juliana* comes, and She
> What I do to the Grass, does to my Thoughts and Me.

Greenness in this poem, as so often in Marvell's verse, represents hope and vitality and virility, the fertile promise of life which man desires and destroys. The mower, angry that there is no true sympathy between man and nature, "fictionally" determines to destroy nature to make the symbolism more complete:

> Unthankful Medows, could you so
> A fellowship so true forego,
> And in your gawdy May-games meet,
> While I lay trodden under feet?
> When *Juliana* came, and She
> What I do to the Grass, does to my Thoughts and Me.
>
> But what you in Compassion ought,
> Shall now by my Revenge be wrought:
> And Flow'rs, and Grass, and I and all,
> Will in one common Ruine fall.
> For *Juliana* comes, and She
> What I do to the Grass, does to my Thoughts and Me.

The Mower poems conveniently define the crucial terms of Marvell's most frequent poetic use of nature. Marvell did not discover an impulse from the vernal wood which spoke unambiguously to the human heart and which offered a possibility for man's at-oneness with all. Nor did he, like George Herbert, usually see in nature patterns of a distinguishable and logical divine will, the *paysage moralisé* which offered a way to the understanding and imitation of God. Human moral criteria do not apply to most of Marvell's landscapes. In his poems nature apart from man is usually "green," vital, fecund, and triumphant. Since it affirms life it is, as part of the divine plan, "good," but its goodness is neither available nor quite comprehensible to man. Man is barred from long or continuous spiritual communion, and his intellect cannot comprehend the natural language. Since his alienation with the departure from Eden, man can only live in nature either as its observer or its destroyer; since he partially partakes of nature, he is, if he acts at all, also his own destroyer. His capacity for self-destruction is clearly implied by the contrast between nature's fecundity and man's harassed and frustrated attempts at love. Faced with unrequited love, man the mower only sharpens his scythe for the destruction of the grass and sharpens the "Woes" which destroy himself:

> How happy might I still have mow'd,
> Had not Love here his Thistles sow'd!
> But now I all the day complain,
> Joyning my Labour to my Pain;
> And with my Sythe cut down the Grass,
> Yet still my Grief is where it was:
> But, when the Iron blunter grows,
> Sighing I whet my Sythe and Woes.
>
> > ("Damon the Mower")

But man destroys the natural and dies not only because he is inferior but also because, suspended between the natural and divine, he is superior to the green world. In "A Dialogue between the Soul and the Body" each of the protagonists charges wittily and convincingly that the other is the source of human misery; of the first 40 lines, each speaks 20, and points are made and capped so expertly as to produce a forensic stalemate. But the Body wins and ironically resolves the argument with its final additional four lines:

> What but a Soul could have the wit
> To build me up for Sin so fit?
> So Architects do square and hew
> Green Trees that in the Forest grew.

Without the soul the body would be truly a part of nature and could not sin. Yet architecture, whether external or internal, is the product and desire of a higher part of man, even though many "Green trees" may be destroyed for it. Whether the building is used for good or ill, man's capacities for reason, for structure, for creation outside the carnal, are not natural but Godlike. Man's distinctive gifts are as destructive within the post-Eden garden as are his weaknesses and his corruption.

It is, moreover, exactly man's superiority to the vegetative world which allows him to recognize his alienation. Nature does not possess the capacity for man's choices between the active and contemplative lives: it can only act. The rival claims of those two chief modes of man's life are ever present in Marvell's poetry, and they are closely related to his themes of nature and time. Man must act and he must contemplate, and he must do each in accordance with the demands of time. Yet the contemplative life is usually the more desirable way—at least for the poet. The poet surpasses most men in the degree and consistency of his recognition of man's alienation, for he is chiefly concerned with the contemplation of the condition of man. In Marvell's poetry, significantly, natural beauty is usually described and appreciated as if it were an imitation of the works of man. The fort and artillery of the garden in "Upon Appelton House" are not simply factual or fanciful. In "The Mower to the Glo-Worms" nature is the gracious and kindly courtier to man, so lost in love "That I shall never find my home." In one of the most memorable descriptions in "Bermudas" God Himself is the manlike decorator:

> He hangs in shades the Orange bright,
> Like golden Lamps in a green Night.
> And does in the Pomgranates close,
> Jewels more rich than *Ormus* show's.

It is the artifacts, the "golden Lamps" and the "Jewels more rich than *Ormus* show's," which contribute most of the sensuous richness to the passage. In relation to the garden man is the judge and the measure as well as the accused.

Whatever the immediate resolutions, man is usually suspended between the greenness and God at the conclusions as well as at the beginnings of Marvell's poems. Within "A Dialogue between The Resolved Soul, and Created Pleasure," the Soul deftly propounds the orthodox thesis that the sensuous and worldly pleasures are only appearances, that the soul possesses the quintessence of all pleasures in his resolution. Yet the tensions are still felt, and the soul's conclusions, while "true," are also partial. At the moment of death "The rest" (both the ease and the remainder of all the pleasures) *does* "lie beyond the Pole, / And is thine everlasting Store." But before that moment, Marvell and most of his contemporaries believed that no man enjoyed fully and continuously either the flesh or the spirit, that the battle was constantly renewed so long as a living spirit inhabited a living body. This did not imply that the battle lacked interest nor that decisions and momentary achievements were impossible. Such decisions and such achievements were, in fact, the poet's subjects, not only in "A Dialogue" but also "To his Coy Mistress." The speaker of the latter poem seems to resolve clearly for sensuality: *Carpe diem* appears to be all. The image of the "birds of prey," however, makes us realize the costs of a resolution to "devour" time, to choose destructive brevity of life since eternity cannot be sensually chosen.

The reader's awareness of Marvell's complex use of nature should cast light on almost any one of the poems. Within such light, the presentation of Cromwell in "An Horatian Ode" as a force of nature seems not perplexing but inevitable. "Upon Appelton House" is Marvell's most ambitious and in many respects his most interesting poem. A full consideration of it would require another essay, and I only wish to suggest here that it is a mistake to read it as an artificial "public" poem interesting chiefly for a few "personal" passages. Similarly, "The Picture of little T. C. in a Prospect of Flowers" is not a graceful trifle which somehow goes wrong. It is a fine poem, and it elucidates Marvell's central vision of man and nature. [Quotes poem.]

The opening stanza of the poem tells us of the child's alienation from and superiority to nature, as well as of her delight in it. Her apparently successful imposition of her own order and value on nature raises inevitably the question of the prospect of time, and we see prophetically in the second stanza her future triumph over "wanton Love"—and over man. Not a combatant, the speaker of the poem resolves to observe the dazzling scene from the shade which allows vision, for the god-like glories cannot be viewed immediately by profane man. If he is to admire her triumph, it must be from a distance where there is no fear of its destructiveness. With the "Mean time" of the fourth stanza we are back at the present prospect, and the observer from his advantageous point of view advises the present T. C. At the golden moment when "every verdant thing" charms itself at her beauty, she is instructed to prepare for her future career by reforming the "errours of the Spring." At first it seems, or perhaps would seem to a child, an almost possible command. With the talismanic power of her "fair Aspect" she already "tames / The Wilder flow'rs, and gives them names," and she tells the roses "What Colour best becomes them, and what Smell." At least within the circle of her immediate view she may, perhaps, by a judicious bouquet arrangement cause the tulips to share in sweetness, and it is possible to disarm roses of their thorns with assiduous labor. But the thing which should be "most" procured is impossible for the human orderer even within his small area. And all of it is, of course, impossible if all the "errours of the Spring" are in question. For, in comparison either with the triumph of T. C. or the vision of Eden, Spring is full of errors; the decorative details suggest exactly how far nature fails to sustain human visions of propriety, delight, and immortality. T. C. and the idealizing aspect of man wish delight and beauty and goodness to be single, but they cannot find such singleness within the promising verdancy of nature; if they desire it they must impose it on nature or must seek it in an "unnatural" or supernatural world. The tulips show how improperly the delights of the senses are separated in this world; the roses with their thorns traditionally indicate the conjunction of pain and pleasure, the hidden hurts lying under the delights of the senses; and the transience of the violets is a perpetual reminder of the mortality of life and innocence and beauty. The description of the preceding triumph is placed in a doubtful light. If T. C.'s reformation of floral errors is so doomed, how much real hope or fear can there be of her reformation of the errors of that higher order, man? Is the former description a fantasy, ideal yet frightening, of what might happen if the superhuman power as well as the superhuman virtue were granted, a fantasy proceeding from the observer's sharing for one moment the simplicity of the nymph?

In the exclamatory warning of the final stanza the observer and the reader see the picture of little T. C. in the full prospect of time which the flowers have furnished. At the present moment "Nature courts" her "with fruits and flow'rs" as a superior being; she represents the promise of an order higher than we have known. But she is also the "young beauty of the Woods," and she is a "Bud." The child of nature as well as its potential orderer, she shares the mortality as well as the beauty of the flowers; her own being, in the light of the absolute, is as "improper" as are the tulips or the roses. The former vision of her triumph implied full recognition of only one half of her relationship to the fruits and flowers. The introduction of Flora reminds us more sharply than anything else in the poem of the entire relationship. However lacking in the ideal, Flora has her own laws which man violates at the peril of self-destruction. Flora decrees that life shall continue: the infants shall not be killed "in their prime"—either in their moment of ideal promise or in their first moment of conception. The sexual concerns which have been suggested throughout the poem are made explicit in the final stanza. The picture in the central stanzas of the complete triumph of T. C., the absolute rule of human notions of propriety, has inevitably meant that "wanton Love's" bow will be broken, his ensigns torn: there will be no more marriages. With a recognition of mortality and of the power of Flora, we recognize also the doom of such a triumph, for both the ideal and the reality will soon die, and there is no prospect of renewal in future "T. C.'s." The conclusion, however, is neither a Renaissance nor a modern "naturalism." Because perfect fulfillment is impossible, man is not therefore to abandon his attempts at perfection. T. C. is allowed and even commanded to "Gather the Flow'rs," to expend her present and her

future energies in ordering the natural nearer to the ideal pattern—
so long as she spares the buds. The qualification is all important.
Man must beware of attempting to anticipate heaven by imposing
the ideal absolutely on earth. The killing of the infants in their
prime is not only a crime against Flora but against all the gods, for
man is never free to commit either murder or suicide in the pursuit
of the abstract ideal. The human triumph must function within and
wait upon the fulness of time. It must recognize the real and individual as well as the ideal and the general or it becomes a horror.
The ending of the poem revalues everything which has gone before.
"Ere we see" may mean something equivalent to "in the twinkling
of an eye"; it certainly means, "Before we see what will become of
you and the vision of a new and higher order." What will be
nipped "in the blossom," in the first full flowering, unless the warning is heeded will be not only "all our hopes" (our hopes of the
idealized child and of a possible new order, our hopes of love and of
a new generation), but also "Thee," the living child.

"The Picture of little T. C. in a Prospect of Flowers" is characteristic of Marvell's poetry both in its complexity and in its subtle
use of superficially "romantic" or decorative detail. It may remind
us of modern poetry, but ultimately Marvell is both more complex
and more assured of his meanings than are most of the moderns.
Marvell does not present a *persona* simply and finally torn between
this world and the next, distracted by the sensuous while attempting to achieve a spiritual vision. For Marvell, as for most Renaissance poets, the perception of a dilemma was not considered a
sufficient occasion for a poem. Marvell made precise the differences
between the values of time and of eternity. He recognized that man
exists and discovers his values largely within time; he also believed
that those values could be ultimately fulfilled only outside time.
The recognition and the belief did not constitute a paralyzing
dilemma. Each of his early poems implies the realization that any
action or decision costs something; yet each presents a precise
stance, an unique position and a decision taken at one moment
with a full consciousness of all the costs. The costs are counted, but
not mourned; the position is taken, the poem is written, with
gaiety.

When we have understood what the "prospect of flowers"
implies, "The Coronet" does not seem a churchly recantation of all
that Marvell valued, but an artful recognition of the ultimate issues.
Here the decision is taken in the full light of eternity, and, as in
George Herbert's "A Wreath" (which Marvell probably remembered), the intricate and lovely form of the poem provides an index
to the joy. The speaker of the poem describes his attempt to create
a coronet for Christ. He dismantles "all the fragrant Towers / That

once adorn'd my Shepherdesses head" to gather the necessary
flowers, but he discovers that the Serpent has entwined himself into
the proposed offering, "With wreaths of Fame and Interest." The
poet prays that Christ would untie the Serpent's "slipp'ry knots,"

> Or shatter too with him my curious frame
> And let these wither, so that he may die,
> Though set with Skill and chosen out with Care.
> That they, while Thou on both their Spoils dost tread.
> May crown thy Feet, that could not crown thy Head.

The poem is moving as well as orthodox in its expression of willing-
ness to sacrifice man's sensuous and aesthetic structures to a divine
necessity. But Marvell's most Miltonic line, "Though set with Skill
and chosen out with Care," ruefully insists that, whatever his vision
of ultimate value, the living poet also values the structures of time.

ROBERT ELLRODT

[Henry Vaughan]†

Whether inspired by the gloom of defeat in a Puritan common-
wealth, or grief at the death of a dearly loved younger brother, by
the influence of George Herbert—acknowledged in the Preface—or
a keener interest in the spiritual alchemy of Thomas Vaughan, a
sense of conversion pervades the first part of *Silex Scintillans*. It is a
record of private experience: secretive self-communings. The best
poetry of Vaughan is subjective: 'A sweet *self-privacy* in a right
soul" ('Rules and Lessons'). He addresses God—'Thou that
know'st for whom I mourne'—not the reader who will only discover
incidentally that the loved one is now a brother, now a wife. The
elegiac, *In Memoriam* note is insistent and 'unseen tears' blend
with the theme of retirement and solitude—a retreat 'from the Sun
into the *shade*' (advocated in the prose treatise *Flores Solitudinis*),
a refuge in the Circle of the Cell ('Misery') or a deeper seclusion,
the life 'hid above with Christ in God' or the 'Dear, secret Greenness' of the Seed growing secretly, 'unseen and dumb'.

Vaughan only meets himself in solitude, not in dialogue with a
Mistress or his Master. His self-awareness is a self-expression in reverie and sympathy. Donne and Herbert focussed their attention on
a centre. Vaughan may long for the 'Centre and mid-day' but he
can only 'see through a long night / Thy edges, and thy bordering
light!' ('Childe-hood'). His diffusive imagination will 'Rove in that

† From "George Herbert and the Reli-
gious Lyric," in *English Poetry and*   *Prose 1540–1674*, ed. Christopher Ricks
(London, 1970), pp. 192–99.

mighty, and eternall light' ('Resurrection and Immortality') or seek 'that night! where I in him / Might live invisible and dim!' ('Night').

Another expression of his subjectivity is his belief in Hermetic *sympathies*, proclaimed with a personal intensity of emotion in 'Sure, there's a tye of Bodyes'. The mysterious attraction which was still scientific truth to the seventeenth century mind is much more than a source of conceits or intellectual perplexity to Vaughan: it is the nostalgic apprehension of a bond with 'Absents', an animistic experience of 'the strange resentment after death' of the 'Timber', wasting 'all senseless, cold and dark',

> Where not so much as dreams of light may shine,
> Nor any thought of greenness, leaf or bark.

Vaughan's intercourse with Nature has been aptly described by Elizabeth Holmes as 'a kind of interpenetration of himself with a spirit which his special philosophy taught him to find in the objects of Nature'. But, as the same critic pointed out, 'he not only believed with the Hermetists in the 'tye of bodies', but he felt the tie; and the expression of his sense of kinship with the creatures of Nature leaves a curious impression in the reader's mind of a tie as strong as the physical or even the uterine link'.

In such projections, or in the dispersion of reverie, Vaughan unlike Herbert, first goes out of himself; but, unlike Crashaw he returns to himself. In his self-diffusing he remains self-centred, but without a keen interest in his states of mind, without the feverish self-obsesssion of Donne or the self-probings of Herbert. He is apt to generalize his experience: 'Such is man's life, and such is mine' ('Miserie'). This oscillation from the universal to the individual occurred in *The Temple*, but the dramatic impact of personality was not so often diluted by impersonal reflection. Many of Vaughan's poems centre on a natural object ('The Waterfall', 'The Showre') or on a Biblical episode, a verse from Scripture, as if his meditation was provoked by some occasion from outside, whereas Donne's and Herbert's poems mostly sprang from the sudden awareness of an inner experience, a state of mind. Accordingly there will be little psychological complexity in *Silex Scintillans*. Similes do not aim at defining but intensifying the emotions, as in 'Unprofitableness':

> 'Twas but just now my bleak leaves hopeless hung
>> Sullyed with dust and mud;
> Each snarling blast shot through me, and did share
> Their Youth, and beauty, Cold showres nipt, and wrung
>> Their spiciness, and bloud . . .

Self-examination, when attempted, is conducted through allegory and the search is not ultimately directed to self-discovery. In 'Vanity of Spirit', an epitome of his mystic quest and favourite symbolism, the poet leaving his 'Cell' by 'dawn' lingered by a 'spring' (of living waters) and 'gron'd to know' the Author of Nature. The alchemist in vain 'summon'd nature' and rifled her 'wombe'. He 'came at last / To search [him] selfe'. Yet not after the manner of Donne seeking 'the *Ego*, the particular, the individual, I' (*Eighty Sermons*, xxxiv, p. 338). The 'traces' and 'Hyerogliphicks' he discovers in a 'nook' of his own soul, like the 'Ecchoes beaten from the eternall hills', are intimations of a Divine mystery and only build up another fantastic world of 'weake' beames' and 'Mooneshine night'. Thus the poet's thought first turns to Nature, then from the contemplation of Nature moves to self-exploration, but with no Augustinian sense of opposition. In his comparison of Vaughan's quest with the questioning of Nature by Augustine in book X of the *Confessions*, Martz slurs over the movement of recoil, because it cannot be found in the poem: 'Interrogavi terram et dixit non sum'.[1] Unlike Augustine, or Herbert at that, Vaughan leaves no clear boundary between the world of objects and the subjective experience; unlike Traherne he does not enclose the outer world in the sphere of soul. His longing for a fuller revelation in death, unlike Donne's, is not a search for his own identity but a yearning for the discovery of the Divine, were it 'but one half glaunce', through the rending of 'these veyls' ('Vanity of Spirit') or 'mists' ('They are all gone into the world of light') in either Nature or the soul. This is closer to the Hermetic approach than to Augustine's close analysis of memory in his journey of the mind towards God as a reality 'interior intimo meo'.

What Vaughan has in common with many Christian mystics is a yearning to recapture something lost. It may be connected with his particular intuition of time. Not for him the 'here and now' of Traherne, or, with a difference, Herbert. The present is always filled with the remembrance of things past or the expectation of future things. When momentary, the 'moment' is integrated to 'time's silent stealth' like the 'lingring' of the 'Waterfall'. The present is emotion recollected in tranquillity. Compare Donne's 'What if this present were the worlds last night?' and Vaughan's 'I saw Eternity the other night'. A sense of distance is forced upon us: 'Silence and stealth of dayes! 'tis now / Since thou art gone, / Twelve hundred hours . . .' There is no instant projection: the imagination seems to move up a continuous stream, in full awareness of duration: 'So o'er fled minutes I retreat / Unto that hour . . .' Indeed, 'The Retreate'

---

1. 'I questioned the earth, and she said, "I am not." ' [*Editor*.]

and 'Looking back' are intimations of this fundamental mode which unifies the poet's essential longings for childhood, Eden and the Biblical ages.

Yet Vaughan does not 'long to travell back' merely to revive the past. Retrospection is inseparable from expectation, and the 'backward steps' towards Eden only supply an assurance that the 'forward motion' will ultimately take us to 'That shady City of Palme trees'. The distinctive note is the sense of delay and resistance: 'Tyme now / Is old and slow'. Therefore the intuition of the eternal cannot be a present apprehension: eternity is *beyond* time and *above* the World, as 'The Evening-watch', 'The Agreement' and 'The World' show. To Donne and Herbert eternity was a mode of being and a metaphysical concept. To Vaughan, as in the more naïve interpretations of Plato, it is the 'country beyond the stars', a world of light, calm and insubstantiality. The 'great Ring' gathers into itself all the impressions dear to the poet: 'Joys / Active as light, and calm without all noise' ('Mount of Olives').

'Beauteous shapes, we know not why, / Command and guide the eye' ('The Starre'). A feeling for sensuous beauty does command Vaughan's allegiance to Christian Platonism and his preference for natural theology. The aesthetic emotion in spiritual natures becomes an intuition of transcendence. The light of Creation is but the shadow of God, *umbra Dei*. The aesthetic contemplation of the created world only feeds the poet's dreams of Eden, his nostalgia for a diviner world, meditating 'what transcendent beauty shall be given to all things in that eternall World, seeing this transitory one is so full of Majesty and freshnesse' (*The World Contemned*). Hence the 'gazing soul' will dwell on 'the living works' of God

> And in those weaker glories spy
> Some shadows of eternity.
>
> ('The Retreate')

The mystic naturalism of the 17th century Hermetists suited this poet's sensibility. It implied an unbroken continuity in the material and spiritual world, not the abstract relation of form and matter in the contemplations of Marvell. 'Spirit' is the keyword. It is more than 'that subtile knot, which makes us man', effecting the conjunction of body and soul as in Donne's 'Exstasie' or Herbert's 'The H. Communion'. It is the 'fire-spirit of life', the 'preserving spirit . . . Which doth resolve, produce, and ripen all' ('Resurrection') in the natural cycle, but is none other than 'the knowing, glorious spirit' ('The Book'), the Divine Intelligence 'whose spirit feeds / All things with life' ('The Stone'). The spirit that passes untainted through Nature still quickens, 'refines' and transmutes matter, raising it to immateriality, 'Till all becomes [God's] cloudless glass, / . . . Fixt by [His] spirit to a state / For evermore immaculate' ('L'Envoy').

Vaughan, like the Hermetists, spurns the grossness of matter, yet obscures the distinction between 'spirit' as refined matter and the immaterial soul or mind. Accordingly his response to Christian dogma will be different from Donne's and Herbert's. He almost explains away the Resurrection when he discovers '*prolusions* and strong *proofs* of our *restoration* laid out in *Nature*, besides the promise of the *God* of nature' (*The Mount of Olives*; compare 'Resurrection and Immortality'). On the other hand, his exclamation 'O that I were all Soul!' contrasts with Donne's conviction that 'the body is not the man, nor the soul is not the man, but the union of these two make up the man'. He has therefore little interest in the paradox of the Incarnation as the meeting of two natures in Christ. The presence of the Redeemer in 'the fields of *Bethani* which shine / All now as fresh as *Eden*' ('Ascension-day') or his roaming at night 'where *trees* and *herbs* did watch and peep / And wonder' ('The Night') move him deeply through these associations with Nature and Paradise. His attention and hopes are not focused on the historical fulfilment of the Atonement, but on the 'mystic birth' of the Lord of Life in the individual soul ('Christ's Nativity'), on the process of regeneration described in the symbolism of the 'spiritual alchemists' ('Regeneration').

The religious poet at times imitates the conceited style of his predecessors, but a personal intensity is only felt in the mystical paradoxes that enlarge the imagination rather than perplex the mind:

> Most blest believer he!
> Who in that land of darkness and blinde eyes . . .
> Did at mid-night speak with the Sun! . . .
> There is in God (some say)
> A deep but dazzling darkness

> ('The Night')

The peculiar reverberation of Vaughan's poetry, when contrasted with Herbert's, its emotional impact and stronger appeal, at least for the Romantically inclined, proceed from a closer connection between his natural symbolism and the deeper layers of the archetypal imagination. From such hidden sources spring his dreams of Eden and Paradise, his yearning for a far-off 'country' or 'home' (a frequent word in *Silex*), his constant quest or 'search', ascent or 'Ascension', and the recurrent image of the archetypal Mount, the holy Hill and 'those *clear heights* which above tempests shine' ('Joy'). His light imagery is insistent and individual through the perception of light as substance—the 'firie-liquid light' of heaven ('Midnight')—as life or soul—the 'Sunnie seed' ('Cock-crowing') or Hermetic star-soul in each creature—and through the poet's sensitiveness to dawn as a new birth: 'mornings, new creations are' Day-spring'; compare 'Rules and Lessons'). The frequent association of light with silence or the starry heavens rather than the radiance of noon is remarkable. Hence the poet's ability to strike the deeper chords in his celebration of 'Night'.

The pervasive water-symbolism suggests a longing for purity and lustration, but is related to the feeling for life and growth expressed in the symbols of vegetation. The reader of Vaughan 'shall feel / That God is true, as herbs unseen / Put on their youth and green' ('Starre'). The analogical imagination alone was at work in the Biblical parable which suggested 'The Seed growing secretly', but the poem achieves the perfect fusion of the sensible and the spiritual through the emotion awakened in the poet's soul by the actual life of the seed underground: 'Dear, secret *Greenness*! nurst below / Tempests and windes, and winter-nights . . .' Fancy plays with outward form. Imagination here pierces at once to the heart of matter and the heart of life: life, '*a quickness which my God hath kist*' ('Quickness'). This realism of the symbolic imagination extends to all the recurrent images and lends substance to spiritual emotions. Since 'not a wind can stir' but straight the poet thinks of God ('Come, come . . .'), the sensuous reality of breath and wind may be given to the Spirit who first moved upon the face of the waters ('Midnight', 'Water-fall').

Neither the modes of sensibility nor the symbolic imagination invite ambiguity or ambivalence in the poetry of Vaughan. His 'sad delight' has nothing in common with Crashaw's. A unity of tone and feeling prevails. Emotions freely mingle in a nostalgic pensiveness without sharp contrasts or changes. Vaughan is the poet of osmosis rather than transubstantiation. His debased use of 'mystical' in 'The Water-fall' has been criticized by Empson, but it is the only apt word to convey this emotional halo about things, this sense of their spiritual depth, at once intense and vague, though more precise than the later Romantic emotions because of its associations with a definite theology or philosophy.

Therefore, Vaughan's greater moments are moments of balance between mystery and clarity, symbolic suggestion and precise allusion:

> God's silent, searching flight:
> When my Lords head is fill'd with dew, and all
> His locks are wet with the clear drops of night;
> His still, soft call;
> His knocking time; The souls dumb watch,
> When Spirits their fair kinred catch.
>
> ('The Night')

With a few exceptions, isolated lines rather than poems have this
haunting power, for the author of *Silex Scintillans* has neither the
unerring artistry of Herbert nor the sustained intensity of Donne.
Emotion cools and the style flags when vision or intuition fade into
moral meditation. Despite a feeling for aural beauty—'How shril
are silent tears?' ('Admission')—the music of the verse is uneven.
In the association of colloquiality and imaginative vision, Vaughan
may reach heights unattained by the more conceited 'metaphysicals': 'I saw Eternity the other night' ('The World'). However,
the lack of wit is felt when his plain utterance—in description or
meditation—is no longer the language of the imagination. His literal conception of poetic sincerity, unlike the sophisticated simplicity of Herbert, looks towards the Romantic ideal; 'O! 'tis an easie
thing / To write and sing; / But to write true, unfeigned verse / Is
very hard!' ('Anguish').

E. C. PETTET

[Henry Vaughan's "Regeneration"]†

To him that hath designed a superstructure of true blessings the
fundamental must be Salvation.

The World Contemned (p. 315)

'Regeneration' lies at the beginning of *Silex Scintillans* somewhat
like *The Wreck of the Deutschland* at the beginning of Hopkins'
Poems—an undoubted major work of its author, filled with his
most admirable and characteristic qualities (though narrative in pattern) but, at the same time, a little daunting, especially to the new
reader, because of its length, complexity and obscurity.

Of course the difficulties of *Regeneration* are not so great as
those of *The Wreck of the Deutschland*, nor are they of the same
kind. Unlike Hopkins' poem, *Regeneration* has a beautifully translu-
cent surface, its obscurities arising chiefly from its allegorical intention and its unusual amount of largely private symbolism, those

> hidden, dispers'd truths that folded lie
> In the dark shades of deep allegory.
>
> *Monsieur Gombauld*

Once we have unravelled these allegorical 'truths' the poem is readily accessible, and certainly, following the guidance of its title, its
significant position as the opening of *Silex Scintillans*, and the close
parallel between its last stanzas and the conclusion of *The World*,

† From *Of Paradise and Light* (New York, 1960), pp. 104–17.

344 · E. C. Pettet

we should never be in any serious doubts about its main theme. It is a poetic record of Vaughan's recovery—and in a large sense discovery—of religious faith; of his return to grace and his hope of election. Above all, of his hope of election, which is also seen against the general mystery of election and predestination[1]—the inspiration of God's spirit blowing where it listeth.

Though the first two lines of the poem indicate clearly enough the start of some spiritual journey, in their detail they are rather puzzling. 'In bonds' presumably refers to sin. But if that is the meaning, how are we to reconcile this idea of hateful imprisonment with 'ward', which, used in its common sense, would imply some kind of desirable, protective guardianship? Possibly Vaughan is extending the Old Testament use of 'ward' ('imprisonment', 'the condition of being a prisoner') to mean 'prisoner'. Again, he may be saying that, for all his bondage to sin, he is still under the guardianship of God. This would probably have been an acceptably orthodox point of view. But the expression of the idea through two closely joined but different metaphors would be awkward. And is the spiritual condition (whatever it is) that is described in the first line something that the pilgrim is escaping from or that he takes with him?

The rest of the stanza, which expresses the poet-pilgrim's acutely divided state of being, is quite straightforward. On the surface his life seems to be one of 'high-Spring'—of youth and enjoyed pleasure; but underneath there is the winter of sin and spiritual desolation, in which the divine spark within him is entirely obscured. The description of these two states is linked by a common, and highly characteristic, vegetal imagery, with 'Primros'd' probably carrying the deliberate ambiguity of youth and the path of destruction; and the blighted soul is represented by the typical metaphor of the frost- and wind-ravaged plant. (There is a particularly close parallel to lines 5–7, with a similar context of 'Breaking the link 'Twixt Thee and me', in *Disorder and Frailty*:

> though here tost
> By winds, and bit with frost. . . .)[2]

Further adding to the densely characteristic quality of the first stanza there is also the recurrent image of the eclipsing cloud, with

1. The urgency of this theme for a religious poet of Vaughan's time is clearly brought out by H. C. White [*The Metaphysical Poets* (New York, 1936)—*Editor*.], p. 285: 'Predestination was at the beginning of the century the official theory of the English Church, but in practice . . . men like Donne had seriously modified it in the direction of free will. The state of mind, however, for which it was of first importance to make sure that one had within himself the immediate and certain confidence of his own salvation, lingered long after intellectual accommodations were pretty widely accepted, and undoubtedly this was reinforced by the conversion and regeneration theories that came to play so large a part in the thought of the more "Enthusiastic" groups of the time.'

2. For another parallel, see *Mount of Olives II*, ll. 11–14.

which * * * we may relevantly associate the latent detail of the star and therefore the divine spark. Certainly, when Vaughan speaks of his 'eclips'd' mind, he is not thinking of his intellectual faculties, but, as the penultimate stanza makes plain, of his soul that, were all well with him, would be open to the Divine 'ray'.

The second stanza records the first advance in the poet's pilgrimage, when, realising his divided condition, he perceives that his 'high-Spring' is an illusion. ('Show', which may echo Psalms 39.6 —'Surely every man walketh in a vain show'—almost certainly carries the double meaning of illusory, external appearance and of spectacle, pageant, etc., while 'stage', besides being synonymously linked with the second meaning of 'show', may also include the sense of 'phase'.) In the only reality that matters the pilgrim's walk is

> a monstrous, mountain'd thing,
> Rough-cast with rocks, and snow

—an image that powerfully concentrates suggestions of appalling alienation from the true and natural order of things ('monstrous'), of something fearsome and even horrible (for that was how mountains seemed to the common sensibility of the time), of sterility, and of impending destruction. This notable advance brings with it, through an overwhelming sense of sin, the temptation of despair.[3] But there is no indication that the pilgrim is seriously troubled by this temptation, unless that is the implication of the phrase "Twixt steps and falls' (l. 18). Even in grief his sighs have been significantly 'upwards', and while it is unlikely that 'pinnacle' bears any special suggestion, the line, 'I reach'd the pinnacle,' clearly implies that, in spite of some suffering and set-back, the poet has struggled to a state above and beyond despair.

At this point there is a momentary halt in the progress of the poem as the pilgrim reflects on the pains of his recent ascent. The focus of this reflection is a discovered 'pair of scales'—a familiar object from the emblem books[4] but treated by Vaughan in such a way that it runs into some obscurity of reference—and of syntax. As commonly used, by Quarles for instance, this emblem is simple enough: the scales demonstrate the worthless lightness of the things of the world, etc., balanced against the substantial weight of spiritual things.[5] Vaughan appears to reverse this usage in two ways, for in his treatment of the emblem what is rejected is the heavier side of

---

3. Ll. 13–16 are somewhat reminiscent of a passage in one of Vaughan's translations from Casimirus—lib. 3, Ode 22, 15–18. The first two lines of this translation might be taken as a summary of the first two stanzas of *Regeneration*.

4. Rosemary Freeman, *English Emblem Books* [London, 1948—*Editor*.],. p. 150.

5. The *Epigram* to Quarles's *A Pair of Balances* (bk. 1 no. IV) reads: 'My soul, what's lighter than a feather? Wind. / Than Wind? The fire. And what, than fire? The mind. / What's lighter than the mind? A thought. Than thought? / This bubble world. What than this bubble? Nought.'

the scales, and the heavier side is constituted of worldly pleasures, which, with a further complicating paradox, are 'smoke'! However, the main confusion of these lines is created not so much by the reversal of the usual emblem as by Vaughan's adaptation of it to an unsuitable purpose. We may read the passage in one of two ways: in the first, we understand that whereas the 'late pains' carried the poet upwards, to the pinnacle, his worldly 'pleasures' would have borne him down to earth, hell and damnation—to the 'centre' that he speaks of later in the poem; in the second, the 'late pains' are considered as of small consequence against weightily damning pleasures. In the first, Vaughan would be expressing an idea for which his emblem is unsuitable; in the second, he would be violently straining the emblem into a false measurement, since the 'pains' can have no weight, no earthward and hellward tendency, whatsoever.[6]

Sufficient probably to take the lines in the brief and essential paraphrase that all the pilgrim's ordeals, in his ascent to the pinnacle, were of small account against what was to follow.

The voices at the pinnacle, though they may be angelic, are probably of no particular significance, merely a narrative device. But in obeying them and continuing a stage further in his journey, the poet-pilgrim is afforded a revelation of God; and this revelation constitutes the central theme of stanzas 4–6. The 'East' towards which the pilgrim travels symbolises the dawn of light and illumination in general and of the Scriptures, especially perhaps the Old Testament, in particular. The first intimation of communion with the revealed God is given by a straightforward allusion to Jacob's vision of God in a dream before Bethel (Gen. 28. 11 ff.); and this field of revelation is described as 'fresh' and 'virgin' because for each individual soul the moment of illumination comes as an eternally original experience. The last four lines of stanza 4 express a familiar idea in *Silex Scintillans*: that in earliest Old Testament days men enjoyed a particularly close intimacy with God, 'Friends of God' referring explicitly to the patriarchs (James 2. 23).

However, the intimations of communion with God that follow are much more subtle and private and require some knowledge of the whole of Vaughan's poetry for their full appreciation. For instance, the significance of the 'grove' that the pilgrim soul enters (stanza 5) is not likely to be apparent until we understands the peculiar but strong association that existed in Vaughan's imagination between God and groves. Nothing better illuminates this stanza than the opening of *Religion* (a poem printed in the first

6. There is perhaps yet another way of taking this obscure figure: that at this stage in his spiritual development the poet resents the 'pains' of his pilgrimage, and that his heart still chiefly values the 'pleasures', even though they are 'smoke'. He has not yet found the true joy of the religious life.

few pages of *Silex Scintillans* and therefore possibly composed in
the same period as *Regeneration*) where Vaughan nostalgically pictures the earliest Old Testament days as a time when man was in
familiar, speaking contact with God and his angels under a canopy
of trees:

> My God, when I walk in those groves
>   And leaves, Thy spirit doth still fan,
> I see in each shade that there grows
>   An angel talking with a man, etc.

(It is also interesting to notice, for the parallel, that where the
'grove' stanza in *Regeneration* immediately follows the reference to
'Jacob's Bed', *Religion* also has, shortly after its opening, the line,
'Here Jacob dreams, and wrestles.')

This link between groves and religious experience, especially of
communion with God, is certainly a strange one, since a poet who
knew his Bible so well as Vaughan must have been thoroughly
aware of the recurrent, almost ominous, associations in the Old Testament between groves and pagan worship. Something of its establishment may have been due to the influence of Herbert, for the
opening of *Religion* is certainly a reminiscence of Herbert's poem,
Decay:

> Sweet were the days, when Thou didst lodge with Lot,
> Struggle with Jacob, sit with Gideon. . . .
>
> One might have sought and found Thee presently
> At some fair oak, or bush. . . .

Again, as several writers have suggested, following the note in L. C.
Martin's edition, the 'grove' reference in *Regeneration* may be one
of several echoes from his brother's treatise, *Lumen de Lumine*:[7]
'Being thus troubled to no purpose, and wearied with long endeav-
ours, I resolved to rest myself, and seeing I could find nothing, I
expected if anything could find me. I had not long continued in
this humour, but I could hear the whispers of a soft wind that travelled towards me, and suddenly it was in the leaves of the trees, so
that I concluded myself to be in some wood, or wilderness.'[8] Later
in *Lumen de Lumine* there is the sentence: 'I found myself in a
grove of bays.' But along with these possible echoes we must also
take into consideration an obvious feature of Vaughan's poetic
development in *Silex Scintillans*—his adaptation of images and sensuous delights of his unregenerate days to the 'sacred poems' of his
conversion. He had always loved trees and woods and felt something of the mystery of woodland places, as we may see from such
early poems as *Upon the Priory Grove* and from passages in *Ad*

7. *"Light from Light."* [*Editor.*]
8. Waite's ed., pp. 243–4. However, if
Vaughan was recollecting this passage, it
is surprising that he did not take up the
impressive description of light that immediately follows it.

Echum[9] and *To the River Isca*, and it is not difficult to trace the
probable source of the 'grove' stanza in such a pagan fancy as

> May vocal groves grow there, and all
> The shades in them prophetical,
> Where laid men shall more fair truths see
> Than fictions were of Thessaly!
>
> > *To the River Isca*

Possibly stanza 5 carries yet another implication. This grove

> Of stately height, whose branches met
> And mix'd, on every side,

is also suggestive of the interior of some church or cathedral, with
all its columns, pillars, and arches. Whether or not Vaughan deliberately intended this suggestion it is hard to say, but the entry into
the grove might, just possibly, signify entrance into church worship.
Another pointer (admittedly a slight one) in the direction of this
reading is the allusion in the following and closely connected stanza
to *The Song of Songs*, a book currently interpreted as celebrating
the marriage between Christ and his Church.

The transition from the grove of stanza 5 to the flowery bushes
and spicy air of stanza 6 was no doubt inspired by Vaughan's
epigraph from *The Song of Songs* 4. 16—'Arise O North, and
come thou South-wind, and blow upon my garden, that the spices
thereof may flow out.' This verse, echoed in stanza 6, and, in its
allegorical interpretation, a key to the whole poem, was almost certainly running in Vaughan's head right from the start of the composition. At the same time the development may also have been
prompted to some extent by a suggestion from *Lumen de Lumine*,
for the first passage already quoted is followed by: 'With this gentle
breath came a most heavenly, odorous air, much like that of sweet
briars, but not so rank, and full.'[1]

So far as its meaning is concerned, stanza 6 is certainly another
symbolical representation of the pilgrim's experience of the Divine
illumination.[2] This interpretation is perhaps sufficiently established
by the line,

> The unthrift sun shot vital gold,

9. See especially the lines (in Edmund
Bluden's translation): 'O Nymph, that
through the drowsy thicket fliest, / And
boughs beloved, and sauntering there
repliest / Out of the deeps: Spirit of this
old grove. . . . / Show me the mystery
of this tangled maze, / The happy secret
of these his green ways, / Thy home, thy
walks!'

1. It is also to be noticed that stanza 6
contains a word, 'chequer'd', that is rare
in Vaughan's vocabulary but occurs in
his brother's treatise—'The ground both
near and far off presented a pleasing
kind of chequer.'

2. Cf. Thomas Vaughan's *Anima Magica
Abscondita*, p. 85: 'we might enter the
Terrestial Paradise, that encompassed the
Garden of Solomon, where God de-
scends to walk and drink of the Sealed
Fountain.'

since the sun here is undoubtedly to be connected with the Divine 'ray' of illumination in stanza 9. Further, with the alchemic reference to the sun's action in generating precious stones and gold, we must also take that hermetic analogy between chemical transmutation and spiritual regeneration that makes the allusion an extremely apt one in its context. But once again a really convincing demonstration of Vaughan's meaning and intention depends on familiarity with the body of his poetry, which * * * reveals a very clear connection between scents, occasionally flowers, the sun, and divine visitation.

The echo from *The Song of Songs* suggests another significance in stanza 6 besides the main one of spiritual illumination. Like stanza 5, with which it is so closely linked, it may celebrate the pilgrim's entrance into Christ's Church. And there are several other important implications. 'Vital gold' may also be used for its common symbolical significance of eternal life, its incorruptibility, while the choice of the word 'heaven' for sky[3] and 'snowy' (here probably indicative of purity as 'snow' in stanza 2 is of sterility) might imply a glimpse of the beatitudes of the after-life. Again, from the explicit statement at the end of stanza 5, the paradisal garden that Vaughan depicts (one of the most richly sensuous descriptions in the whole of his poetry) is certainly to be taken as an intimation of the 'new spring' that is in contrast with the false spring at the outset of pilgrim's journey. This strand of meaning is closely woven with another that is of the utmost importance for the development of the poem. This delightful garden of sweet airs and flowering bushes represents, quite simply, the beauty of religion. Just so that other poem of Vaughan's regeneration, *Mount of Olives II*, begins with:

When first I saw True Beauty. . . .[4]

By this revealed beauty of the religious life the pilgrim's eyes are fed. But he has a stage further to go in his path towards salvation: 'All the ear lay hush'—he has still to receive the word of Christ, and Christ himself. This vital but obscure link in the development of the poem is clearly illuminated by a passage in *The World Contemned*: 'Why with so much dotage do we fix our eyes upon the deceitful looks of temporal things? . . . Is it the Eye alone that we live by? Is there nothing useful about us but that wanderer? We live also by the ear, and at that inlet we receive the glad tidings of Salvation, which fill us with earnest groans for our glorious liberty and the consummation of the promises. . . . That faithful one, the

---

3. Though there is nothing conclusive in the refernce we should perhaps notice the line describing God in heaven in *Retirement*—'Who on yon throne of azure sits', for 'azure' is a rare word in Vaughan's poetic vocabulary.

4. There is another passage in *Mount of Olives II* (ll. 17–20) that points straight to stanza 6.

blessed Author of those promises, assures us frequently of his fidelity and performance; let us covet earnestly his best promises.'[5] In *Regeneration* Vaughan is not condemning the eye, nor has he been concerned with its regard for temporal things; but the ear that 'lay hush' is certainly waiting for the 'glad tidings of Salvation' and the 'blessed Author of those promises'.

The 'fountain' image in stanza 7 was probably 'given' to Vaughan at this point in the poem by preceding developments. For one thing, reminiscence of the fourth chapter of *The Song of Songs* during the composition of stanza 6 may very well have stirred an echo of verse 12—'a a Spring shut up, and a fountain sealed up.'[6] Again, the mention of 'Jacob's Bed' in stanza 4 may already have brought into his mind the idea of Jacob's well, the fountain beside which Christ spoke to the woman of Samaria, for he was certainly very familiar with this allusion to Jacob's well in John 4, as we may see from *The Mount of Olives* and his poem *The Search*.[7] Finally, the 'fountain' may have come in direct association with the 'grove' of stanza 5 since there are at least half a dozen instances of this image conjunction in his poetry.[8]

Apart from the clue given us by the passage already quoted from *The World Contemned*, numerous other passages in Vaughan's prose and poetry (in the two *Jesus Weeping* poems, for instance) make it reasonably certain that the 'fountain' in the first part of stanza 7 symbolises Christ—the 'fountain of life', who, in his Incarnation, is the man of sorrows weeping with tears of grief and pity for the blind sinfulness of man. (The 'her' in line 53 in no way invalidates this interpretation, since Vaughan commonly uses nouns with their Welsh gender.) Unfortunately this reading of the symbol is complicated by a difficult and possibly corrupt line—'And on the dumb shades language spent'. Without attempting any emendation, we may perhaps roughly paraphrase the line as follows: 'And, in addition to the message of the dumb shades, Christ himself expends on us the solace of his tears.' 'On' could be taken in the sense of 'over and above,' 'in addition to'; and the 'shades' language would refer to the beauty of religion, all the significance of the grove-garden, which is 'dumb' because it is addressed to the eye, not to the ear.

However, what matters in this poem is not so much Christ himself as his symbolical significance as the fountain of life, which Vaughan elaborates to describe a further stage in the pilgrim's prog-

5. *Works*, p. 326.
6. This is Vaughan's own wording as appended to *Religion*. If he is echoing this verse, he is drastically transforming the image, for besides being 'sealed', the fountain represents the Bride (the Church) not the Bridegroom (Christ).
7. *Works*, p. 162, and *The Search* (ll. 22–32).

8. See the interpolated lines 47–8 from the translation of Ovid's *De Ponto*, lib. 3, *The Search*, ll. 69–70; *Corruption*, ll. 23–8; 'They are all gone into the world of light', l. 23; *The Queer*, l. 8; *The Retirement* (*Thalia Rediviva*), l. 6.

ress—his discovery of the spiritual condition of mankind in general and of the fact and mystery of predestination.

The symbolism and reference in Vaughan's first statement of this theme (ll. 53–60), though complex and a little strained in some respects, is easily accessible. The 'cistern' (probably not to be distinguished in any special way from the 'fountain' or the 'flood') is almost certainly a pointer to Jeremiah 2. 13, a reference that is singularly apt in one way but inappropriate in another: 'they have forsaken me the fountain of living waters, and hewed them out cisterns, broken cisterns, that can hold no water.' Stones as a symbolical representation of souls is not a common one, either generally or in Vaughan's writing; but the symbol has some Scriptural precedent[9] and is close to Vaughan's emblematic figure of the heart of 'flint' (even in the regenerate). The souls of the elect are 'bright' and 'round' because they are pure and perfect; while—possibly with some reminiscence of pebbles tossed and carried along by a vigorous mountain stream—Vaughan pictures them as dancing through the fountain of life, which is Christ, towards God and heaven. The souls of the unelect, in sharpest contrast, are 'ill-shap'd', 'dull', and 'nail'd to the centre', by which Vaughan means, as elsewhere in his writing,[1] earth and ultimately hell, located in the centre of the globe. This antithesis is intensified by two further details—the echo of the Scriptural 'first' and 'last', and the contrasting, highly characteristic similes of 'light' and 'night'. Fairly close parallels to this passage may be found in *Corruption*—

> Sin triumphs still, and man is sunk below
> The centre, and his shroud.
> All's in deep sleep and night

—and also in *Man in Darkness*: 'The flesh . . . draws us back to the Earth, as to its proper centre and original; but the soul being descended from the Father of Lights is like the sparks of fire still flying upwards.'[2]

Line 63, 'My restless eye, that still desir'd,' poses some small difficulty of interpretation. It may perhaps be taken as a simple narrative bridge, but the pointed description of the eye as restless and desiring seems to indicate some significant meaning. Probably Vaughan is referring to the poet-pilgrim's still unsatisfied quest for God, who has so far been experienced only in momentary revelations and who is not present in the first vision of the elect and unregenerate. The discovery of the 'ray' and the 'rushing wind' has yet to come; while even at the end of the pilgrimage the descent of the Holy Spirit can only be prayed for and awaited.

9. See Ezekiel 36. 26; Matthew 3. 9; and —though the reference is to living souls in the new Temple—1 Peter 2.4–5.
1. E.g. *Corruption*, l. 36. Herbert also uses 'centre' to mean earth and its interior (e.g. *The Search*, l. 7).
2. *Works*, p. 315.

This small detail apart, the poem moves towards its close on a fairly simple and straightforward course. Stanza 9 commences with a second symbolical representation of the poet's belief in predestination. God is figured as the 'ray', and human souls are divided between those who stand open, 'broad-eyed', to the influence of the celestial light, and those who are 'fast asleep' (or in a state of spiritual torpor). This repetition of the theme of stanzas 7–8 is certainly compact and poetically effective; and the 'ray', the 'bank of flowers' —as well as the later 'leaves'—provide some satisfying recapitulation of earlier imagery. Perhaps, too, the restatement of theme adds something to the poem since the reference this time to the active ministration of God, reinforced by the phrase "twas mid-day', emphasises the hopeless blindness of those who remain 'nail'd to the centre'. On the other hand, as a whole the stanza cannot be completely defended against a charge of redundancy.

The final development in the poem is introduced by the 'rushing wind' that the pilgrim suddenly hears. This image, which brings the second of the two main hermetic representations of God[3] into one and the same poem, is undoubtedly an echo of Acts 2. 2: 'there came a sound from heaven as of a rushing mighty wind.' But much more significant in the concluding lines of the poem is the allusion, prompted most likely by the allegorical reading of The Song of Songs 4. 4, to one of the central New Testament texts on election and salvation, John 3. 3–8, and especially to verse 8: 'The wind bloweth where it listeth, and thou hearest the sound thereof, but canst not tell whence it cometh, and whither it goeth: so is everyone that is born of the spirit.' All through the last three stanzas the intellectual perplexity of the pilgrim, confronted with the mystery of election, is reiterated—'I wonder'd much', 'musing long', 'while I list'ning sought My mind to ease'; and Vaughan uses this text from John to point his conclusion. All musing and wondering is in vain, he intimates, for there is no rational human explanation of the mystery. The Christian can only submit to the inscrutable will and purpose of God, to the divine breath that whispers 'Where I please'. In exactly the same way he resolves the foiled questioning in his other important poem about election, The World; and the parallel between the two poems is particularly close since The World also contains the image of the Divine Sun:

> Yet some, who all this while did weep and sing,
> And sing, and weep, soar'd up into the ring;
> But most would use no wing.
> O fools—said I—thus to prefer dark night
> Before true light!

3. It is also probable that Vaughan was intimating the third manifestation of the Trinity—God, Christ, and now the Holy Spirit.

To live in grots and caves, and hate the day
    Because it shows the way;
The way, which from this dead and dark abode
    Leads up to God;
A way where you might tread the sun, and be
    More bright than he!
But as I did their madness so discuss,
    One whisper'd thus,
'This ring the Bridegroom did for none provide,
    But for His bride.'

As it began, so the poem ends with a somewhat enigmatic line. 'And let me die before my death' cannot be Vaughan's constant thought, plainly expressed in several other poems,[4] of the Christian's need to be continuously remembering his sojourn in the grave and so reconciling himself to death, for the 'one breath' (of divine grace) that he is invoking can have little to do with the discipline of mortification. Possibly he is alluding to the mystical 'mors raptus'[5] that Donne speaks of in one of his sermons: 'I will find out another death, mortem raptus, a death of rapture, of ecstasy, and that death which St Paul died more than once' (**LXXX** *Sermons,* No. 27). But from the total context of the poem, and its title, it seems much more likely that Vaughan is speaking here of the death of the old Adam in him that, in the dialectical process of Christian spiritual growth, must always precede the rebirth of the soul. We die in spirit to be reborn; and we can only be reborn after a spiritual death. As he writes in one of his translations from Paulinus:

So blest in death and life, man dies to sins,
And lives to God; sin dies, and life begins
To be revived: old Adam falls away,
And the new lives, born for eternal sway.[6]

Yet these lines, which concern baptism, do not provide a perfect gloss on the concluding couplet of *Regeneration*, for in *Regeneration* Vaughan is speaking of the spiritual death and rebirth that are dependent upon the 'one breath', upon predestination and the grace of God. Not completely sure of his election, in spite of abandonment of his old sinful ways and the revelations of God and Christian religion, the pilgrim-poet can only conclude with the humble prayer that the Holy Spirit will descend on him[7] and that he will be numbered among the elect.

4. E.g., *Rules and Lessons*, ll. 125–6.
5. Itrat-Husain (*The Mystical Element in the Metaphysical Poets of the Seventeenth Century*, p. 214) interprets the lines in this way as an intimation of that death of ecstasy that marks the final 'unitive' stage of mystical experience, the stage of oneness with the Absolute. ·
6. *Works*, p. 365. See also *Ascension*

Hymn, ll. 7–12, and the line in another translation from Paulinus—'I have died since, and have been born again' (p. 349, l. 10).
7. This would have been the accepted allegorical reading, sometimes indicated in the margin, of the text, *The Song of Songs* 4. 16, that Vaughan prints as his epigraph.

S. SANDBANK

Henry Vaughan's Apology for Darkness†

Among several commendatory poems prefixed to Henry Vaughan's *Thalia Rediviva* (1678), I. W.'s "To my worthy Friend, Mr. Henry Vaughan the Silurist"[1] makes a critical point beyond mere commendation. Vaughan's muse is praised here for wisely demeaning herself to express, not only the supreme bliss of "radiant Worlds," but also the "hollow Joyes" of earthly life; not that the latter have any intrinsic value: "hollow Joyes" here obviously means "the hollowness of joys." If hollowness nevertheless deserves to be expressed, it is mainly because it can serve to set off fullness. The king's majesty is "burnished" by his own eclipse and suffering. His luster is best read in the shade, his greatness best found in the shroud. Two analogues are then quoted—from nature and from religion:

> So lightning dazzles from its night and cloud;
> So the first Light himself has for his Throne
> Blackness, and Darkness his Pavilion.

Lightning, King and God—the brightest manifestations of the physical, the human, and the spiritual—owe much of their brightness to a background of night, suffering, or primeval Darkness, respectively. I. W. here points to an image and an idea very central to Vaughan's poetry: what may be called Vaughan's apology for darkness.

There is no need to show once again that terminology of light and darkness is prominent in Vaughan's vocabulary. Light, as often pointed out, is associated with God, Election, Heaven, life, happiness; darkness—with the Devil, Damnation, death, misery. The two images, or groups of images, thus serve to re-inforce a dramatic world-picture in which the opposition between heaven and earth, Grace and nature, is a very basic distinction. This more or less conventional use of light-darkness imagery in Vaughan's poetry has been traced back to numerous possible sources: Hermeticism, the Bible, Christian mysticism, the Christian Meditation etc.

Essentially more important, however, though statistically less prevalent, is another, less conventional, treatment of darkness, which critics often neglect. Darkness, to Vaughan, is not only the absence of light—and, figuratively, of all the values light stands for.

† *Studies in English Literature 1500–1900*, VII (1967), 141–52.
1. *The Works of Henry Vaughan*, ed. L.   C. Martin (Oxford, 1957), 620. All references in my text are to this edition.

It is also a necessary condition of light, the background which sets
it off. As such, it cannot be branded as merely evil. Vaughan's popular epithet of "poet of light" needs some qualification. He is by no
means a Boehme[2] or a Blake, but the consciousness of darkness,
indeed, the conviction that light cannot do without darkness, is
essential to the understanding of what he says and of how he says
it. This affirmation of darkness gives his work much of its unity, in
that it is the embodiment in an image of several separate aspects of
his thought. A visual experience here gives rise to a whole complex
of analogous experiences: psychological, theological, mystical.

The visual experience itself has been noticed often, notably by E.
C. Pettet, who speaks of the recurrence of the cloud-star image-clus-
ter in Vaughan's poetry.[3] The phenomenon of starlight intensely
shining forth from among dark clouds seems to have been particularly attractive to Vaughan. It produces parallel images, such as that
of sun shining at midnight, or darkness at noon. A chamber in the
Globe Tavern, "painted over head with a Cloudy Skie, and some
few dispersed starres," gives rise to the playful paradox of "Darkness, & Stars i'th' mid day!", while outside, towards twilight, "the
soft stirs / of bawdy, ruffled Silks, turne night to day" (pp. 10–11).
Nicodemus speaks with the Sun at midnight (p. 522), and it is at
midnight that Christ's "all-surprizing light" may break (p. 451).

Time and again Vaughan stresses the "value" light gains from
night (p. 678). "Light," he says, "is never so beautifull as in the
presence of darknes" (p. 217), and "stars never shine more glorious, then when they are neare black Clouds" (p. 370);[4] "one
beam i'th' dark outvies / Two in the day" (p. 439). Darkness, here,
is obviously more than the negation of light. One cannot discern
light—one cannot, at any rate, do justice to its beauty—without a
dark background to set it off. This visual experience—and the formula it can be reduced to—namely, the value of the negative as a
foil for the positive—has several repercussions in Vaughan's
thought. It is the object of this paper to consider some of these analogues.

A) *The Cosmological Analogue.*

Henry Vaughan's brother Thomas, practically obsessed by cosmo-
gony and cosmogonical speculation, assigns a central place to dark-

2. Jakob Boehme (1575–1624), philosopher and mystic, claimed that his writings were based on what he learned personally through divine illumination.
[*Editor.*]
3. *Of Paradise and Light: a Study of
Vaughan's Silex Scintillans* (Cambridge,
1960), 24–26, 135–136.

4. These words are from *Primitive Holiness,* a work which is largely a translation of the *Vita diui Paulini Episc. No-
lani ex scriptis eius & veterum de eo
Elogiis concinnata* (Antwerp, 1621); the
quoted words, however, seem to be
Vaughan's own. See editor's note to p.
370.

ness and night in his numerous accounts of creation.[5] Great as his influence on Henry be,[6] I cannot find any trace of such cosmogonical theories in Henry's work. Cosmologically, however, darkness plays an important part—and is vindicated—in Henry's work.

The cosmological vindication of darkness was an integral part of both the religious and the philosophical traditions Vaughan was working in. The God of the Bible is the creator of darkness as well as light, and darkness, originally a chaotic power, has been integrated, in creation, into the constitution of the universe. The alternation of day and night becomes essential to the world-order, and darkness finds its legitimate place within this order.[7] Philosophically, the idea that universal harmony is based on reconciled opposites goes back to the Aristotelian definition of beauty as "discordia concors."

Both aspects appear in Vaughan. God is the creator of darkness as well as light: "Did not he, who ordain'd the day, / Ordain night too?" (p. 459). "Light, and darkness," "days, nights" are all God's works (p. 436). But the religious aspect is inseparable from the philosophical. For not in vain did God "Ordain night too":

> Were all the year one constant Sun-shine, wee
> Should have no flowres,[8]
> All would be drought, and leanness; not a tree
> Would make us bowres;
> Beauty consists in colours; and that's best

5. Central to Thomas Vaughan's accounts of creation is the meeting between masculine fire and the feminine darkness of the Materia Prima. He identifies the biblical primeval darkness with the Kabbalistic "Ensoph" and the Orphic "Night," and subscribes to "that position of all famous poets and philosophers—that 'all things were brought forth out of the night.'" (*The Works of Thomas Vaughan: Eugenius Philalethes*, ed. A. E. Waite [London, 1919] p. 216.) His description of both subrational Materia Prima and super-rational God as "Darkness" (ibid., p. 269) seems to lead him astray in that it makes him mix up Materia Prima with the pseudo-Dionysian "nothingness" of God, and he says of the former that "It is that Transcendent Essence whose theology is negative" (ibid., p. 214). Darkness plays a central role in his thought as the mother of all things.
6. I find the long controversy about whether the twin-brothers had anything to do with one another after adolescence rather futile. The biographical fact that Henry was not sure whether his brother had an M.A. (see his letter to John Aubrey, p. 687), or what the name of the village was where he had been buried (p. 691), by no means disproves in-

fluence. After all, Henry did know his brother's work (pp. 687–688), and apparently sympathized with his brother in his ludicrously bad-tempered controversy with Henry More ("Daphnis," ll. 35–38, p. 677). Thomas Powell's homage to the brothers—"Not only your faces, but your Wits are Twins" ("Upon the most Ingenious pair of Twins . . .", p. 36) would have been absurdly tactless, had the brothers been completely estranged from each other. Above all, the many thoughts, terms, and images they share in common clearly point to mutual knowledge and influence. A comparison such as Miss Elizabeth Holmes makes tween Henry's "Cock-crowing" and a passage from Thomas' *Anima Magica Abscondita* (see editor's note to "Cock-crowing," p. 746) is an irrefutable proof of the latter's influence on the former.
7. See Sverra Aalen, *Die Begriffe 'Licht' und 'Finsternis' im Alten Testament, im Spätjudentum und im Rabbinismus*, Skrifter utgitt av Det Norske Videnskaps-Akademi i Oslo. II, Hist.-Filos. Klasse, 1951, no. 1 (Oslo, 1951) 9–19.
8. Cf. "Affliction" (*Thalia Rediviva*), p. 662: "Flow'rs that in Sun-shines riot still, / Dye scorch'd and sapless"; cf. also Traherne, *Centuries* III, 21.

Which is not fixt, but flies, and flowes;
The settled Red is dull, and whites that rest
   Something of sickness would disclose.
      Vicissitude plaies all the game,
         Nothing that stirrs,
         Or hath a name,
      But waits upon this wheel,
Kingdomes too have their Physick, and for steel,
   Exchange their peace, and furrs.

(p. 459)[9]

"Though temper'd diversly," elements are reconciled to each other in "sweet Concord," the cold assisting the hot etc. (p. 651). Night, far from taking away the use of light, "urgeth the Necessity of day (p. 628). Darkness is not only inevitable. It is necessary for the success of its opposite.

B) *The Psychological Analogue: Conversion.*

The cosmological principle of harmony-based-on-contraries has for its counterpart, on the religio-psychological plane, the conviction that the bliss of the pious contains the consciousness of vanquished sinfulness. This experience of conversion, so central to Vaughan's world, is another version of the light-in-darkness image. A related theme is that of chastisement and affliction as essential to religious bliss. The main image to express this last theme is that of the "silex scintillans," or sparkling flint, again a variation on the light-out-of-darkness motif.

One source of Vaughan's conviction, that in the same way as lights is brighter against darkness, holiness too is holier against the background of past sins and repentance, seems to be suggested in the poem "St. Mary Magdalen" (p. 507). Speaking of Mary's conversion, Vaughan refers to the story of Mary and Simon the Pharisee (Luke VII), rebuking the "Self-boasting Pharisee" for calling her a sinner. The relevant passage in Luke includes the following words, spoken by Christ: "Her to whom little is forgiven, the same loveth little."

Sin and forgiveness are thus closely associated with eventual Glory. The connection between the two is explained in a passage from Anselm's *Man in Glory*, translated by Vaughan, in which faith is said to grow out of a profound consciousness of one's own corruption and from the consequent gratitude to a redeeming God: "That therefore thou mayst for ever take delight in the singing of his

9. Cf. Sylvester's Du Bartas (1621 ed.) 12–13: "But yet, because all Pleasures wex unpleasant, / If without pause we still possesse them, present; / And none can right discerne the sweets of Peace, / That have not felt Wars irkesome bitterness; / And Swans seem whiter if swart crowes be by / (For, Contraries each other best discry) / Th'All'sArchitect, alternately decreed / That Night the Day, the Day should Night succeed."

prayses, thou wilt (I believe) have alwayes in thy mind those great transgressions and eternal miseries from which he delivered thee" (p. 201). This theme is then developed in many of Vaughan's divine poems. The paradox of "Sighs make joy sure" (p. 491), "pious griefs Heavens joys awake" (p. 511), "through thick pangs, high agonies / Faith into life breaks" (p. 512), finds its concrete embodiment in the image of light shining out of, and set off against, darkness. True joy, overcast with clouds and rain, is likened to "those clear heights which above tempests shine" (p. 491), while true grief is, paradoxically, bright enough to "outshine all joys" (p. 505). The simile is made explicit in "The Timber":

> But as shades set off light, so tears and grief
> (Though of themselves but a sad and blubber'd story)
> By shewing the sin great, shew the relief
> Far greater, and so speak my Saviors glory.
>
> (p. 498)

A similar image used in this context of repentance is that of light-in-dew, where dew, like darkness, stands for grief and tears, out of which the light of glory shines, but also for the tears of merciful Grace.[1] "Dew" is then further associated with Christ's blood, on the one hand, and with blooming and budding, on the other hand.[2]

Finally, a motif related to that of the awareness of past sins as essential to true Glory is that of discipline and chastisement as breaking the armor of darkness, thus bringing forth the hidden light. The seeming darkness of affliction paradoxically leads to the light of happiness; man is rendered "most Musicall" through "Wholesome" sickness (p. 459), through "restorative" diseases (p. 662); truth, when afflicted, thrives like that light which "gains a value from the Night" (p. 678). There are many metaphoric variations on this theme: the bird that sings best when its nest is broken (p. 501), the tree which being bent grows best (p. 490), liberty in imprisonment (p. 472), or God's "easie yoke" (p. 516). Above all, the idea

---

1. "Dew" in both its figurative senses is used in "The Sap" (p. 475) ll. 3–4 and 39–41, "Jesus Weeping" (p. 503) ll. 11, 48–49, "Admission" (p. 453) ll. 29–32, or "The Timber" (p. 497) in which there is a gradual progression from the tears of repentance to the spiritual waters of the celestial springs. The twofold sense of "dew" is discussed in Pettet's *Of Paradise and Light*, p. 133.

2. Pettet, pp. 30, 42–47. Vaughan's association of water with light is persistent: in "Midnight" (p. 421), God's Heaven is described as a "fierie-liquid light," both flaming and streaming, and the poet asks Heaven to make his own blood, or water, both "burne and streame." The star, in "The Starre" (p. 489), is said to "stream or flow," while God's emana-tions of light, in "The Importunate Fortune" (p. 634) are "Sacred streams," "A glorious Cataract," and they "flow." Also in "The Eagle" (p. 626), the beams of the sun rush upon the eagle "like so many Streams." The combination, in Heaven, of light, or fire, and water, may have something to do with the Jewish traditional interpretation of Shamayin (heaven) as derived from a combination of Esh (fire) and Mayim (water), an interpretation cited by Henry's brother Thomas (*The Works of Thomas Vaughan*, p. 278) and by two authors he admired: Pico della Mirandola, in *Heptaplus*, "Ad Lectorem Praefatio," and J. Reuchlin, in *De Arte Cabalistica* (in Johann Pistorius' *Artis Cabalisticae*, [Basel, 1587], p. 633).

of bliss out of affliction is rendered through the famous "silex scintillans," or sparkling flint, image, in which sudden light breaks out
of the dark stoniness of the sinful heart.

C) *Night for Prayer and Vision.*

Darkness also spells silence, rest, peace, refuge. Night is the
antithesis of the fussiness and distraction of daylight, it is "this
worlds defeat" (p. 522). Vaughan's favorite word here is "shade"
rather than "darkness,"[3] and its use is often complex: for it stands
not merely for shelter from the heat of earthly ill-guiding light, and
as an epithet for "that shady City of Palme trees" (p. 419), but it
also means "copy" or "image." When Sundays, therefore, are
described as the "Bright shadows of true Rest" (p. 447), the oxymoron is justified because "shadows" stands for both refuge from
the heat (shade) and "image" of the light of God's glory. More
naturally, "shadow" stands for the image of death, in which its
meaning as "copy" and its meaning as "darkness" combine. This
use appears in a section from Nierembergius's *Of Life and Death*,
translated by Vaughan. The section discusses sleep as a copy of
death; the underlined words are Vaughan's additions:

> So life, by reason of the importunity, and the multitude of
> humane troubles, cannot endure or hold out till it reacheth the
> Inne, which is death; but is driven to rest *in the shade* upon the
> way-side; for sleep (*the shadow of death*) is nothing else but a
> reparation of weary and fainting life. . . . If death *in its shadow
> and projection* be the recreation of life, how delightfull will it be
> at home, or in it self!

(p. 285)

But night, beyond its being the antithesis of the heat of gaudy
sunlight, is also the channel that leads to another light, the true
Light of the spirit. Here, again, light shines out of darkness and
needs the "shade" to be revealed. Night is the time of prayer and
vision.

The dialectic of light-of-the-world→darkness→divine Light is
particularly worked out in the two prefaces to *Flores Solitudinis*:
the Epistle Dedicatory and the "To the Reader." The transition
which the reader may expect from "the Sun into the Shade," will
lead him, not to the deadly "Occidentem & tenebras," but to "that
happy starre, which will directly lead you to the King of light" (p.
213). Similarly, the "shine of this world" is contrasted to the other
light that grows out of darkness—"this light I live by in the Shade"
(p. 216). It was at midnight that Nicodemus spoke with the Sun of
Christ (p. 522), and it was the other night that the poet himself

---

3. In *The Mount of Olives* (p. 152) night as "shadow," as "rest and secu- rity," is even contrasted to night as "the hours and the powers of darknesse."

saw the endless light of eternity (p. 466). The soul's ascent to God at night is likened to a star shining behind the "mistie shroud" of clouds (p. 425).

Night being the "day of Spirits" (p. 522), or the "working-time of Spirits" (p. 305),[4] no wonder that it is, in accordance with Luke XXI, 37,[5] Christ's "prayer time" (p. 522), and that it should be our own prayer-time as well (p. 143). For it is "the mother of thoughts" (p. 169), and of all other times "the most powerful to excite thee to devotion" (p. 187). But it is not only the concrete peace and quiet of night that makes it the most practical time for vision and prayer. Blocking the way to the ordinary senses, it frees man from the subjection to sense and makes possible purely spiritual meditation, thus becoming a metaphor similar to St. John of the Cross's Night of the senses and of the understanding. It is only when the eye of sense and reason closes that the mystical eye opens. Darkness is again vindicated as the gateway to the light, as that blindness which makes real sight possible:[6] one's eyes never open except when God closes them (p. 488). The man who walks in God is the man whose eyes are both put out (p. 525), and the poet is resolved to "seal my eyes up" (p. 520).

D)   The Darkness of God.

St. John of the Cross adds a third Night to the Nights of the senses and of reason—the Night of God Himself; for God "is dark night to the soul in this life."[7] That is, the incomprehensibility of God to man's mind finds its embodiment in the image of light too dazzling to look at, that is, dark; as Milton puts it: "Dark with excessive bright thy Skirts appear."[8] The ultimate source of this much-discussed image is pseudo-Dionysius's "darkness above light,"[9] meant, as Thomas Vaughan understands it, not in an absolute sense, "but in a relative sense or, as the schoolmen express it, 'in respect of us,'" for He is "invisible and incomprehensible."[1] This "Dark Aleph" of the contracted pre-creative God later manifests itself in the "Bright Aleph" of Creation, or of Christ.[2]

Henry Vaughan's own much-discussed reference in "The Night," to the "deep, but dazzling darkness" which is in God, may have

4. These are words Vaughan added to his translation of Nierembergius.
5. Quoted on the title-page of *The Mount of Olives*, p. 137; cf. Vaughan's marginal note to "The Night," l. 29.
6. This paradox is popular with the Metaphysicals: "To see God only, I goe out of sight" (Donne, "A Hymne to Christ, at the Authors last going into Germany"); "Shutt our eyes that we may see" (Crashaw, "In the Glorious Epiphanie of our Lord God, a Hymn . . .").
7. *Ascent of Mount Carmel*, as quoted by Ross Garner, *Henry Vaughan, Experience and the Tradition* (Chicago, 1959), pp. 55–56.
8. *Paradise Lost*, III, 380.
9. ὑπέρφωτος γνόρος—De Myst. Theol. II.
1. *The Works of Thomas Vaughan*, p. 269.
2. *Works*, p. 15.

been inspired by pseudo-Dionysius,[3] or by his own brother. Like Thomas, he makes it clear that the darkness derives from our own inability to see: "some say" there is darkness in God—in the same way as men say it is dusky, not because there is "obejctive" darkness in God, or because it is "objectively" dusky, but "because they / See not all clear." The final two lines, however, seem to "objectivize" God's darkness:

> O for that night! where I in him
> Might live invisible and dim.

But "dim," elsewhere used by Vaughan to describe the extinguishing effect of the greater on the smaller light,[4] could indirectly show these words to mean the very opposite: I wish I were united to God, so that His excessive *light* would dim my little candle.

E) *The Darkness of Incarnation.*

The darkness of Incarnation is a motif both opposed and complementary to the darkness of God. For if the inaccessibility of God's light makes Him dark, the darkness—or veil—of the Incarnate Christ makes God's light accessible. Man cannot see God's light and live; therefore—as well as for other reasons, of course—God puts on a dark veil of flesh that makes His sight possible.

The veil-image, elsewhere used by Vaughan to symbolize the limitations connected with existence in the flesh, here serves as a metaphor for the "epistemological" advantage of the incarnate phase of God, which makes possible the knowledge of God by dimming His dazzling light.[5] Vaughan speaks of Christ's "entrance through the veile," of His putting on "Clouds instead of light," of the breaking of the veil on Christ's death which gave man sight and led him to the knowledge of God.[6] Above all, the much discussed first stanza of "The Night" clearly states that Nicodemus could recognize God "through"—which undoubtedly means also "by means of"[7]—the "sacred vail" of flesh He had put on. We cannot see God unless He is shrouded, eclipsed, veiled; and the veil is Incarnation.[8] Glow-

3. His reference to "Hierotheus" in the preface to the second edition of *Silex Scintillans* (p. 392) shows that he knew at least the *De divinis nominibus*, in which this fictitious writer of hymns is mentioned, though he could have picked up the name from a later writer. .

4. E.g. p. 472: "But to this later light they saw in him, / Their day was dark, and dim."

5. Cf. Hebrews X, 19–20. This motif is recurrent in 17th century poetry. Milton, in "Il Penseroso," ll. 11–16, applies it to his admired Melancholy.

6. *Flores Solitudinis,* p. 288; "The Incarnation, and Passion," p. 415; "The Holy Communion," p. 457.

7. Cf. R. A. Durr, *Of the Mystical Poetry of Henry Vaughan* (Cambridge, Mass., 1962), p. 115.

8. The underlying assumption here seems to be that pure spirits must put on material "garments" when they descend to earth: "No spiritual thing descending below can operate without a garment," says Pico della Mirandola in the 35th of his "Conclusiones Cabalisticae," quoted as a "Kabalistic maxim" by Thomas Vaughan (*The Works of Thomas Vaughan,* p. 46) and paraphrased by Henry Vaughan (p. 366).

worms can shine only when facing the semi-darkness of the moon, for daylight would extinguish them; man can live only when facing the semi-darkness of Incarnation, for the naked light of God would drown his light. But the wish to "live" by looking at the "sacred vail," instead of the "glorious noon" itself, later in the poem develops into a wish to "die before his death"—as he puts it in "Regeneration"—and "live invisible and dim" in the "night," or "dazzling darkness" of God, which actually is the very same "glorious noon" of the first stanza.

F) *Light in Darkness and Life in Death.*

The paradox of God in the flesh is superseded by the sharper paradox of divine death for the sake of human life. The saving Crucifixion is the core of Vaughan's light-in-darkness dialectic, and the climax of his apology for darkness.

Death, besides being traditionally associated with darkness, also leads to a world of light, and it is in this sense that "the jewel of the just (shines) nowhere, but in the dark" (p. 484), i.e., death is the dark corridor, the passage through which is indispensable for the vision of the Light. Above all, Christ died to give life to man; the paradox of this life-giving death is often inseparable in Vaughan's poetry from the act of Incarnation itself: "a God Enclos'd within [a] Cell" (p. 415) is both a God incarnated and a God buried. It finds its traditional type in the phoenix whose "custom 'tis / To rise by ruin" (p. 657), but above all, in the light-in-darkness image. Christ's death, "dark and deep pangs" to Himself, "to me was life and light" (p. 394). Less directly, in "Disorder and frailty" (p. 444), the "grave and womb of darkness," from which Christ beckons to the poet's "brutish soul" at the beginning of the poem, is later replaced by "Thy stars, and spangled hall" at which the poet aims and stretches from his cell of clay; thus an implied picture emerges of a lowly dark grave containing a high heaven of stars. As the source of true light, the death of Christ is an eye-opener. His blood has cleared our eyes and given us sight (p. 458). Like the setting sun, the dead set in the west only to be reborn in the east (p. 59).

"As time one day" (p. 512), probably a lament over the death of his first wife, combines the paradox of light-in-darkness with that of green branches budding out of dry dust and of the "bleaching" blood of Christ. The latter is an image Vaughan is particularly fond of. From a more pedestrian use of the snow-blood cluster—for blood-stained truth as soiled snow (p. 673), or carnations washing their bloody heads in snow-white streams (p. 644),—he progresses (in thought, not in time) through Revelations VII, 4, prefixed to his translation of *Man in Glory* (p. 193), to the typically paradoxical "bleaching" blood.[9]

In Vaughan, as in the Bible, darkness, though integrated into the world-order, is naturally further from the divine plan and will than is light. It is light and day, not darkness and night, that represent Providence, Redemption, hope and life. None of the metaphorical uses that make darkness so significant in Vaughan's poetry implies a "Romantic" attraction to darkness as such. If Glory is set off against past sins and repentance, it is Glory, not repentance, that ultimately wins the day. If night, both literally and figuratively, is the mother of thoughts and of mystical vision, it is the final sudden ray of light that is the much-expected goal. If God is darkness, it is only to our imperfect mind that darkness must be His sole attribute. If death is the only way to true life, and Crucifixion the only way to salvation, it is true life and salvation, not death and Crucifixion, that Vaughan "groans" for. As in the Bible, in which the elimination of day-night alternation is an integral part of eschatological visions,[1] Vaughan, too, can occasionally visualize that state of Glory in which the earthly light-darkness dialectic is overcome and light alone reigns. If here on earth a "wreath of grief and praise" must be offered to Christ, "Praise soil'd with tears, and tears again / Shining with joy, like dewy days," Christ's "quickning breath" ultimately bears

> Through saddest clouds to that glad place,
> Where cloudless Quires sing without tears,
> Sing thy just praise, and see thy face.
>
> (p. 539)

Silex Scintillans ends with a powerful description, in "L'envoy" (p. 541), of the disappearance of the veils of physical light, and the overflow into this world of the immaculate brightness of ultimate light, absolute, which is freed from the need to be set off against its opposite:

> Arise, arise!
> And like old cloaths fold up these skies,
> This long worn veyl: then shine and spread
> Thy own bright self over each head,
> And through thy creatures pierce and pass
> Till all becomes thy cloudless glass,
> Transparent as the purest day
> And without blemish or decay,

9. See "Ascension-Hymn," p. 482; "To my most merciful . . . Christ," p. 394; "As time one day," p. 512.

1. E.g. Zechariah XIV, 6–7; see Sverre Aalen, pp. 20–27.

Fixt by thy spirit to a state
For evermore immaculate.
A state fit for the sight of thy
Immediate, pure and unveil'd eye.

Vaughan's muse here rises to the "radiant Worlds" of which I. W. speaks in his commendatory poem, for once leaving all "hollow Joyes" behind. But the dazzling force of rare lines such as these depends, for its effectiveness, on their general context, on the long passage through the semi-darkness which is Vaughan's more usual theme.

ROBERT ELLRODT

[Thomas Traherne]†

* * *

* * * In the association of colloquiality and imaginative vision, Vaughan may reach heights unattained by the more conceited 'metaphysicals': 'I saw Eternity the other night' ('The World'). However, the lack of wit is felt when his plain utterance—in description or meditation—is no longer the language of the imagination. His literal conception of poetic sincerity, unlike the sophisticated simplicity of Herbert, looks towards the Romantic ideal; 'O! 'tis an easie thing / To write and sing; / But to write true, unfeigned verse / Is very hard!' ('Anguish').

Yet this is how Thomas Traherne (1637–1674), parson, poet, and mystic, wrote with ease among Restoration gentlemen:

A simple Light, Transparent Words, a Strain
That lowly creeps, yet maketh Mountains plain,
Brings down the highest Mysteries to sense
And Keeps them there, that is Our Excellence:
At that we aim. . . .
('The Author to the Critical Peruser')

The true importance of Traherne, however, is not in the history of poetry, but in the history of thought and religious sensibility. Alone among the 'metaphysicals' he expounds a philosophy and delivers a message. Though influenced by the Hermetic writings, Plato and the long line of Platonists, from Alexandria to Florence and Cambridge, though well-read in the moralists of antiquity and probably acquainted with the more daring sects of the Puritan age, he only borrowed what responded to the needs of his mind and sen-

† From "George Herbert and the Religious Lyric," in *English Poetry and Prose 1540–1674*, ed. Christopher Ricks (London, 1970), pp. 199–202.

sibility. He modified and made his own such ideas as entered into his Gospel of Felicity—including the Biblical texts he turned to his own ends.

His originality proceeds from a conjunction of self-centredness and expansiveness. The solipsistic absorption of the newborn child was the image of his own consciousness:

> Unfelt, unseen let those things be
> Which to thy Spirit were unknown,
> When to thy Blessed Infancy
> The World, thy Self, thy God was shewn.
>
> ('The Instruction')

Then indeed, 'The World was more in me, than I in it' ('Silence'). The child and the mystic, both inflamed 'With restlesse longing Heavenly Avarice' ('Desire') discover that 'self LOV is the Basis of all Lov' (*Centuries of Meditation*, iv. 55). But since the poet is 'a lover of company, a delighter in equals' whose Soul 'hateth Solitude' ('A Thanksgiving and Prayer for the Nation')—almost a Whitman figure—self-love overflows in a love directed to all men. A love still egocentric, for Traherne looks on his 'lovely companions' as his 'peculiar treasures' and seeks society in order that others may glorify him as he glorifies God.

Out of this intense awareness of his individual existence springs the poet's 'Insatiableness' (a revealing title): 'There's not a Man but covets and desires / A Kingdom, yea a World; nay, he aspires / To all the Regions he can see / Beyond the Hev'ns Infinity' ('Misapprehension'). However, man's desire is infinitely satisfied: 'all is yours', as Saint Paul and Seneca had proclaimed, for the world is seated in your soul. Distance is illusion; perception is spiritual possession since every object 'Was present in the Apple of my Eye' and 'in my Soul a Thought / Begot, or was' ('My Spirit'). Traherne anticipates Berkeley's theory of vision and the celebrated *esse est percipi*.[1]

The poet, however, does not really call in question the reality of the outer world. His main point is that 'not to appear is not to be.' Thus his subjectivism supports the Christian and Hermetic notion that the prime function of man is to contemplate the Creation and glorify the Creator. But the mystic presses his claim further. A 'Mind exerted, will *see* infinity ('My Spirit'), for 'We first by Nature all things boundless see' ('The City'). Though the astronomical discoveries and the theory of endless space fired his imagination, like Henry More's,[2] Traherne's passion for the unbounded

---

1. The philosopher George Berkeley (1685–1753) published his *Theory of Vision* in 1709, denying the objective existence of material objects and advocating a kind of subjective idealism according to which things "exist" only when they are perceived. [*Editor.*]

2. Henry More (1614–87), a Cambridge Platonist who argued against the materialistic views of Hobbes. [*Editor.*]

really proceeds from the dilation of an 'enlarged Soul', his vivid sense of the unlimited 'capacity' of the mind and his quenchless thirst for infinite treasures. The same instinct directs the contemplation of eternity by the soul 'whose Glory it is that it can see before and after its Existence into Endless Spaces' (*Centuries*, i. 55). At other times, however, Eternity is a more mystical experience, a vision of the world in glory, of the works of God in their changeless essence and beauty:

> 'The Corn was Orient and Immortal Wheat, which never should be reaped, nor was ever sown. I thought it had stood from everlasting to everlasting . . .'
>
> (*Centuries*, iii. 3)

In the illumination of 'Innocence' (primal or recaptured) 'the ancient *Light of Eden*' shines over the present world and in the poet's soul. Paradise is here and now, not a distant dream. Even when the themes are alike, Traherne and Vaughan speak from a different point of view. Both poets herald the Romantic glorification of childhood, though Traherne's message alone is consistently based on the illumination of infancy and the conviction of original innocence. To both, however, childhood is essentially a symbol of a spiritual state. But Vaughan only longs to travel back: Traherne lives in a Paradise regained.

Religious contemplation in the Gospel of Felicity becomes a contemplation of the universe. Despite the idealistic transmutation of things into thoughts, attention is focused on what sense and the imagination can reach and apprehend. Though free from sensuality, the celebration of the senses in the 'Thanksgiving for the Body' strikes a note as yet unheard. The Christian mysteries are still an occasion for wonder, but the significance of the Redemption has suffered a sea-change when Christ is presented as the 'Heir of the whole world' who taught us 'how to possess all the things in Heaven and Earth after His similitude': 'To this poor Bleeding Naked Man did all the Corn and Wine and Oyl, and Gold and Silver in the World minister in an Invisible Manner, even as he was exposed Lying and Dying upon the Cross' (*Centuries*, i. 60).

In his absence of sin-consciousness, in his faith in the natural instincts, in his reliance on Reason and his conviction that 'Things pure and true are Obvious unto Sence' ('Ease') and irresistibly taught by Nature as long as it is uncorrupted by Custom, Traherne departs from the Christian tradition of Herbert, Crashaw and Vaughan. Despite his confidence in intuition (or because of it) he stands on the threshold of the age of *Christianity not Mysterious* and already looks in the direction of eighteenth-century primitivism. In his sense of wonder and illuminated vision he stands alone.

'Amazement was my Bliss' cried the mystic in 'Wonder', and the poet claimed * * * that 'Affections are the greatest Wits.' The purity of impression will shine through the transparency of the style:

How like an Angel came I down!

('Wonder')

Order the Beauty even of Beauty is

('The Vision')

Lyrical ejaculation, though fitfully Blake-like in 'The Rapture', is usually artless to the point of formlessness. Rhapsodical accumulation, of Whitman-like amplitude in the 'Thanksgivings', proves wearisome in the shorter lyrics. Only the prose of the *Centuries of Meditation* reaches a higher excellence when it beats with rapture and burns with beauty, as in the record of the child's intimations of immortality.

* * *

H. M. MARGOLIOUTH

[Traherne the Writer]†

Traherne, both in the *Poems* and in the *Centuries*, is the poet of Felicity. He tells of his Felicity as an infant, of his temporary loss of it and of his Paradise regained ('He called his Hous the Hous of of Paradice', C IV. 22, lines 3–4). It was regained with a richness unknown in infancy. The child among 'his new-born blisses' (it is impossible to read Traherne without thinking of Wordsworth's *Ode*) had singleness of eye and keenness of sense-perception unblunted by reflexion or knowledge of evil. The 'gleam' (Wordsworth again) was on everything he saw. This was lost awhile because neither his companions nor his educators had right values; but Traherne became a child again in the sense in which that is necessary for entering the Kingdom of Heaven (*Innocence* 60).

Yet to an adult who is 'Heir of the World', to whom the whole phenomenal world is given as his Garden in Eden, two things are added, and, unless they are added, there is no Felicity for him. First, he must be conscious of his happiness: he not only enjoys the World but loves the 'Beauty of Enjoying it' (C I. 31, line 2). This consciousness of Felicity is an enrichment not possible for the

† From 'Introduction' to Margoliouth's *Poems, and Thanksgivings* (Oxford, edition, *Thomas Traherne: Centuries,* 1958), I, xxxix–xli.

infant, and from it spring a whole mental development and creation
—for Traherne his *Poems* and *Centuries*. Secondly, the adult is
aware that the phenomenal world is not all: it is not even primary
or infinite. Primary and infinite is Spirit, that is God, a Trinity of
Love. There is nothing conventional, second-hand, or merely 'orthodox' about Traherne's Christianity. That is clear from the great sections on Love in the middle third of the second *Century*. His consciousness of Spirit and of his contact therewith and part therein is
described in *My Spirit*. It may or may not be right to attribute to
Traherne actual mystical experience, but he had that living and permanent awareness of Spirit which is necessary for Felicity in the
adult.

This double awareness, of enjoying the phenomenal world and of
belonging to a spiritual life, is the foundation of Traherne's philosophy as seen, for example, in *The Circulation* and *Amendment*. I am
Heir of the World. That is God's bounty. But everything in the
World is the better for being enjoyed by me. In this way I make a
return to God for his bounty. I return his gifts to him with interest.
God enjoys the World through me.

> Thy Soul, O GOD, doth prize
> The Seas, the Earth, our Souls, the Skies,
> As we return the same to Thee;
> They more delight thine Eys,
> And sweeter be,
> As unto Thee we Offer up the same,
> Then as to us, from Thee at first they came.
>
> (*Amendment* 36–42.)

That is Traherne. Is he a great poet? What are his limitations?
He had nothing of the dramtist: he has not attempted to create a
single character. He is not a poet of detailed 'observation of nature':
he counts the streaks of no tulips. Even if he wished to count them,
he might be dazzled by the gleam. He is not a poet of wide-ranging
esemplastic imagination: he reaches no Xanadu. He can make the
mistake of arguing in verse, and in complicated stanzaic verse at
that, and the result is not poetry.

> The End Compleat, the Means must needs be so.
> By which we plainly Know,
> From all Eternitie,
> The Means whereby God is, must perfect be.
>
> (*The Anticipation* 46–49.)

He is, of course, an ecstatic poet. He has fine openings ('How
like an Angel came I down', *Wonder* 1): even *The Anticipation*
opens finely. No one—not Vaughan, not Wordsworth—is more
vivid or convincing about his felicity as an infant. No one, in my

limited experience, has so married the worlds of sense and spirit, leaving the objects of sense undimmed and showing the potencies of spirit as 'all Act'.

ARTHUR CLEMENTS

[On Traherne's "My Spirit"]†

* * * Whereas "The Salutation" articulates the more accessible idea of the necessity of prizing for the sake of true possession, "The Preparative" and "My Spirit" express the profounder idea that the single-eyed, undivided, unfallen or redeemed Self truly is at one with the world he creatively and fully appreciates. The Dobell poems[1] do not of course baldly assert this most difficult concept. Rather, by means of different symbols and poetic techniques, the careful "critical peruser" gradually, subtly, repeatedly, variously "discovers" and thereby more fully and deeply actually realizes this idea and its development in the whole sequence.

Since "My Spirit" concerns "beginnings" and creation in a special sense, I would suggest that a particularly helpful context in which to read this rich poem is Genesis I, John I, and Eckhart's masterpiece, *Commentary on the Gospel according to St. John*.[2] In his short Prologue to this work, Eckhart reminds us that in Book VII of the *Confessions* Augustine says he read "a great part of this first chapter of John's Gospel in the works of Plato."[3] Throughout his *Commentary*, Eckhart quotes and alludes to Augustine more frequently than he does any other writer; Aristotle is the second most frequently cited author. In the first words of Chapter I, Eckhart draws our attention to the parallel between Genesis I and John I: "It must be pointed out in the first place that this very statement, 'In the beginning was the Word, and the Word was with God,' and several of the ensuing statements are contained in the words: 'And God said, let there be light: and there was light. And God saw the light, that it was good, and He separated the light and the darkness' (Genesis I, 3–4)."[4] "My Spirit" is a Neoplatonic poem, but more precisely it is a Christian, biblical Neoplatonic poem, and the con-

---

† From *The Mystical Poetry of Thomas Traherne* (Cambridge, Mass., 1969), pp. 121–30.
1. So called because discovered by Bertram Dobell: see Textual Notes. [*Editor.*]
2. It is not necessary to claim that Traherne was familiar with Eckhart's *Commentary*, although it was written in Latin rather than in Eckhart's native German. Whether or not Traherne read it, my

point is only that this *Commentary* is very helpful to the critic for understanding "My Spirit." [Johannes Eckhart (1260–1327) was the founder of German mysticism.—*Editor.*]
3. Clark, *Meister Eckhart*, p. 232. [*Meister Eckhart: Selected Treatises and Sermons*, ed. James M. Clark and John V. Skinner (London, 1958)—*Editor.*] And see Augustine's *De Beata Vita*, IV.
4. Clark, *Meister Eikhart*, p. 232.

text just suggested (as opposed, say, to an exclusively or predominantly Neoplatonic one) provides, I believe, the various religious and philosophic elements of Traherne's thought, including the Aristotelian elements, essentially in their proper and just proportions. Unless we have some idea of how a contemplative, like Eckhart, who was familiar with the Church Fathers and classical philosophy, read Genesis I and John I, we cannot, I think, fully understand and appreciate "My Spirit."

To speak generally, the poem "My Spirit" explains further, in its own unique and distinctive way, the meaning of pneuma primarily by articulating and developing the idea that unfallen and redeemed activity are perfectly "imitative" of God's creative activity through his Word as expressed by Genesis I and John I—providing we understand those biblical texts in an Eckhartian and Augustinian sense, a sense consistent with Traherne's other works. The main concepts found at length in the prose *Centuries*, II 40–46, 73–91, III 62–68, and IV 4 have been distilled, refined, and economically and poetically expressed in "My Spirit." It should at once be made explicit that on one level, let us say the literal level, Genesis I, John I, and "My Spirit" concern different matters: Genesis I is about God's creation of the world at the beginning of time; John I is about the unique Word or Son of God, who was with God, and who was God, and who in the beginning made all things and then at some later time entered the world; "My Spirit" is primarily about the beginning or childhood of the speaker, his creative vision, who he truly was and who, redeemed, he truly is. But on the poetic or mythic level, this poem makes it clear that the speaker or, more precisely, his essential Self is "without Hyperbole, The Son and friend of God," and that this divine Spirit "makes" or "re-makes" the otherwise dead material world in the eternal Now-moment, for "evry Moments Preservation is a New Creation" (C II 91). As the Son of God, he willingly does the joyful work of God, sustaining or recreating God's very good works, the universe, which wise work is also truly play—Wisdom, as it were, playing before the throne of God.

The two major relationships of the poem are those of *my Spirit* to God and of *my Spirit* to the so-called external world, the "Material World" which in itself "is Dead and feeleth Nothing" (C II 90). These relationships are complex and paradoxical in that *my Spirit* is both identical and not identical with God, and identical and not identical with the external world which it quickens. Throughout the poem Traherne maintains this delicate balance of distinguishable but ultimately indivisible natures. Eckhart's commentary on the Word and its relationships to God and the world provides the contemplative context which helps to explicate the relationships of *my Spirit* to God and the world. Indeed, Eckhart's last sentence in the following lengthy passage invites and justifies our procedure:

We have, accordingly, four considerations, namely that the thing issuing is in the producer, that it is in it as the seed is in its source, as the word is in the speaker, and that it is in it as the idea, in which and through which the product issues from the producer.

In the fifth place, however, we must realize that by the very fact of a thing's issuing from something else it is distinguished from it. Hence follows the statement: 'The Word was with God'. It does not say 'below God', nor 'it came down from God', but 'the Word was with God'. For the expression 'with God' indicates a certain measure of equality. In this connexion it should be noted that in analogical relations the product is always inferior, less, more imperfect than, and unequal to the producer, whereas in homogeneous relations it is always equal to it, not sharing the same nature but receiving it in its totality, simply and integrally and on an equal footing, from its principle.

Hence, sixthly, that which issues forth is the 'son' of the producer. For a son is one who becomes another in respect of personality but not other in nature.

From this it follows, seventhly, that the son or the word is identical with the father or principle. And so we have next: 'The Word was God'. Yet here it must be noted that, although the product in analogical relations derives from the producer, it is nevertheless below its principle, not with it. Furthermore, it is other in nature and so is not the principle itself. Yet in so far as it is in the latter, it is not other in nature nor yet in substance. A chest in the mind of an artist is not a chest but the life and intelligence of the artist, his actual concept. My purpose in mentioning this point is to bring out the implication contained in these words on the procession of the divine Persons, namely, that the same thing holds good and is found in the procession and production of every being in nature and in art.[5]

Eckhart's terms producer, product, and issuing (which suggest Neoplatonic emanationism[6] are parallel to Traherne's distinction in stanza 4 between a "Transeunt Influence" and an "Immanent" Act and to Traherne's "Proceeding" and "Dilate" of stanza 6. In Eckhart, the Word is the product which issues from God, the producer; and the world (as later passages in Eckhart make still clearer) is the product which issues from the Word or Son, the producer, for "All

5. Clark, *Meister Eckhart*, pp. 233–234.
6. And see Clark, *Meister Eckhart*, p. 247: "there is a personal emanation and generation of the Son from the Father." Also *C* II 40–46 and "Church's Year-Book," f. 5lv.

things were made by him" (John 1 : 3). Similarly in Traherne's poem, *my Spirit* is the product which issues from "its Creator" to which it is "so near . . . In Greatness Worth and Nature" (lines 80–83); and the "World within" (which paradoxically is also the world without—see lines 35–40 in particular) is the product of the creative spirit acting upon the material world. Most notably, the relationship between the Word and God (that is, the Word's being identical with but distinguishable from God) that Eckhart pains-takingly describes is essentially the same relationship between *my Spirit* and God that Traherne carefully but also poetically describes throughout the poem and perhaps most clearly in stanza 5, the first of the three conclusive stanzas. Throughout the poem, Traherne distinguishes *my Spirit* from God, but also indicates that it is "nigh of Kin To" and "like the Deitie"; he applies traditional sym-bols for God to *my Spirit*, and ascribes to *my Spirit* attributes, such as infinity, which are traditional attributes of God. Just as God is, so the true Self or pneuma is all Act, all Spirit, and

> being Simple like the Deitie
> In its own Centre is a Sphere
> Not shut up here, but evry Where.

Writing on the nature of Being, St. Bonaventure concludes that because Being is "most simple and greatest [see also line 74: "That Being Greatest which doth Nothing seem!"], therefore it is entirely within and entirely without all things and, therefore, is an intelligible sphere whose center is everywhere and whose circumfer-ence nowhere."[7] There can be no doubt as to Traherne's meaning and his full awareness of it, when we compare his "Thanksgivings for God's Attributes": "O the wonderful excellency of thine eternal Nature! It is a Sphere, O Lord, into which we were born, whose Centre is everywhere, circumference no where" (p. 318; and see C II 80).

The speaker's essential being, then, is an Act which consists in the full realization of its eternal and infinite potentialities, an eternal and infinite Act. In Traherne's day, the word Act had the now obsolete senses of both Reality and Active Principle (OED). Like the God of Aristotle and the Scholastics, *my Spirit* is pure Actual-ity, Thought-Thinking-Thought: "The Thought that Springs Ther-from's it self." (We read in the first stanza of "Thoughts I" that Thoughts are the "Machines Great Which in my Spirit God did Seat"—p. 169—which interrelates the "Thoughts" poems with "My Spirit.") In stanzas 1 and 3 of "My Spirit" Thought, the spir-

---

7. St. Bonaventure, *The Mind's Road to God*, tr. George Boas (Indianapolis, 1953), p. 38. [*Editor.*]

itual connection (so to speak) between God and the world, is contemplative or noetic and creative, not meditative, abstract, or rational; can be either sensuous or nonsensuous; and corresponds to Eckhart's "idea" in the lengthy passage cited above and, with qualification, to the Platonic Idea. (Nor should this be surprising, for it is precisely in his conception of God that Aristotle is closest to Platonism.) Later in his *Commentary*, Eckhart cites Augustine on the Greek *logos* signifying in Latin *idea* (that is, *ratio*) as well as *word*, and then goes on to clarify what he means by "idea":

> it should be noted that 'idea' is taken in a double sense. For there is the idea received or abstracted by the intellect from things, the idea in this case being subsequent to the things from which it is abstracted. There is also an idea which is prior to things, the cause and idea of the things, which is indicated by the definition and is grasped by the intellect in the innermost ground of the things themselves. The latter is the idea now under discussion. Therefore it is said that the logos, that is, the idea, is in the beginning. 'In the beginning', he says, 'was the Word.'[8]

Like Eckhart's "idea," Traherne's "Thought" is neither discursive nor abstract. We saw in our discussion of "The Preparative" that Traherne holds, with Plotinus and others, that discursive thought cannot apprehend God, the absolutely simple. Now, it is very important to realize also that, for Traherne, the mystic or Felicitous experience does not involve or consist of ideas "received or abstracted by the intellect from things." Since there is a tendency in some non-Christian Neoplatonists toward rationalistic abstraction —or at least their articulation of the matter has been interpreted as such—we must here make some careful distinctions concerning extrovertive, sensuous mysticism and introvertive nonsensuous mysticism. Traherne writes of and apparently enjoyed both kinds, as also we saw in "The Preparative." In "My Spirit," both kinds again seem to obtain, but extrovertive mysticism, particularly involving the sense of sight, clearly predominates. When mystics write of not being able to apprehend ultimate reality with the bodily, fleshy, or conventional eyes or senses (C II 76, "Innocence," line 16, and "Thoughts I," stanzas 6–7, for example) they are referring to either (1) nonsensuous introvertive mysticism or (2) the necessity of purgation so that the veil of custom and selfish solicitude will be removed, so that eventually one may sensuously perceive ultimate reality with a pure heart through cleansed senses. In *The City of God*, St. Augustine writes: "Thus, it was with 'heart' that the

8. Clark, *Meister Eckhart*, pp. 243–244. Eckhart's translators have translated *ratio* in Eckhart's text and citations as *idea*.

Prophet says he saw . . . Now just think, when God will be 'all in all,' how much greater will be this gift of vision in the hearts of all! The eyes of the body will still retain their function and will be found where they now are, and the spirit, through its spiritual body, will make use of the eyes."[9] This is the kind of creative and apocalyptic vision that Traherne writes of in "My Spirit" and elsewhere, when God in the eternal Now-moment is all in all, when Christ or pneuma in us sees. He does not mean seeing objects in some generalized, rationalistic, abstract way. This, I believe, ultimately comes to thinking about objects rather than actually looking at them with the heart through the eyes. As I understand him, Traherne means seeing with fully open eyes rather than with closed or indifferent eyes; or seeing felicitously into the particular-universal suchness or quiddity of an object with regenerated or enlightened heart and eyes rather than seeing in such a way as mentally to abstract an "essence" from the object, as if essence and object could ever really (that is, in fact, not just in mind) be dualistically separated.[1]

That Traherne's Spirit or Thought, like Eckhart's *Logos* and idea, is, among its other meanings, essentially a Christ-like creative Act and all that is "made" through this active, creative power (the product being, in some important sense, in the prior, causing producer, or, putting it another way, "so is the Soul Transformed into the Being of its Object"—C II 78) becomes most apparent by stanza 3 of "My Spirit."[2] Noting that stanza 3 ends on the word "shind," a key biblical word[3] in the sequence, a word that, echoing "shineth" in John 1 : 5, practically opens the poem, occurs repeatedly, and then literally closes the poem, we again have recourse to

9. *The City of God*, ed. V. J. Bourke (Garden City, 1962), p. 535. It is noteworthy that in line 45 of "My Spirit" ("And evry Object in my Soul a Thought") Thomas changed "Soul" to "Heart." See Margoliouth, II, 350. Although we cannot determine whether or not Traherne made the change with the biblical or Augustinian passages in mind, this revision appears to be one of several instances in D of changes made by Thomas which Margoliouth should have respected.

1. Many Neoplatonists are both extrovertive and introvertive mystics, though Plotinus is not as clearly and definitely an extrovertive mystic as Eckhart and Traherne are. (See, for example, W. T. Stace, *Mysticism and Philosophy*, p. 77.) With exceptions, Neoplatonists in general tend to reduce or not to share Plato's depreciation (relatively speaking) of the physical sensuous universe, although they can be and have been misinterpreted that way, particularly when the extrovertive purging away of conventional seeing (for

the sake of real, regenerated seeing) is mistaken as the introvertive voiding of all sensuous content. What apparently is missing in or insufficiently stressed by Plato and some Neoplatonists is the extrovertive Hebraic-Christian praise of and joy in God's "very good" visible creation.

2. This controversial stanza could also be validly and valuably, though anachronistically, explained in Berkeleian terms, providing we understand Berkeley not in a Johnsonian sense nor in the usually garbled textbook fashion but rightly in accord with the interpretation of, for example, A. A. Luce, in his *Berkeley's Immaterialism* (London, 1945) and *Sense Without Matter: Or Direct Perception* (London, 1954).

3. Shine is a biblical word especially associated with Christ as well as with the First and Third Persons: see my "Donne's Holy Sonnet XIV," *MLN*, 76 (1961): 484–489, esp. 486, reprinted in my *John Donne's Poetry* (New York, 1966), pp. 251–255.

Eckhart's elucidating remarks: "Indeed, it would be more correct to say that in the case of created things nothing 'shines' but their ideas . . . The idea, then, is 'the light shining in darkness'—that is to say in created things—yet not enclosed, intermingled or comprehended by it."[4] Eckhart then concludes:

> We can see then how this passage, from 'in the beginning was the Word' down to 'There was a man sent from God', may be expounded by means of the ideas and properties of natural things. It is clear too that the actual words of the Evangelist, if subjected to careful scrutiny, teach us about the nature and properties of things whether in being or in operation and so in addition to establishing our faith provide us with instruction on the nature of things. For the Son of God Himself, 'the Word in the beginning', is the idea, 'a sort of creative power charged with all living and immutable ideas, which are all one in it', as Augustine says in the last chapter of Book vi of his *De Trinitate*.[5]

In the opening of the first stanza we read that in the beginning of the speaker's life the Act (which is "the Substance of My Mind," is "My Spirit") "so Strongly Shind Upon the Earth, the Sea, the Skie." Having in mind Traherne's conception of pure vision and the principle "That evry Moments Preservation is a New Creation" (C II 91), this is tantamount to, as Genesis I puts it, the creation or re-creation "in the beginning" of "the heaven and the earth," to the moving of "the Spirit of God . . . upon the face of the waters," and to the letting there be light. Considering stanza 3, especially the alternatives presented by lines 45–51, "That Act" is also tantamount to, as John I puts it, "in the beginning . . . all things" being "made by him," in whom is "the life" which is "the light of men," the light which "shineth in darkness." ("My Naked Simple Life was I," "My Spirit Shind," "A pure Substantial Light!" are some of the biblically resonant lines of the poem, lines which are particularly echoic of those words in John I that are associated with or symbolic of Christ.) This creative Act is, in other words, "a repetition in the finite mind of the eternal act of creation in the infinite I am"; for the pure vision of which Traherne and the contemplatives speak is, I believe, comparable to Coleridge's view of the imagination. Like Traherne, Coleridge conceives of objects in themselves as essentially fixed and dead; the imagination, essentially vital, is the God-like faculty in man, "the living Power and prime Agent of all human Perception."[6]

* * *

4. Clark, *Meister Eckhart*, p. 236.
5. Clark, *Meister Eckhart*, p. 237.

6. *Biographia Literaria*, ed. J. Shawcross (Oxford, 1907), I, 202.

STANLEY STEWART

[Traherne the Poet]†

* * * "The Salutation" (pp. 5–6) purports to be a poem about birth and the period shortly thereafter. But the poem actually deals with an anxiety similar to Augustine's: Where was the self before time?

> These little Limmes,
> These Eys and Hands which here I find,
> These rosie Cheeks wherwith my Life begins,
>   Where have ye been? Behind
> What Curtain were ye from me hid so long!
> Where was? in what Abyss, my Speaking Tongue?

When Philip alters "Speaking" to "new-made Tongue" he shows that he misses his brother's point. Originally and rightly the language suggests a paradoxical state of affairs in which the speaker's tongue was owned but owned without his knowing it. The stanza has a surreal quality that tends to blur the distinction between the times before and after the moment of birth. Personal existence seems to precede cognition: "Rosie cheeks" are temporally prior to "Life." Implicit in these rhetorical questions is the assertion that for aeons the speaker lay, along with his "Speaking Tongue," in "Chaos." Malcolm Day has recently pointed out Traherne's belief in the doctrine of the preexistence of the soul.[1] In this stanza we find a hint of the preexistence also of the body. The opening poem is the speaker's salute to his bodily parts which for "So many thousand thousand yeers / Beneath the Dust did in a Chaos lie." In the infinite expanse of this eternity before time, the "I" remained silent because of the alienation of part from part. We encounter the striking notion of a tongue, "Speaking" in the void of eternity, without the willed participation of the self.

The speaker seems to suggest that the tongue speaks but is not heard. Various parts of the body appear from the speaker's vantage point in the present to have been hidden from each other, behind curtains or in vast reaches of physical space. If Philip's revision is therefore not completely wrong-headed, he did miss the fact that the "newness" hinted at in Stanza 1 belongs to the apprehensions of the speaker:

> I that so long
> Was Nothing from Eternitie,

† From *The Expanded Voice: The Art of Thomas Traherne* (San Marino, Calif., 1970), pp. 171–82.

1. "Traherne and the Doctrine of Pre-existence," *Studies in Philology*, LXV (1968), 81–97.

> Did little think such Joys as Ear or Tongue,
> To Celebrat or See:
> Such Sounds to hear, such Hands to feel, such Feet,
> Beneath the Skies, on such a Ground to meet.

What is new is the organizing consciousness, the "I," composed from "Nothing." This disengaged ego could not "think" of the full satisfactions lying in store for his fragmented sense receptors. Stanza 4 is an apostrophe to the new sense of "Joy" which emerges coeval with the "Lims," the "Organized Joynts" of the child. Before time or organized consciousness or wholeness, the veins and limbs of the body possess this joy.

The opening poem is not a "composition of place" but rather a blurring of the sense of place and time; the moment of birth loses its temporality as it is pushed back into the timelessness of chaos. Indeed, it seems that the self was present as witness to the body's birth:

> From Dust I rise,
> And out of Nothing now awake,
> These Brighter Regions which salute mine Eys,
> A Gift from GOD I take.
> The Earth, the Seas, the Light, the Day, the Skies,
> The Sun and Stars are mine; if those I prize.

First a stranger to his parts, the speaker now presents himself as a stranger to the world. The heroic proportions of the ego (seen in the speaker's habitation of chaos) enable him to occupy the universe: "The Earth, the Seas, the Light, the Day." In the last stanza of "The Salutation," some variant of "strangeness" appears six times. What once appeared as merely new is now construed as awesome; the fragmented has been resurrected as the wonderful, a quality that provides coherence between the first two poems. "How like an Angel came I down," the speaker exclaims, only to repeat the theme of "The Salutation": again, the skies are bright, the body like a little world, the world full of treasure.

* * * In this early section, generally, the focus is not on childhood in the autobiographical sense, but rather on infancy as a way of responding to the world: "The World resembled his *Eternitie*, / In which my Soul did Walk" (lines 5–6). "Wonder" (pp. 6–8) deals with this quickened awareness:

> A Native Health and Innocence
> Within my Bones did grow,
> And while my GOD did all his Glories shew,
> I felt a Vigour in my Sence
> That was all SPIRIT. I within did flow
> With Seas of Life, like Wine;
> I nothing in the World did know,
> But 'twas Divine.

In this fine stanza Traherne emphasizes metaphors of physical and emotional plasticity. "Health and Innocence" are not just "Native," they are alive, burgeoning like a plant within the hardest substances of the body. The very sense of life is entirely—"all"—"SPIRIT." But the "I" not only apprehends this "Vigour" within; in a marvelous shift Traherne stresses the malleable nature of the "I" by use of fluid imagery. The "I" moves within the infant self in the most elastic of all forms: with physical likeness to the irrepressible ocean tides, or with the unpredictable emotional effects of wine. Hence, the vitality of movement within corresponds to the Divinity pervading the macrocosm. In the following stanza the same theme is treated in antithetical terms; "Weeping Eyes" provide the only semblance of motion, as Traherne depicts the static, mundane world of adult commerce with "The State of Innocence." From the idyllic world of vital, liquid movement we are thrust into the restrained and dead world of the fallen senses.

In the remaining stanzas of "Wonder" the speaker describes this prelapsarian consciousness. On the one hand the world seemed like the Heavenly City, and it seemed also that the infant was the joyful possessor of all:

> The Streets were pavd with Golden Stones,
>   The Boys and Girles were mine,
> Oh how did all their Lovly faces shine!
>   The Sons of Men were Holy Ones.
> Joy, Beauty, Welfare did appear to me,
>   And evry Thing which here I found,
>   While like an Angel I did see,
>   Adornd the Ground.

This stanza seems to blot out all possibility of evil. But as we read in stanza 7, the child fails to perceive the fallen world only because it literally flees from "the splendor of [his] Eys":

> Cursd and Devised Proprieties,
>   With Envy, Avarice
> And Fraud, those Feinds that Spoyl even Paradice,
>   Fled from the Splendor of mine Eys.
> And so did Hedges, Ditches, Limits, Bounds,
>   I dreamd not ought of those,
>   But wanderd over all mens Grounds,
>   And found Repose.

In the final stanza the contrarieties set up in the poem (plenitude and deprivation, innocence and experience, Paradise and limitation, treasure and "ragged Objects") are drawn into accord. Even the figures of enclosure, which Traherne often uses with negative overtones ("Hedges . . . / Walls, Boxes, Coffers") "shine," like the faces of the children of Paradise. They shine because the infant fails to understand the human intentions underlying their functions in the "real" or adult world. The child projects his own sense of beauty outward: "Proprieties themselves were mine." He invests the universe with the liberty of his own "Health and Innocence."

Like Milton, Traherne was a learned man. But like the Milton of *Paradise Regained*, he had grave doubts about the efficacy of knowledge, at least insofar as knowledge implied sophistication or disunity. The truth does not divide, but reconciles. The only residue of division in the poem is that between the fallen and Edenic visions. As in Thomas'[2] "Fern Hill," or Blake's *Songs of Innocence*, Traherne's Eden is that blissful time before time-consciousness. The coffin represents limits only to one schooled in death. Pristine ignorance of time and mortality was the "Original Simplicitie" lost by Adam at the Fall: "Those Things which first his Eden did adorn, / My Infancy / Did crown. Simplicitie / Was my Protection when I first was born" ("Eden"). Structurally, "Eden" is like a parenthetical meditation on the "Happy Ignorance" which "Divided" the child from any sense of sin. As such, it is also a poem in praise of ignorance and naïveté. Traherne did not think of knowledge as the appropriate end of human life. Indeed, he shared with Montaigne and Pierre Charron[3] a belief that knowledge was a potential source of danger and anxiety. Thus, in the opening suite of poems most frequently anthologized ("The Salutation," "Wonder," "Eden," "Innocence") Traherne examines the ideal sense of union between subject and object. He determines that the ideal perception is in the subject, and he is led to see the infant's ignorance as closely linked to innocence and security. Conversely, knowledge and complexity are features of the fallen, adult world. We need not construe this theme as anti-intellectual, however; it represents, instead, Traherne's assumption that Truth and Goodness are identical. This was his theme in "Shadows in the Water": adult perceptions must not be insulated from the quickening illuminations of the child's vision, for where such fragmentation of viewpoint exists, an arbitrary limit has been mistakenly imposed, or the single part has been confused with the whole. The theme of unity, or of essentialism, is a clear expression of Traherne's Platonism: particularity and division are not consonant with perfection. Traherne would have agreed with Thomas Jackson's comment on God's perfection:

Wee must not conceipt a multitude or diversity of excellencies in his *Essence*, answering to the severall natures of things created: We must not imagine one excellencie sutable to *elementary*

---

2. Dylan Thomas. [*Editor.*]
3. Pierre Charron (1541–1603), French

preacher and philosopher, wrote on wisdom: *De la sagesse* (1601). [*Editor.*]

bodies, another to *mixt*, a third to *vegetables*, a fourth to *sense*, &c. one to humane nature, another to Angelicall.[4]

After a rather complicated discussion of the plural, the total, and the universal, Jackson concludes that the divine Essence precludes all quantification: hence,

> Hee speaks more fully and more safely, that saith, *God is being itselfe, or perfection itselfe*. . . . So all *plurality* be excluded, we express his *being* and *perfection* best, by leaving them, as they truly are, without all quantity.
>
> [I, 36]

The continual use of repetition, and the piling up of syntactic elements (especially of synonyms) appropriately conveys this Platonic sense of perfection by way of the inadequacy of language. Accordingly, Jackson explains, qualifiers which suggest "illimited Essence" are appropriate, "In that Hee [God] is without beginning [and] without end" (I, 37). So, we might point out, is the speaker of Traherne's poems. In this sense Traherne's conception and his dramatization of the inadequacies of language to express it meet happily in his love of abstract nouns and adjectives, a love shared by Jackson:

> The indivisible unity of illimited *being* or *perfection*, is, in every respect imaginable, more excellent and soveraigne than all infinite *perfections*, by imagination possibly could be. . . . From this fundamentall truth of Gods absolute infinity by indivisible unity, we may inferre, He is *powerfull* above all conceit of infinite power, . . . *Wise He is*, beyond all conceit of infinite wisdome . . . *Good* likewise *He is* above all . . . Lastly, the immensity of his Majesty, and infinity of duration . . . infinitely exceed all conceipt of *infinite* succession or extension, whose parts cannot be actually and indivisibly the same, one with another, or with the whole.
>
> [I, 39–40]

In this context the very use of language at all becomes paradoxical, for the purport specifically negates the efficacy of language. Thus in the opening sequence of the Dobell *Poems* the speaker decides that the closest approximation of divine essence is the wordless "Serious Meditation" which occupies the child. What Jackson calls the "unity of illimited *being*" (I, 39) is like the self-contained eye of the child, into which "All Objects . . . feed" ("Innocence"). Just as "Eden" parenthetically focuses on the paradisical imagery of "Wonder," so is the thematic material of "Innocence" recursive: "But that which most I Wonder at." In effect, the speaker reiterates the reiterative substance of "Eden." The entire poem themati-

4. *A Treatise of the Divine Essence and Attributes* (1628), I, 34 [Thomas Jackson (1579–1640) was an Anglican theologian.—*Editor*.]

cally parallels "Eden," and both are in syntactic apposition to "Wonder."

Part I ends with a resolve that is also a confession: "I must becom a Child again." Into the tensed world of experience the speaker has fallen from grace. His affirmation, drawn from a text in Matthew, presents the future as antidote to the present. Though as a child he was "A little Adam in a Sphere," now he must go forward by returning to the source. Thus "The Preparative" (pp. 12–14), which begins the second section of the sequence, returns to the very beginning, to the egoless non-being described in "The Salutation":

> My Body being Dead, my Lims unknown,
>   Before I skild to prize
>   Those living Stars mine Eys,
> Before my Tongue or Cheeks were to me shewn,
>   Before I knew my Hands were mine,
> Or that my Sinews did my Members joyn,
>   When neither Nostril, Foot, nor Ear,
>   As yet was seen, or felt, or did appear;
>   I was within
> A House I knew not, newly clothd with Skin.

The last two lines here may remind us of the soul in Herbert's "The Flower," which during the long winter of afflictions withdraws to keep "house unknown" until the approach of spring. But they are more strongly reminiscent of Vaughan's "The Retreat":

> Happy those early dayes! when I
> Shin'd in my Angell-infancy.
> Before I understood this place
> Appointed for my second race,
> Or taught my soul to fancy ought
> But a white, Celestiall thought,
> When yet I had not walkt above
> A mile, or two, from my first love,
> And looking back (at this short space,)
> Could see a glimpse of his bright-face; . . .
> Before I taught my tongue to wound
> My Conscience with a sinfull sound . . .
> But felt through all this fleshly dresse
> Bright *shootes* of everlastingnesse.[5]

In both poems the diction and imagery stress the debilitating aspects of experience. But in "The Retreat" the child looks back at ever-increasing time intervals into the still glowing face of a personalized Deity, whose impression slowly disappears from the visible

5. *The Works of Henry Vaughan*, ed. L. C. Martin (Oxford, 1957), p. 419. *Silex Scintillans* appeared in 1650, and so was available to Traherne, who may have meant openly to echo "The Retreat."

world; this process of attenuation is the outward sign of the speaker's self-inflicted punishment in the form of verbalized guilt. In Traherne, the child's sense of limitlessness derives from the fact that in the earliest moments of his life he can accord to the various parts of his body no specialized functions. With particularization come limits: the codifying of the human intellect.

In "The Preparative,"[6] again, we see the child's sense of reality as intrinsically godlike; he seems anesthetized to the perception of mundane differences which so pervade the adult and secular worlds. Only division of eternity into temporal units allows the child to distinguish his body from the world perceived. Earlier (before human time existed), the "I" was present, but in an unknown "House." In the Fall that followed, the seer was divorced from the scene. Characteristically, Traherne reaches back to the preceding poem for his imagery: "I was an Adam there, / A little Adam in a Sphere." The proper preparative is a reiteration of already stated and expanded motifs. The spheral imagery of the earlier poem contradicts the idea of movement and development suggested by the following poem's title. To reinforce this atemporality the world is again depicted virtually without a transitive verb:

> Then was my Soul my only All to me,
>> A Living Endless Ey,
>> Far wider then the Skie
> Whose Power, whose Act, whose Essence was to see.
>> I was an Inward *Sphere of Light*,
> Or an Interminable Orb of *Sight*,
>> An Endless and a Living Day,
> A *vital Sun* that round about did *ray*
>> All Life and Sence,
> A Naked Simple Pure *Intelligence*.
>
> [Stanza 2]

The infinite universe, the "All," is present to the child as his "Soul," which is a sphere. His being is represented by the emblem "A Living Endless Ey." The "Ey-I" perceives and encompasses the spatio-temporal world. The diction attempts to articulate the indefinable qualities of extension in time and space: "All," "Endless," "Wider," "Interminable," "Essence," "Pure." The "Sphere" of Adam takes on a new aspect: "I was an inward Sphere of Light." The "I" is either a microcosmic sphere of light (perceived), "Or" a universally extended "Ey." The two are one, for one place is like all space, and one present embraces eternity. God and the "I" are one, and only time and knowledge (being "shewn," becoming "skild")

6. For an admirable analysis of "The Preparative," see A. L. Clements, "On the Mode and Meaning of Traherne's Mystical Poetry: 'The Preparative'," *Studies in Philology*, LXI (1964), 500–521.

from the "Learned and Happy Ignorance" instilled at birth, dividing essence into power and act.

In *Christian Ethicks* Traherne associated the sphere with divine omnipresence,[7] and again, he may have had Thomas Jackson's *Treatise of the Divine Essence and Attributes* in mind: "God is a sphere, whose Center is everywhere, whose circumference is no where" (I, 55).[8] Jackson's discussion is tantalizing not only because we know that Traherne read it, but also because in it he uses many of Traherne's favorite abstract nouns. Thus, God is rightly compared to a sphere because "of all figures" the sphere is the most "capacious" (I, 56). The metaphor has perplexed certain men, apparently for two reasons. Most obviously, how can a circle's center be everywhere, and still remain the center? Secondly, in what sense is it appropriate to speak of God's presence as a center? According to Jackson, the answer involves a suprarational understanding of both space and time.

Both Jackson and Traherne try to make language express the unspeakable. In "The Preparative," the child is born to limits he at first does not or will not recognize. In a like manner the poet is forced into acceptance of an imprecise medium of expression: the emblem of fallen man, language. Ideally, both in experience and art, limits and differences do not exist. Yet the child without knowing it—and the poet too—have to some degree been compartmentalized and restricted almost from the beginning. Hence, the poet's use of paradox, whose function it is to violate the ordinary expectations and limits of commonsense experience. Thus Jackson writes, "Wheresoever He is (and Hee is every where,) He is *unity* it selfe, *infinity* it selfe, *immensity* it selfe, *perfection* it selfe, *power* it selfe" (I, 58). Except in the realm of fantasy, "place" logically excludes "every where"; and by the same token, "where" the speaker "is" or "was" when he perceived "an Inward *Sphere of Light*" becomes a set of atemporal and aspatial qualities. Further, if we take the "is" seriously we grasp the paradoxical function of piling up abstract nouns. If X *is* Y, and if Y is not the same as Z, how can X also *be* Z? The answer is that the mystic's declaration of equivalences is like the poet's reconciliation of the adult's analytical (if limited) view of reality with the unifying and charismatic quali-

---

7. *Christian Ethicks* (1675), pp. 18–20, 60–62, and esp. 448–449.
8. The figure itself goes far back in the mystical tradition; Georges Poulet traces this particular phrase to a twelfth-century source, but the idea in one form or another is at least as old as *Timaeus: The Dialogues of Plato*, tr. B. Jowett (Oxford, 1871), II, 528 [33], 538 [44]. For a few of the many pertinent discussions of the figure, especially as it applies to Dante's *La Vita Nuova*, see

Poulet, *The Metamorphoses of the Circle*, tr. Carley Dawson and Elliott Coleman (Baltimore, 1966); Robert Fleissner, "Donne and Dante: The Compass Figure Reinterpreted," *Modern Language Notes*, LXXVI (1961), 315–320; John Freccero, "Dante's Pilgrim in a Gyre," *PMLA*, LXXVI (1961), 168–181; Freccero, "Donne's 'Valediction Forbidding Mourning'," *Journal of English History*, XXX (1963), 335–376.

ties of the child's appreciative powers. The victim of this rhetorical thrust is the category "center." It is inappropriate and finally ineffective to apply too stringently a word which rightly is meant to approximate only one aspect of divinity. To insist upon this center as a literal point or "place" might suggest a denial of God's infinite extension by requiring simultaneously a conception of infinite movement from one place to another. And if God moves from place to place, he must exist temporally as well as spatially, and consequently, he must change—clearly an impossibility: "He is every where, because no body, no space, or spirituall substance can exclude his presence, or avoid penetration of his Essence" (I, 53). The qualifiers in "The Preparative" consistently stress the inexplicable qualities of infinity: space without boundary, time without duration, subject without object. The "Ey" does not see; it lives, and lives interminably—extended beyond all objects in space: "I / . . . was all Sight, or Ey."

Not surprisingly, then, the entire poem develops paradoxically. Part of the soul's preparation is to recognize the speaker's vision as not in the natural order of life, that order in which "Iron Fate" and life's trivialities (intensely underlined in stanza 5 by the rhyme between "Dross" and "gross") impose upon the early unity of the soul and the "All." The universe in which the child dwelt is destroyed, and with it disappears the operative unity between feeling and the self: "Vain Affections . . . Seduce" the soul from its earthly paradise, where *"Feeling Feeling* Wounds / With Pleasure and Delight."* The catalog of senses and their operations reiterates the Edenic qualities, particularly unity in simplicity seen in the earlier poems. But the stanza does more than reiterate this. Traherne tries to suggest the inexplicable identification of different objects or senses. Syntactically, *"Feeling,"* contiguous to *"Feeling"* in the sentence, becomes both subject and object of the verb "Wound," as if to suggest that the poet would bind the two words while insisting on their separateness and distinctness:

> For *Sight* inherits Beauty, *Hearing* Sounds,
>   The *Nostril* Sweet Perfumes,
>   All *Tastes* have hidden Rooms
> Within the *Tongue*; and *Feeling Feeling* Wounds
>   With Pleasure and Delight, but I
> Forgot the rest, and was all Sight, or Ey.
>   Unbodied and Devoid of Care,
> Just as in Heavn the Holy Angels are.
>   For Simple Sence
> Is Lord of all Created Excellence.

> [Stanza 4]

The intensity of this poem, one of Traherne's best, derives from an effective pathos. Since preparation of the soul depends on the recognition of the Fall, the speaker confronts again the image of a lost world:

> Divine Impressions when they came,
> Did quickly enter and my Soul inflame.
> Tis not the Object, but the Light
> That maketh Heaven; Tis a Purer Sight.
> Felicitie
> Appears to none but them that purely see.
>
> [Stanza 6]

Quickness here reminds the reader that the "Ey" lived, expelling light, like the cock in Vaughan's poem, whose "Sunnie seed" could not resist the magnetism of Paradise. But Traherne's poem does not end in prayer for spiritual union. Instead, the speaker addresses himself: "Get free, and so thou shalt even all Admire" (line 70). As in the garden of[9] "Burnt Norton," here the lost and timeless world remains "a perpetual possibility." But the speaker by implication rehearses the true condition of man; in the tensed world of the English sentence, when the speaker expatiates on his past unfettered existence he implicitly introduces a future and potentially opposite possibility. "I was as free . . ." the speaker says in stanza 5; but this is the rhetorical "preparative" for his almost immediate resolve: "My Soul retire, / Get free."

9. T. S. Eliot's. [*Editor.*]

Annotated Bibliography

ABBREVIATIONS

BUSE	Boston University Studies in English
ELH	Journal of English Literary History
ELR	English Literary Renaissance
HLQ	Huntington Library Quarterly
JEGP	Journal of English and Germanic Philology
JWCI	Journal of the Warburg and Courtauld Institute
MLQ	Modern Language Quarterly
MP	Modern Philology
PLL	Papers on Language and Literature
PMLA	Publications of the Modern Language Association of America
RES	Review of English Studies
SP	Studies in Philology
SR	Sewanee Review
SEL	Studies in English Literature 1500–1900
UTQ	University of Toronto Quarterly
YES	Yearbook of English Studies

I. GENERAL

The scholarly and critical literature on our poets (not to mention edifying tributes or pious rhetoric) is vast; this bibliography is selective. For earlier materials, the standard source is Douglas Bush's magisterial *English Literature in the Earlier Seventeenth Century 1600–1660*, Oxford History of English Literature, second edition (Oxford, 1962). But so much has been done since Bush that the bibliographies need to be supplemented. The standard *Cambridge Bibliography of English Literature*, compiled by G. Watson, is more trouble than it is worth; the lists are bare, illogically organized, and unindicative of content or orientation. *English Literary Renaissance* contains bibliographical surveys of Renaissance English writers.

The following annual surveys can be very helpful: *The Year's Work in English Studies;* the *Modern Humanities Research Association: Annual Bibliography of English Language and Literature;* the *Modern Language Association Annual Bibliography and Abstracts;* the periodical *Studies in Philology (SP)*, which, until 1969, published an annual "Recent Literature of the English Renaissance"; and *Studies in English Literature 1500–1900 (SEL)*.

There are two specialized journals to consult: *Seventeenth-Century News* and the newly established *George Herbert Journal.*

Two bibliographies are devoted to seventeenth-century poetry: Theodore Spencer and Mark Van Doren, *Studies in Metaphysical Poetry* (New York, 1939); and Lloyd E. Berry, *A Bibliography of Studies in Metaphysical Poetry, 1939–1960* (Madison, 1964).

II. HISTORICAL AND CULTURAL BACKGROUND

Ashley, Maurice. *England in the Seventeenth Century*. Baltimore, 1963.

Boas, Marie. *The Scientific Renaissance, 1450–1630*. (Harper Torchbooks.) New York, 1962.

Burtt, Edwin Arthur. *The Metaphysical Foundations of Modern Physical Science*. London, 1925.

Cassirer, Ernst. *The Platonic Renaissance in England*. Trans. J. P. Pettegrove. London, 1953.

Davies, Godfrey. *The Early Stuarts, 1603–1660*, 2nd ed. Oxford, 1959.

Friedrich, Carl J. *The Age of the Baroque, 1610–1660*. (Harper Torchbooks.) New York, 1952.

Grierson, Sir Herbert. *Cross Currents in English Literature of the Seventeenth Century*. London, 1929.

Hill, Christopher. *Puritanism and Revolution*. London, 1958.

——. *The Century of Revolution, 1603–1714.* Norton Library History of England. New York: Norton, 1966.

Hollander, John. *The Untuning of the Sky: Ideas of Music in English Poetry, 1500–1700.* Princeton, 1961.

Jones, Richard Foster. *Ancients and Moderns. Seminal Studies in the History of Ideas.* St. Louis, 1936.

Lewis, C. S. *The Discarded Image: An Introduction to Medieval and Renaissance Literature.* London, 1964. The best brief introduction to the Medieval-Renaissance world view.

Lovejoy, Arthur O. *The Great Chain of Being: A Study of the History of an Idea.* Cambridge, Mass., 1936.

Patrides, C. A., ed. *The Cambridge Platonists.* Cambridge, Mass., 1970.

Raven, Charles E. *Natural Religion and Christian Theology.* Cambridge, Mass., 1953.

Stone, Lawrence. *The Causes of the English Revolution 1529–1642.* New York, 1972.

Tillyard, E. M. W. *The Elizabethan World Picture.* London, 1943.

Westfall, Richard S. *Science and Religion in Seventeenth-Century England.* New Haven, 1958.

Whitehead, Alfred North. *Science and the Modern World.* New York, 1925.

Willey, Basil. *The Seventeenth Century Background: Studies in the Thought of the Age in Relation to Poetry and Religion.* London, 1934.

Winny, James. *The Frame of Order: an Outline of Elizabethan Belief Taken from Treatises of the Late Sixteenth Century.* London, 1957.

III. REFORMATION, RELIGION, AND SPIRITUALITY

Major reference works in the areas of religion and spirituality include:

Dictionnaire de Spiritualité. Ed. M. Villier, S. J., et al. 9 vols. so far, to letter L. Paris, 1937–1976.

Dictionnaire de Theologie Catholique. Ed. A. Vacant, E. Mangenot, and E. Amann. 15 volumes. Paris, 1903–1950.

Hastings Encyclopedia of Religion and Ethics. 12 vols. New York, 1908–26.

Oxford Dictionary of the Christian Church. 2nd ed., rev. Ed. Frank L. Cross and E. A. Livingstone. Oxford, 1974.

——

Allison, C. F. *The Rise of Moralism: The Proclamation of the Gospel from Hooker to Baxter.* London, 1966.

Bettenson, Henry, ed. *Documents of the Christian Church.* 2nd ed. London, 1963.

Bouyer, Louis, et al. *History of Christian Spirituality.* 3 vols. Trans. by Mary Ryan, Barbara Wall, and others (London, 1963–69). See especially the second part of the first tome of the third volume (1965) which surveys Protestant spirituality in the sixteenth and seventeenth centuries (pp. 81–225), including discussions of the poets and the Cambridge Platonists.

Bremond, Henri. *Histoire Litteraire du sentiment religieux en France.* 11 vols. Paris, 1915–1936. A massive and full work, for serious and extended study. Essays on individual figures, heavily relying on contemporary sources; emphasis on the French seventeenth century, but relevance to the larger questions. See A. Guinan, "Portrait of a Devout Humanist," *Harvard Theological Review,* 47 (1954), 15–53.

Chandos, John, ed. *In God's Name: Examples of Preaching in England 1534–1662.* Indianapolis, 1971. Large sampling of sermons with generous headnotes on the preachers.

Clarke, W.K.L., ed. *Liturgy and Worship: A Companion to the Prayer Books of the Anglican Communion.* London, 1932.

Cohn, Norman. *The Pursuit of the Millenium.* (Harper Torchbooks.) New York, 1957; rev. 1961. An historical view of messianic extremism.

Davies, Horton. *Worship and Theology in England.* 5 vols. Princeton, 1961–75. The final chapters of vol. I, *From Cranmer to Hooker, 1535–1600* (1970) and the entire vol. II, *From Andrewes to Baxter, 1600–1690* (1975) are the most relevant.

Dickens, A. G. *The English Reformation.* London, 1964. Sound, lucid; the standard work on the early period of 1529–59.

George, Charles H. and Katherine. *The Protestant Mind of the English Reformation 1570–1640.* Princeton, 1961. Emphasizes English theology and the "specific social and institutional character of the ideology of the English pulpit."

Heppe, Heinrich. *Reformed Dogmatics: Set Out and Illustrated from the Sources.* Foreword by Karl Barth. Rev. and ed. Ernst Bizer. Trans. G. T. Thomson. London, 1950. Originally compiled in 1861, still an important source book on early theologians of the Reformation, copiously and impartially presented.

Knox, Ronald. *Enthusiasm: A Chapter in the History of Religion with Special Reference to the Seventeenth and Eighteenth Centuries.* Oxford, 1950. On recurrent waves of charismatic reform in the institutional church.

Leonard, Emile G. *A History of Protestantism.* 2 vols. Ed. H. H. Rowley. Trans. Joyce M. H. Reid. London, 1965. Substantial chapters on basic Reformation themes and on the English experience.

McAdoo, Bishop H. R. *The Structure of Caroline Moral Theology.* London, 1949.

―――. *The Spirit of Anglicanism: A Survey of Anglican Theological Method in the Seventeenth Century.* London, 1965. Deals with Hooker and Calvinism, the Cambridge Platonists and the Latitudinarians; uses contemporary sources extensively.

Mitchell, W. Fraser. *English Pulpit Oratory from Andrewes to Tillotson: A Study of Its Literary Aspects.* London, 1932. Contains a massive bibliography, especially of English sermons of the seventeenth century (pp. 411–52).

More, Paul Elmer, and Cross, Frank Leslie, editors. *Anglicanism: The Thought and Practice of the Church of England, Illustrated from the Religious Literature of the Seventeenth Century.* Milwaukee, 1935. A long introduction on "The Spirit of Anglicanism" and "Anglicanism in the Seventeenth Century"; the book is a kind of sampler—the body (800 pages) contains over 360 excerpts on a wide range of subjects.

Murdock, Kenneth B. *Literature and Theology in Colonial New England.* Cambridge, Mass. 1949. Theological ideas and literature, with relevance to English seventeenth century.

New, John P. H. *Anglican and Puritan: The Basis of their Opposition 1588–1640.* Stanford, 1964. Analytical on Man, Church, Sacraments, Ethics.

Stranks, C. J. *Anglican Devotion: Studies in the Spiritual Life of the Church of England Between the Reformation and the Oxford Movement.* London, 1961.

White, Helen. *English Devotional Literature (Prose) 1600–1640.* Madison, 1931. Chapters on religious background and devotional life, and on translations of important works, particularly the *Imitation of Christ* and works of Saint Augustine and Saint Bernard.

IV. MAJOR RELIGIOUS WORKS

Kempis, Thomas à. *The Imitation of Christ.* First written in the early fifteenth century, this is one of the great central books for Renaissance spirituality. It was published in two hundred or more Latin editions by the mid-seventeenth century, and translated into English often from the mid-fifteenth century on: see the Early English Text Society editions of the first translation, ed. J. K. Ingram (London, 1892) and of Richard Whitford's translation, ca. 1530, ed. E. J. Klein, with full introduction and notes (London, 1941). Composed by the monk, Thomas à Kempis (ca. 1380–1471), the work has four parts, the first two providing general counsels for the spiritual life, the third examining the interior dispositions of the soul, and the fourth discoursing on the Sacrament of the Eucharist. The work was central to the *Devotio moderna,* the revival of spirituality which began in the late fourteenth century and contributed greatly to the development of spiritual practice (especially Lutheran and Anglican) during the following centuries. There are several modern translations, including the Penguin Classics volume by Leo Sherley-Price (1952: but lacking notes or other helpful apparatus) and those published in the Image Book series (New York, 1955) and Everyman's Library (New York, 1976).

Loyola, Saint Ignatius. *Spiritual Exercises.* The founder of the Jesuit order, Ignatius (1495?–1556) composed the *Spiritual Exercises* at Manresa during the 1520s and revised the work several times; gradually it became a detailed and systematic manual of spiritual direction. The work describes the Ignatian system of meditation, organized into four weeks for methodical and intensive consideration of (1) sin (*deformata reformare*); (2) the Kingdom of Christ (*reformata conformare*); (3) the Passion of Christ (*conformata confirmare*); and (4) the Risen and Glorified Christ (*confirmata transformare*). The method calls upon the imagination and memory, the intellect, and the will, and this involves all three faculties (according to Renaissance psychology) in the meditative process. The critical edition, with full introduction, notes and bibliography, is that in the *Monumenta Historica Societatis Jesu, Monumenta Ignatiana*, series 2, vol. I, 2nd edition (Rome, 1969). Among the many English translations, two are most useful: that by T. Corbishley, S. J. (London, 1963), with commentary; and the paperback in Image Books (New York, 1964), translated by Anthony Mottola with introduction by Robert W. Gleason, S. J.

The importance of Ignatius's *Spiritual Exercises* for much seventeenth-century religious verse has been discussed at length by Louis Martz in his basic and indispensable study, *The Poetry of Meditation*, rev. ed. (New Haven, 1962).

Saint Teresa of Avila (also known as Saint Teresa of Jesus), 1515–82, also had an immense influence on spirituality. The most important work is her *Autobiography*. The critical edition in the *Biblioteca Mistica Carmelitana*, nine volumes (Burgos, 1915–19), ed. by Silverio de Santa Teresa, contains the *Vida* and other works in the first six volumes and her letters in the last three. E. Allison Peers, the leading English scholar on Teresa, has published a five-volume translation (1946–51), some of which is available in Image paperbacks; J. M. Cohen translated the *Autobiography* for the Penguin Classics.

Also of importance:

Saint John of the Cross (a contemporary of Teresa), whose poems, especially "The Dark Night of the Soul" have been translated several times in recent years, particularly by Roy Campbell. All his works have been translated by E. Allison Peers (London, 1935; rev. 1953). Gerald Brenan's study, *St. John of the Cross: His Life and Poetry* (Cambridge, 1973), is sound, fresh, and direct; it includes translations of the poetry by Lynda Nicholson.

Saint Francis de Sales (1567–1622). *The Introduction to the Devout Life of St. Francis de Sales* (first edition, Lyons, 1609; revised and definitive edition, 1619) was originally a small manual for the private use of a relative, aimed at fostering a Christian life in the world; cultivating, as Francis put it, the "Presence of a Friend." The work is readily available in Image Books, translated and edited by John K. Ryan (New York, 1955).

V. LITTLE GIDDING

An important part of the religious experience of both George Herbert and Richard Crashaw was Little Gidding and the Ferrar family associated with it. Celebrated in our time by T. S. Eliot in the last of his *Four Quartets*, Little Gidding was a modest religious community in Huntingdonshire north of Cambridge, presided over by Nicholas Ferrar from 1625 until his death in 1637. King Charles I visited the community, as did Herbert and Crashaw, both of them friends of Ferrar. Devoted to spiritual growth, the community at Little Gidding emphasized prayer, work on the farm, meditation, charity, and certain other kinds of activities, including the copying and binding of books. A splendid example of their calligraphy is the Bodleian manuscript of Herbert's *The Temple*.

In 1646, Little Gidding was shut down by the Puritans, the remaining members dispersed, and many papers and books burned, including many of Nicholas Ferrar's papers. A contemporary book, *The Arminian Nunnery: or a Brief Description and Relation of the late erected Monastical Place, called the Arminian Nunnery, at Little Gidding in Huntingdonshire*, denounced the community as an attempt to reintroduce Roman Catholicism into England.

John Ferrar wrote a life of his brother Nicholas, part of which survives in an eighteenth-century manuscript. In *The Ferrar Papers* (Cambridge, 1938), Bernard Blackstone provides a critical edition of this manuscript, supplemented by material from the other biographies based on John Ferrar's work and by a selection of family letters. The Ferrar papers are in the Old Library at Magdalene College, Cambridge. The fundamental biography is by Alan Maycock, *Nicholas Ferrar of Little Gidding* (London, 1938).

VI. MYSTICISM

One important development in the study of these religious poets in recent decades has been the emphasis on "mystical" poetry. The area—as critics do not often recognize—is difficult and complex, and too easily open to distorting analysis and reductive comment. For this reason, I cite some of the basic, solid studies here.

The fundamental work is still that of Evelyn Underhill (1875–1941), large, demanding, but necessary: *Mysticism: A Study in the Nature and Develop-*

ment of Man's Spiritual Consciousness, first published in 1911, and currently available in a Dutton paperback. The scope is large—Miss Underhill ranges from Christian mystical teaching and experience to Neoplatonism, from Teresa of Avila to Jakob Boehme—and the study is marked by intellectual rigor and disciplined clarity. Miss Underhill also translated and edited *The Cloud of Unknowing* (1912), *Walter Hilton* (1939), *The Scale of Perfection* (1923), and *Prayers from the Ancient Liturgies* (1939). Her narrative *The Mystics of the Church* (1925; available in a Schocken paperback) is a readable survey.

Useful also are: E. Cuthbert Butler, *Western Mysticism: The Teaching of Sts. Augustine, Gregory and Bernard on Contemplation and the Contemplative Life* (London, 1922), which has recently been reissued with a long, careful, corrective introduction (New York: Harper Torchbooks, 1966); M. David Knowles, O.S.B. *The English Mystical Tradition* (London, 1961; repr. Harper Torchbooks, 1965); the introduction by Eric Colledge to his collection *The Medieval Mystics of England* (London, 1962), which includes a substantial primary bibliography. Stanley Stewart's study, *The Enclosed Garden: The Tradition and the Image in Seventeenth-Century Poetry* (Madison, 1966) surveys the development of mystical imagery from the Song of Songs.

A popular and useful work is F. C. Happold, *Mysticism: A Study and an Anthology* (Baltimore: Penguin Books, 1963), which is divided into two parts —a general study by Happold, whose claims are modest and unpretentious; and an anthology of selections, usually brief (sometimes unhappily too brief), from thirty-one sources, including Plato, Plotinus, Saint John, Dionysius, Meister Eckhart, Nicholas of Cusa, and Teresa of Avila. The selections are preceded by brief and often useful headnotes.

VII. LITERARY STUDIES AND BOOKS ON SEVERAL POEMS

Allen, Don Cameron. *Image and Meaning.* Baltimore, 1960; rev. 1968. Ch. 4, "George Herbert—'The Rose'" (pp. 67–79); ch. 6, "Andrew Marvell—'The Nymph Complaining for the Death of Her Faun'" (pp. 93–114); ch. 7, "Andrew Marvell—'Upon Appleton House'" (pp. 115–53); ch. 8, "Henry Vaughan—'Cock-Crowing'" (pp. 154–69).

Alvarez, A. *The School of Donne.* London, 1961. Ch. 3, "The Poetry of Religious Experience" on Herbert (pp. 67–83); on Vaughan (pp. 83–90); ch. 4, "Metaphysical Rhetoric: Richard Crashaw" (pp. 91–103); ch. 5, "The Poetry of Judgement: Andrew Marvell" (pp. 104–20).

Bennett, Joan. *Five Metaphysical Poets.* Cambridge, 1964. (Originally *Four Metaphysical Poets*, Cambridge, 1934, omitting Marvell.) Ch. 4, "George Herbert, 1593–1633" (pp. 49–70): ch. 5, "Henry Vaughan, 1622–1695" (pp. 71–89); ch. 6, "Richard Crashaw, 1613?–1649" (pp. 90–108); ch. 7, "Andrew Marvell, 1621–1678" (pp. 109–33).

Colie, Rosalie L. *Paradoxia Epidemica: The Renaissance Tradition of Paradox.* Princeton, 1966. Part II, ch. 6, "Logos in 'The Temple'" (pp. 190–215).

———. *The Resources of Kind: Genre-Theory in the Renaissance.* Berkeley, 1973. Illuminates "Upon Appleton House" and several poems of Herbert with apt illustrations from the emblem tradition in ch. 2, "Small Forms" (pp. 32–75).

Duncan, Joseph E. *The Revival of Metaphysical Poetry.* Minneapolis, 1959. Ch. 5, "The Catholic Revival of the Metaphysicals," on Crashaw and Herbert (pp. 89–112).

Eliot, T. S. "The Metaphysical Poets," *Times Literary Supplement,* 20 (October, 1921), 669–70; repr. in *Homage to John Dryden: Three Essays on Poetry of the Seventeenth Century* (1924); and in *The Hogarth Essays* (1928); and in *Selected Essays, 1917–1932* (1932, and later editions); and in *Criticism: the Major Texts,* ed. Walter Jackson Bate (1952), pp. 529–34; and in *Discussions of John Donne,* ed. Frank Kermode (1962), pp. 42–47; and in *Seventeenth Century English Poetry,* ed. William R. Keast (1971), pp. 23–31.

Ellrodt, Robert. *Les Poètes Métaphysiques Anglais.* 2 vols. 2nd ed. Paris, 1973. Originally published in three volumes in 1960, the full title is *L'Inspiration Personelle et l'Esprit du Temps chez Les Poètes Métaphysiques Anglais.* The 1973 edition does not contain the second part. For students who can manage French, this is probably the most important single work on the subject; it is a pity the book has not been translated. Vol. I deals with Donne, Herbert (pp. 267–373), and Crashaw (pp. 375–449). Vol. II studies Lord Herbert, Cowley, Marvell (pp. 107–70), Vaughan (pp. 173–260), and Traherne (pp. 261–398)—the latter two as "Poètes mystiques." These two volumes were to be the first part of a projected five-part study of the poetry and the age. They remain invaluable.

Freeman, Rosemary. *English Emblem Poets.* London, 1948. Still the basic study of the topic, this includes a chapter, "George Herbert," pp. 148–72.

Grant, Patrick. *The Transformation of Sin: Studies in Donne, Herbert, Vaughan, and Traherne.* Montreal, 1974. Ch. 3, "Augustinian Spirituality and George Herbert's 'The Temple'" (pp. 73–99); ch. 4, "George Herbert and Juan de Valdes: The Franciscan Mode and Protestant Manner," pp. 100–33; ch. 5, "Henry Vaughan and the Hermetic Philosophy," pp. 134–69; ch. 6, "Irenaean Theodicy and Thomas Traherne," pp. 170–97. Grant discerns tension between the Augustinian concepts of sin and guilt and the Renaissance emphasis on reason and tolerance. Grant sees Herbert as a kind of Franciscan mixed with Lutheran, harmonizing "self-determination" with "God's foreordained mercy;" Vaughan modifies basic Augustinianism by Hermeticism; in his richest chapter, he places Traherne in the context of both the Cambridge Platonists and the pre-Nicene Fathers.

Grierson, Herbert J. C. "Introduction" to his *Metaphysical Lyrics & Poems of the Seventeenth Century: Donne to Butler.* Oxford, 1921; repr. often. The "Introduction" is still an important essay; it is available in several collections, including *Seventeenth-Century English Poetry,* ed. William R. Keast (1971).

Halewood, William. *The Poetry of Grace: Reformation Themes and Structures in Seventeenth-Century English Verse.* New Haven, 1970. Ch. 4, "Herbert" (pp. 88–111); ch. 5, "Marvell and Vaughan: The Psalm model of Reconciliation" (pp. 112–39). Emphasizes Reformation theology of opposites and reconciliations, insisting on the "essential Protestant and Augustinian nature of George Herbert's "preoccupations." In Marvell, he finds the outlines of "moderate Calvinism." In Vaughan, he finds the "Blessedness of created things." He opposes the emphasis placed by Rosemond Tuve on continuity.

Keast, William R., ed. *Seventeenth Century English Poetry: Modern Essays in Criticism.* New York, 1962; rev. 1971. This collection includes in the 1971 edition: Jeffrey Hart, "Herbert's *The Collar* Re-read," pp. 248–65; Frank Kermode, "The Argument of Marvell's 'Garden,'" pp. 333–47; Louis L. Martz, "Henry Vaughan: The Man Within," pp. 388–413; Leo Spitzer, "Marvell's 'Nymph Complaining for the Death of Her Faun:' Sources versus Meaning," pp. 372–87; Arnold Stein, "George Herbert: The Art of Plainness," pp. 257–78; Joseph H. Summers, "The Poem as Hieroglyph," pp. 225–47; Harold E. Toliver, "Pastoral Form and Idea in Some Poems of Marvell," pp. 356–71; Frank J. Warnke, "Play and Metamorphoses in Marvell's Poetry," pp. 348–55; Austin Warren, "Symbolism in Crashaw," pp. 312–23. In the 1962 edition are also the following: Robert Martin Adams, "Taste and Bad Taste in Metaphysical Poetry: Richard Crashaw and Dylan Thomas," pp. 264–79; Margaret Bottrall, "Herbert's Craftsmanship," pp. 238–51; Cleanth Brooks, "Marvell's 'Horatian Ode,'" pp. 321–40 and (on the same topic) pp. 352–58; Douglas Bush, "Marvell's 'Horatian Ode,'" pp. 341–51.

Mahood, M. M. *Poetry and Humanism.* New Haven, 1950. Ch. 8, "Vaughan: The Symphony of Nature," pp. 252–95.

Martz, Louis L. *The Paradise Within: Studies in Vaughan, Traherne, and Milton.* New Haven, 1964. Martz sees a tradition of "Augustinian" poetry.

———. *The Poetry of Meditation: A Study in English Religious Literature of the Seventeenth Century.* New Haven, 1954; rev. 1962. Ch. 1, "The Method of Meditation": part five, "Meditative Structure in Poems by Herbert," pp. 56–61; part six, "Similar Structure in Poems by Crashaw and Vaughan," pp. 61–67. This is the single most important book on the subject, containing numerous discussions of, and explications of poems by, Herbert, Crashaw, and Vaughan. There are only a few pages on Marvell. Two major chapters deal entirely with Herbert: ch. 7, "George Herbert: In the Presence of a Friend," pp. 249–87, and ch. 8, "George Herbert: The Unity of 'The Temple'" pp. 288–320.

———. *The Wit of Love: Donne, Crashaw, Carew, Marvell.* Notre Dame, 1970. With illustrations. Ch. 3, "Richard Crashaw: 'Love's Architecture,'" pp. 113–47; ch. 4, "Andrew Marvell: 'The Mind's Happiness,'" pp. 151–90. Martz relates poetry to Mannerist and Baroque esthetics.

Miles, Josephine. *The Continuity of Poetic Language: The Primary Language of Poetry in the 1640s.* Berkeley, 1948.

Miner, Earl. *The Metaphysical Mode from Donne to Cowley.* Princeton, 1969. Stresses the privateness and the use of dramatic technique.

Miner, Earl, ed. *Illustrious Evidence: Approaches to English Literature of the Early Seventeenth Century.* Berkeley, 1975. Contains Barbara Lewalski's important essay, "Typology and Poetry: A Consideration of Herbert, Vaughan, and Marvell," pp. 41–69.

Mulder, John. *The Temple of the Mind: Education and Literary Taste in Seventeenth-Century England.* New York, 1969. In ch. 6, "The Spiritual Temple of Herbert," pp. 138–42; "Vaughan: 'Isaac's Marriage,'" pp. 147–50.

Nicolson, Marjorie Hope. *The Breaking of the Circle: Studies in the Effect of the 'New Science' upon Seventeenth-Century Poetry*. Rev. ed. New York, 1960.

Praz, Mario. *Studies in Seventeenth-Century Imagery*. Rev. ed. Rome, 1964.

Ross, Malcolm Mackenzie. *Poetry and Dogma: The Transfiguration of Eucharistic Symbols in Seventeenth-Century English Poetry*. New Brunswick, N.J., 1954. Ch. 6, "George Herbert and the Humanist Tradition," pp. 135–57. Ross sees an evolution from Anglo-Catholic to Puritan uses of imagery.

Summers, Joseph. *The Heirs of Donne and Jonson*. Oxford, 1970. Ch. 3, "Gentlemen at Home and at Church: Henry King and George Herbert," pp. 76–101; ch. 4, "A Foreign and a Provincial Gentleman: Richard Crashaw and Henry Vaughan," pp. 102–29; ch. 5, "The Alchemical Ventriloquist: Andrew Marvell," pp. 130–55; ch. 6, "Private Taste and Public Judgement: Andrew Marvell," pp. 156–81.

Swardson, H. R. *Poetry and the Fountain of Light*. Columbia, Mo., 1962. Ch. 3, "George Herbert's Language of Devotion," pp. 64–82; ch. 4, "Marvell: A New Pastoralism," pp. 83–109. Emphasizes tensions between the Classical and the Christian traditions.

Tuve, Rosemond, *Elizabethan and Metaphysical Imagery: Renaissance Poetic and Twentieth-Century Critics*. Chicago, 1947. Difficult but invaluable.

Wallerstein, Ruth. *Studies in Seventeenth-Century Poetic*. Madison, 1950. "Marvell and the Various Light," pp. 151–324.

White, Helen C. *The Metaphysical Poets: A Study in Religious Experience*. New York, 1936. Introductory chapters on "Mysticism and Poetry," "The Intellectual Climate," "The Religious Climate," and two chapters each on Herbert, Crashaw, Vaughan, and Traherne: ch. 6, "George Herbert and the Road to Bemerton," pp. 144–65; ch. 7, "George Herbert and 'The Temple,'" pp. 166–88; ch. 8, "Richard Crashaw: Little Gidding to Rome," pp. 189–213; ch. 9, "Richard Crashaw: 'Poet and Saint,'" pp. 214–39; ch. 10, "Henry Vaughan: The Country Doctor," pp. 240–60; ch. 11, "The Poetry of Henry Vaughan," pp. 261–88; ch. 12, "Thomas Traherne: The Pursuit of Felicity," pp. 289–313; ch. 13, "Thomas Traherne: Poems and Meditations," pp. 314–41.

Williamson, George. *A Reader's Guide to Six Metaphysical Poets*. New York, 1967. Paraphrases and glosses. Ch. 5, "George Herbert: 1593–1633," pp. 94–118; ch. 8, "Henry Vaughan, 1621 / 2–1695," pp. 175–209; ch. 9, "Andrew Marvell, 1621–1678," pp. 210–42.

VIII. GEORGE HERBERT

The first edition of *The Temple, Sacred Poems and Private Ejaculations* (Cambridge, 1633) is available in a 1968 Scolar Press facsimile. Scholars Facsimiles & Reprints has published the invaluable Williams manuscript with introduction by Amy M. Charles (Delmar, New York, 1977), and has in press a facsimile of the beautiful Bodleian manuscript (Tanner 307: "The Original of Mr. George Herbert's Temple; as it was at first Licenced for the presse"), a superb example of the work done at Little Gidding; the volume will be published in 1978, with introduction by Amy M. Charles and Mario A. Di Cesare.

The major modern edition of *The Temple* remains F. E. Hutchinson's *The Works of George Herbert* (Oxford, 1941, rev. 1945) with full critical apparatus and commentary. Numerous other excellent editions are available, especially:

Joseph H. Summers, *The Selected Poetry of George Herbert* (New York, 1967), which includes the entirety of *The Temple*.

Barbara K. Lewalski and Andrew J. Sabol, *Major Poets of the Earlier Seventeenth Century* (New York, 1973) which uses the Bodleian manuscript as the base text.

C. A. Patrides, *The English Poetry of George Herbert* (London, 1974), which contains an exhaustive bibliography.

Besides the bibliography in Patrides's volume, the following are useful: Samuel and Dorothy Tannenbaum, *George Herbert: A Concise Bibliography* (London, 1964); Jerry Leath Mills, "Recent Studies in Herbert," *ELR*, 6 (1976), 105–18, which covers the period 1945–1973. A full annotated bibliography has been prepared by John R. Roberts (forthcoming, Columbia, Mo., 1978).

A Concordance to the Complete Writings of George Herbert (Ithaca, 1977) compiled by Mario A. Di Cesare and Rigo Mignani, includes the texts of the Williams manuscript.

Critical study of Herbert has been rich and vigorous in the last quarter-century, beginning with Rosemond Tuve's dense and full *A Reading of George*

Herbert (Chicago, 1952), a response to William Empson's tight reading of "The Sacrifice" in *Seven Types of Ambiguity* (1930). Miss Tuve's book analyzes "The Sacrifice" in terms of the familiar liturgical and iconographic traditions, and extends these traditions to other poems. Shortly after this appeared Joseph H. Summers's *George Herbert: His Religion and Art* (London, 1954), still the fullest and most perceptive study of the poetry. While Tuve, Summers, and Martz provided the major directions and emphasis for criticism since, a parallel tradition emphasizes textual explication and poetic technique—see e.g. Rickey, Stein, and Vendler, below.

Asals, Heather. "The Voice of George Herbert's 'The Church.'" *ELH*, 36 (1969), 511–28. Herbert as psalmist.

Blanchard, Margaret M. "The Leap into Darkness: Donne, Herbert, and God." *Renascence*, 17 (1964), 38–50. Emphasizes the differences between the religious experiences of Donne and Herbert.

Bottrall, Margaret. *George Herbert*. London, 1954. Partly biographical, partly analytical.

Bradbrook, M. C. "The Liturgical Tradition in English Verse: Herbert and Eliot." *Theology*, 44 (1942), 13–23.

Bowers, Fredson. "Herbert's Sequential Imagery: 'The Temper.'" *MP*, 59 (1962), 202–13. On relationships among the poems of *The Temple*.

Brown, C. C. and W. P. Ingoldsby. "George Herbert's 'Easter Wings,'" *HLQ*, 35 (1972), 131–42.

Burke, Kenneth. "On Covery, Re- & Dis-." *Accent*, 13 (1953), 218–26. Discusses Tuve and Empson as well as Herbert.

Carnes, Valerie. "The Unity of George Herbert's *The Temple*: A Reconsideration." *ELH*, 35 (1968), 505–26.

Charles, Amy M. *The Life of George Herbert*. Ithaca, 1977.

Clark, Ira. "Lord, in Thee the Beauty Lies in the Discovery: 'Love Unknown' and Reading George Herbert." *ELH*, 39 (1972), 560–84.

Colie, Rosalie L. "Logos in the Temple." *JWCI*, 26 (1963), 327–42. Also ch. 6 of her *Paradoxia Epidemica: The Renaissance Tradition of Paradox* (Princeton, 1966).

Dundas, Judith. "Levity and Grace: The Poetry of Sacred Wit." *YES*, 2 (1972), 93–102.

Endicott, Annabel M. "The Structure of George Herbert's *Temple*: A Reconsideration." *UTQ*, 34 (1965), 226–37.

Ericson, Edward E., Jr. "A Structural Approach to Imagery." *Style*, 3 (1969), 227–47.

Fish, Stanley. "Letting Go: The Dialectic of the Self in Herbert's Poetry." In his *Self-Consuming Artifacts* (Berkeley, 1972), pp. 156–223.

Hart, Jeffrey. "Herbert's 'The Collar' Re-read." *BUSE*, 5 (1961), 65–73.

Hayes, Albert McHarg. "Counterpoint in Herbert." *SP*, 35 (1938), 43–60.

Hughes, Richard E. "Conceptual Form and Varieties of Religious Experience in the Poetry of George Herbert." *Greyfriar*, 3 (1960), 3–12.

―――. "George Herbert's Rhetorical World," *Criticism*, 3 (1961), 86–94.

Knieger, Bernard. "The Purchase-Sale: Patterns of Business Imagery in the Poetry of George Herbert." *SEL*, 6 (1966), 111–24.

Mahood, M. M. "Something Understood: The Nature of Herbert's Wit." In *Metaphysical Poetry*. Ed. Malcolm Bradbury and David Palmer (London, 1971), pp. 122–47.

McGuire, Philip C. "Private Prayer and English Poetry in the Early Seventeenth Century." *SEL*, 14 (1974), 63–77. Concentrates on "The Altar."

McLaughlin, Elizabeth, and Thomas, Gail. "Communion in *The Temple*." *SEL*, 15 (1975), 111–24.

Merrill, Thomas F. "'The Sacrifice' and the Structure of Religious Language." *Language and Style*, 2 (1970), 275–87.

Mollenkott, Virginia R. "George Herbert's 'Redemption.'" *ELN*, 10 (1973), 262–67.

Mulder, John R. "George Herbert's *The Temple*: Design and Methodology." *SCN*, 31 (1973), 37–45.

Ostriker, Alicia. "Song and Speech in the Metrics of George Herbert." *PMLA*, 80 (1965), 62–68. Important analysis of Herbert's poetic craftsmanship.

Paynter, Mary, "'Sinne and Love': Thematic Patterns in George Herbert's Lyrics." *YES*, 3 (1973), 85–93. Traces the images of love as a feast and sin as a hard heart or closed box.

Rickey, Mary Ellen. *Utmost Art: Complexity in the Verse of George Herbert*. Lexington, Ky. 1966. Close reading, emphasizing poetic devices.

Sanders, Wilbur. "'Childhood is Health': The Divine Poetry of George Herbert." *Melbourne Critical Review*, 5 (1962), 3–15.

Stambler, Elizabeth. "The Unity of Herbert's *Temple*." *Cross Currents,* 10 (1960), 251–66.

Stein, Arnold. *George Herbert's Lyrics*. Baltimore, 1968. Difficult; emphasizes style, metrics, technique.

Stewart, Stanley. "Time and *The Temple*." *SEL,* 6 (1966), 97–110.

Tuve, Rosemond. "George Herbert and *Caritas*." *JWCI,* 22 (1959), 303–31. Repr. in her *Essays,* ed. Thomas P. Roche (Princeton, 1970), pp. 167–206.

Vendler, Helen. *The Poetry of George Herbert*. Cambridge, Mass., 1974. Close explications, often revisionist, emphasizing Herbert's subtle expression of his own psychology.

Warren, Austin. "George Herbert." In his *Rage for Order: Essays in Criticism*. Chicago, 1948, pp. 19–36.

Ziegelmaier, Gregory, "Liturgical Symbol and Reality in the Poetry of George Herbert." *American Benedictine Review,* 18 (1967), 344–53.

(See also Section VII; virtually all the items listed there contain sections on Herbert.)

IX. RICHARD CRASHAW

The major editions are those by L. C. Martin, *The Poems in English, Latin and Greek of Richard Crashaw*, 2nd ed. (Oxford, 1957), and George Walton Williams, *The Complete Poetry of Richard Crashaw* (New York, 1970).

Three older works remain fundamental for Crashaw criticism: Austin Warren's *Richard Crashaw: A Study in Baroque Sensibility* (1939, Ann Arbor, 1957), still the best single work; Ruth Wallerstein's *Richard Crashaw: A Study in Style and Poetic Development* (Madison, 1935); and Mario Praz's substantial essay, "Richard Crashaw and the Baroque," in *The Flaming Heart: Essays on Crashaw, Machiavelli and Other Studies* (New York, 1958).

Adams, Robert M. "Taste and Bad Taste in Metaphysical Poetry: Richard Crashaw and Dylan Thomas." *Hudson Review,* 8 (1955), 61–77.

Allison, A. F. "Crashaw and St. Francis de Sales." *RES,* 24 (1948), 295–302. Discusses Crashaw's mysticism in the context of Francis's *Treatise on the Love of God*.

Bertonasco, Marc F. *Crashaw and the Baroque*. University, Alabama, 1971.

Cirillo, A. R. "Crashaw's Epiphany Hymn: The Dawn of Christian Time." *SP,* 67 (1970), 67–88. The hymn invokes several dawns, including the eternal dawn that concludes history.

Eliot, T. S. "Richard Crashaw." *The Dial,* 84 (1928), 246–50.

Farnham, Anthony E. "Saint Teresa and the Coy Mistress." *BUSE,* 2 (1956), 226–39.

Jacobus, Lee A. "Richard Crashaw as a Mannerist." *Bucknell Review,* 18 (1970), 79–88.

McCanles, Michael. "The Rhetoric of the Sublime in Crashaw's Poetry." In *The Rhetoric of Renaissance Poetry from Wyatt to Milton*. Ed. Thomas O. Sloan and Raymond B. Waddington (Berkeley, 1974), pp. 189–211.

Manning, Stephen. "The Meaning of 'The Weeper.' " *ELH,* 22 (1955), 34–47.

Neill, Kerby. "Structure and Symbol in Crashaw's 'Hymn on the Nativity.' " *PMLA,* 63 (1948), 101–113.

Nelson, Lowry, Jr. "Embodied Ecstasy." *Yale Review,* 60 (1971), 444–49.

Peter, John. "Crashaw and 'The Weeper.' " *Scrutiny,* 19 (1953), 258–73.

Petersson, Robert T. *The Art of Ecstasy: Teresa, Bernini, and Crashaw*. London, 1970.

Raspa, Anthony. "Crashaw and the Jesuit Poetic." *UTQ,* 36 (1966), 37–54. Relates Crashaw to poetic theories of continental Jesuits.

Rickey, Mary Ellen. *Rhyme and Meaning in Richard Crashaw*. Lexington, 1961.

Swanston, Hamish. "The Second 'Temple.' " *Durham University Journal,* 56 (1963), 14–22. Detailed discussion of Crashaw's poetic relationship to Herbert.

Willey, Basil. *Richard Crashaw. Memorial Lecture on the Tercentenary of Richard Crashaw's Death*. Cambridge, 1949.

Williams, George W. *Image and Symbol in the Sacred Poetry of Richard Crashaw*. Columbia, S.C., 1963.

(See also Section VII, especially Alvarez, Bennett, Ellrodt, Keast, Martz, Summers, and White.)

X. ANDREW MARVELL

The basic text, *Miscellaneous Poems* (1681), has been published in facsimile by Scolar Press (1969). H. M. Margoliouth's standard two-volume edition, *The*

Poems and Letters of Andrew Marvell, has been revised by Pierre Legouis and E. E. Duncan Jones (Oxford, 1971, 3rd ed.) with useful commentaries. Other editions include:

Dennis Davison, *Andrew Marvell: Selected Poetry and Prose* (London, 1952), with notable introduction, minimal commentary.

Joseph Summers, *Marvell* (New York: The Laurel Poetry Series, 1961), with notable introduction, minimal commentary.

Frank Kermode, *Selected Poetry of Andrew Marvell* (New York: Signet Classics, 1967), with introduction containing discussions of individual poems, and useful commentary.

George de Forest Lord, *Andrew Marvell: Complete Poetry* (New York, 1968).

Elizabeth Story Donno, *Andrew Marvell: The Complete Poems* (Baltimore: Penguin Books, 1972).

Barbara Lewalski and Andrew J. Sabol, *Major Poets of the Earlier Seventeenth Century* (New York, 1973).

The basic biography is Pierre Legouis' *André Marvell: poéte, puritan, patriote* (Paris, 1928), revised, abridged, and translated by Legouis as *Andrew Marvell: Poet, Puritan, Patriot* (Oxford, 1965). Legouis studies both the life and times, and Marvell's place in literary and political history. When he reads poems, he is emphatically conservative: see his "Marvell and the New Critics," *RES*, 8 (1957), a witty assertion of the primacy of historical study and attack on modern criticism.

There is a concordance to the English poems by George R. Guffey (Chapel Hill, 1974). The only recent bibliographies are Dennis Donovan, *Elizabethan Bibliographies Supplements XII: Andrew Marvell, 1927–1967* (London, 1969); Gillian Szanto, "Recent Studies in Marvell," *ELR*, 5 (1975), 273–86; and D. B. Smith, "Marvell, 1621–1673," in A. E. Dyson, ed., *English Poetry: Select Bibliographical Guides* (Oxford, 1971), pp. 96–110.

There are several useful collections of critical essays:

George de Forest Lord, *Andrew Marvell: A Collection of Critical Essays* (Englewood Cliffs, 1968), which contains mainly essays of the 1950s and 1960s; Michael Wilding, *Marvell: Modern Judgements* (London, 1969); John Carey, *Andrew Marvell: Penguin Critical Anthology* (Baltimore, 1969), which contains both older and recent criticism.

Besides Legouis and T. S. Eliot, the most influential early critic was Ruth Wallerstein, most of whose book, *Studies in Seventeenth-Century Poetic* (Madison, 1950) is commentary on the intellectual background, especially neo-Platonic and medieval. Attempting to save Marvell from the new critics, she gives particular attention to the "Garden," the "Horatian Ode," and "Upon Appleton House." See pp. 151–342, "Marvell and the Various Light." Study of Marvell has been so vigorous and prolific in the past fifty years that the following lists and comments must be highly selective.

Berthoff, Ann E. *The Resolved Soul: A Study of Marvell's Major Poems*. Princeton, 1970. Deals with the soul's life in time.

Bradbrook, Muriel C. and M. G. Lloyd-Thomas. *Andrew Marvell*. Cambridge, 1940.

Colie, Rosalie. *"My Ecchoing Song": Andrew Marvell's Poetry of Criticism*. Princeton, 1970. Major study of "Upon Appleton House," emphasizing pictorial aspects, "exuberant" and "ecphrastic." She views Marvell's poems as poems about writing poetry.

Creaser, John. "Marvell's Effortless Superiority." *Essays in Criticism*, 20 (1970), 403–23. Levity and seriousness: Marvell's serenity is not callowness but courage.

Cullen, Patrick. *Spenser, Marvell, and Renaissance Pastoral*. Cambridge, Mass., 1970. Emphasizes the religious lyrics, asceticism, and acceptance of created nature.

Eliot, T. S. "Andrew Marvell." In his *Selected Essays* (New York, 1932). First published in *Times Literary Supplement*, 20 (October 1921). Fundamental.

Friedman, Donald. *Marvell's Pastoral Art*. Berkeley, 1970.

Hyman, Lawrence W. *Andrew Marvell*. New York, 1964. Elementary; emphasizes the conflict between action and withdrawal, with psychological readings of the love poems.

Leishman, J. B. *The Art of Marvell's Poetry*. London, 1966. Marvell in context of his times and literary tradition: his relationship to other poets, especially Donne and Crashaw.

Lerner, Lawrence. "Pastoral v. Christianity: Nature in Marvell." In *Seven Studies in English*, ed. Robert Gildas (London, 1970), pp. 20–43.

Lord, George de Forest. "From Contemplation to Action: Marvell's Poetical Career." *Philological Quartery*, 46 (1967), 207–24.

Nevo, Ruth. "Marvell's Songs of Innocence and Experience." *SEL*, 5 (1965), 1–21.

Rosenberg, John D. "Marvell and the Christian Idiom." *BUSE*, 4 (1960), 152–61. Sees Marvell as one of the great Christian poets of his century.

Spencer, Jeffry B. *Heroic Nature: Ideal Landscape in English Poetry from Marvell to Thomson*. Evanston, 1973. Links with emblem books and with Bosch and Breughel the Elder.

Summers, Joseph H. "Andrew Marvell: Private Taste and Public Judgement." In *Metaphysical Poetry*, ed. Malcolm Bradbury and David Palmer (London, 1971), pp. 181–210. Lyrical and political poetry form an integrated body of work.

Tayler, Edward W. "Marvell's Garden of the Mind." In his *Nature and Art in Renaissance Literature* (New York, 1964), pp. 142–68.

Toliver, Harold. "Pastoral Form and Idea in Some Forms of Marvell." *Texas Studies in Language and Literature*, 5 (1963), 83–97. Successful pastoral fuses real and ideal.

Wallace, John M. *Destiny His Choice: The Loyalism of Andrew Marvell.* Cambridge, 1968. Historical study of Marvell's political and literary careers.

ON INDIVIDUAL POEMS

"The Nymph Complaining . . ."

For detailed and analytical history of the controversy over this poem, see Edward S. LeComte in *Poets' Riddles: Essays in Seventeenth-Century Explications* (Port Washington, N.Y., 1975), pp. 161–79.

Allen, Don Cameron. "Marvell's 'Nymph.'" *ELH*, 23 (1956), 93–111. Repr. in his *Image and Meaning: Metaphoric Tradition in Renaissance Poetry* (Baltimore, 1968), ch. 6. Emphasizes genre and classical antecedents, allusions, and references.

Allen, Michael J. "The Chase: The Development of a Renaissance Theme." *Comparative Literature*, 20 (1968), 301–12.

Guild, Nicholas. "Marvell's 'The Nymph Complaining for the Death of her Faun.'" *MLQ*, 29 (1968), 385–94.

Hartman, Geoffrey, "'The Nymph Complaining for the Death of her Fawn': A Brief Allegory." *Essays in Criticism*, 18 (1968), 113–35. "An apotheosis of the diminutive powers of poetry."

Miner, Earl. "The Death of Innocence in Marvell's 'Nymph Complaining . . .'" *MP*, 65 (1967), 9–16; expanded in his *Metaphysical Mode from Donne to Cowley* (Princeton, 1969), pp. 246–71. Parallels between betrayed love and the death of the old order; and between these and Marvell's divided loyalties. Sees the poem as truly "enigmatic."

Spitzer, Leo. "Marvell's 'Nymph Complaining for the Death of her Faun': Sources versus Meaning." *MLQ*, 19 (1958), 231–43. Combines psychological interpretation with structural analysis.

"To His Coy Mistress"

Cunningham, J. V. "Logic and Lyric." *MP*, 51 (1953), 33–41. Repr. in his *Tradition and Poetic Structure: Essays in Literary History and Criticism* (Denver, 1960), pp. 40–58.

Farnham, Anthony E. "Saint Teresa and the Coy Mistress." *BUSE*, 2 (1956), 226–39.

Hartwig, Joan. "The Principle of Measure in 'To His Coy Mistress.'" *College English*, 25 (1964), 572–75. Vegetable and animal love slow down and speed up time.

Hogan, Patrick G., Jr. "Marvell's 'Vegetable Love.'" *SP*, 60 (1963), 1–11.

King, Bruce. "Irony in Marvell's 'To His Coy Mistress.'" *Southern Review*, 5 (1969), 689–703. Not a hymn to the flesh; Marvell's ironic mask satirizes the *carpe diem* tradition and its pagan assumptions.

Low, Anthony and Pival, Paul J. "Rhetorical Pattern in Marvell's 'To His Coy Mistress.'" *JEGP*, 68 (1969), 414–21. The speaker is an ironic persona.

Stewart, Stanley. "Andrew Marvell and the *Ars Moriendi*." In *Seventeenth-Century Imagery: Essays on Uses of Figurative Language from Donne to Farquhar*, ed. Earl Miner (Berkeley, 1971), pp. 133–50.

"The Garden"

Berger, Harry Jr. "Marvell's 'Garden'; Still Another Interpretation." *MLQ*, 28 (1967), 285–304. Retirement into the garden (the poem) and return to the world, the real garden.

Carpenter, Margaret A. "Marvell's 'Garden.'" *SEL*, 10 (1970), 155–69. Locates the garden in the traditions of Romans and Genesis.

Godshalk, William Leigh. "Marvell's Garden and the Theologians." *SP*, 66 (1969), 639–53. Suggests Christian analogues and outlines the theological background: Christianity "taught men how to find God in nature."

Hartman, Geoffrey H. "Marvell, St. Paul, and the Body of Hope." *ELH*, 31 (1964), 175–94. Argues for a Pauline context, not completely successfully.

Klonsky, Martin. "A Guide Through 'The Garden.'" *SR*, 58 (1950), 16–35. The Plotinian sources described.

Poggioli, Renato. "The Pastoral of the Self." *Daedalus*, 88 (1959), 686–99. Repr. in his *The Oaten Flute* (Cambridge, Mass., 1975), pp. 166–81. Emphasizes the poet-figure.

Røstvig, Maren-Sofie. "Andrew Marvell's 'The Garden': A Hermetic Poem." *English Studies*, 40 (1959), 65–76. Following Klonsky and Wallerstein, attempts to establish the Hermetic books as basis for Marvell's androgynous Adam.

Siemon, James E. "Generic Limits in Marvell's 'Garden.'" *PLL*, 8 (1972), 261–72. The pastoral form and the Neoplatonic ideas are uneasy with each other.

Solomon, J. "A Reading of Marvell's 'Garden.'" *English Studies in Africa*, 11 (1968), 151–60. Sees the poem as a "series of lyrical commentaries on experience."

Stempel, Daniel. "'The Garden': Marvell's Cartesian Ecstasy." *Journal of the History of Ideas*, 28 (1967), 99–114. On the influence of the Cartesian new philosophy and theory of knowledge.

Williamson, George. "The Context of Marvell's 'Hortus' and 'Garden.'" *Modern Language Notes*, 76 (1961), 590–98. Repr. in his *Milton & Others* (London, 1965), pp. 140–9.

"An Horatian Ode"

Cleanth Brooks's new-critical essay, "Marvell's 'Horatian Ode.'" *SR*, 55 (1947), 199–222 (also published with title "Literary Criticism," *English Institute Essays, 1946*, ed. W. K. Wimsatt, Jr. [New York, 1947], pp. 127–58, and in *Explication as Criticism: Selected Papers from the English Institute, 1941–1952*, ed. W. K. Wimsatt, Jr. [New York, 1952], pp. 99–130), performs close textual analysis and finds a dramatic and partly ironic structure. Douglas Bush replied spiritedly in "Marvell's 'Horatian Ode,'" *SR*, 60 (1952), 362–76 (reprinted in Keast) that the Brooks reading is too complex, too ambiguous, not unified: "Historical conditioning has a corrective as well as a positive value," to prevent us from turning a seventeenth-century liberal into a modern poet. Brooks responded in "A Note on the Limits of 'History' and the Limits of 'Criticism,'" *SR*, 61 (1953), 129–135. The three essays together (reprinted in the first edition of Keast's collection, see Section VI) are highly instructive on the possibilities and limits of both historical and new-critical approaches. Also valuable are:

Coolidge, John. "Marvell and Horace." *MP*, 63 (1965), 111–20.

Edwards, Thomas R. *Imagination and Power: A Study of Poetry on Public Themes*. New York, 1971, pp. 66–82.

Lerner, Laurence D. "An Horatian Ode." In John Wain, *Interpretations: Essays on Twelve English Poems* (London, 1955), pp. 59–74.

Mazzeo, Joseph A. "Cromwell as Machiavellian Prince in Marvell's 'An Horatian Ode.'" *Journal of the History of Ideas*, 21 (1960), 1–17. Repr. in his *Renaissance and Seventeenth-Century Studies* (New York, 1964), pp. 166–82.

Nevo, Ruth. *The Dial of Virtue: A Study of Poems on Affairs of State in the Seventeenth Century*. Princeton, 1963, pp. 97–109.

Patterson, Annabel. "Against Polarization: Literature and Politics in Marvell's Cromwell Poems." *ELR*, 5 (1975), 251–72. Like Wallace, she links the "Ode" to the other Cromwell poems.

"Upon Appleton House"

Allen, Don Cameron. "Andrew Marvell, 'Upon Appleton House.'" In his *Image and Meanings Metaphoric Traditions in Renaissance Poetry* (Baltimore, 1960), pp. 115–53, Explication with copious classical analogues.

Evett, David. "'Paradice's Only Map': The Topos of the *Locus Amoenus* and the Structure of Marvell's *Upon Appleton House*." *PMLA*, 85 (1970), 504–13.

Goldberg, S. L. "Andrew Marvell." *Melbourne Critical Review*, 3 (1960), 41–65.

Hibbard, G. R. "The Country House Poem of the Seventeenth Century." *JWCI*, 19 (1957), 159–74.

McClung, William A. *The Country House in English Renaissance Poetry.* Berkeley, 1977. A full survey, both modifying and adding much to Hibbard's essay, especially on the Classical tradition and on English architectfure.

Røstvig, Maren-Sofie. " 'Upon Appleton House' and the Universal History of Man." *English Studies,* 42 (1961), 337–51. Parallels to Exodus; philosophical implications.

Scoular, Kitty (Datta). *Natural Magic: Studies in the Presentation of Nature in English Poetry from Spenser to Marvell.* Oxford, 1965. Ch. 3.

(See also Section VI; most works listed there include discussion of Marvell.)

XI. HENRY VAUGHAN

The basic texts are L. C. Martin, *The Works of Henry Vaughan,* 2nd ed. (Oxford, 1957) and French Fogle, *The Complete Poetry of Henry Vaughan* (New York, 1964) which builds on and improves Martin. *Silex Scintillans,* the major work, is published in full in Barbara K. Lewalski and A. J. Sabol, *Major Poets of the Earlier Seventeenth Century* (New York, 1973). F. E. Hutchinson wrote the only full-length biography, *Henry Vaughan: A Life and Interpretation* (London, 1947). For bibliography, there are E. L. Marilla, *A Comprehensive Bibliography of Henry Vaughan* (University, Ala., 1948); E. L. Marilla and James D. Simmonds, *Henry Vaughan: A Bibliographical Supplement, 1946–60* (University, Ala., 1963); and Robert E. Bourdette, Jr., "Recent Studies in Henry Vaughan," *ELR,* 4 (1974), 299–310. All are annotated.

Bethell, S. L. *The Cultural Revolution of the Seventeenth Century.* New York, 1951. This has a major chapter, "The Poetry of Henry Vaughan, Silurist," pp. 121–61.

Brooks, Cleanth. "Henry Vaughan: Quietism and Mysticism." In *Essays in Honor of E. L. Marilla,* ed. T. A. Kirby and W. J. Olive (Baton Rouge, 1970), pp. 3–26. Explicates "Man," "Quickness," "The Retreat," and "The Night."

Chambers, Leland H. "Henry Vaughan's Allusive Technique: Biblical Allusions in 'The Night.' " *MLQ,* 27 (1966), 371–87.

Childe, Wilfred R. "Henry Vaughan." *Transactions of the Royal Society of Literature,* 22 (1945), 131–60.

Christopher, Georgia B. "In Arcadia, Calvin . . .: A Study of Nature in Henry Vaughan." *SP,* 70 (1973), 408–26. Seeing God in nature; Vaughan's theology is Calvinist.

Durr, Robert A. *On the Mystical Poetry of Henry Vaughan.* Cambridge, Mass., 1962. Focussing on Vaughan as mystic, this emphasizes the major image systems. Indispensable.

Eliot, T. S. "The Silurist." *The Dial,* 83 (1927), 259–63.

Garner, Ross. *Henry Vaughan: Experience and the Tradition.* Chicago, 1959.

———. *The Unprofitable Servant in Henry Vaughan.* Lincoln, Neb., 1963.

Holmes, Elizabeth. *Henry Vaughan and the Hermetic Philosophy.* Oxford, 1932.

Kermode, Frank. "The Private Imagery of Henry Vaughan." *RES,* I (1950), 206–25. Separates Vaughan from Christian and mystical traditions.

MacCaffrey, Isabel G. "The Meditative Paradigm." *ELH,* 32 (1965), 388–407.

Marilla, E. L. "The Secular and Religious Poetry of Henry Vaughan." *MLQ,* 9 (1948), 394—411. Emphasizes excellence of secular poetry and the continuity of secular and religious verse.

Martz, Louis L. "Henry Vaughan: The Man Within." *PMLA,* 78 (1963), 40–49. Also in his *The Paradise Within: Studies in Vaughan, Traherne, and Milton* (New Haven, 1964). Vaughan is a meditative poet in Augustinian-Bonaventuran tradition; Martz favors poems of 1650. See MacCaffrey review for qualifications.

Pettet, E. C. *Of Paradise and Light: A Study of Vaughan's* Silex Scintillans. Cambridge, 1960. Sensitive explication of major poems.

Rickey, Mary Ellen. "Vaughan, *The Temple,* and Poetic Form." *SP,* 59 (1962), 162–70.

Rudrum, Alan. "An Aspect of Vaughan's Hermeticism: The Doctrine of Cosmic Sympathy." *SEL,* 14 (1974), 129–38.

Sandler, Florence. "The Ascents of the Spirit: Henry Vaughan on the Atonement." *JEGP,* 73 (1974), 209–26.

Simmonds, James D. *The Masques of God: Form and Theme in the Poetry of Henry Vaughan.* Pittsburgh, 1972. Deals with both the secular and the sacred poetry, and emphasizes lesser-known poems to the exclusion at times of the major works.

Smith, A. J. "Henry Vaughan's Ceremony of Innocence." *Essays & Studies*, 26 (1973), 35–52.

Spitz, Leona. "Process and Stasis: Aspects of Nature in Vaughan and Marvell." *HLQ*, 32 (1969), 135–47.

Summers, Claude J., and Ted-Larryh Pebworth. "Vaughan's Temple in Nature and the Context of Regeneration." *JEGP*, 74 (1975), 351–60.

Underwood, Horace H. "Time and Space in the Poetry of Vaughan." *SP*, 69 (1972), 231–41.

(See also Section VI; most of the books there contain sections on Vaughan.)

XII. THOMAS TRAHERNE

Discovered less than a century ago, Traherne's works are still in process of definition. The main edition is H. M. Margoliouth's two-volume *Centuries, Poems and Thanksgivings* (Oxford, 1958); Anne Ridler alters the organization and modifies some of the readings in her *Poems, Centuries and Three Thanksbivings* (Oxford, 1966). George Guffey has compiled *A Concordance to the Poetry of Thomas Traherne* (Berkeley, 1974).

There is no reliable biography; Gladys Wade's *Thomas Traherne* (London, 1944) must be used with care. For bibliography: Arthur Clements, "Thomas Traherne: A Chronological Bibliography," *The Library Chronicle*, 35 (1970), 36–51, and Jerome S. Dees, "Recent Studies in Traherne," *ELR*, 4 (1974), 189–96; the latter is annotated.

The best available study of Traherne's work as a whole is Stanley Stewart, *The Expanded Voice: The Art of Thomas Traherne* (San Marino, 1970). Arthur L. Clements, *The Mystical Poetry of Thomas Traherne* (Cambridge, Mass., 1969) studies the poems of the Dobell folio; John M. Wallace, "Thomas Traherne and the Structure of Meditation," *ELH*, 25 (1958), 79–89, is also seminal. Whereas Clements focuses on the elusive and sometimes blurred questions of the mystical tradition, Wallace sees "regeneration" as the central motif of the poems which, he says, "constitute a complete five-part meditation."

Bottrall, Margaret. "Traherne's Praise of the Creation." *Critical Quarterly*, 1 (1959), 126–33. General description and evaluation.

Colie, Rosalie L. "Thomas Traherne and the Infinite: The Ethical Compromise." *HLQ*, 21 (1957), 69–82.

Cox, Gerald H., III. "Traherne's Centuries: A Platonic Devotion of 'Divine Philosophy,' " *MP*, 69 (1971), 10–24.

Day, Malcolm M. "Traherne and the Doctrine of Pre-existence." *SP*, 65 (1968), 81–97. Traherne a Neoplatonist.

———. " 'Naked Truth' and the Language of Thomas Traherne." *SP*, 68 (1971), 305–25.

Drake, Ben. "Thomas Traherne's Songs of Innocence." *MLQ*, 31 (1970), 492–503. Review article on Clements: the poems were not botched by Philip Traherne; Thomas was not a wholly capable poet.

Ellrodt, Robert. "Scientific Curiosity and Metaphysical Poetry in the Seventeenth Century." *MP*, 61 (1964), 180–97.

Guffey, George Robert. "Thomas Traherne on Original Sin." *Notes & Queries*, 14 (1967), 98–100.

Jordan, Richard D. *The Temple of Eternity: Thomas Traherne's Philosphy of Time*. Port Washington, N.Y., 1972.

Marks, Carol L. "Thomas Traherne and Cambridge Platonism." *PMLA*, 81 (1966), 521–34.

———. "Thomas Traherne and Hermes Trismegistus." *Renaissance News*, 19 (1966), 118–31.

Martz, Louis L. *The Paradise Within: Studies in Vaughan, Traherne, and Milton*. New Haven, 1964. An Augustinian reading of the *Centuries* as iterative and circling.

Peers, E. Allison. "Thomas Traherne: Poems." In his *Behind That Wall: An Introduction to Some Classics of the Interior Life* (Toronto, 1947), 118–26. An intelligent appreciation.

Ridlon, Harold G. "The Function of the 'Infant-ey' in Traherne's Poetry." *SP*, 61 (1964), 627–39.

Salter, K. W. *Thomas Traherne: Mystic and Poet* (London, 1964). Emphasizes, somewhat controversially, the stages of mysticism outlined by Evelyn Underhill.

Trimpey, John E. "An Analysis of Traherne's Thoughts.' " *SP*, 68 (1971), 88–104.

Uphaus, Robert. "Thomas Traherne: Perceptions as Process." *University of Windsor Review*, 3 (1968), 19–27.

Webber, Joan. "'I and Thou' in the Prose of Thomas Traherne." *PLL*, 2 (1966), 258–64.

––––––. *The Eloquent "I": Style and Self in Seventeenth-Century Prose.* Columbus, 1968. Traherne's complex use of "I" in his style and devotional method.

Willy, Margaret. "Thomas Traherne: 'Felicity's Perfect Lover.'" *English*, 12 (1959), 210–15.

(See also Section VI, especially Ellrodt, Grant, Martz, Nicolson, and White.)